James Hutchison Stirling

**Philosophy and Theology**

Being the First Edinburgh University Gifford Lectures

James Hutchison Stirling

**Philosophy and Theology**
*Being the First Edinburgh University Gifford Lectures*

ISBN/EAN: 9783337079703

Printed in Europe, USA, Canada, Australia, Japan

Cover: Foto ©Thomas Meinert / pixelio.de

More available books at **www.hansebooks.com**

# PHILOSOPHY AND THEOLOGY

BEING

*THE FIRST EDINBURGH UNIVERSITY
GIFFORD LECTURES*

BY

JAMES HUTCHISON STIRLING, LL.D. (EDIN.)
FOREIGN MEMBER OF THE PHILOSOPHICAL SOCIETY OF BERLIN
GIFFORD LECTURER TO THE UNIVERSITY OF EDINBURGH, 1888-90

EDINBURGH
T. & T. CLARK, 38 GEORGE STREET
1890

[*All Rights Reserved.*]

These Lectures are published at the request of the Senatus Academicus of the University of Edinburgh in agreement with the terms of the Gifford Bequest. Further, they explain themselves.

# CONTENTS.

---o---

## GIFFORD LECTURE THE FIRST.

### THE BEQUEST OF LORD GIFFORD—ITS CONDITIONS.

PAGE

Introductory—Lord Gifford—The bequest—The lectureships—God really all in all to Lord Gifford—The lecturers—Natural theology the only science—The immediate lecturer—The three Churches — Feeling — Understanding — Both — Intolerance — Reason as reason—The positive—Rationalism—Aufklärung—"Advanced" views—The temper of the time—Tom Paines of the tap—No-God men—What is really the new—The prejudice against belief—Duty of philosophy now—Sacred books—Those of the Hebrews—Discrepancies—Buckle, Hume, Voltaire—Historical anachronism, . . . . . . . 3-20

## GIFFORD LECTURE THE SECOND.

### NATURAL THEOLOGY—HOW TO BE TREATED.

Natural theology, what is it?—Usual answers—Hutcheson—Varro—The Middle Ages—Raymund of Sebonde—Rays, Paleys, etc.—Till 1860—Since—Philosophies of religion—Pagan gods—De Quincey, Augustine, Cicero, Pliny, Juvenal, Herodotus, Aulus Gellius—The proofs historically treated—That the theme—Plotinus, Augustine—Natural theology not possibly a physical science—Understanding and faith, Augustine, Anselm—Monotheism alone religion proper—The course, affirmative, negative—China, India, Colebrooke, Rás bihárí Mukharjí—Hindu texts (Gnostics)—Hesiod, . . . . . 21-40

## CONTENTS.

### GIFFORD LECTURE THE THIRD.
#### HISTORICAL TREATMENT OF THE PROOFS—ANAXAGORAS.

PAGE

Final causes—The four Aristotelian causes—Are there final causes in nature—Matter and form—Other causes only to realize the final causes—Cudworth—Adam Smith—The proofs, number, order, etc.—Teleology—Anaxagoras—Socrates in the Phædo—Xenophon—Plato—Socrates on Anaxagoras—The causes together, concrete — "Abstract" — Forces, Clerk Maxwell—Heraclitus—Newton—Buckle—Descartes—Gassendi—Bacon on causes, metaphysics, and forms—The νοῦς (*nous*) of Anaxagoras—Bacon on design—Reid, Newton, Hume on design—Newton,    41–59

### GIFFORD LECTURE THE FOURTH.
#### ANAXAGORAS AND DESIGN.

Anaxagoras, the νοῦς—Aristotle—Understanding—Pythagoreans—Pantheism—Lord Gifford—Baghavad Gita—The νοῦς to Socrates, Plato, Aristotle—Grote, Schwegler, Zeller—The world a life—Berkeley, Cudworth, Plato, Zorzi—Subject and object—Nature and thought—Externality and internality—Bruno—Universal and particular—Spinoza—Physical theories—Space and time—Hodgson, Carlyle, Berkeley, Reid, Leibnitz, Kant—But for an eye and an ear, the world utterly dark, utterly silent,   . 60–78

### GIFFORD LECTURE THE FIFTH.
#### DESIGN GENERALLY—SOCRATES.

Astronomy, space, time, the νοῦς—Kant, Fichte, Schelling—Carlyle, the *Sartor*—Emerson — Plato—Aristotle—A beginning — The want of eye and ear again — Deafness and blindness together —Design restored—Thomson—Diogenes of Apollonia—Socrates —Meteorology and practical action—Morality and ethicality—The first teleological argument — Proofs of design—Bacon—Socrates finally, .   .  .  .  .  .  .  .  . 79–96

### GIFFORD LECTURE THE SIXTH.
#### DESIGN—PLATO.

Plato—His position—His prose—Indebted to Socrates—Monotheism —The popular gods—Socrates' one principle—His method—Universalized by Plato—Epinomis—The *Timaeus*—The eyes, etc.—Kant here—Subject and object—Mechanical and final causes—The former only *for* the latter—Identity and difference—Creation, the world—Time and eternity—The Christian Trinity—The two goods—Religion, the *Laws*—Prayer—Superstition—Hume, Dugald Stewart, Samuel Johnson, Buckle—The Platonic duality—Necessity and contingency—Plato's work, 97–114

## GIFFORD LECTURE THE SEVENTH.

### THE SOPHISTS—THEIR NEGATIVE. ARISTOTLE.

Sophists—Aufklärung—Disbelief, Simon of Tournay, Amalrich of Bena, David of Dinant—Italian philosophers, Geneva Socinians, Bacon, Hobbes, the Deists, Locke, Descartes, Spinoza—Hume, Gibbon—Germany, Reimarus, etc.—Klopstock, Lavater—Lessing, Hamann, Herder, Jacobi—Goethe, Schiller, Jean Paul—Carlyle—France—Kant and his successors—Necessary end of such movements—Cosmological argument—Locke, Clarke, Leibnitz—Aristotle—Dependency—Potentiality and actuality — A beginning—Aristotle and design—Mr. Darwin's mistake—Empedocles and the survival of the fittest, . . . . 115–134

## GIFFORD LECTURE THE EIGHTH.

### ARISTOTLE AND THE PROOFS.

Aristotle and design—Matter and form—Abstraction—Trinity—The ascent—The four causes—A first mover—Lambda of the *Metaphysic* — The hymn of Aristotle — Speculation — Mankind—Erdmann—Theory and practice—Nature—Kant, Byron, Mme. de Genlis—Aristotle's ethic and politic—God—Cicero—Time—Design—Hume, Buffon—Plato and Aristotle—Immanent Divinity and transcendent Deity—Schwegler—Bonitz—The soul—Unity—Homer—The Greek movement up to Aristotle, Biese—The Germans and Aristotle—Cuvier, Owen, Franzius, Johann von Müller—Darwin—Aristotle in conclusion, . . . 135–156

## GIFFORD LECTURE THE NINTH.

### THE SECTS AND THE PROOFS—CICERO.

The Sects—The Skeptics—The Epicureans—Epicurus—Leucippus and Democritus—Aristotle, Plato—Stoics, Pantheism—Chrysippus—Origin of evil—Antithesis—Negation—Epictetus—The Neo-Platonists—Important six hundred years—Course of history—Reflection at last—Aufklärung, Revolution—Rome—The atom, the Caesar—The despair of the old, the hope of the new—Paganism, Christianity—The State—The temple—Asceticism—Philosophy, the East, Alexandria—The Neo-Platonists—Ecstasy—Cicero—Paley and the others all in him—All probably due to Aristotle—Sextus—Philo Judaeus—Minucius Felix—Cicero now as to Dr. Alexander Thomson and the Germans—A word in defence, . . . . . . 157–176

## GIFFORD LECTURE THE TENTH.

### THE FATHERS—ANSELM.

Cicero—To Anselm—The Fathers—Seneca, Pliny, Tacitus—God to the early Fathers—Common consent in the individual and the race—Cicero—Irenaeus, Tertullian, Chrysostom, Arnobius, Clement of Alexandria, Lactantius, Cyril of Alexandria, Julian, Gregory of Nyssa, and others, Athanasius—Reid, religion, superstition—The Bible—F. C. Baur—Anselm—His argument—The College Essay of 1838—Dr. Fleming—Illustrations from the essay—Gaunilo—Mr. Lewes—Ueberweg, Erdmann, Hegel—The Monologium—Augustine and Boethius—The Proslogium—Finite and infinite—What the argument really means—Descartes—Knowledge and belief, . . . . . . 177–193

## GIFFORD LECTURE THE ELEVENTH.

### INTRODUCTORY—LORD GIFFORD'S ESSAYS.

Lectures by Lord Gifford—By whom edited—Germane to, and illustrative of, natural theology—Number and nature—Their literary excellence—Even poetical—*Der laute Lärm des Tages*—On attention—On St. Bernard of Clairvaux—(Luther, Gibbon)—What Lord Gifford admires—The spirit of religion—The Trinity—Emerson, Spinoza—Substance—Brahmanism—Religion—Understanding and reason—Metaphysical terms—Materialism—Literary enthusiasm—Technical shortcomings—Emerson and Carlyle—Social intercourse—Humanity—Liberality and tolerance—Faith—Mesmerism—Ebenezer Elliott—An open sense to evidence, . . . . . . . . 197–216

## GIFFORD LECTURE THE TWELFTH.

### THE NEGATIVE—HUME.

A settlement for faith Lord Gifford's object—Of our single theme the negative half now—Objections to, or refutations of, the proofs—Negative not necessarily or predominatingly modern, Kant, Darwin—The ancient negative, the Greeks, Pythagoreans, Ionics, Eleatics, Heraclitus, Empedocles, Democritus, (Bacon), Anaxagoras, Socrates, Sophists, Diagoras, Aristotle, Aristoxenus, Dicaearchus, Strato, (Hume, Cudworth), Aristophanes, etc.— Rome—Modern Europe, France, Hume and the seventeen atheists—Epochs of atheism—David Hume, his influence—To many a passion and a prejudice—Brougham, Buckle—Style!— Taste!—Blair—Hume's taste, Pope, Shakespeare, John Home —*Othello*—The French to Hume—Mr. Pope!—Some bygone *litterateurs*—Personality and character of Hume—Jokes, stories, Kant, Aristotle—The Scotch—The *Epigoniad*—America —Germany—Generosity, affection, friendship, hospitality— Smollett—Burke—but Hume, honest, genuine, and even religious and pious, . . . . . . . . 217-242

GIFFORD LECTURE THE THIRTEENTH.

THE NEGATIVE AND HUME (*continued*).

The Dialogues concerning Natural Religion—Long consideration and repeated revision of them—Their publication, Hume's anxiety for, his friends' difficulties with—Style, Cicero—Words and things, Quintilian—Styles, old and new—The earlier works— The *Treatise*—The *Enquiry*, Rosenkranz—Hume's provision— Locke, Berkeley—Ideas—Connection in them—Applied to the question of a Deity—Of a Particular Providence—Extension of the cause inferred, to be proportioned only to that of the given effect—Applied to the cause of the world—Natural theology to Hume—Chrysippus in Plutarch—Greek—The order of argumentation—The ontological—Matter the necessary existence— The cosmological answers that—Infinite contingencies insufficient for one necessity—The teleological—Analogy inapplicable— Hume's own example, . . . . . . . 243-264

GIFFORD LECTURE THE FOURTEENTH.

THE NEGATIVE AND HUME (*concluded*).

The teleological argument—Two moments—First, the alleged necessity of thought—It has itself no end—So matter enough— Thought itself only a part, limited, imperfect, and in want of explanation—Thought as thought common to us all, Grote, Hume, Erigena, Heraclitus—The sole necessity—Second, the

xii                           CONTENTS.

PAGE

analogy—The supreme cause not situated as other causes—
Other principles, vegetation, generation—The world an animal
—The Empédoclean expedient—The effect only warrants great
power, not Almighty power—Evil—Free opinion—Hume's
friends — Epicurus's dilemma — Superstition results — Four
suggestions—No pain—Special volitions—Greater strength—
Extremes banished from the world—Creation on general prin-
ciples—Erasmus Darwin—Mr. Froude, Carlyle—Finitude as
such, externality as such—Antithesis—Charles V.—Abdal-
rahman III. — Septimius Severus — Johnson — *Per contra*—
Wordsworth, Gibbon, Hume—Work, Carlyle—The trades—
Comparison—Self-contradiction — Identity — Hegel —"As regards Protoplasm"—The Hindoos—Burton on cause—Sir John
Herschel — Brown, Dugald Stewart — Spinoza — Erdmann—
Notions and things, Erigena—Rabelais—Form and matter—
Hume in conclusion, . . . . . . . . 265-285

## GIFFORD LECTURE THE FIFTEENTH.

### KANT ON THE PROOFS.

Transition, Hume to Kant—Effect of Kant on natural theology
—The centre of Kant's thought—Hume led to this—Causal
necessity—That necessity objective—Still in matters of fact—
Relations of ideas—Hume on one side, Kant on the other, of the
dilemma—Hume quite as Reid, on natural necessity—But what
the explanation to intellectual insight—Synthetic addition—
Analytic implication—Change—Kant's explanation is, There
are *à priori* syntheses native to the mind—The whole Kantian
machinery in a sentence—Time and space—The twelve categories and the three ideas—A toy house—A peculiar magic
lantern — A psychology — A metaphysic — Analysis of the
syllogism for the ideas—Simple apprehension missed—An idea
—The ideal—The teleological proof, . . . . 286-304

## GIFFORD LECTURE THE SIXTEENTH.

### KANT AND THE PROOFS (*concluded*).

The cosmological proof—Contingency—*Ab alio esse* and *esse a se*—
The special contingency an actual fact in experience—This
Kant would put out of sight—Jehovah—Two elements in
the argument, experience and ideas—The generality of the
experience — Also of the idea — Contingency *is* a particular

empirical fact—*Ens realissimum*—Only the ontological argument
in disguise—Logical inference—But just generally the all-
necessary being of such a world—Hume anticipated Kant—
Why force analogy—Why transcend nature—No experience of
such cause, which must not exceed the effect—Hume's early
memoranda—The "nest"—All Kant dependent on his own
constant sense of school-distinctions—His entire world—The
system being true, *what* is true?—The ontological argument—
No thinking a thing will bring it to be—What it all comes to,
the single threefold wave—Hegel—Middle Age view from
Augustine to Tauler—Meister Eckhart—Misunderstanding of
mere understanding—The wickedest then a possible divine
reservoir—Adam Smith and the chest of drawers—Absurd for
Kant to make reason proper the "*transcendent shine*"—The
Twelfth Night cake, but the *ehrliche* Kant, . . . 305-322

## GIFFORD LECTURE THE SEVENTEENTH.

### DARWIN AND DESIGN.

The three degrees, positive, comparative, superlative in negation of
the proofs, or Hume, Kant, Darwin—*The Life and Letters of
Charles Darwin*, chapter viii. of the first volume—Darwin one
of the best of men—Design—Uniformity and law—Darwin's
own words—He himself always gentle—But resolute to
win—Concessiveness—Religious sentiment—Disbelief—Jokes—
Natural selection being, materialism is true, and ideas are only
derivative—The theory—A species what—Sterility—What
suggested natural selection to Darwin—Bakewell's achievements
as a breeder—Darwin will substitute nature for Bakewell, to the
production, not of new breeds, but, absolutely, of new species—
His lever to this, change by natural accident and chance : such
*necessarily* proving either advantageous, disadvantageous, or
indifferent—*Advantage* securing in the struggle for life survival
of the fittest, *disadvantage* entailing death and destruction,
*indifference* being out of count—The woodpecker, the mistletoe
—But mere variation the very fulcrum—Variation *must* be, and
consequences to the organism *must* be : hence the whole—But
never design, only a mechanical pullulation of differences by
chance that simply *prove* advantageous or disadvantageous, etc.
—Conditions—Mr. Huxley—Effect of the announcements of
Sir Joseph Hooker and Sir Charles Lyell—Mr. Darwin insists
on his originality—His difficulties in winning his way—Even
those who agree with him, as Lyell, Hooker, and others, he

demurs to their expressions; they fail to understand—Mr. Darwin's own qualms—"What makes a tuft of feathers come on a cock's head, or moss on a moss-rose?"—That the question —Still spontaneous variation both universal and constant, 323-342

## GIFFORD LECTURE THE EIGHTEENTH.

### DARWIN AND DESIGN (*continued*).

The theory—Individual variation—Darwin early looked for natural explanation of design—Creation, its senses—Antisthenes, Colebrooke, Cudworth—Creative ideas—Anaxagoras—Aristotle— Mr. Clair Grece and Darwin—For design Mr. Darwin offers a mechanical pullulation of individual difference through chance, but with consequent results that as advantageous or disadvantageous *seem* concerted—The Fathers—Nature the phenomenon of the noumenon, a boundless externality of contingency that still is a life—Nature, the object will only *be* when it reaches the subject—That object be, or subject be, *both* must be—Even the crassest material particle is already both elementarily—As it were, even inorganic matter possesses instincts—Aristotle, design and necessity—Internalization— Time space, motion, matter—The world—Contingency—A perspective of pictures—The *Vestiges* and evolution—Darwin deprecates genealogies, but returns to them—The mud-fish— Initial proteine—There are so many mouths to eat it up now —Darwin recants his pentateuchal concession to creation— Depends on "fanciers and breeders"—The infinitudes of transition just taken by Mr. Darwin in a step—Hypothesis— Illustration at random—Difference would go on to difference, not return to the identity—Mr. Lewes and Dr. Erasmus—The grandfather's filament—Seals—The bear and the whale—Dr. Erasmus on the imagination, on weeping, on fear, on the tadpole's tail, on the rationale of strabismus, . . . 343-362

## GIFFORD LECTURE THE NINETEENTH.

### DARWIN AND DESIGN (*continued*).

Dr. Erasmus Darwin—Student scribbles on *Zoonomia*—Family differences, attraction and repulsion—The Darwins in this respect—Dr. Erasmus of his sons, Mr. Charles and Dr. R. W.— Dr. R. W. as to his sons—Charles on his grandfather, father, brother—Mr. Erasmus on his brother's book—On the *à priori* —On facts—Darwin's one method—Darwin and Hooker on

facts — Family politics — Family religion — Family habits—
Family theories—Mr. Darwin's endowments—His *Journal*—
The *Zoonomia*—Theories of Dr. Erasmus—Paley—Instinct—
An *idea* to Dr. E. — Dugald Stewart — Picture-thinking—
Dr. E.'s method—Darwin's doubts — His brave spirit—The
theory to his friends—Now—Almost every propos of the grandson has its germ in the grandfather (Krause)—Yet the position
of the latter—Byron on—Mr. Lewes also—The greater Newton,
original Darwinism now to be revived—Dr. E. admirable on
design—Charles on cats made by God to play with mice!—
Dr. E. on atheism—The apology—But will conclude with a
single point followed thoroughly out: the Galapagos—Darwin
held to be impregnably fortified there—The Galapagos thrown
up to opponents at every turn—But we are not naturalists!—
Dr. E. rehabilitates us — Description of the Galapagos from
the *Journal* — The islands, their size, number, position,
geographical and relative—Depth of water and distance between
—Climate, currents, wind—Geology, botany, zoology—Volcanoes, dull sickly vegetation, hills, craters, lava, pits, heat,
salt-pools, water—Tortoises, lizards, birds—Quite a region to
suggest theory, . . . . . . . . 363–381

GIFFORD LECTURE THE TWENTIETH.

DARWIN AND DESIGN—*(conclusion).*

The action—South American types, left here to themselves, change
into new species from accumulation of their own individual
spontaneous differences—The birds—Differences in the times
and modes of arrival between land and sea birds—Carte and
tierce—Contradiction—Parried by a word—An advocate's proof
—The printer and Mr. Darwin's *woulds*—The sea-gull—The
finches—Sir William Jardine—The process to Darwin—What
was to him "a new birth"—Where the determinative advantage for these *different* beaks—The individual central islands *not*
incommunicably separate—French birds at Dover—Isolation—
*Ex-contrario*—Individual difference the single secret, that is
the "law" which has been "discovered" of "natural selection"
—Apply influence of external conditions to the Galapagos—
Kant—The Galapagos rat and mouse—New beings but yet the
old names—If difference goes always on only to difference
without return to identity, why are there not infinitely more
species?—Bowen—Darwin only empedoclean—Parsons—Lyell
—Monsters (giants and dwarfs) sterile—Frederick's grenadiers,

the pygmies—Divergent species at home—The Galapagos but the Mr. Jorkins of the Darwinians—The tortoise, where did it come from?—The amblyrhyncus similarly inexplicable—Lizards of the secondary epoch—The Galapagos Islands absolutely without a vestige of the struggle for life in any direction—The breeder, and nature, can act only on what is already there—The breeder deals in identity, not difference, and his breeds would all turn back to the original—No breeder a new species—Nature acts not on Darwin's method, but design—Toothed birds, the hipparion, the otter-sheep—Accidental individual difference to be the sole creator in the end of all that enormous and infinitely complicated concert to unity!—Farewell, . . . . . . . . . 382–400

INDEX, . . . . . . . . 401

# THE FIRST COURSE OF LECTURES:
## THE AFFIRMATIVE.

1889.

# PHILOSOPHY AND THEOLOGY.

## GIFFORD LECTURE THE FIRST.

Introductory--Lord Gifford—The bequest—The lectureships—God really all in all to Lord Gifford—The lecturers—Natural theology the only science—The immediate lecturer—The three Churches — Feeling — Understanding — Both — Intolerance— Reason as reason—The positive—Rationalism—Aufklärung— " Advanced " views—The temper of the time—Tom Paines of the tap—No-God men—What is really the new—The prejudice against belief—Duty of philosophy now—Sacred books—Those of the Hebrews—Discrepancies—Buckle, Hume, Voltaire—Historical anachronism.

Mr. Principal and Fellow-Students,—The first word that is due from a man in my position is necessarily one of thanks. I owe it to the Senatus of this University respectfully to tender it my best thanks for the high honour it has done me in electing me to the distinguished office of its first Gifford Lecturer.

Again, a word is no less due from me in respectful acknowledgment of the rare liberality and signal generosity of him who disinterestedly sought to bestow what best boon he could think of for the public, in the founding of this and the other University lectureships which bear his name.

I have had but few opportunities of acquaintanceship with the late Lord Gifford. I *have*, however, met him over the dinner-table and elsewhere; and I could not but like what I saw in him. He had eminently the bearing of an honourable gentleman who held his own ground. With a smile, there was humour on the mouth; but there was at the same time a look of shrewdness in the eyes, with a certain firm stability of the chin and the whole countenance, that intimated as plainly as any words could: I am accessible, open, willing; but, have a care that you neither trespass nor exceed. He was frank, loyal, warm, generous in his affirmation of merit; but neither bitter nor unjust in his negation of demerit and insufficiency. He was good-natured: he could listen to what was out of place, or doubtfully offensive even, in a personal regard, and keep silence with a smile on his lips. That he was skilful and successful as a lawyer; esteemed, respected, honoured as a judge,—that is a matter of public recognition. To me it belongs rather to note that he was a lover of books. The hours he loved best were those he spent with the writings of his favourite authors; foremost among whom were the heroes of his own day and generation: and, of them all, that it was Emerson for whom, perhaps, he entertained specially a predilection, vouches for his love of philosophy. Further, now, indeed, we know that not philosophy only, but religion also, lay at his heart, and must have constituted there a very familiar theme of reverent and persistent meditation. I did not think of that then as I met him often in my walks about Granton. I did not think of that then as I saw him trailing his poor semi-paralytic limbs along, but holding his head bravely aloft and looking imperturbably before him, as, within his open coat, he still placed a broad chest, as it were, in front of all the accidents of time. That, in these circumstances, was always the impression he exactly and vividly made upon me. He was for months confined to the house before his death; but, doubtless, even in these walks at that time he was meditating this bequest that is the occasion of our being at present together.

And to that bequest it is now my duty to turn; for, clearly, the very first necessity of the case is to know what that service specially is which the Testator expected to be rendered to the University and the public in return for his own munificence.

I have spoken of Lord Gifford as pondering in his mind what best boon he could find it within his power to bestow upon the public; and about the very first words of the Extracts from his Trust Disposition and Settlement bear me out in this. "I, having fully and maturely considered my means and estate, and the modes in which my surplus funds may be most usefully and beneficially expended, and considering myself bound to apply part of my means in advancing the public welfare and the cause of truth:" from these words it is plain that Lord Gifford, finding himself in possession of what appeared to him more than was necessary for the satisfaction and fulfilment of all his private duties, claims, wishes, or intentions, felt himself in presence with the rest of a public burden which he was bound to discharge. How, for the public welfare and the cause of truth, that could be most usefully and beneficially effected, was the next thought. And so, as he says further, "being of opinion that I am bound if there is a 'residue' as so explained, to employ it, or part of it, for the good of my fellow-men, and having considered how I may best do so, I direct the 'residue' to be disposed of as follows:—I, having been for many years deeply and firmly convinced that the true knowledge of God, that is, of the Being, Nature, and Attributes of the Infinite, of the All, of the First and the Only Cause, that is the One and Only Substance and Being; and the true and felt knowledge (not mere nominal knowledge) of the relations of man and of the universe to Him, and of the true foundations of all ethics and morals,—being, I say, convinced that this knowledge, when really felt and acted on, is the means of man's highest well-being, and the security of his upward progress, I have resolved, from the 'residue' of my estate as aforesaid, to institute and found, in connection, if possible, with the Scottish Universities, lectureships or classes for the promotion of the study of said subjects, and for the teaching and diffusion of sound views regarding them." From these words there can be no doubt that the conclusion of Lord Gifford's mind as to how, in satisfaction of a public obligation which he felt lay upon him, he could best employ an expected "residue" of his estate, was the institution and foundation of certain lectureships in Natural Theology. The lectureships in question, in fact, are, within inverted commas, formally described as established for "Promoting, Advancing, Teaching, and Diffusing the Study of Natural Theology." That is express; there is no possible mistake of, or possible escape from, the bare term itself; and just as little are we allowed any possible mistake of, or possible escape from, what Lord Gifford himself literally prescribes as his own whole will and meaning in the term. Natural Theology is, for Lord Gifford, in precise "other words," and with the same distinction of inverted commas, "The Knowledge of God, the Infinite, the All, the First and Only Cause, the One and the Sole Substance, the Sole Being, the Sole Reality, and the Sole Existence, the Knowledge of His Nature and Attributes, the Knowledge of the Relations which man and the whole universe bear to Him, the Knowledge of the Nature and Foundation of Ethics or Morals, and of all Obligations and Duties thence arising." All here, we see, is formal and express; and everything is done that can be done by capital letters and inverted commas, by word upon word and phrase upon phrase, to cut off the very possibility of any failure to understand. That is the technical scroll, style, title, and designation of the business that is in hand. That is the Purview of the Lecturer: these are his Instructions.

Further, indeed, and more expressly as regards the lecturers, he says this: "I have intentionally indicated the general aspect which *personally* I would wish the lectures to bear, but the lecturers shall be under no restraint whatever in their treatment of their theme . . . provided only that the 'patrons' will use diligence to secure that they be able, reverent men, true thinkers, sincere lovers of, and earnest inquirers after, truth." These, then, briefly are Lord Gifford's views in regard to the lecturers; while, as for the lectures, we have already learned that they are to promote the teaching and diffusion of "sound views" in respect of Natural Theology. Now the whole question here is—What did Lord Gifford mean by "sound views"? This, in the first place, is plain, that Lord Gifford wished the "sound views" he desiderated to be independent of Revelation; but, in the second place, Revelation apart, he undoubtedly expected the phrase to be understood as it is ordinarily understood —and that is on the serious and affirmative side.

Unless we can suppose that Lord Gifford could, in such serious and solemn circumstances, descend to a paltry quibble and an unworthy irony, we must believe that the phrase bore for him, and must have borne for him, the only signification that is given to it in current usage. But we can say more than that. Lord Gifford himself expressly tells us, "I have intentionally indicated, in describing the subject of the lectures, the general aspect which *personally* I would expect the lectures to bear;" and with such an avowal as that before us, there can be no great difficulty in coming to a certainty of assurance as regards what was peculiarly meant by the expression "sound views." Lord Gifford tells us that his personal expectation as regards the general aspect of the lecturers has been "intentionally indicated " by himself, and that we shall find as much in his description of *the* " subject " of the lectures. We are not even allowed a moment's hesitation in the reference, then ; for not only do we know that the subject is Natural Theology, but we know also, and that, too, in all fulness and completeness of detail, Lord Gifford's own definition of the subject. We need but recall a phrase or two here to have the whole before us again, and to feel relieved from all doubt relatively. " The First and Only Cause," " the Sole Being," " the greatest of all possible sciences,—indeed, in one sense, the only science, that of Infinite Being,"—surely when Lord Gifford solicits " sound views " on such subjects, and so expressed, he is speaking affirmatively, and not negatively ; seriously, and not mockingly. The whole tone of any relative wording all through is one of reverent belief in, and reverent desire for, the realization of religion. His solemn last words are these : " I give my body to the earth as it was before, in order that the enduring blocks and materials thereof may be employed in new combinations ; and I give my soul to God, in Whom, and with Whom, it always was, to be in Him, and with Him for ever in closer and more conscious union." These sublime and solemn, almost awe-ing, last words comport but ill with " sound views," in the construction that would make them only ironical and a mock. I have no desire to strain the situation to any undue extreme ; it is not my wish to make a Saint Simeon Stylites of Lord Gifford in the matter of Revelation, nor yet an antique ruling elder in rigidity of Confession and the Creed. As to that I know nothing. How it was situated with Lord Gifford as regards any particular religious body or persuasion, is beyond my ken. I know only this, and the document so long before us bears ample testimony to the fact, that, during these suffering last years of Lord Gifford, it must have been the subject of religion that occupied his whole mind and heart. The proof is his Testament and Will, in which he is not content to concern himself only with the things of earth and his worldly relations, but in which he draws nigh also to his God and his heritage on the other side. " I give my soul to God," he says, "in Whom, and with Whom, it always was, to be in Him, and with Him for ever in closer and more conscious union." What, in a religious sense, Lord Gifford personally felt, and what, in a religious sense, as regards his lecturers, he personally expected or desired, I shall hold now to have been made conclusively plain. It is equally plain, at the same time, that Lord Gifford had no wish in any way to trammel his lecturers, or to bind them down to any express articles, provided always that whatever they advocated was advocated only by them as " reverent men, true thinkers, sincere lovers of, and earnest inquirers after, truth." No doubt that is true ; though I think we may also take it for granted, from the whole tone and general drift of his expressions, that it was the serious side he would wish to see triumphant in the world, and prevailing in the lives of men. " My desire and hope "—this is his own, most unambiguous declaration towards the close— "my desire and hope is that these lectureships and lectures may promote and advance among all classes of the community the true knowledge of Him Who is, and there is none and nothing besides Him, in Whom we live and move and have our being, and in Whom all things consist, and of man's real relation to Him Whom truly to know is life everlasting."

Now, coming from such considerations as these, it is not unnatural that the question should suggest itself, And how of the lecturer,—how is he situated in regard to the momentous interests which have been before us ? Of course there is no necessity in the bond that the lecturer, whom it has been the care of the patrons to appoint, should declare himself before he lectures, or, simply, further and otherwise than as he lectures. Still it might be convenient did he contrive to let his hearers have some inkling beforehand, generally, of what spirit and drift they might expect from him. Fielding, in one of his novels, tells us that, when we dine with a gentleman who gives a private treat, we must not find fault, but cheerfully accept whatever fare he pleases; whereas, in the case of an ordinary, with a bill of fare in the window, we can see for ourselves, and either enter or turn away as it suits us. This hint, which only bears on physical food, Fielding does not disdain to borrow in respect of food otherwise. Following his example, then, let us prefix, not exactly now a bill of fare (which will come later), but an explanation, so far, in regard to creed. But that amounts to a religious confession, whereas it may seem that Lord Gifford himself deprecates or disapproves all such. It is certain that, according to the terms of the document, all previous declarations are unnecessary; but still it cannot be said that there is any actual prohibition of them, either expressed or understood. Lord Gifford himself, as I have attempted to show, has made no secret of his own convictions on the general question; and without at all desiring to set up a compulsory precedent for others, we may, without impropriety, follow his example. I am a member of the National Church, and would not willingly run counter to whatever that involves. Again, as is seen at its clearest and most definite in the sister Church farther south, perhaps,—there are three main sections of that Church, or rather, as actual speech has it, in that one Church,—there are three Churches. There is Broad Church, High Church, Low or Evangelical Church. I daresay it has been by some — few or many, I know not—supposed that I am Broad, and it is very certain that it is not with my own will that I shall be narrow. I am an utter foe to religious rancour—religious intolerance of any kind. In that respect I am absolutely as Lord Gifford himself would appear to have been from his own statements, which are now, I hope, clearly in our minds. Nevertheless, I have to confess that I would quite as soon wish to be considered High as Broad, and that the party to which I do wish to be considered to belong is the Low or Evangelical one. No doubt there is deeply and ineradicably implanted in the human soul an original *sentiment* which is the religious one ; and no doubt also there is as deeply and ineradicably implanted there a religious *understanding*. We not only *feel*, we *know* religion. Religion is not only buoyed up on a sentiment of the heart, it is founded also on ideas of the intellect. So it is that, if for me High Church seems too exclusively devoted to the category of feeling, Broad Church, again, too much accentuates the principle of the understanding. Now, if as much as this be true, as well for the one Church as the other, it will not be incorrect to say that while the Low or Evangelical Church is neither exclusively High nor exclusively Broad, it is in essential idea both ; and so it is that it is on its side that I would wish to be considered to rank. I know not at the same time but that all three Churches have a common sin, the sin of absolute intolerance and denial, the one of the other. That I would wish otherwise for them in a mutual regard, and that I would wish otherwise from them in my own regard when I point out *this difference* between them and me, that what they possess in what is called the Vorstellung, I rely upon in the Begriff. What they have *positively* in the feeling, or *positively* in the understanding, or *positively* in a union of both, I have reflectively, or ideally, or speculatively in reason. What the term *positive* amounts to will be best understood by a reference to other religions than our own.

The very edge and point of the *positive* may be placed in bare will, the bare will of another. Mormonism is a positive religion. There, says Joseph Smith, holding up the book of Mormon, take that, believe whatever it says, and do what it tells you. That is positive: the religion—the book—is just given, and it is just received as given. There is not a shadow of explanation, not a shadow of reasoning, not a shadow of stipulation on the one side or the other. So it is with Mahomet and the Koran. Book in hand, he just steps forward, and there, on the instant, the Mahometan is at his feet, simply repeating the precise words he hears read out to him. It is for the same reason that laws are positive. They rest on authority alone, another will than his who must obey them: as the dictionary has it, They are prescribed by express enactment or institution. Nevertheless, it is implied in laws and law that *they* as particulars, and *it* as a whole, are as much the will of him or them who receive, as of him or them who give. Law is but a realization of reason, of the reason common to us all, as much yours as his, as much his as yours. So it is, or so it ought to be, with religion; and there you have the whole matter before you. He whose religion rests only on the *Vorstellung* possesses it positively — believes it positively only; whereas he with whom religion rests on the *Begriff*, has placed beneath it a philosophical foundation. You may illustrate this by a reference to the Shorter Catechism. If you get its specifications by heart and, making them your own only so, straightway act upon them, then that is an illustration of what is positive. To dwell on each specification separately by itself again, making it to flow and coalesce, and live into its own inmost meaning—that is to transmute it into the Begriff, for the Begriff is but the external material words made inward intellectual notion or idea—thought—something from without converted into one's own substance from within. Not but that the positive has its own rights too. We *positively* muzzle our dogs, we *positively* bridle our horses, and we *positively* install our cattle; and we have right on our side. In the same way, and for the same reason, we *positively* teach our children; and we have no other resource—we *positively must*. But what we teach them is only their own; they follow only their own *true* selves when they follow us. We make it only that they are *free*—that it is absolutely only their own true wills they have, follow, and obey when we give them the wills of maturity and experienced reason. So it is that it has been a custom of a Sunday in Scotland to make our children learn by heart verses of the Bible or the specifications of the Shorter Catechism. They take what they learn only into the Vorstellung; they are unable as yet to convert it into Begriff; but the trust is that they will do so later. Nor is there any reason that they should not do so, at least on the whole. I do not mean to say that earnest reflection will remove every difficulty connected with the various articles of the Book of Articles or of the Larger or Shorter Catechisms; but I do say that many of these articles mean at bottom the very deepest and most essential metaphysical truths.

But it is not with that that we have to do at present, at the same time that *it*, and what else I have said in this connection, will all serve to 'realize to you the religious position of the lecturer as what we *are* concerned with at present. And in that reference I ought to explain that, when I have opposed what is *positively* held in feeling, or understanding, or a union of both to what is reflectively, ideally, speculatively held in *reason*, it is not the system of belief technically known as Rationalism that I have in mind, whatever relation there may exist between the two words etymologically. As the sentence itself shows, indeed, the term reason is opposed by me, not only to feeling, but also to understanding; and understanding is the faculty, special, proper, and peculiar, of Rationalism. Rationalism, in fact, means—in its religious application—nothing but Aufklärung, *is* nothing but *the* Aufklärung, though claiming a certain affirmative side in its bearing on religion. The prevailing mind of the Aufklärung, namely, as in Hobbes, Spinoza, Hume, Voltaire, is seen to be, in a religious direction, negative, so far at least as Revelation is concerned; whereas the Aufklärung in the form of Rationalism, as in such a writer as the German Reimarus, for example, while planing away much, or perhaps almost all, that is essential in religion, makes believe still to have an affirmative attitude to Revelation. Of course, I need no more than *mention* the *distinction between understanding and reason*, as I have no doubt it is now well known and familiar. It is current in Coleridge. I think, then, there will no longer be any possibility of misapprehension or mistake when I oppose religion as in reason to religion as in understanding; while the latter, in the form of Rationalism say, has to do only with what is conditional and finite, the former, in ideal or speculative religion, would attain to converse with the unconditional and the infinite itself.

But though I am thus careful to preclude the danger of a religion in reason being confounded with Rationalism, it seems to me that I must be equally careful to provide against another and opposing danger. There is a great prejudice against old forms now-a-days; and it is not usual for the advocates of them to find themselves listened to. Advanced views, that is, what are called advanced views, are very generally, because advanced, supposed to represent the truth—at least the truth in its highest contemporary form. The supporters of them have been fighting a battle against the old, it has been conceived—a battle of enlightenment, progress, and improvement against received prejudice, traditional bigotry, and stereotyped obstruction. It is the new only that is to be hailed as the true. He who, in any way, may seem now to stand for the old must be but a hired spadassin, a gladiator, a Prætorian guard, a bravo, a bully upon wages. He cannot have anything to say worth hearing. He must simply be going to babble the orthodoxy he is paid for.

These words, I doubt not, will be found to strike a true note now. If a man would have any success with the general public now-a-days, almost it would seem as though, very commonly, he must approve himself, on the whole, as an Aufgeklärter, a disciple of the "advanced" thinking we all understand so well. That is the temper of the time, and the time—let critics say as scornfully as they like, "whatever that may mean"—the time *has* a a temper; and, suppose it even in the wrong, it is as much in vain to move against it as for Mrs. Partington to stave out the Atlantic with her besom. The reason, of course, is that the Aufklärung,—call it if you will Secularism, Agnosticism, or even Rationalism,—the reason is that the Aufklärung which, to our greatest thinkers, was old and worn-out, and had completely done its task, by the beginning of this century has descended upon the generality.

In our large towns in these days, in our capitals, in our villages, we are confronted by a vast mass of unbelief. The Aufklärung, the historical movement called Aufklärung, as I say, dead among thinkers, has descended upon the people; and there is hardly a hamlet but has its Tom Paines by the half-dozen—its Tom Paines of the tap, all emulously funny on the one subject. I witnessed such a thing as this myself last summer in the country

—the bewildered defeat of my landlady under the crowing triumph of her son, a lad of seventeen or so, who had asked her to explain to him where Cain got his wife! In such circumstances we cannot expect to find a large portion of the Press different. I recollect I was once warned by a publisher, that I must remember it was the No-God men who had the pull at present. One is glad to think, however, that in this the dawn of a change begins to show. There are those among our highest, best, and most influential organs that have ceased to think that it is any longer necessary only to follow. They will teach now, inform, instruct, educate, lead. Still, on the whole, we may lay our account with this, that there is a prejudice in the mass for what *appears*, at least, to come to it as new. These are the words of the *advanced*, it thinks, of those, as I have said, who have been fighting the battle of time, in which, of course, it is always the new is the true. I am sorry for this. It is only a radical mistake of what *is* the new and what *is* the true. "Distinguished Paine, rebellious staymaker, rebellious needleman," as Carlyle calls him, cannot at least be new in these days, seeing that it is now about a hundred years since, by his chalked door on the wrong side, he just escaped the very last tumbrils of the French Revolution. I suppose *deep* with Paine was but shallow at its best: it is not likely that the shallowness of a hundred years ago is less shallow now.

That, however, is the other danger. If there was a danger that reason might be confounded with the understanding, and philosophical faith with Rationalism, there is also a danger that said philosophical faith, just in this that it is *faith*, should, by the followers of what they consider the new, not be listened to. It is to be suspected, indeed, that many good men, who know quite well what and where the Aufklärung is, are now-a-days reduced to silence precisely by such a consideration. Why speak if no one will listen? Nothing succeeds like success, and a failure remains a failure. Human nature is but weak; and it cannot be wondered at, that it very soon gets hoarse in the throat, if it finds itself to be bawling only in a desert. It takes patience and a *long life* for men like the Carlyles and the Brownings to be overwhelmed with plaudits in the end that can only spoil themselves.

What I mean by all this, however, is only to protest against such religious views as I have, not expounded, but indicated, being regarded as something too old to be listened to. I, for my part, very stupidly, perhaps, but still, as even the adversary will hasten to allow, not unnaturally, am apt to look upon them as the very newest of the new, as precisely *the* message which the votaries of philosophy have to give the world at present.

And so it is that, to my mind, such votaries of philosophy must not allow themselves to be browbeat by the vulgarity that cries, and can only cry, as Cervantes tells us, " Long live the conqueror," meaning, of course, by that, only the side that is uppermost for the moment. What is really out of date, what is really behind the time, is to insist on regarding as still alive an interest that, as is historically known, had, so far as the progress of thought is concerned, fully come to term a hundred years ago. Not, at the same time, that there is any call for us to be either narrow or intolerant. What is in place now is a large and wise liberality that shall not fail at any time in the wish and the will to face and admit the truth. If any man confessed to me, for example, that, when the walls of the city were said to have fallen at the blast of the trumpet, his own belief was that this was merely the Oriental phantasy expressing in a trope the signal speed of the event—if any man confessed such attitude of mind to me *with fears for his orthodox security*, I do think that I should not feel justified in bidding him despair! In fact, our relative riches are such that, to my belief, we may readily allow ourselves as much. *For the sake of comparison*, let us even do this—let us consent, so far, and for this purpose, to place the sacred books of the Hebrews on the same level as the other sacred books of the East, and what have we lost? Will they lose in the regard? Is it not amusing at times to note the exultation with which our great Cochinese and Anamese scholars, our great Tonquin explorers, will hold up some mere halting verse or two, or say some bill of sale, certificate of feu, against the Hebrew Scriptures. Suppose the state of the case reversed. Suppose we had been rejoicing all this time in these bills of sale, certificates of feu, and halting verses—nay, give them all, give them their own best, suppose we had been rejoicing all this time in the Confucian Kings and the very oldest Vedas, and suppose, in the face of all these possessions, the Hebrew Scriptures, unknown before, were suddenly dug up and brought to light! Then, surely, there might be a cry, and a simultaneous shout, that never before had there been such a glorious—never before had there been such a miraculous find! The sacred writings of the Hebrews, indeed, are so immeasurably superior to those of every other name that, for the sake of the latter, to invite a comparison is to undergo instantaneous extinction. Nay, regard these Scriptures as a literature only, the literature of the Jews—even then, in the kind of quality, is there any literature to be compared with it? will it not even then remain still as the sacred literature? A taking simpleness, a simple takingness that is divine—all that can lift us out of our own week-day selves and place us, pure then, holy, rapt, in the joy and the peace of Sabbath feeling and Sabbath vision, is to be found in the *mere nature* of these old idylls, in the full-filling sublimity of these psalms, in the inspired Godwards of these intense-souled prophets. With all that in mind, think now of the tumid superiority of Mr. Buckle! If any one can contradict me, he magnanimously intimates when perorating against all that, "I will abandon the view for which I am contending!" With the Hebrew Scriptures lying there before us in their truth, as I have attempted to image it, is it not something pitiably small to hear again the jokes even of a Voltaire about the *discrepancies?* I do not apprehend that it is pretended by any one that there are not discrepancies; but what are they in the midst of all that grandeur? He, now, who would boggle at the wife of Cain, or stumble over the walls of Jericho, is not an adult: he is but a boy still. For my part, I do believe—I feel sure—that David Hume, that Voltaire himself were he alive now, and were he cognizant of all the education that we have received since, even on prompting of his own, would not for a moment be inclined to own as his these laggards and stragglers of an army that had disappeared. He would know that the new time had brought a new task, and he would have no desire to find himself a mere anachronism, and historically out of date.

But with whatever general spirit we may approach the subject, it is to be considered that that subject, that Natural Theology itself, makes no call on Revelation— nay, that the Lecturer is under an express stipulation to treat it in independence of Revelation. Natural Theology, indeed, just as *Natural* Theology, means an appeal to nature, an appeal that is only natural. In it the existence of a God is to be established only by reference to the constitution of the universe, even as that universe exhibits itself within the bounds of space and time; and not in anywise farther than as it is reflected also in the intellect and will of man.

Having thus exhausted what appeared necessary preliminaries of the subject so far as the respective persons seem concerned, their claims, wishes, intentions, views, powers, and understandings in its regard, we shall, in the next lecture, proceed to what more directly bears on the subject itself.

# GIFFORD LECTURE THE SECOND.

Natural theology, what is it?—Usual answers—Hutcheson—Varro—The Middle Ages—Raymund of Sebonde—Rays, Paleys, etc.—Till 1860—Since—Philosophies of religion—Pagan gods—De Quincey, Augustine, Cicero, Pliny, Juvenal, Herodotus, Aulus Gellius—The proofs historically treated—That the theme—Plotinus, Augustine—Natural theology not possibly a physical science—Understanding and faith, Augustine, Anselm—Monotheism alone religion proper—The course, affirmative, negative—China, India, Colebrooke, Rás bihárí Mukharjí—Hindu texts (Gnostics)—Hesiod.

HAVING discussed and settled, so far as seemed desirable, the personal aspects in connection with the matter in hand—what, viz., may have been the wishes, intentions, and general spirit of the Testator himself in the reference, as well as what expectations it may be in place to form in regard to the immediate lecturer, and the mood of mind in which he avows himself to enter upon this theme,—questions, it is hoped, all viewed with feelings and considerations not alien from, but so far in harmony with, the subject,—to that subject itself it only now remains for us more directly to turn.

It—that subject—is formally dictated and expressly prescribed to us under the name of Natural Theology. We are met at once, in the first place, then, by the question, What is it—what is Natural Theology? I daresay we have all some idea, more or less correspondent to the interest itself, of what Theology is. Theology, by the etymology of the mere expression, is the logos of God. The Greek *logos*, to be sure, like the Latin *ratio*, has quite an infinitude of applications; but the application that comes pretty well at once to the surface here, suggests, as in some degree synonymous with itself, such words as description, narrative, account, report, rationale, theory, etc. Geology is a description, narrative, account, report, rationale, theory of all that concerns the earth in itself and in its vicissitudes. Zoology is such an account of all that concerns animals; and astrology, supposing it to mean, as it ought, all that astronomy means, is a description, narrative, account, report, rationale, theory of all the objects we perceive in the heavens, and of their various movements and general phenomena. Theology, then, is to expound to us God, the fact of His existence, and the nature of His Being. Now, the qualifying word, *Natural*, when applied to *Theology*, must have a limitative, restrictive, and determinative force. What is still in hand is Theology, the account of God; but that account is to be a natural account. In short, Natural Theology means that we are to tell of God all that we can tell of Him *via naturæ*, by the way of nature,—we are to tell of Him all that we can tell of Him from an examination of mere nature— of nature as we perceive or find it to be without us, of nature as we perceive or find it to be within us. The information so acquired will sometimes be found to be named, as by the Scholastics, and by Descartes and Leibnitz after them, the *lumen naturæ, lumen naturale, lumière naturelle*, the light of nature; and consequently, by very name, is opposed to the supernatural light which is to be understood as given us by express revelation.

Francis Hutcheson, in the third part, *De Deo*, of his excellent little Latin *Synopsis of Metaphysics*, says that "although all philosophy is pleasant and profitable, there is, nevertheless, no part of it more productive and rich than that which contains the knowledge of God, *quæque dicitur Theologia Naturalis.*" This Natural Theology he goes on to describe as due to "philosophers who support themselves on the sole powers of human reason, and make no reference to what God has supernaturally revealed to inspired men." And the thing itself confirms the definition. We have only to look to what treatises have been actually written on the subject to perceive that the attempt in all of them is to demonstrate the existence and attributes of the Deity by reason alone, in application to nature itself as it appears within us or without us. Any sketch of the history of these treatises—of the history of Natural Theology—usually begins with the mention of Varro, the contemporary of Cicero, a man, as it appears, of encyclopædic knowledge. I cannot see, however, much in his connection that is in application here. All that is known of Varro on this head is to be found in the sixth book of St. Augustine's *City of God*, the greater part of which is taken up with Varro and his relation to the gods. Augustine praises Varro, and says, "he will teach the student of things as much as Cicero delights the student of words." There shall have been on his part also "a threefold division of theology into fabulous, natural, civil." And here Varro says himself, "they call that kind mythical (or fabulous) which the poets chiefly use; physical, that which the philosophers use; civil, that which the people use;" and again he says, "the first theology is especially adapted to the theatre, the second to the world, the third to the city." But without going any further into this, it may be said at once that the Natural, rather Physical Theology here, only considered the principles of the philosophers, as the fire of Heraclitus, the numbers of the Pythagoreans, the atoms of Epicurus; and was merely a rationalizing of what was alleged of the gods into these—these principles, and had no claim whatever to the title Natural Theology as understood by us. At all to allude to Varro in this connection is on the whole idle.

Of the power and majesty, as well as of the love of God, exhibited in the spectacle of the creation, we know that in the Old and New Testaments there is much both of awing sublimity and heart-touching gentleness. And, accordingly, we may as readily surmise that such marvels of poetry and inspiration would not escape the early Fathers, but would be rapturously used by them. And so indeed it was. Not but that there was a religious teaching, sooner or later, in vogue also, that despised nature, and turned from it as something inferior or wicked. All through the Middle Ages, and in most of their respective writings, there occur traces of references to nature that may be claimed in any professed history of the subject; but in point of reality there is no veritable "Natural Theology" till the work expressly so named by the Raimond Sebond, the Raimondus de Sebonde, of Montaigne. The place he is named from is supposed to be somewhere in Spain, but nobody seems to know where it is to be found; every new authority has a new name for it, Sebonde, Sabunde, Sabeyda, Sabieude, etc.

Raymund flourished in the middle of the fifteenth century, and his book was called *Theologia Naturalis sive Liber Creaturarum ex quo homo in Dei et creaturarum suique ipsius cognitionem assurgit*—*Natural Theology or Book of the Creatures*, from which a man rises to a knowledge of God and the creatures and his own self. This is sufficiently promising; but, after all, there is not a great deal in the book. Nevertheless, it appeared of such importance to the Roman Curia that we find its Prologus in the list of forbidden books; this in 1595, more than a century and a half after its presumed composition. Montaigne, too, who translated it into French for his father, speaks in the highest terms of it. "Many folks amuse themselves reading it," he says, "and especially the ladies." I had noted some passages to quote, but they are hardly worth the time. In the ascent of things to God, man is on the fourth grade, he remarks: he *is*, he *lives*, he *feels*, and he *understands*. This is a fourfold distinction taken from Aristotle, which we find in most writers throughout the Middle Ages; it is the *esse, vivere, sentire, intelligere*, so universally applied in exposition of the stages of creation during the Hexaemeron—the six days of it.

After Raymund, or his commentator Montaigne, I fancy we need hardly mention any other writers on the subject till we come to the Grews, Rays, Cudworths, Stillingfleets, Derhams, Clarkes, and Fénélons nearer our own times; in which (times) all previous authorities have been superseded by our Paley and our Bridgewater Treatises.

These last, then,—this now is the important consideration, and here is the critical pause,—these last, then, represent Natural Theology, and, as a whole, exhibit it—is it their contents that shall constitute the burden of these lectures, and be reproduced now? It is Natural Theology we have to treat—*Paley* is Natural Theology. Shall we just give Paley over again? I fear the question will be met by most of us with a shudder. For many years back it would seem as though the Natural Theology of the Rays and the Derhams, of the Paleys and the *Bridgewater Treatises* had vanished from our midst. "Where," asked a metaphysician some fourscore years ago,—" where may or can now a single note of former Natural Theology be heard—all that has been destroyed root and branch, and has disappeared from the circle of the sciences?" His own question, all the same, did not hinder the same metaphysician from lecturing affirmatively on Natural Theology a considerable number of years later; while, at about the same time in England, there was a revival of interest in the subject, principally in consequence, perhaps, of a new edition of Paley's work, to which Sir Charles Bell and Lord Brougham had, each in his own way, contributed. From that time, quite on indeed till 1860, we may say, there was the old interest, the old curiosity, admiration, reverence, awe, as in presence of the handiwork of God, when the descriptions of Natural Theology were before us, whether in lecture or in book. But now, again, a new wave has come and washed, for some twenty years back, Natural Theology pretty well out of sight. He who should take it up now as Paley took it up, or as Lord Brougham took it up, would simply be regarded as a fossil.

In such circumstances the resource seems to be to turn to what is called the Philosophy of Religion, and has been introduced into Great Britain almost quite recently in the form of one or two translations from the German. There are other philosophies of religion in existence besides any as yet translated. Perhaps, indeed, there is no department of philosophy, so far as publishers' lists are in evidence, which claims a greater number of books at present. Even here, however, *with a special view to the requirements of Lord Gifford's Bequest*, I do not find my look of inquiry quite hopefully met. In one of the translated books, for example, what we find as a philosophy of religion is pretty well a series of biographies; while, in the other, there are two parts—a part that is general, and a part that is biographical. Now, I do not apprehend that a mere series of biographies would suit the requirement which we have in view; and, as for the general part, it does not seem to satisfy me in that consideration either. That part may be said to consist of three divisions— one division being given to what we may call alien religions, another to our own Christianity, and a third to what may be regarded as specially general. Now, as regards Christianity, I do not feel that I should be happy did I philosophize it to you, even if that were competent to us on Lord Gifford's foundation, in the way in which it has been usual to do so, as, in fact, we find at once in the example readiest to hand— I mean in the Raymund of Sabunde we have just spoken of. This writer holds that there must, of necessity, be a plurality of persons in the Godhead, *quia in Deo debet esse communicatio, quæ nequit esse sine dante, et recipiente atque communicante* (that is, "because in God there must be communication or community, which, again, is impossible unless there be a *Giver*, a *Receiver*, and a *Communicator*"). Of course, as is obvious at once, Raymund means that the Father should be the Giver, the Son the Receiver, and the Third, Person in the Godhead the Communicator. I do not mean to say that it is literally thus our modern writers philosophize to us the Trinity; but it is an example in point, and perfectly illustrates the general method actually in use. I do not know that it is popularly known; it is quite true, nevertheless, that in the greater number of the Fathers of the Church, and the other ecclesiastical, especially mystical, writers of the Middle Ages, some such method of philosophizing the persons of the Godhead is commonly to be found. In them, for example, as in more modern philosophical writers, it is quite usual for Christ to stand as the existent world. Now, I am not at all a foe to a warranted religious philosophizing; I am not at all a foe even to the carrying of trinity—trinity in unity—into the very heart of the universe in constitution of it. But it strikes me that in these days, and as we are here in Great Britain, so to attempt to philosophize the Christian Godhead would only repugn. I, for my part, cannot feel at home in it. I feel quite outside of it. There is such a naked *naïveté* in the Old Testament, and there is such a direct trust of natural simplicity in the New, as comport but ill with the apparent artifice and mere ingenuity of these seeming externalities. Again, as regards the division which, in these books, is devoted to other religions than our own, one finds it hard to put faith in that adjustment of them, the one to the other, that would make a correlated series of them, and a connected whole. With whatever attempt to philosophize them, there appears little for us that is vital in these religions now. They are not lively these nondescript divinities. My reading of these parts of these philosophies has been careful enough; but I always found that a *Gesindel* (a rabble) of gods would not prove to me, as a Gesindel of ghosts had proved to a German professor, entertaining, that is, and refreshing. My experience rather seemed to be something like that of De Quincey in his dreams. " I fled from the wrath of Brahma; Vishnu hated me; Siva lay in wait for me; I came suddenly on Isis and Osiris. I had done a deed, they said, which the ibis and the crocodile trembled at." Milton's " Lars and Lemures," and " wounded Thammuz," and " the dog Anubis," and " that twice-battered god of Palestine," were only delightful to me in his own most glorious poem. Apart from it, I was as grimly content to see them turn tail and flee as he was. I quite sympathized with Augustine in his contempt or horror of such gods as Jugatinus and Domiducus, and Domitius and Manturna, and Subigus and Prema and Pertunda. I agreed with Cicero that it was "detestable," that it was to be "repudiated," and not to be "tolerated," that there should be such gods as Fever and Mischance, Insolence and Impudence. I did not wonder at Pliny's disgust with the human folly that would believe in such gods. And did not Juvenal tell us of the Leek and the Onion as the gods whom, inviolably, the Egyptians swore by ? "Oh, the holy nation," exclaims Juvenal,—"oh, the holy nation whose very gods grow in their gardens!" One remembers, nevertheless, that in the erection of the pyramids, according to Herodotus, these same Egyptians ate up ever so many hundred talents' worth of those gods of theirs. As for the divinity of the onion in particular, Aulus Gellius informs us that the Egyptian priests believed it, because the onion reversed for them the usual order of sublunary things, growing, namely, as the moon declined, and declining as the moon grew. I am not aware that modern science has confirmed the supposition; but, no doubt, they knew a great many more things then than we know now! A Gesindel, a canaille, a rabble of gods truly! And Pliny has it that there was, in his time even, a greater population of gods and goddesses than of human beings! The Greek poets and the Roman poets—I am just recounting my relative experiences here—were all as pleasing to me, no doubt, as to another; but I could not say that the special gods, Jupiter and the rest, made any very appreciable part of the pleasure. I had no interest in the gods of polytheism at all: after strange gods I suppose it formed no part of my idiosyncrasy to run. In short, in the division under reference of the said philosophies of religion, the philosophizing of the various gods of the various nations failed to move me or inspire me with a will to follow in the same direction. This, of course, cannot be without some natural exaggeration; for, in the end, I by no means deny a certain affinity of the religions, the one to the other, and a consequent possibility of philosophically bringing them together. I only wish that for the purpose of use the actual attempts in this direction, so far as possibility of presentation is concerned, were better suited for our public. But, for the mere histories of the various popular divinities, I failed to see that I could make any application of them in the charge I had accepted in connection with Lord Gifford's bequest. Natural Theology as Natural Theology I could not in any way find in them.

But, besides the divisions philosophizing,—the one Christianity and the other paganism,—there was the intermediate division of a more general philosophical matter, discussing, for example, the question of the seat of religion, whether it was a sentiment, or whether it was a knowledge—even here I failed to find myself satisfied as to its sufficient availableness in respect of the conditions in view. The best performances in this regard had in them, assuming all else to be unobjectionable, such a mode of presentation and treatment as hardly could be acceptably and intelligibly conveyed.

Recurring perforce from the Philosophy of Religion to Natural Theology again, it suggested itself that, after all, Paley's way of it did not exhaust the subject. The field was really a larger field than Paley occupied. Paley entertained no questions of the proofs as the proofs, and the proofs as the proofs constituted the subject. The arguments, the proofs for the Being of a God—that was Natural Theology. And, again, not less are these proofs the very essential elements and bases of the philosophy of religion itself. There is no philosophy of religion that, extricating itself from mere biography, possesses a general part, but finds room—the best of them large, important, and essential room—for the subject of the proofs. Whence come these proofs, then? They must have had a beginning. But begin where they might, they could have had no place where paganism and polytheism obtained. Side by side with religion, there might have been vague, crude, general philosophizings, but there could have been no Natural Theology as Natural Theology, and no proofs as proofs of Natural Theology. Polytheism, therefore, must fade, monotheism must dawn, before there could be even a thought of Natural Theology or its proofs. What, then, is the history of these proofs, and in this relation?

Suppose, at long and last, we take up this,—suppose we take up consideration of the known, received, tabulated, traditional proofs, *and in connection with their history*,—that would be an escape at once from what is alleged to be antiquated, and to what brings with it an element that promises to be new; for there may be in existence sketched suggestions in regard to those who have written on the subject; but it seems unknown that any attention has been paid as yet to the historical derivation of the proofs themselves. In this way, too, there would be no abandonment of the subject itself. Natural Theology—God as the sole content of Natural Theology—would never fall from sight nor cease to be before our eyes. Nor yet are we any more in this way excluded from philosophy: we are at once here in the very heart of the philosophy of religion itself; and, in a personal regard, there can be no want of every opportunity to say everything whatever that one may have a wish or ability to say on such theme generally. With four men, at four universities, all declaiming, year after year, on the same text, there *may* come necessity for diversion and digression; but now, in this first year, it would ill become the lecturer who was first elected on the whole foundation, and in the university at least *of* the capital—it would ill become him, so signalized and so placed, to set the example of an episode, while it was the epic he was specially engaged for. There can be no doubt that Lord Gifford was very serious in his bequest,—there can be no doubt of the one meaning, end, aim, intention, and object of all those emphatic specifications and designations of his,—there can be no question but that the Testator's one wish, in these days of religious difficulty and distrust, was for some positive settlement in regard to the Being of a God. One cannot read that last Will and Testament of Lord Gifford's, indeed, without being reminded of what Porphyry tells us of Plotinus. Plotinus died, he says, with these last words in his mouth: Πειράσθω τὸ ἐν ἡμῖν θεῖον ἀνάγειν πρὸς τὸ ἐν τῷ πάντι θεῖον (strive to bring the God that is in us to the God that is in the All). Kepler, apparently in contrast to this, says : "My highest wish is to find *within* the God whom I find everywhere *without.*" In such a matter, however, it does not signify from which side we take it. There can be no doubt that the last thoughts of Lord Gifford concerned his own soul, and the God who made it. To know that, was to Lord Gifford to know all. It was with him just as though he soliloquized with St. Augustine (*Soliloq.* i. 7): *Deum et animam scire cupio* (I desire to know God and the soul). *Nihilne plus* (Nothing more)? *Nihil omnino* (Nothing at all)!

It is true at the same time—and it may be well for a moment to meet this point—that Lord Gifford wished the subject to be treated as a strictly natural science, just as astronomy or chemistry is. But *natural* obviously is only opposed here to *supernatural*, only to what concerns Revelation. It were idle to ask me to prove this: every relative expression is a proof in place. If it were said that astronomy is to be treated as a strictly natural science just as chemistry is, would it be necessary to substitute in the former the method of the latter—to roast Jupiter in a crucible, or distil Saturn over in a retort? Things that are identical in the genus are very unlike in the species, as in the Aristotelian example of the ox and the man, where each is an animal. The apparatus of chemistry is for chemistry, and the apparatus of astronomy is for astronomy: neither can be substituted for the other; and both are powerless in regard to the object of Natural Theology. Our transatlantic brothers, as we hear at this moment, are going to have object glasses, or reflectors, or refractors, of ever so many feet; but the very tallest American, with the very tallest of telescopes, will never be able to say that he spied out God. Natural Theology is equally known as Rational Theology; and Rational Theology is equally known as the Metaphysic of God. That last phrase is acceptable enough; it repugns not; but fancy the Physic of God! The Greek term, doubtless, has an identity with the Latin one; but it has also a difference. Natural Theology may be considered a strictly natural science; but it were hardly possible to treat it as a strictly physical science. *Physical* Theology sounds barbarous, and carries us no farther than Mumbo-Jumbo and the fetich in general.

What we have to aim at, wholly and solely, here, in our science, is the *knowledge* of God, a knowledge that can come to us only *metaphysically*; for it is a knowledge that, with whatever reference to nature, is still beyond nature; —a knowledge, in fact, whose very business in the end is to transcend nature—the knowledge, namely, to which the Finite is only the momentary purchase that gives the rise to the Infinite. It can come to us, then, as said, only metaphysically, and for that matter, too, only religiously. The old way of it is not without its truth, the old way of it, as in the time of Augustine, or as in the time of Anselm. To both Augustine and Anselm there may be a necessity for a cultivation of the understanding; but to both also there is a necessity that faith precede. Augustine (*Civ. Dei*, ix. 20) has in mind the verse (1 Cor. viii. 1), " Know-

C

ledge puffeth up, but charity buildeth up." "And this can only be understood," he says, "as meaning that without charity, knowledge does no good, but inflates a man, or magnifies him with an empty windiness." So it is that to Augustine faith, love, charity must precede knowledge. Even as the ground must be loosened and softened for reception of the seed, so must the heart be made tender by faith, charity, and love, if it would profitably receive into itself the elements of knowledge. The same necessities, to the same end, *with* humility, occur in Anselm. So here we have only to recollect his most frequent expressions to know that the general object of Lord Gifford, too, was faith, belief—the production of a living principle that, giving us God in the heart, should, in this world of ours, guide us in peace.

How inapplicable mere Physics are to Natural Theology is obvious also from this, that Lord Gifford directly styles the latter "the only science, the science of Infinite Being." It is not in a science of Infinite Being that the lever or the pulley or the screw can have any place; in respect of such a science, there is no power to deal with it but what lies in philosophy. And thus in meeting an objection that may rest on such expressions as astronomy, chemistry, natural science, etc., we are brought back to where we were in connection with the proofs and their appearance in history. Natural Theology as Natural Theology, the philosophy of Infinite Being as the philosophy of Infinite Being, neither the one nor the other can be found in Physics, and just as little in paganism or in polytheism; but both are to be found, and found together, when on the stage of history polytheism is melting into monotheism, and paganism is drawing nigh to Christianity. I have been met with surprise when I have said that religion *proper* only begins with monotheism. But you will realize what I mean, if you will only consider the idea of sin. In mere mythology, which is superstition only, there may be fear for an evil in threat, or hope for a good that is desired, but there is no moral sense of sin, no moral anguish and conflict in one's own conscience. Moral responsibility comes only with the doctrine of the one God that has made man in His image. For then man is no longer a slave; he is a free man, and is referred to his own standard as a rational being, in regard to whether he is in unison with his Maker or not. Had ever any Greek or Roman struggles within himself as to his belief or unbelief? Many a modern has given to this world soul-thrilling testimonies of struggles as to God; but never a Greek or a Roman in regard to Jupiter or Juno. Men, of course, will tear you like wild beasts, and rend you into a thousand fragments, should you spit upon their fetiches, in whose good-will they trust; but that is a different matter. These men may hate *you;* but they have no struggles in themselves.

And now, after all these meetings of objections and all these explanations, in which, I trust, you will still kindly acknowledge a certain treatment of the subject itself,—after all this, it remains for me to state finally and formally what our further course shall be both for this session and the next. I take the theme as it is prescribed to me—Natural Theology and the proofs for the Being of a God. These proofs I follow historically, while the reflection, at the same time, that we have still before us "the only science, the science of Infinite Being," may bring with it a certain breadth and filling, tending to preclude, perhaps, what possible insufficiency of philosophical matter a mere consideration of the proofs themselves might chance to involve. This is one half of my enterprise. The other half—the negative half—shall concern the denial of the proofs. This session I confine myself to the affirmative; next session, I shall conclude with what concerns the negative. In this way we shall have two correspondent and complementary halves—one irenical, and the other polemical; one with the ancients, and the other with the moderns. For I shall bring the affirmative half historically down only till we come again in sight of Raymund of Sabunde, with whom in a way our explanations opened. I shall not trouble you with any formal exposition of the proofs themselves till we come to the negative that denies them; and I do not think it necessary to deduce the historical part farther than Raymund. I hold the Grews, the Rays, the Derhams, etc., to have been all absorbed in your familiar Paley, who, for his part, needs no exposition of mine.

Now, of the historical reference in question, I know not that there is much to be said till the first faint rise of monotheism begins to show itself among the Greeks; for I shall presume the writings of the Hebrews to have stood fairly on the world-stage only after Christianity came to the struggle with heathenism; though certainly, some 250 years before the commencement of our era, the Jews had attained, in Alexandria, to a decided influence on, to say so, the universal historical life.

Before Greece, and in regard to possible philosophizings spoken of as side by side with the religions, we have to cast our eyes only on India; for, as regards China, there does not seem anything for us there, unless the declaration of the sect of Lao-tse, that a material naturalism need not alone be the object of knowledge and belief, but that the superiority lies with the things of reason and the soul. Henry Thomas Colebrooke, in his essays on the philosophy of the Hindus, published in the *Transactions of the Royal Asiatic Society*, and reprinted in his *Miscellaneous Essays*, has collected for us all that bears on the philosophical theology of India; for what is philosophical in that reference alone concerns us—we have no call to turn to that Gesindel of gods themselves. I may allow myself to lament to you that I have not an assistance here, which I had at least much hoped for. I have in correspondence with me an Indian gentleman of the greatest philosophical promise, who has for years been engaged upon, and will soon publish, a great historical work in reference to the philosophy and philosophies of the Hindus—Mr. Rás Bihárî Mukharji. In the meantime, while we wait, we must be glad that we have Colebrooke. Here among his translations is one in which the beginning of all things is represented very much as it is in the first chapter of Genesis: "The earth was without form and void; and darkness was upon the face of the deep. Then, was there neither entity nor nonentity; no world, nor sky, nor aught above it . . . darkness there was . . . but THAT breathed without afflation—other than Him nothing existed . . . this universe was enveloped with darkness . . . but that mass, which was covered by the husk, was at length produced by the power of contemplation and desire, the original productive seed." It is observed in a note to the passage in Colebrooke that darkness and desire here (Tamas and Kárna) bear a distinct resemblance to the Chaos and Eros of Hesiod. But that mighty formless void, as it were the nebula of a world, breathed out like an exhalation around the Supreme Being, who then was simply contemplation and desire, reminds of similar ideas in the Gnostics, who also were mainly Orientals. Thus to Valentinus God was as the Bythos, the deeply-brooding abyss, the syzygy of which was ἔννοια, meditation; and meditation was σιγή, silence, or χάρις, bliss. All these ideas seem to go together; and, as Thomas Taylor might say, are not *paradigmatic* only, but *parental*. They are not merely schematic—merely in effigy or scheme, but they are substantially productive, procreative, parturient.

Almost we get the thought from them that God *must* be, and *with* God His world. There is the βυθός, the deep, the eternal deep, the abysmal deep—is it not very striking that with such first principle, the second should be ἔννοια, meditation? And that meditation is σιγή, silence, deep, eternal, infinite; and that silence is' χάρις, bliss, the mighty secret, the deep, silent, mystic felicity of the all-blessed God hidden and shut up into Himself. One cannot think of that first of things, that unfathomable profound, all-silent there, all-blissful there, —one cannot think of it but as full—the æon world is its πλήρωμα, and its πλήρωμα, its filling, is the universe that *is* to be. All the thoughts go together, and they come to us as but the necessary nisus of the mighty prime, the prime that is itself a necessity and a nisus. The Gnostics proceed to add here, perhaps, a discordant note. They call this βυθός, ἀρρενο-θηλυς, man-woman; but still it is not incongruous that it should be as yet the all-one, the all-indifferent, the all-neutral, the simple infinite, the ἄπειρον of Anaximander. Another syzygy of the Gnostics here is ἀλήθεια truth, and truth also is in place. To all mankind, as to Democritus, it has seemed only fit that truth should be hidden in a well (βυθῷ).

These gnostic ideas are evidently very much in consonance with the conceptions of the Indians in regard to their Supreme Being, who at first for them "breathed without afflation." And I refer to such ideas now not as formally illustrative of the proofs as such, but as being at least akin to them. If there be a creating God as there is both to the Indians and the Gnostics, then what is called Teleology is irrepressible, design confronts us on the spot. But however it be with Teleology, with the proofs, how much such a passage as that Indian passage is as a voice from what to Lord Gifford is "the only science—the science of Infinite Being," must of itself be obvious at once. As might be expected too, it is not a passage left to Colebrooke alone; it is to be found in all writers of the class, as, prominently, in the texts and translations of that eminent Orientalist Dr. John Muir. In his *History of Ancient Sanscrit Literature*, at page 546, there is also an admirable poetical rendering of it at the able hands of Mr. Max Müller, who, as we all know, is not only a passed master in linguistic science, but in comparative mythology as well the chief authority.

Further, here, it may not be out of place, indeed, that I should name a few more of these Indian assonances. This, for example, is very notable: "Looking around, that primeval being saw nothing but himself, and he first said, 'I am I.' Therefore his name was 'I.'" Here, too, is a remarkable passage: "Brighu approached his father, Varuna, saying, 'Venerable! make known to me Brahma;'" and on the third asking, it is said, "He (Varuna) meditated in deep contemplation, and discovered intellect to be Brahma; for all these beings are indeed produced from intellect; when born they live by intellect; towards intellect they tend; and they pass into intellect." Anaxagoras on the νοῦς could hardly have been better abbreviated. The declarations of Hindu philosophy in regard to causality may be referred to as having a relation as well to Teleology as to Ontology, or the Science of Being. But for them we shall have a fitter place elsewhere. Continuing our illustrations from Colebrooke, here is another proposition which I think we shall yet find of the greatest relevance and reach in what constitutes for us our special interest: "There must be one to enjoy what is formed for enjoyment: a spectator, a witness of it; that spectator is soul." There is also to be found, similarly, in these communications this remarkable statement in regard to the final cause of the world, or rather simply of nature, nature as such.

It (nature) is not there independently, self-subsistently, and on its own account; it is there only for a purpose and as a means. "As a dancer," it is said, "having exhibited herself to the spectator, desists; so does nature desist, having manifested herself to soul. . . . He (the spectator) desists because he has seen her; and she (the dancer) desists because she has been seen." That is, the work has been accomplished; what was to be done has been done; and the implements withdraw.

As regards the reference on the part of Colebrooke to the *Theogony* of Hesiod and certain resemblances in its traditions to those of the Indians, there cannot be a doubt of its correctness. Both ring with assonances to the cosmogony of the Pentateuch; and it is impossible to avoid believing, in reference to all three, that they echo to us some of the most ancient utterances of the race. Mr. Paley, the learned editor of Hesiod, observes in his preface (xv.) that in the *Theogony* we have "traces of what appear to be primitive and nearly universal traditions of the human family . . . traditions so immensely ancient, that all traces of anything like a history of them had, long before Hesiod's time, been utterly and irretrievably lost. The coincidences between the earliest known traditions of mankind and the Mosaic writings are much too numerous and important to be purely accidental, and much too widely dispersed to have been borrowed solely from that source." So writes Mr. Paley. The traditions in Hesiod, therefore, in regard to primitive being, infinite and divine, are in nowise discordant from those of the East. We shall allow Hesiod, accordingly, to be, so far, the bridge from the East to the West, from the Indian to the Greek, where and among whom we shall find at last the scientific beginning, historically, as well of Teleology as of Ontology, with all the ethical and other consequences desiderated by Lord Gifford.

# GIFFORD LECTURE THE THIRD.

Final causes—The four Aristotelian causes—Are there final causes in nature—Matter and form—Other causes only to realize the final causes—Cudworth—Adam Smith—The proofs, number, order, etc.—Teleology—Anaxagoras—Socrates in the Phædo—Xenophon — Plato — Socrates on Anaxagoras — The causes together, concrete — "Abstract" — Forces, Clerk Maxwell — Heraclitus—Newton—Buckle — Descartes — Gassendi — Bacon on causes, metaphysics, and forms—The νοῦς (*nous*) of Anaxagoras—Bacon on design—Reid, Newton, Hume on design—Newton.

FEARING that we should find the present lecture dull, I have been at considerable pains this week in the re-writing of it; for I desire to be at least intelligible, if not interesting or popular. My reason for fear was that I had been led to speak at some length of final causes, and the subject appeared a somewhat dry one. Still, let it be as it may, it is one that in such a course as this is unavoidable. For the very existence of our science, the very existence of Natural Theology, is bound up with the existence of final causes. Destroy final causes once for all, and you destroy Natural Theology for ever.

The origin of the term, as is well known, lies in the Aristotelian quadruplicity of causes as such; final causes being but one of its members. We are told in our class-rooms, namely, of *material* causes, *formal* causes, *final* causes, and *efficient* causes; and the usual example given is that of a watch, in regard to which, the metals are the *material* causes; the wheels, pinions, cylinders, etc., the *formal* causes; the watchmaker, the *efficient* cause; and the pointing of the hour, the *final* cause. Warmth is the final cause of a blanket; but so much sheep's wool is its material cause. The final cause of a bridge is the passage of a river; its material cause, the stones; its formal cause, the arch; and its efficient cause, the architect with his workmen. Now, though we can hardly say with Dr. Reid (*IV W.* 526) that these four causes are but four shades of the same meaning, we can certainly maintain that, for the most part, they constitute together but a single concrete; as we can readily see in the examples of the watch and the bridge. It is evident, however, that such examples as these, let them be as explanatory as they may, can have no application to, or vitality in, Natural Theology, so far as, in its very terms, it is to be considered a manifestation of nature. That there are these causes existent in human affairs, even to an almost endless extent, is not the question. We have only to know a house, or a ship, or a canal, or a railway, or a telegraph, or a garter, or a shoe tie, or a button, or a knife, fork, and spoon, to understand all that. But are there also such things in nature?—that is the question; and there are those who answer it in the affirmative; while there are others, again, who meet it with a direct negative. And this is the *clash:* here is the very edge —here is the very knot, and point, and core of the battle. The whole business of Natural Theology lies there—is there, or is there not, design? Is there, or is there not, a final cause in nature? If there be anything such in nature—if there be anything in nature that, by very formation, shows design, purpose, intention to have been its origin, then there is also proof in nature of an efficient cause that gave at least form to matter. And in this way, even in nature, the four causes would be seen to constitute together but a single concrete quite as much and as manifestly as they do in art. Already, indeed, we can see as much as this to be at least the case with the material and the formal causes, let it be as it may with the others. That is, either apart is at once seen to be null. If matter were without form, it would be incognizable, a nonentity, a void, something nowhere to be seen or touched or heard. Lump-paste, lump-clay, lump-metal may seem formless to us, and yet cognizable; but this is not so. Lump-paste, lump-clay, lump-metal are substances, each with its own qualities; and these qualities are to each its form. The qualities of paste are not the qualities of clay; nor are these the qualities of metal. Consequently, all three are distinguishable the one from the other. A substance without a quality were a non-ens, and a quality without a substance were but a fiction in the air. *Matter*, if to be, must be permeated by *form;* and equally *form*, if to be, must be realized by *matter*. Substance takes being from quality; quality, actuality from substance. That is metaphysic; but it is seen to be as well physic,—it is seen to have a physical existence; it is seen to be in *rerum natura*. *Form* is, as it were, the thought, the soul of *matter;* and *matter*, as it were, the body, the externale of *form*. So it is that a thing is understood when we see the externale in the internale; and, quite as much, the internale in the externale. Form and matter are the same synthesis, or, what is equally true, they are the same antithesis. But, taking it for granted that this will be readily admitted to be the case as regards matter and form, it will not be so readily acknowledged, we may assume, that final causes are in similar vital relation with the material and formal ones. That these latter causes are but the vehicles in realization of final causes,—this, in fact, is but the matter in dispute, and can never be expected to be accepted by those who oppose final causes themselves. What we have presently historically to see, however, is precisely this doctrine in Greece — that material causes (with formal) are but the implements, and instruments, and scaffolding of final causes. It is in this mood that Cudworth says, "To take away all final causes from the things of nature is the very spirit of atheism: it is no prejudice or fallacy imposed on ourselves to think that the frame and system of this whole world was contrived by a perfect understanding and mind." As another modern illustration, we may say that there is a passage in the *Theory of Moral Sentiments* which almost bears out the supposition that even Adam Smith saw the one set of causes to be but the complement of the other. "In every part of the universe," he says, "we observe means adjusted with the nicest artifice to the ends which they are intended to produce; and in the mechanism of a plant or animal body, admire how everything is contrived for advancing the two great purposes of nature, the support of the individual, and the propagation of the species. But in these, and in all such objects, we still distinguish the efficient from the final cause of their several motions and organizations. The digestion of the food, the circulation of the blood, and the secretion of the several juices which are drawn from it, are operations all of them necessary for the great purposes of animal life; yet we never endeavour to account for them from those purposes as from their efficient causes, nor imagine that the blood circulates, or the food digests, of its own accord, and with a view or intention to the purposes of circulation or digestion." That is, we never fancy that the one side suffices. The "purposes," which are the final causes, do not, alone and by themselves, realize themselves; neither do we imagine of the blood and the food, which are the material causes, that the one circulates, or the other digests, of its own accord. Plainly, Adam Smith here has excellently caught sight of the two sides, abstract, idle, dead, apart, but concrete, energetic, busy, living and life-giving in unity. Of course, I need not remark that his *efficient* is the usual *material:* he says *efficient* here, because what he speaks of is the matter or material *operant.*

With these anticipatory explanations, I may now proceed. In regard to the history of the proofs for the Being of a God, we are now arrived, as has been said, within sight of Greece. As I am not intending at present to expatiate on these proofs themselves; so I shall not take up your time with any rehearsal of the various classifications and designations proposed in their regard by the various authorities. It shall be enough for us that all of these, with whatever peculiarity of dressing, come, in the end, to the three arguments in and with which Kant assumes to comprehend and exhaust the subject. That is, there is, first, the Cosmological; second, the Teleological; and, third, the Ontological argument. There is no dispute as to the position of this last. That argument, the ontological one, does not appear in history until in the time of Anselm Christianity has been for centuries the dominant religion in Europe. About the order of the two others there has been some little difference; Kant characterizing the teleological argument as the oldest, and Hegel postponing it to the cosmological. It has been usual, however, to speak of the latter in connection with Aristotle, and at all events it seems, on the whole, more convenient to begin with the teleological argument. Begin with which we may, however, and let them be separated from each other as they may be in time, the three, after all, do constitute together but the three undulations of a single wave, which wave is but a natural rise and ascent to God, on the part of man's own thought, with man's own experience and consciousness as the object before him.

The word Teleology (due as a word probably to Wolff) has, in its meaning at all events, always been associated with the name of Anaxagoras. He, so far as history teaches, is the acknowledged originator of the idea. That is to be admitted. There can be no doubt that, whatever others may seem to have said in the same direction, it was Anaxagoras who, for the first time in Greece, perhaps in the world, spoke of the beauty and order in the universe being due to a designing mind. We have but to look to the single fragment of his lost work, περὶ φύσεως, which (the fragment) has been preserved to us by Simplicius, to become aware of such clearness and fulness on the part of Anaxagoras in his conception of the νοῦς, *nous*, as could not fail to impress on his successors the necessary problem, generally, of what is meant by teleology, and must perfectly justify, as well, the position which has been assigned to him at their head. "Nous (Intelligence)," he says there, "is infinite and absolute, free from admixture with anything else, alone by itself; it is omniscient and omnipotent, and has disposed all things, in order and in beauty, within the encompassing whole, where the stars are, and the sun, and the moon, and æther, and the air." This, beyond doubt, is fairly to characterize Mind as the ultimate causality of the universe, and of the order and design we see in it; and, very certainly, most amply, does the general voice of antiquity confirm the gloss. For one, Socrates, in the *Phædo*, gives very full testimony to this effect. He had heard a book of Anaxagoras' read, he says, in which it was maintained that νοῦς, which may be translated mind, understanding, reason, was the disposing and arranging principle in the universe, and he had been mightily pleased therewith. For it seemed to him right and excellently well that an intelligence should be recognised as the cause of all things, inasmuch as, in that case, everything would find itself precisely where it was best that it should be; so that, accordingly, such consideration would directly lead us to a perfect explanation of anything in the world around us which we might be curious to understand. In a personal reference, for example, it became a man to ask, whether for himself or others, only what was best. To know that was the same thing as to know what was worst; for in a single cognition both lay (the proposition which is more familiar to us now-a-days, perhaps, as the *dictum de vero;* that the truth, namely, is the index *sui et falsi*). But it is this that has specially struck the mind of Socrates. What an inestimable good it will be to come to understand everything by being made to see that an intelligence has placed it precisely where it is best for it! Nothing could better have suited him than such a doctrine. What was as it should be, justice, right, reason, moral and intellectual truth — that was the special quest of Socrates at all times. Socrates is understood to have had no favour for *Meteorologia*, speculation into things celestial. Nay, Xenophon introduces him as calling this very Anaxagoras mad in the special reference (*Mem.* iv. 7. 6). Not but that Socrates, as we may see further, has his own interest in cosmologia, if not in meteorologia. It is only as characteristic of him, indeed, that he should be made to say here: " It appeared to me εὖ ἔχειν—it appeared to me to be excellently well that the Nous should be the cause of all things;" for it certainly belonged to his very inmost and dearest thought that all things should be found to be framed and arranged by intelligence, and disposed according to what is best. There are other expressions in Plato, not always in the mouth of Socrates, quite to the same effect as regards the Nous of Anaxagoras holding and disposing all things at its own sovereign best. Such expressions are to be found in the *Laws* (967 B), for example, and in the *Cratylus* (400 A, 413 C) more than once. But it is this great passage in the *Phædo* that must be considered the *locus proprius* on the point. Socrates, in it, dwells at very considerable length on the whole matter. It may almost be referred to, actually has been referred to, as an example and proof of Socrates' *polylogia*, his *Redseligkeit*, his loquacity, and, as Smollett says, *clack*. In point of fact, there is no fuller reference to the consideration in debate to be found anywhere, and Socrates does seem to have taken occasion from it to deliver himself in full freedom, unrestrictedly at large. He expatiates, positively, on the expectations which Anaxagoras had conjured up in him, expectations quite contradictorily meteorological, after all, seeing that, in great measure, they concern the shape of the earth, the sun, and the moon, and the comparative courses of the stars,—he expatiates at great length on these expectations, positively, and he would not have given them up, he says, πολλοῦ, for a great deal. Then he expatiates at equal length on his disappointments, negatively, when, most eagerly possessing himself of the books and most keenly reading them, he found the man making no use whatever of the Nous, but, on the contrary, in all actual explanations of things, calling in only mechanical causes, airs, and æthers, and waters, and other ἄτοπα the like, quite as before!—just as though, says Socrates, it should be first affirmed of Socrates that he did all that he did by his own understanding, and then sapiently subjoined as if by way of example, that it was because of such and such bones and tendons, so and so constructed, that he sat there, the real reason being that it seemed to the Athenians best to condemn Socrates, and to himself best to abide the result. "Else, by the dog," he exclaims, "methinks these bones and tendons would, long ere this, have been somewhere about Megara or the Bœotian confines, transported thither on the thought of what seemed best."

We see here that Socrates not only understood the principle of Anaxagoras with Anaxagoras' own further stultification of it, but also, perfectly, the distinction between final and mechanical causes. Proximately, it was certainly because of certain bodily antecedents that Socrates remained, as he did, sitting in prison; but, as certainly, for all that, it was the resolution of his own mind that was the final cause. Here, too, this also is to be seen, that the two sorts of causes do not *remain* abstract, that is, as Bacon (compare the *De Augmentis* in its correspondent part with *The Advancement of Learning*, ii. 8. 2) explains the word *abstract*, "severed," or "dissevered," from all else; but that they are, in *rerum natura*, concretely associated. The centrifugal force, in the revolution of the planets, is not the same as the centripetal: rather, the one is directly the reverse or the opposite of the other. Nevertheless, in the words of Mr. Clerk Maxwell, they are "merely partial and different aspects of the same stress." In point of fact, as already seen in regard to form and matter, this synthesis in antithesis, this one of two, this breadth of a duality in the unity of strain, seems to be the cosmical truth, and alone valid. There cannot be action without reaction; and the one abiding reality is the single nisus between, that conjoins no less than it disjoins. It is the τὸ ἀντίξουν συμφέρον, the coherent disherent, attributed to Heraclitus by Aristotle, who adds "that the fairest harmony results from differents, and that all things are produced from strife" (*Eth. Nic.* viii. 1). The two sides, it would seem, though they stand over against each other, and are absolutely opposed the one to the other, do not, for all that, subvert or destroy each other, but, on the contrary, even in and by their opposition, conserve and maintain each other.

And so it precisely is with Socrates here. The bones and tendons that keep him in prison would in themselves be no better than null were it not for the volition that animates them; and neither would this volition itself be anything were it not for the bones and tendons that realize it. Reaction depends on action, centrifugal force on centripetal force, repulsion on attraction, and even energy must have its support in corporeity. It is Newton himself who says, *Virtus* sine *substantia* subsistere non potest.

Authorities, however, are largely neglected now-a-days, and it is widely the fashion at present to have changed all that—it is widely the fashion, indeed, not only to separate final and efficient (or mechanical) causes as irreconcilable the one with the other, but even to destroy those before these. And this even by reference to such philosophers as Descartes and Bacon. Mr. Buckle, for one, is very apt to rise authoritatively on triumphant toes in this matter as regards both. And, indeed, both philosophers *can* be quoted, as though they were minded, each, to dispute the truth of final causes. But, for all that, suppose we do not simply accept the allegation—suppose, on the contrary, that, as in the case of Charles II. and the dead fish, we examine, rather, into its truth, perhaps we shall find that the accompaniment of a grain of salt may not prove altogether superfluous. As regards Descartes, for example, it will not be found that he at all denied the existence of final causes; and if he discouraged, which he undoubtedly did, the inquisition of them, his reason, his motive was not that he respected them less, but that he respected the place and perfection of the Deity more. Any prohibition in the case of the former arose wholly and solely from devotion in the case of the latter. In fact, there can be no doubt that what wholly and solely determined him here, was the peculiarity of his conception in regard to the Divine Being. That conception was so high that it appeared presumptuous to Descartes to make one, as it were, in the counsels of the Eternal as regards the creation of the world, at the same time that our limited faculties ran the risk, in such a daring, of seeing imperfection where there was perfection alone. Gassendi, I may observe, has a remarkable answer to Descartes here, the foundation of which is entirely the reference to design (see in Descartes at *Med.* IV.).

As regards Bacon, it is on him that the greatest stress is laid for the rejection of final causes; but perhaps, even in his case, as I have suggested, it may not be necessary to take the allegation *au pied de la lettre*. Formal causes, final causes, metaphysic itself,—and it is in place here to name metaphysic, for such causes, *with* the whole logos of God, constitute the very contents of metaphysic,—formal causes, final causes, metaphysic itself, Lord Bacon would seem to have thought of and respected as much as anything whatever in physic itself. I hold *The Advancement of Learning* alone to be sufficient to prove this. That work, in numberless editions, is quite possibly in the hands of everybody, and it constitutes the original English form of what is known as the *De Augmentis Scientiarum*. Really, one has only to look at it to be immediately impressed with an utter surprise that any one should ever have considered its author an enemy of what is known as the metaphysical region of inquiry. By the easy trick of isolating words and clauses, we may make any writer argue on any side we please; and so it has been done with Bacon. The seventh section of the seventh chapter of the second book of *The Advancement of Learning*, for example, he begins in this way: "The second part of metaphysic is the inquiry of final causes, which I am moved to report, not as omitted, but as misplaced. And yet if it were but a fault in order, I would not speak of it . . . but the handling of final causes, mixed with the rest in physical inquiries, hath intercepted the severe and diligent inquiry of all real and physical causes." The correspondent Latin is to the same effect : "Tractatio enim causarum finalium in physicis, inquisitionem causarum physicarum expulit et dejecit." There can be no doubt from such words, then, but that it was a decided opinion of Bacon's that the "handling," the tractatio of final causes, "mixed with the rest in physical inquiries," has expelled and ejected the inquisition of physical causes. And I do not suppose there is any one who will deny this. It is matter of the commonest information that the earliest physical explanations were largely rendered impure and untrustworthy by the reference of phenomena, not to literal antecedents, but to figured agencies. Perhaps we have not lost the same habit even in these days of enlightenment. Falling bodies do not any longer seek the earth by appetite, perhaps; but we have still many other such like tropes in abundance.

It is matter, then, of the commonest information that the earliest physical explanations were apt to be disfigured, or sublimed, by all manner of metaphors, tropes, and personifications. So it was, as Bacon righteously complains, that real physical causes were apt to be pushed out or overlaid. We will all readily grant that ; but we must also say with Bacon, despite any such abuse, and Bacon points to no more, that the general problem of final causes is sufficiently to be respected. Final causes constitute to Bacon the second part of metaphysic, as the subject of forms constitutes to him the first. And Bacon does not at all speak ill of metaphysic. "Natural science or theory," he says in *The Advancement of Learning* (ii. 7. 2), is divided into physic and metaphysic." The latter word, metaphysic, he adds, is used by him "in a differing sense from that that is received." For us here, then, it becomes necessary to know what that "differing sense" is; and Bacon, on that head, leaves us in no difficulty. In the first place, we have (3) this: "I intend *philosophia prima*, summary philosophy and metaphysic, which heretofore have been confounded as one, to be two distinct things;" and, in the second place, these words: "Natural theology, which heretofore hath been handled confusedly with metaphysic, I have inclosed and bounded by itself." It appears thus, that, in the eyes of Bacon, metaphysic must lose two main sciences or disciplines that formerly belonged to it. Nevertheless, it must be said that even to Bacon metaphysic must still remain a very sovereign region of human intelligence. In " what is left remaining for metaphysic " (his own words) he directly rules that " physic should contemplate that which is inherent in matter, and therefore transitory; and metaphysic that which is abstracted and fixed; and again, that physic should handle that which supposeth in nature only a being and moving and natural necessity; and metaphysic should handle that which supposeth further in nature a reason, understanding, and platform or idea. . . . Physic inquireth and handleth the material and efficient causes: metaphysic handleth the formal and final causes." This, then, is to give to metaphysic a serious and principal *rôle*. While physic contemplates in nature only what is external, metaphysic contemplates in the same nature, the reason, the understanding, the idea. It is important to observe that reference to nature: the reason, the understanding, the idea of metaphysic, according to Bacon, is a reason, an understanding, an idea that is actually in nature, and no mere figure of speech, no mere figment of phantasy. But what under metaphysic are called reason, understanding, and idea, are also called, and precisely in the same pages, formal and final causes. Formal and final causes are to Bacon, therefore, each a reason, an understanding, an idea that is in nature; and I can hardly think that any metaphysician, even in these days, would wish for them a deeper place or a more essential function. Bacon insists very much on formal causes: he is even inclined to place them in a region by themselves, a region that is to be a sort of reformed, and improved, and renovated "natural magic," as he calls it. Bacon laments (5) that formal causes "may seem to be nugatory and void, because of the received and inveterate opinion that the inquisition of man is not competent to find out essential forms and true differences." He, for his part, holds that "the invention of forms is of all other parts of knowledge the worthiest to be sought, if it be possible to be found. And, as for the possibility, they are ill discoverers that think there is no land, when they can see nothing but sea." Of these forms, "the essences (upheld by matter) of all creatures do consist." In short, Bacon would seem to have in mind both Plato and Aristotle when they will have us pass beyond all externality to the internality itself which reason alone touches (οὗ αὐτὸς ὁ λόγος ἅπτεται), the ὄντως ὄντα which are, as Schelling interprets, the very "subjects of what is predicted of the ὄντα." Such, then, are the forms of Bacon, the very subjects of things which reason itself touches. And no less decided is Bacon as regards metaphysic in its reference to final causes. "Both causes," he says (7), "physical and metaphysical, are true and compatible, the one declaring an intention, the other a consequence only," for "men are extremely deceived if they think there is an enmity between them." "Physic carrieth men in narrow and restrained ways, subject to many accidents of impediments, imitating the ordinary flexuous courses of nature;" but everywhere broad are the ways for the wise in metaphysic "which doth enfranchise the power of man unto the greatest liberty and possibility of works and effects" (6). Bacon, in fact, has not a word to say against metaphysic or final causes, but only against their "abuse," when they happen to be "misplaced."

We have now left Anaxagoras and his commentators a long way behind us, as though we had forgotten them, and started off into quite another region. What concerns us with Anaxagoras, however, is the νοῦς; and the νοῦς means for us design, at the same time that the forces of design, the realizing agents of design, are final causes. It is with Anaxagoras that design comes in, that final causes first make their appearance; and it is here and now, where there is question of Anaxagoras, that there should be question also of that part of metaphysic which embraces the consideration of such causes. And here, evidently, it was impossible to avoid the relative discussion, especially of Bacon, in regard to whom it has hitherto been received as an established commonplace that he is the declared foe—the foe à l'outrance of anything and everything that concerns the subject of final causes. It is indeed surprising that, with such a common English book before us as *The Advancement of Learning*, any such opinion should ever have been so unconditionally expressed. Even of Natural Theology, Bacon's deliberate utterances are such as may surprise not a few. He directly says, for example, "As concerning divine philosophy or natural theology, it is that knowledge or rudiment of knowledge concerning God, which may be obtained by the contemplation of His creatures; which knowledge may be truly termed divine in respect of the object, and natural in respect of the light. . . . Wherefore, by the contemplation of nature, to induce and enforce the acknowledgment of God, and to demonstrate His power, providence, and goodness, is an excellent argument, and hath been excellently handled by divers" (*Adv. of Learn.* ii. 6. 1). " It is an assured truth, and a conclusion of experience," he says elsewhere in the same work (i. 1. 3), " that a little or superficial knowledge of philosophy may incline the mind of man to atheism, but a further proceeding therein doth bring the mind back again to religion. For in the entrance of philosophy when the second causes, which are next unto the senses, do offer themselves to the mind of man, if it dwell and stay there it may induce some oblivion of the highest cause ; but when a man passeth on farther, and seeth the dependence of causes and the works of Providence, then, according to the allegory of the poets, he will easily believe that the highest link of nature's chain must needs be tied to the foot of Jupiter's chair." Lastly, here, as regards Bacon, we may refer to that grand passage in the *Essays* that begins : " I had rather believe all the fables in the ' Legend,' and the ' Talmud,' and the ' Alcoran,' than that this universal frame is without a mind." Even of the fool it is not credible to Bacon that he hath *thought*, if he hath *said*, in his heart, There is no God. Even the fool, Bacon thinks, must have said it only, as it were, " by *rote* to himself." That is an excellent idea, the only speaking by rote ! " Atheism," as he says further, " is rather in the lip than in the heart of man." " For, certainly, man is of kin to the beasts, by his body ; and if he be not of kin to God, by his spirit, he is a base and ignoble creature." Surely, then, in every way it is a noble testimony that Bacon bears to final causes, to metaphysic, and to Natural Theology.

Of the teleological argument, Dr. Reid says that " it has this peculiar advantage, that it gathers strength as human knowledge advances, and is more convincing at present than it was some centuries ago." This was all very well when the "present" was a present that had before it a second edition of the *Principia* of Newton, in which it was mentioned as a thing understood that said *Principia* were a *praesidium munitissimum*, a most perfect defence against the *impetus atheorum*, the sallies of atheists— and a present that had before it also, at the hands of Lagrange, an irrefutable demonstration of the stability of the universe : it was all very well for that "present," with its Newtons and Lagranges, to hug itself on its own security, and more or less directly gird at Alphonso of Castile, but what of *this* "present" that is *our* present ? Our task now is not as the task then. Then even a Hume, who sought in his somewhat narrow ingenious way to reason us out of both soul and body, and the universe out of God, felt forced even by necessity to speak thus : " Were men led into the apprehension of invisible, intelligent power by a contemplation of the works of nature, they could never possibly entertain any conception but of one single being, who bestowed existence and order on this vast machine, and adjusted all its parts, according to one regular plan or connected system. . . . All things in the universe are evidently of a piece. Everything is adjusted to everything. One design prevails through the whole. And this uniformity leads the mind to acknowledge one author. . . . Adam, rising at once, in Paradise, and in the full perfection of his faculties, would naturally, as represented by Milton, be astonished at the glorious appearance of nature—the heavens, the air, the earth, his own organs and members ; and would be led to ask whence this wonderful scene arose " (*Nat. Hist. of Rel.* sections i and ii.). When it is the sceptical Hume that speaks thus, we do not wonder to find the pious Newton always expressing himself with the profoundest reverence and admiration of the divinity he saw everywhere in the mighty scheme of the universe, that was for the first time, perhaps, discovered in all its mightiness only to him. The writers that treat of the life and works of Newton always refer to this. There are his queries in his *Optics*, as, " Whence is it that nature does nothing in vain ; and whence arises all that order and beauty which we see in the world ? How came the bodies of animals to be contrived with so much art; and for what ends were their several parts ? Was the eye contrived without skill in optics, and the ear without knowledge of sounds ? " Then, with all else, there is that marvellous scholium generale in the third book of the *Principia* : " Cum unaquaeque spatii particula sit *semper*, et unumquodque durationis indivisibile momentum sit *ubique*, certe rerum omnium Fabricator et Dominus non erit *nunquam, nusquam.*" (" As every particle of space is *always*, and every indivisible moment of duration is *everywhere*, assuredly the Fabricator and Lord of all things will not be *never, nowhere.*") Quite in place here is that colossal conception on the part of Newton of the vast infinity of space being the sensorium of Deity. In the course of what follows the above words, Newton exclaims : " Deus est unus et idem Deus semper et ubique ; " and, farther on, " hunc cognoscimus solummodo per proprietates ejus et attributa ; " and he adds, " et per causas finales "—" God is the one and the same God always and everywhere—Him we know by His qualities and attributes—and by final causes." I ought to translate all that refers to God in this grand scholium ; but I must content myself now by declaring of the scholium itself that it requires to be neglected by no student of philosophy. As thought is the principle of spirit, so is gravity the principle, the essence, the formal cause, the very self of matter as matter. It was Newton discovered that—that and the system of the heavens. There have been some unique men in this world, as—say Shakespeare! but never, probably, was there a man more unique than Newton: in his peculiar faculty he rises higher, more remote from, more unapproachable of, ordinary men, than any other, perhaps, that ever lived. Newton is the priest and interpreter of the orbs that roll—the Brahmin of the universe.

# GIFFORD LECTURE THE FOURTH.

Anaxagoras, the νοῦς — Aristotle — Understanding — Pythagoreans — Pantheism — Lord Gifford — Baghavad Gita — The νοῦς to Socrates, Plato, Aristotle — Grote, Schwegler, Zeller — The world a life — Berkeley, Cudworth, Plato, Zorzi — Subject and object — Nature and thought — Externality and intervality — Bruno — Universal and particular — Spinoza — Physical theories — Space and time — Hodgson, Carlyle, Berkeley, Reid, Leibnitz, Kant — But for an eye and an ear, the world utterly dark, utterly silent.

RETURNING to Anaxagoras, it is still a question how we are to decide him to have regarded his principle of the νοῦς, whether as a power immanent, that is, dwelling *in* matter, or as a power transcendent, that is, outside of and above matter. It really seems to me difficult, however, to give any other interpretation than the latter to the words of Diogenes Laertius at all events. As though actually quoting from the very work of Anaxagoras, Diogenes says, πάντα χρήματα ἦν ὁμοῦ, all things were together, εἶτα νοῦς ἐλθὼν αὐτὰ διεκόσμησε, then νοῦς coming, orderly disposed them. We seem to see here one thing lying by itself apart, and another, at some certain moment of time, coming, moving towards it, and adding itself to it. But that being so, νοῦς is not immanent in matter, but transcendent over it. Aristotle, near the beginning of the eighth book of the *Physics*, makes the distinction between the two positions, what was first and what came second, even stronger. His words are, " Anaxagoras says that all things being together, and having remained so at rest an endless time, νοῦς set motion into them and separated them." That, plainly, is to the effect that the movement was set into things from without, and not developed in them from within; that νοῦς, namely, was a transcendent, not an immanent principle.

The Germans seem to incline, on the whole, however, to adopt the mere immanence of the νοῦς. To some of them the fault of theology is its rigorous separation of the opposites. In the relation of God and the world they would wish to see, not a fixed inconceivable sunderedness, but a living transition. Others would wish us to see in the νοῦς, not reason, but understanding. What they mean by understanding is what some time ago I endeavoured to figure under the word λόγος. You see that inexplicable thing a reel in a bottle; suppose now it were all explained to you, every step in the idea that generated it clear before your eyes, then that λόγος (for the explanation would be a λόγος),—then that λόγος would be the Verstand, the understanding of the reel in the bottle. This reel would no longer be a mere piece of inexplicable matter; it would now be impregnated with the notion, so that all its parts were held together by it, and, as it were, one in it. Now that is what the νοῦς is held by some to be in relation to the world. The world were an unintelligible externality and material chaos, did not the understanding enter into it as a connecting and explaining tissue. So it is that even the Pythagoreans, too, explain the world; it is a congeries of externalities; but into that congeries of externalities, mere disjunct atoms, proportion enters; and that proportion gives them subsistence, connection, meaning, and unity. In this way it will be intelligible what is meant by an understanding being sunk into the things of the universe. To certain Germans, then, νοῦς is such understanding—an immanent ideal bond, not a fashioning creator apart from, and independent of it. This, in general, and on its own account, is a point of view necessary for us to know, even with reference to our general subject of Natural Theology. I mean that the doctrine of the immanence of the *νοῦς* involves what is called *pantheism*. This is the more interesting to us here inasmuch as some of the expressions in which Lord Gifford characterizes his idea of God may seem to have in them a pantheistic echo. As, for example, these, that God is the Infinite, the All, the One, and the Sole Substance, the Sole Being, the Sole Reality, and the Sole Existence. Some of these expressions no doubt, even *as* pantheistic, suggest criticism. *Reality* and *existence*, it may be said, for instance, are both doubtful words. An iron nail or a brass button is, as we generally speak, a *reality;* but God's reality must be a much other reality than the reality of such as these. *Existence,* too, at least in certain philosophical works, has been pretty well exclusively used in identically the same sense as *reality* in the case of either nail or button. A brass button is an *existence,* and an iron nail is an *existence,*—the word existence being here taken in its strictly etymological sense as a compound from the Latin words *ex* and *stare.* Whatever finitely *stands out* to sense, as an actual object seen of eye or touched of hand, etc., is an *existence;* it stands up and out. But existence in no such sense as that, plainly, can be predicated of God. God is not an object for eye, or ear, or touch, or any sense. We cannot see God as we see a statue or a house, or hear Him as we hear the blowing of the wind or the dashing of the wave. In a word, God is to be thought as infinite, not finite, as immaterial and not material, as a spirit and not as a body. In the sense alluded to, then, He may not *exist;* but He will still *be.* The soul of a man will be granted to *be*—let us conceive its *nature* to be, how we may. Even the crudest judge of character has not his idea of a man as such and such a body merely. There really is an entity that is logically distinguishable from the body, and is, on its side, as much a one, or more a one, than, on the other side, the body itself. An ego is a unity, and a unity of the whole of its infinite contents, take it how you may. Logically, then, an ego is an entity on its own account—an integer, self-contained and self-complete *teres, totum, ac rotundum*. An ego, of course, makes itself known only through and by means of its body, but, with whatever difference, it is precisely so with God; it is the very contention of these lectures that God makes Himself known through His body, which is the visible world without and the intelligible world within. As for Lord Gifford's term, *substance*, again, it reminds at once of Spinoza; *substance* is the God of Spinoza, and Spinoza, as we know, is the archpantheist. The word *All*, again, is certainly a word in pantheistic parlance, and *may*, as the others *may*, be so used by Lord Gifford. Even pantheistically, however, we may stop to say, it is a very objectionable word; for, even so, it is at once too much and too little. Too much! *All*, in its use by Lord Gifford, God as the All, cannot mean stars and planets, sun, moon, earth, air, seas, and continents, minerals, plants, animals, men,—collectively, that is, as so many individual objects in a ring, a mere outside aggregate, there materially in space, and now materially in time. Etymologically, no doubt, such a description of an *All* as God, or of God as an *All*, may seem but a necessary inference from the very word pantheism; but it is difficult to believe that any pantheist, Oriental or Occidental, religious or philosophical, ever thought of his God as any such clumsy miscellaneousness. In some of the books of the Bhaghavad Gita, as the seventh, the ninth, and the tenth, Krishna, indeed, may be heard exclaiming to Arjoon: "I am sunshine, and I am rain;

I am the radiant sun, the moon, the book of hymns, Meru among the mountains; I am the lion, the vowel A," etc. etc. No doubt, however, these are but as so much spray from the overflow of the Oriental phantasy. Hardly ever is it the case, indeed, that they occur in that bare categorical form. More commonly the phrasing itself shows that the term is but a trope: "I am moisture in the water, light in the sun and moon, sweet-smelling savour in the earth. I am the sacrifice, I am the worship, I am the spices, I am the invocation, I am the provisions, I am the fire, I am the victim," etc. etc. In such form as that it is quite evident that there is no thought of an assemblage of mere outer objects as constituting the All that is to be conceived as God. But if such expressions as are in question, and so taken, are too much, they are, as evidently, all too little. No such names, and no such names even if they were multiplied a thousandfold, can exhaust the infinity in unity, and the unity in infinity, of God. That, too, is a way of the Orientals, that they would seek by mere numberless namings to ascend to the infinite that is God; but, again, the Orientals themselves confess, even in the numberlessness of their namings, the impotence of the numberlessness itself. The visible is but an accident and fringe of the invisible; no myriad namings of the seen can reach the unseen.

To certain Germans, then, almost, we may say, to the German philosophical historians generally, the immanence of the νοῦς is the established doctrine. With νοῦς, they say, there certainly comes in, and for the first time in acknowledged history, the principle of an understanding, and the principle of an understanding that is self-determinative; but still we are not to think of the νοῦς in nature as of a mind and thinking consciousness in the way we find it in ourselves. Νοῦς is to be conceived of in nature as we see laws are: we know by the inquiries of our sciences that in the universe of things there is law, and consequently, so far, reason.

In a good deal of all this, however, there enters the thought that there is the danger of supposing that what Anaxagoras, after all, meant was merely a *deus ex machina* that came and ordered the chaos, a Zeus, a Jupiter, or other merely mythological personage of the early crude imagination. So far as such conception is concerned, I think it is right to contend against that. Certain it is that Anaxagoras did make no other use, so far as the application is concerned, of his principle the νοῦς than such *deus ex machina* that was no more, despite all his description of it, than the first cause of motion. It seems that he had no sooner announced it in general, than he set himself, in particular, to the usual mechanical expedients. It does not follow, however, that *we* must think the νοῦς a merely immanent principle, as it were, of lineamentation and proportion in the material mass, and that it was not to be conceived, at the same time, as a self-centred fount of intelligence and of intelligent action, so to speak, on its own account and in its own self-dependence.

It seems to me that even the advocates of the immanence of the νοῦς, themselves, do not regard it as, so to speak, a *brutely* immanent principle, but as an intelligent and conscious principle that has in it the distinction of personality. It seems to me also, that the universal voice of antiquity is to the same effect. Even Socrates, though speaking with disappointment of the *application* of the principle, does not speak differently of the principle itself. To Socrates the νοῦς, in a word, was an intelligent principle that knew the better, and acted on it. Plato repeats this description at least three times further; twice again, indeed, on the part of Socrates, but once on that of another; so that of his own relative sentiments there can be no reasonable doubt.

As for Aristotle, again, it would take up too much time to quote all that, in this connection, his writings show, but we must see a passage or two. In the *De Anima* (404b) he has this on Anaxagoras: τὸ αἴτιον τοῦ καλῶς καὶ ὀρθῶς (the cause of the good, beautiful, and right), τὸν νοῦν λέγει (he calls the νοῦς). A little farther on (405a18), in this same work, we find the νοῦς characterized as "a principle that knows, and as a principle that moves the τὸ πᾶν" (the all). In the *Metaphysic* there are several very distinct passages to a like effect. Anaxagoras, he says once (985a18), "in his explanation of the construction of the world, uses his νοῦς as a mere stage property; that is, he only lugs it in when he is at a loss otherwise." That concerns the application of it. But the main passage in the *Metaphysic* is this (984b8): "These (preceding) principles proved insufficient to explain what *is*; and, in further effort, this now suggested itself. That things are good, and beautiful, and right (εὖ καὶ καλῶς ἔχειν), can assuredly not be ascribed to fire, or earth, or anything else of the kind, nor yet to accident or chance; and so it was that when Anaxagoras came forward with the proposition that, as in animals, so in all nature, νοῦς is immanent as the cause of the world and its whole orderly arrangement, he appeared as though a man that was sober in comparison with mere drunken stutterers that had preceded him. . . . Those, then, who followed him, made the cause of what is good to be the principle of *what is*, and of the movement in it." Especially does Aristotle insist on the unmixedness and unmovedness of the νοῦς, no doubt having in mind himself his own principle of a πρῶτον κινοῦν (a first mover), that, unmixed with other things and itself unmoved, moves all of them.

As for the νοῦς of Anaxagoras, indeed, being a personal self-conscious reason, such as we conceive on the part of the Divine Being, there can be no doubt that such is the natural inference of any of us now-a-days who will impartially read the words that expressly described it; and there can be as little doubt that, as we have seen, such was the general understanding on the part of antiquity. It is certainly impossible to think of this principle as only a natural power sunk into matter, as Mr. Grote does. One, too, must, with Schwegler, give it more spiritual credit, by reason of the attributes of thought and conscious design ascribed to it, than even Zeller does.

It appears to me right, at the same time, even while assuming νοῦς to be capable of an independent existence on its own account, that we should attribute, almost as partly referred to already, more of a life of its own, and more of an instinctive reason of its own, to nature itself than we usually do. The pious Berkeley (*Siris*, 276) vindicates the doctrine; and it is surely, as a doctrine, not by any means necessarily either atheism or pantheism. To me it is quite as certain that there is an absolute subject, God, as it is certain that there is an absolute object, His universe. Still, it appears to me that the object should be brought much nearer the subject than is customary among us. If we view the object as the other of the subject, then we have the two, as I think we ought to have them, in mutual relation. The world, as there at the will of God, is still the work of God, the expression of God; whatever it is, it is still *of* God: there must be relation between them. So it is, in fact, that there is such a science as this very Natural Theology that we have before us. Bacon himself, as we have seen, refers to the two sides of it. He calls it a knowledge " which may be truly termed divine in respect of the object, and natural in respect of the light." Nature is not to be supposed the evil principle, and abandoned of God: rather it is the garment we see Him by. Placed in the midst of beauty itself, it is still the solemn temple most majestical in which it is ours to bend the knee in awe, ours to worship in love. So it is that we shall take nothing from God in commending His work. Nature has a life of its own; it is not simply brute. There is at least relevance for the "plastic nature" of Cudworth, or even the world-soul of Plato. We may exclaim in perfect agreement with Cornelius Agrippa ab Nettesheim: "Supremus et unicus rationis actus religio est;" "Religion is reason's sole and supreme act; in vain we philosophize, know, and understand, if He, who is the essence and author of our intellect, and whose image we are, is left unknown by us;" but we may, not inconsistently, at the same time, feign or figure, with his contemporary Franciscus Georgius Zorzi Venetus, that "the world is an infinitely living individual, maintained by a soul in the power of God." We may even allow ourselves to sympathize with Zorzi's countrymen who came later, and held that "a single soul pervades this living universe." In fact, there is great truth in the old way of it, that the world is the macrocosm of man, as man is the microcosm of the world. We may conceive that it has been the will of God that nature should be the mere externalization of man, as that man should be the mere internalization of nature. The categories which are in man and constitute his thinking furniture—these categories, if in him only subjective and within, are all objective and without in nature. Only so it is that, at once, nature is intelli*gible* and man intelli*gent*. The relation, indeed, between an object that is to be understood, and a subject that is to understand, is precisely as that between matter and form. If form is to take on matter, matter to admit into itself form, form must be *in effect* matter, matter *in effect* form. So it is that nature is but the other of thought; thought, again, but the other of nature. In other words, nature is but the externalization of thought—thought but the internalization of nature. Or nature is externality; thought is internality. Nature is the externality of that internality; thought is the internality of that externality. Nature is difference; thought is identity: the one the difference of that identity; the other the identity of that difference. Nature, as the object, as the externality, as the difference, is a boundless out and out of objects, a boundless out and out of externalities, a boundless out and out of differences—a boundless out and out under physical necessity, which, at the same time, can alone be, and is, physical contingency, fortuitousness, accident, chance. Thought, again, as the subject, the internality, the identity, is a boundless in and in of subjective internalities, subjective identities; and its actuating principle is freedom, free will; for thought as thought, reason as reason, the universal as the universal, is the only freedom, the only free will. "As externality," says Giordano Bruno in the *Della causa principio ed uno*, " As externality, nature is only the shadow of the One, of the first and original principle; for what, in the *principle*, is unseparated, single, and one, appears in *externality* —in *things*—sundered, complex, and multiplex." The thought here, Bruno's thought, as of the one and the many in the language of the Greeks, is, evidently, very much as I have expressed it a moment ago. Thought is the form, and the truth, and the universal— *the one:* nature is only the matter, and the show, and the particular—*the many*. The world is but the negative of the mind; the mind is the affirmative of the world. It is the world that stands up a presence, and the only presence, to the senses; but it is mind that is the soul of that world. No man has *seen* the universal

—it is only the particular that can be *seen*. It is only the objects in the world that can be seen, and heard, and handled. Accordingly, the philosophers of a sensational time will only speak of what they know, they say; and they know only the particular—only what they see. They do not believe there is a universal: a universal they never *saw*. Nevertheless, it is only the universal that is the truth of the particular: the particular only *is* because the universal is. What the particular *is*, that is the universal. Or, it is in the particular that we are to *see* and *know* the universal. That is the way of the truth. As there cannot be a naked outside—an outside that has no inside, so there cannot be a naked particular —a particular that is that and nothing else—a particular that has no universal. We are, all of us that are here, particulars; I wonder what any of us would be if the universal, if *man*, *humanity*, were suddenly allowed to run out of us! The universal is not a single object, a thing which we can touch and handle; nevertheless it *is*, and all these particulars are only *its:* we can touch and handle *them*, only because of *it*. If it is only seen in them, they disappear into it. Separate existence for the universal is only possible in the absolute subject, God. And His is the necessary existence. He is that which cannot *not* be. We can conceive all—all the things of sense—to perish; but still we know that there is God, that He cannot perish, and that they would come again. Extinguish the lamp of this universe, and it is still alight. Crush all into nonentity, and it only smiles an actuality in your face. At the same time that, too, is to be said: we *are*. *We*, too, think; we, too, are universals, but, being in a particular body and a particular world, not infinitely so: we are, as here below, only finitely so. Here, however, the warning is necessary that, even in the position that would give to nature a certain life of its own, it is not for a moment to be understood that it is Spinoza's deification of nature that is meant. I am not one of those who, in these days, *apotheose* Spinoza, though I can very sincerely respect him. He was a gentle, inoffensive, quietly living man, who, for bare bread, contentedly sat polishing his glasses while he pondered the writings of Descartes, and Hobbes, and others the like, which were then before him. For I see no reason to believe that Moses Maimonides, or other *Jewish* philosopher, earlier or later, had such power over Spinoza as men of an imagination of the *Arabian Nights* are profuse in eloquence to lead us to believe. Descartes, with a little of Hobbes, was, after all, quite enough for Spinoza. It is only the peculiarity of its presentation, perhaps, that hides the milk and water in the system, that, for the rest, belonged to the character of the man. It might not be very difficult to look at Descartes geometrically; and then, for the most part, the thing was done—the work was accomplished. Generalized to its ultimate, what was in *rerum natura* was *extension* and *thought*. Space, indeed, was more than extension: it was solid; it was extension in all directions. Even so, however, it was still geometrical. But take it as extension only, then its surface was susceptible of infinite lineamentation, infinite configuration. But infinite configurate lineamentation involved relations, involved ideas, was tantamount to thought. There, then, it was; that was the world—*extension* and *thought*. That also was God: extension, with its involution of thought, geometrical thought—that was God. What, then, of man here? Why, finite things were the figurations, the lineamentations of extension; and one of these was man. Even at the least, even at the worst, consequently, man did occupy, actually *was*, a certain portion of the divine surface. The lines that figured him—the lines that cut him out—might indeed be evanescent and perish; but what of the surface they isolated remained. To that extent man was as God; to that extent man was divine; to that extent man was immortal. Surely, at all events, particularly, while quite in coherence with the general idea, that is the burden and the effect of propositions 22 and 23 in the fifth book of the *Ethic*. We are significantly warned by Erdmann, however, not altogether to trust ourselves to any such concession of immortality on the part of Spinoza, seeing that, if in such propositions we find " a personal God, a personal immortality, and one knows not what else, we must not forget that, according to his (Spinoza's) own express declarations, God has neither understanding nor will; that, according to him, a God who reciprocated love were no God; further, that to him personality and duration are only figments of the imagination, which, even as such, he will not eternalize; finally, that he makes religion and blessedness to consist simply in the self-forgetting resignation through which man becomes only an instrument of God, that, when useless, is thrown away and replaced by another." Evidently, then, on such foundations, what stuff, what portion of the very substance of his God, Spinoza will allow us, cannot come to much, though applying it as, so far, a concession on his part to the general interest of the immortality of the soul, we may feel inclined in our hearts to thank him at least for his good-will. But, to thank him so is not to accept his deification of nature. Nature, as that immeasurable panorama out there, around us, and in front of us, give it what properties we may, is still an externality and a materiality; it is not a spirit; as such it is not even tantamount to the νοῦς of Anaxagoras. To attain even to the νοῦς of Anaxagoras, it is not the externality and the materiality that we have to look to, but what is of the quality of thought—the order, beauty, and designful contrivance of the world. The remarkable consideration is, that all this is otherwise precisely in these sensational days in which our own lot has fallen. We are enormously in advance of Anaxagoras in our knowledge of the sun and moon, which, he said, he was born to speculate—in our knowledge of the whole heaven, to which he pointed as his country ; but increase of knowledge, instead of guiding and directing us, like Anaxagoras, more and more to mind, seems to have completely turned us round to matter. The stars are matter, and the sun, and moon, and planets ; neither is it a principle from within that would give them union and society, but only æther, a matter from without, that, according to some, shall compress them. Matter here, matter there, matter everywhere. Particles of matter that, in mechanical rushing to their clash, shall take fire, and flame out suns. Particles of matter that, in inevitable mechanical swirl and sweep, shall be as worlds around the fires. Worlds and fires, for all that, which, sooner or later, shall be as cold and useless as the spur of Percy. Throw the spur of Percy into space, and let it sink : even as that spur, we are to follow our whole universe into an eternal cold, into an eternal dark, into an eternal wilderness. Astronomy gives us no hint of life. Geology gives us that much— geology does indeed tell of life ; but geology is powerless to save us. Geology transports *weathering* into the sea, and is the while, almost even in the single word, the epic of the elements, piped by the winds, in flash of the sun, to the dash of the rain ; but geology can only join astronomy in the end, and speak our doom. Space is to be an infinite tomb : over that tomb time shall be an infinite pall. Existence may have *been*—a bubble, that no sooner was than it burst, but what properly *is*, what truly *is*, are in everlasting silence, in everlasting cold, in the everlasting dark—two dead corpses, two dead infinitudes, the corpse and the infinitude of space, the corpse and the infinitude of time. But what are space and time themselves? If they *are* the infinitudes, if they *are* the eternities, perhaps it is precisely in them that we shall find some light. And shapes, more ambiguous and equivocal than time and space are, it is impossible to conceive—at once the mockingest of shadows and the toughest of stuffs—now described as the very warp and woof on which the universe is stretched, and now as the most unsubstantial playthings of dream. To one, Mr. Hodgson, they are "immediately and ineradicably certain," the basis of cognition, the "corner-stone of philosophy;" to another, Carlyle, they are but the two "world-enveloping appearances," the "canvass" for all other "minor illusions," if there to "*clothe*" us, there also to "*blind*" us, as it is into *their* quality all that is resolves. Berkeley (*WW*. iv. 468), to whom this "world without thought is *nec quid, nec quantum, nec quale*," declares "time a sensation, and therefore only in the mind; space a sensation, and therefore not without the mind;" while, even to the sober, sensible, and somewhat prosaic Dr. Reid (*WW*. 324, 343), space, looming up there "an immense, eternal, immovable, and indestructible void or emptiness," is "potentially only, not actually," and time is "a dark and difficult object," "a beginning in which is only a contradiction." The monadology of Leibnitz, as is easy to know, could give no authority to the perception of sense, and no external reality to the forms of space and time, which in some way only resulted to us from our perception of the interaction among things. All the early writings of Kant, those, namely, that preceded the

*Dissertatio de mundi sensibilis atque intelligibilis forma et principiis*, which did itself precede and usher in the *Kritik of Pure Reason*—in almost every one of these early writings, there is such mention of time and space as proves the great interest of Kant, from the very first, in their regard.

As is only to be expected, Kant is seen in these writings to be for long in respect of time and space a follower of Leibnitz. In his *Gedanken von der wahren Schätzung der lebendigen Kräfte*, for example, he holds that "there would be no space and no extension, if things had not a power to act out of themselves; for otherwise there would be no connection, while without connection there would be no order, and without order no space." He even goes on to say, "It is probable that the three dimensions of space derive from the law of the interaction of substances; and substances interact so that the force of their action is inversely as the square of their distances." And, eight or nine years later, we have the same doctrine, in his *Nova dilucidatio principiorum primorum cognitionis metaphysicæ*, as where he says: *nexu substantiarum abolito, successio et tempus pariter facessunt* (the connection of substances being withdrawn, succession and time are equally withdrawn). In his *Monadologia physica*, about the same time, he characterizes space as *substantialitatis plane expers*, as plainly devoid of substantiality, and as but the *phaenomenon*, the appearance or show, of "the external relation of the monads in union." What is remarkable, however, is that in 1768, writing his brief paper, *Vom ersten Grunde des Unterschiedes der Gegenden im Raume*, he, as it were, turns his back upon himself, and attempts to prove cogently, and with conviction, that space is an absolute reality and no mere *Gedankending*—that is remarkable; but it is more remarkable still that, in 1770, only a further two years, we find the dissertation " concerning the form and principles of the sensible and intelligible world," in large part, written to prove space a mere subjective appendicle of sense as sense. This is Kant's last position relatively, and in the sequel he never varies from it. Still there are in the writings of the different dates, the vacillation on the part of Kant, and the contradiction in question. What concerns *us*, however, is the fact that Kant did decide in the end both space and time to be but forms of our own sensory within us, into which perceptively received, disposed, and arranged by aid of the categories and their schemata, the contributions of our special senses stood up and out at length, apart from us, as though an infinite universe around us and inhabited by us.

These, then, are great authorities; and there seems *that* even in space and time (on every supposition), which would call a halt to the conclusions of the sensationists. But, unfortunately, we cannot expect every one to be at home with the subtleties of metaphysic, or with what may appear the mere dreams of philosophy. One would like, so far as, in some respects, it seems hostile and obstructive to the interests of Natural Theology—one would like to approach science in that regard, on its own grounds, and to enter into it on its own terms. Suppose we leave aside all questions of a beginning, and equally all questions of an end. Suppose we take the world even as we see it, or rather even as astronomical science sees it at this very moment. Well—there is the sun by day; and there is the spectacle of the heavens by night. What does astronomy say of all that, not as it conceives it to have begun, and not as it conceives it to be predestinated to end, but simply as it is. And as it is, it was seen in his prime by Anaxagoras, more than two thousand three hundred years ago. That is a long time in the life of man; but, in the life of the universe, it would seem, so far as difference is concerned, simply to drop out. The sun and the moon that we see now from the streets of Edinburgh, Anaxagoras saw then from the streets of Athens. Our Sirius was, for Anaxagoras, his Sirius too; and so it was with the Hyades and the Pleiades, and Castor and Pollux, and the Milky Way as well. What he saw led him, the only sober man among mere inebriates, according to Aristotle, to speak of an order and a beauty that could be due to intelligence only. Almost in our own days, the experience of Anaxagoras was precisely that of Kant. The starry heaven above him was one of the only two things that filled his soul with ever new and increasing wonder and veneration the more and the oftener he reflected. "In effect," he says again, "when our spirit is filled with such reflections, the aspect of the starry heavens on a clear night, awakens in us a joy which only noble souls are capable of feeling; in the universal calm of nature, and in the peace of sense, the hidden faculty of the immortal soul speaks to us indescribably, and breathes into us mysterious thoughts, which may be felt, but not possibly named." There, then, it is, that starry heaven —there—in infinite space above us, globe upon globe, in their own light and in the light of each other, all wheeling, wheeling in and out, and round and round, and through each other, in a tangle of motion that has still a law, not without explosions in this one and the other from within, doubtless, that would sound to us, did we hear them, louder, dreader, more awfully terrific than any thunder of the tropics, that would sound to us, did we hear them, veritably as the crack of doom—well, just to think it, all *that* is taking place, all *that* is going on, all these globes are whirling in a darkness blacker than the mouth of wolf, deeper than in the deepest pit that ever man has sunk,—all that is going on, all that is taking place in a darkness absolute; and more, all that is going on, all that is taking place — for exploding globes even—in a silence absolute, in a silence dead, in a silence that never a whisper—never the faintest whisper, never the most momentary echo breaks! Is not that extraordinary? but it is no less true than extraordinary. Undulations there are, doubtless, that are light *to us;* but no undulation will give light to them, the globes. Vibrations there are, doubtless, where there is air, that are sound *to us;* but all vibrations are as the dead to them. It is in a cave, in a den, blacker than the blackest night, soundless and more silent than the void of voids, that all those intermingling motions of the globes go on—but for us, that is; but for an eye and an ear, and a soul behind them! That cannot be denied. The deepest astronomical philosopher, entranced in what he sees, entranced in what he fancies himself to hear, must confess that, but for himself and the few and feeble others that are like himself, all would be as dark as Erebus, all would be as silent as the grave. But as the hour now is, you will allow me to bring this home—you will allow me to point the lesson in a future lecture.

# GIFFORD LECTURE THE FIFTH.

Astronomy, space, time, the νοῦς—Kant, Fichte, Schelling—Carlyle, the *Sartor*—Emerson—Plato—Aristotle—A beginning—The want of eye and ear again—Deafness and blindness together—Design restored—Thomson—Diogenes of Apollonia—Socrates—Meteorology and practical action—Morality and ethicality—The first teleological argument—Proofs of design—Bacon—Socrates finally.

WE resume where we left off at our last meeting. The universal conclusions, we may say, of every writing on astronomical science which we may chance to take up now-a-days, in regard to the eventual entombment of the whole present system of things as a single cold corpse in a perpetual grave of space, under a perpetual pall of time—these conclusions brought us, at the close of our last lecture, to some consideration, firstly, of space and time themselves, and then, secondly, of the heavens above us, at once as, to astronomical observation, they presently are, and, historically, always have been. We have still to bring home what was said then ; and here it may be perhaps well, indeed, not to expand, but just a little to open statements. The subject, certainly, has fairly come to us in connection with the assertion of the presence of νοῦς, intelligence, in the general system around us—an assertion which such a science as this of Natural Theology, with peril of its very life, requires to make good ; at the same time that, obviously, on the contrary supposition, with such an eternity of night and the grave before us as astronomy predicts, it would be just as well to say as little as possible, whether of the νοῦς of Anaxagoras, or of the Natural Theology of anybody else. In regard to time and space, we had strong evidence of their very peculiar nature on many hands, even on the part of Reid, at once the sworn foe of idealism, and equally the sworn friend of common sense. After vacillation, Kant's final opinion was such as we find expressed in these words of his own (*Text-Book to K.* p. 157): "Were our subject abstracted from, or simply the subjective constitution of our senses, all the qualities and all the relations of objects in space and time—nay, space and time themselves—would disappear: for all these are, as mere appearances to sense, incapable of existing in themselves, but only in us." And if such was the doctrine of Kant, it cannot be said, on the whole, that his immediate successors differed from it at least as regards the general ideal quality of space and time. Fichte, for example, laboriously deduces, in his dialectical manner, the construction and setting out of time and space in the imagination. Schelling, again, while simply taking his material from the hands of Fichte, and as Fichte himself gave it him, remained, all through his life, sufficiently an idealist to believe in the ideality of space and time. In a writing, dated 1804 (vi. 223), he will be found saying, "Space, purely as such, is, even for the geometrician, nothing real;" and again, "independently of the particular things, space is nothing." In his *Transcendental Idealism* of 1800, which, however, is little more than a réchauffé of Fichte's *Wissenschaftslehre*, he had already said (iii. 470): "Time is only inner sense becoming to its own self object; space is outer sense becoming object to inner sense."

We referred then to the same belief on the part of Carlyle. In that magnificent chapter of the *Sartor Resartus* which bears the title of "Natural Supernaturalism," he will be found, on a considerable canvass, to speak both fully and grandly on this special topic. Carlyle himself calls this section of his work a "stupendous section;" and it *is* a stupendous section,—I suppose the very first word of a higher philosophy that had been as yet spoken in Great Britain,—I suppose the very first English word towards the restoration and rehabilitation of the *dethroned upper powers*, which, for all that, I fear, under our present *profound* views in religion and philosophy, remain still dethroned. Here it is, as the words are, that the "professor first becomes a seer." Hitherto he has been struggling with all manner of "phantasms," "superannuated symbols, and what not;" but now he has "looked fixedly on existence, till, one after the other, its earthly hulls and garnitures," time and space themselves, "have all melted away," and to "his rapt vision, the celestial Holy of Holies lies at last disclosed." As intimated, it is especially the stripping off of these two "world-enveloping phantasms," space and time, that has enabled him to attain to such grand consummation and blissful fruition. The "deepest of all illusory appearances," he exclaims, they are "for hiding wonder," the wonder of this universe. They hide what is past and they hide what is to come; but yet, as he exclaims again, "Yesterday and to-morrow both *are :*" "with God as it is a universal *here*, so is it an everlasting now." As Carlyle himself says, it is in this chapter that he attains to "Transcendentalism," and to a sight at last of "the promised land, where Palingenesia, in all senses, may be considered as beginning." And certainly, as I say, *Sartor Resartus* itself was a first attempt to reconstruct and revindicate those substantial truths of existence, which are the enduring, firm, fast, fixed, ineradicable foundations of humanity as humanity,—humanity in the individual, humanity in the kind.

F

However much the general testimony of Emerson be in this vein of Carlyle, it is not in my recollection that I can quote him specially in regard to time and space. He does say in that reference, "Therefore is Space, and therefore Time, that man may know that things are not huddled and lumped, but sundered and individual:" that is, time and space are there for "the perception of differences;" but they must disappear, as beams and joists of the mere outward, into his general idealism. Emerson regards "nature as a phenomenon, not a substance." He attributes "necessary existence to spirit," but esteems nature only "as an accident and an effect." He says once, "Even the materialist Condillac, perhaps the most logical expounder of materialism, was constrained to say, 'Though we should soar into the heavens, though we should sink into the abyss, we never go out of ourselves; it is always our own thought that we perceive.'" The quotation in itself is excellent; but it is strange that Emerson should attribute to Condillac, what is so prominent in David Hume; not but that Condillac may have paraphrased Hume, whom Emerson, like most students of his day, under the influence of Coleridge possibly, openly depreciated and disparaged. It is a later series of Kantian studies that has brought up Hume again. Emerson is probably happier when he attributes to a French philosopher the saying that "material objects are necessarily kinds of *scoriae* of the substantial thoughts of the Creator." It is Emerson himself who says, and it is one of the most beautiful things that ever *has* been said, "Infancy is the perpetual Messiah, which comes into the arms of fallen men, and pleads with them to return to paradise."

Before leaving the consideration that we have here, it may be pointed out that there are views in Plato and Aristotle relatively, which are not essentially different.

Apart from the general philosophy of Plato, there is a reference to Time in the *Timaeus* (37 E–38 A) which is manifestly of an ideal import. The parts of time there, the *was* and the *will be*, are called but phenomenal forms, which we wrongly transfer to what is noumenally eternal; "for we say, in a time reference namely, it was, it is, it will be; whereas of what truly is, we can only say it *is*." As regards Aristotle again, what he has to say in this connection would of itself constitute an excellent introduction to metaphysic proper, for it is full of the subtlest turns possible, and requires the intellect that would follow them to have sharpened itself, at least for the nonce, to the fineness of a razor. The mention of one or two of them, however, must here suffice. As regards space, for example, it is enough to point out that to Aristotle it cannot demand for itself a place, so to speak, whether in heaven or in hell. Of the two known elements, that is, it is without a claim upon either. It cannot pretend to mind or soul; for its *extension* excludes it: and just as little can it profess itself corporeal; for it has got no body. The prestidigitation, or jugglery, that time exacts, is subtler and more irritating still. All other things, for example, consist of parts that are; and, on that necessity, time itself cannot be, for, in view of the past and the future, it consists of parts that are not. But leaving all such finenesses aside, we may limit ourselves to the distinct avowal on Aristotle's part, in the last chapter of the fourth book of the *Physics*, that, as to how time is, when viewed in reference to a mind, "one might doubt whether, if there were no mind, time would be or would not be."

Now, the purpose of all this that concerns time and space is to suggest that the constitution of them may be somewhat in the way of the constitution of a universal beginning or a universal end, as postulated by science.

Till the world began, there was, conceivably, neither time nor space; and when the world ends, it is equally conceivable that neither will remain. In short, ideal considerations must be allowed to interfere with all such materialistic conclusions as, excluding νοῦς, intelligence, from any rôle, part, place, or share in the composition of the universe, would summarily truncate all pretensions of a so-called Natural Theology, and concisely close this lecturer's vocation.

But now, again, what was all that about black wolves' throats, and palls, and graves, and Erebus', and what not? How is that to be brought home to us, and what is the lesson that is to be pointed? Well, in a word, all *that* is just this:—kill us all off, and the likes of us, wherever to be found—kill us all off in the universe, I say, and from that moment all is dark, and all is silent as the grave. The in and out, and round about, of all the stars in the firmament, of Arcturus and Aldebaran, of Vega, Spica, and Capella, of Alamak, Alpharat, and Scheat, of Ophiuchus and Fomalhaut, and every myriad spark and sparkle in the Milky Way may go on ceaselessly still, by day, by night, but henceforth in a silence absolute—in a darkness dense, impenetrable. That, let move what move may; that, indeed, will be all—a solid soundlessness, a substantial black! What, you will say, will there not be Charles's Wain still circling in the north, and Cassiopeia's Chair, like a swarm of busy bees, and the glorious constellation of Orion, with his grand belt of three, and in his surpassing brightness Sirius, and the Pleiades in their pallor? Or simply, as regards this earth of ours, do you mean to say that the thunder will no longer roll nor the lightning flash—or just to reduce and confine it to a single point, do you mean to say that, though there were not a single life in the whole solar system, the sun would not continue to shine? Well, now that is just what I do mean to say. But for a living eye, but for a living ear, there would be no light in the sun, no voice in the thunder. Vibration in the air, caused by whatever it may, is sound in the ear; but the vibration itself is soundless, it is but a mechanical tremble, a mechanical quiver; alone and by itself it is in silence only, there is not the very suggestion of a tone or a note in it. So it is with light. Similar to the vibrations of the air there are the undulations of the aether. These undulations are light in the eye, but in themselves— alone and by themselves — they are darkness itself. Without an eye and without an ear all those globes in the heaven around us career among themselves in a single unbroken black that has not a sound in it. The darkness is still in its size monstrous, it is still equal to the infinitude of space. But, all dark, does it not seem to lose its proportions and to contract somehow? What are all these enormous differences in that one dark? Let them be as they may, they are all, as it were, within the hollow of a single den. But if these great globes are only to wheel and wheel, and circle and circle, in a single silent den, why should they be so huge—why should they be at such vast distances? Let them draw nearer each other, let them shrink in themselves: still, to all intents and purposes, there is scarce a change, all everywhere to our minds remains pretty much the same. Quantity is but relative; there is no absolute large, there is no absolute small. The earth, possibly, is but as a pea to Sirius; Sirius, possibly, but as a pin's point to the Magellan clouds. After all, the mighty black of space is no more than an indefinite cave—a den—no more than as a black hole of Calcutta. It is as though it were in a black hole of Calcutta that, without an eye, all the operations of the firmament proceed. Quantity has pruned itself, quantity has retrenched its idle, useless dimensions—very idle, very useless if in a single, soundless dark; quantity has retired into a black hole of Calcutta, but if into a black hole of Calcutta, why not into the butt of a mantuamaker's thimble? There! that is the result! Without an eye to see, and without an ear to hear, the world, whether for magnitude or for use, were no worse or better, did it compress the operation of its dimensions from the infinitude of space into the butt of a mantuamaker's thimble! I have actually seen the world almost so compressed. Years ago, at a Welsh ironwork, I found a man, a fireman, who, from some injury in the course of his occupation, had incurred an inflammation that cost him not only the sight of both his eyes, but even, by its extension, the hearing of both his ears. He was still in the vigour of life. He might have been yoked, like a beast of burden, to some mechanical appliance; but otherwise he was useless. He was left (with a small pension, I fancy) to some poor people who took care of him. Henceforth, for the poor fellow, there was only a life of dream. Night and day, day and night, he lay warm in his bed, shut up, like a cat before the fire, into the bliss of subjectivity, bare subjectivity—so to speak, brute subjectivity, physical, corporeal subjectivity. He rose only when his smell told him that his meals were ready. The senses of smell and taste he enjoyed, evidently, with the intensest avidity; but still there was one pleasure which, during his meals, he seemed to enjoy more than the pleasures of either of these. It was a pleasure of touch; but it was a human pleasure. His poor face wore a smile, a sweet smile, a smile of our common reason, as he fed the cat that rubbed on his legs only, knowing the uselessness of a mew! Now to that man the world was contracted into a silent dark, where his meals were, and the cat that rubbed on his legs. What, then, would the world be were all mankind as he?

What would the world be were there no such things as an eye and an ear within the immeasurable vast of its entire infinitude? So far as any use or purpose is concerned, would it be any bigger or better than a black hole of Calcutta,—would it be any bigger or better than the butt of a mantua-maker's thimble? To any one who will approach to look, an eye, an ear is as much a necessity in the realization, is as much involved in the very plan, of the universe, as matter and molecules, and the immensity of space itself. But the moment we see that, we see design also. We see that intelligence has gone to the composition of the universe. We have come to be sober, like Anaxagoras, in the midst of inebriates, and, like him, we proclaim the νοῦς. There is, then, a reality in our science of Natural Theology, and we can still exclaim with the poet of the *Seasons:*—

> "These, as they change, Almighty Father, these
> Are but the varied God. The rolling year
> Is full of Thee. Forth in the pleasing spring
> Thy beauty walks. . . .
> Then comes the glory in the summer months. . . .
> Thy bounty shines in autumn unconfined. . . .
> In winter, awful Thou! with clouds and storms,
> Majestic darkness!
> Mysterious round! what skill, what force divine,
> Deep-felt, in all appear!"

For our purpose of Natural Theology, it is Diogenes of Apollonia that offers himself next to our consideration; but I leave what I have on him aside, and pass at once to Socrates.

The position of Socrates on the historical roll, as well of civilisation as of philosophy, is, like that of Anaxagoras, a sole and singular one. If Anaxagoras introduced the consideration of *purpose* in an intellectual regard, it was Socrates that turned the attention of mankind to the same principle in practical application. It was with him as though he had said, Anaxagoras cannot apply his principle *meteorologically*—in the heavens, that is; he has only announced it meteorologically; neither can *I* apply it meteorologically, but let us see whether it has an application or not to human life. I do not know that there is anything to be got from the trees and the fields, but there is a good deal to be got from the market-place, and the gymnasia, and the people in them. Accordingly, what new principle Socrates introduced was that of morality. By this word, however, there is something else and more to be understood than it usually suggests. As far as that goes, it is to be hoped, indeed, that there was morality upon the earth, that there was morality in mankind, that there was morality among the Greeks, before even Socrates appeared among them. The old Die-hards of the Medic wars, to say nothing of those of times yet earlier, old Trojans say, were surely not without morality. The distinction is this. The old morality, the old virtue, was an unconscious morality, an unconscious virtue. These men of old only *did* what they did. They did what they did without a thought of themselves. They thought, indeed, and they thought well; but their thoughts were not properly conscious or self-conscious thoughts. Their thoughts were instinctive, natural, as the blood in their veins, as the breath they drew, as the food they ate. They made, in a way, no merit to themselves of what they did. What they did, and why, was but as the institutions of their country, was but part and parcel of their streets and houses, was but as the common voice, the common sound, the common hum of the agora. They and the State were not different individuals, they and the State were one. Their life was, as it were, foetal as yet, foetal in the State, their mother, and there was the common circulation still between them:

the medium of that circulation was the laws familiar to them, the beliefs they all believed, the patrimonial use and wont, and established manners, so to speak, *natured* in them. If we can so name the distinction, morality was then ethicality. Both are right doing, but ethicality is the right doing according to the conscience of the State, of the community, while morality is right doing according to the conscience of the individual. Or both are virtue: the one the virtue of the public, the other the virtue of the private, conscience. As it is in the Bible with the words and the thoughts, which still seem, as it were, *vitally connected;* so it is here with the State and the individual, the universal and the particular: both are still one. Existence is as yet objective; subjectivity has still to appear. Now thus it was in Greece upon the whole, up almost to the time of Pericles and the Peloponnesian war. But, during, say, some two-hundred years before that, the philosophical consciousness had been gradually growing, and, no doubt, during the same time, the common mind correspondently altering. After Anaxagoras, the rate of progress, or, as it may be thought, *regress, regress* especially in a public respect it unquestionably was — after Anaxagoras the rate of change became greatly accelerated. Publicly such men as Alcibiades and Lysander were but poor substitutes for such others as Leonidas and Miltiades. Then there were the Sophists, occupying a position not quite public, nor yet again quite private. In these respects there was regress; but what we have in Socrates, Plato, Aristotle, who came next, is progress, and compared with what result preceded it, progress nameable pretty well infinite. Almost it would seem as though Anaxagoras by his reference to the νοῦς had concentrated all attention on intelligence as intelligence; which was raised, as it were, well-nigh to the position of an Absolute then when the

Sophists said or seem to have said to themselves, That absolute shall be ours, ours in our individual consciousness — if thought is to be the principle, and the authority, and the deciding consideration, then that thought is ours even as we are: it is we alone; it is men alone, who think. Socrates, now, was a reflective, considerate personality who turned over everything in his mind to see what it came to, what was the worth of it. But turning from the fields and the trees to the homes and haunts of men, the interests that were offered for that reflection and consideration of his could only be of a practical nature. That is, what immediately presented itself to him was, as we may term it, the ethicality of the past, which, shaken in the present, promised but poorly for the future. So it was, in his hands, that ethicality became morality—in this way that, ethicality being taken into his consciousness and there looked at, questioned, and examined, had to make good its claim to its authority of heretofore. Virtue, that is, what was right and good, was now before the bar of the single consciousness, but in a universal regard. And it was that regard, the universality of that regard, that, for the first time, realized in history and the life of man, morality as morality. Actions, if they had been ethical before, were now to be moral. On the question of right or wrong, the tribunal of sentence was now within, and no longer without. The individual was now referred to his own self, to his own responsibility, to his own conscience and judgment. But the conscience or judgment must not be, as with the Sophists, a private one, in this sense that the individual was to consider only what was good for himself as this particular individual that he was, Callicles, Cebes, Chaerephon, or another. No; it was not one of these *as* one of these, Callicles *as* Callicles, Cebes *as* Cebes, Chaerephon *as* Chaerephon, that was to be considered—not each as he was in his immediate individuality, but each as he was in his universality, each as he was in his manhood, each as he was in his humanity. The conscience that was to decide, the judgment that was to pass sentence, must be a universal conscience, must be a universal judgment. Now that universality could, as was plain to Socrates, only come by *knowing*. And so it was that to Socrates virtue was knowledge or a knowledge. So far, too, Socrates was perfectly right. The individual will universalize his nature only by knowledge. It is by knowledge that the individual must excavate himself; it is by knowledge that he must dredge and deepen himself; by knowledge that he must widen his walls, and raise his roof, letting in light and fresher air upon himself. It is by knowledge that *man*—man as man—is made of men. Every true growth in a man's garden must singly be gone round about, and tended with as much peculiarity of care as, under the impost, makes a perfect exemplar of every individual tobacco plant in France. Or we may say, in the camera of a man's soul, there falls many a blur on the so sensitive crystal *there;* and it takes the cunning pouring on of chemicals to transmute the haze into transparency and shape. And all that is principally an affair of knowledge; but still we are not to forget that knowledge alone is not enough. Socrates was wrong there; and Aristotle added the training and discipline, the custom and practice that, with all knowledge, were still necessary to make man good—good not only in his knowledge, not only in his thoughts and wishes, but good also in his will, good in the acts and actions of his daily life.

This, then, is what is meant by saying that Socrates was the first to introduce into the State morality as against ethicality. The ethicality of the State was still morality; but it was the material morality of the organized objectivity without, as against the ideal morality of the conscious subjectivity within. This is Socrates in his historical position; but, though averse to what is called *meteorology*, and even expressing himself against it, we know from what he confessed himself to have hoped to learn from Anaxagoras concerning the sun, and the moon, and the other stars, and the causes of all things—we know, from as much as this, I say, that Socrates still entertained a lively curiosity in respect to the constitution of this universe. That, indeed, could not fail the inquirer into the universal will, into the universal good and right. And it was from that side, in fact, that he had his interest in the universe. As an observer who saw, marked, and inwardly digested what he saw and marked, he could not be blind to the innumerable proofs, as he said, of the goodness of the gods in care of animal life in the world around him. Man's body, for example, what a contrivance it was,—what an organism of contrivances it was for the support, protection, and enjoyment of the soul that dwelt in it! And in this way it is that we have from Socrates his various discourses on the evidences of design which he saw in man and in the life of man. In consequence of these discourses on design, indeed, and of the turn he gave them, it has been, so to speak, *officially* entered into the historical record that, of the three theoretical arguments for the existence of God, the argument from design was originated and first used by Socrates of Athens, the son of Sophroniscus the statuary and Phaenarete the midwife. Plato and Xenophon have pretty well deified this Socrates for many virtues and for many excellences; and we have just seen how a very peculiar speciality of well-merited fame is justly his as originator, and first, in regard to a most important stage

—in regard to a main epoch in the progress and development of morals and the moral principle in mankind; but what lustre attaches to his name, in consequence of the argument from design, is only second to that in regard to morality. "This proof," says Kant (*WW*. ii. 485), "deserves to be named always with reverence. It is the oldest, the clearest, and the most suited to our common understanding. It animates the study of nature, which gives existence to it, and acquires thereby ever new power. It shows ends and intentions where our own observation would never of itself have discovered them, and extends our knowledge of nature through guidance of a peculiar unity, the principle of which is above nature. The new knowledge acts back again towards its cause, its originating idea namely, and exalts our belief in a Supreme Originator into an irresistible conviction."

We shall not deny as against this, that power probably *was* what first in the perception or feeling of men led them to the thought and the worship of the supernatural; but we shall incline very much to agree with the opinion as to Greece having been the birthplace of the first teleological argument for the being of a God. Only to men who had reached their majority,—only to men who looked about them in reason, and in full freedom were led in all their doings by reason,—only to such men was it at all probable that the "order" of this universe should, as in the case of Anaxagoras, for the first time, have shown itself. Only *of* reason could reason have been seen. But Kant is still right in regard to the value and importance of the argument itself. We may say, on the whole, it is the key to the position, and only with special satisfaction is it that we take it from the hand of Socrates. The precise source of our information in this respect is the *Memorabilia* of Xenophon. There we find

Socrates conversing again and again on the evidence of design in nature and in the objects of nature. Since Kant, as we know, there are two ways of looking at design. There is a design that is to be named external, and a design as well that is to be named internal, or immanent, indwelling. Of these it is only the latter that is worthy of the name. In truth there is no design that is not internal and immanent. What is meant by external design is a purpose not intrinsic, but quite extrinsic to the relation concerned. The common joke of Goethe or Schiller in the *Xenien* about the cork-tree having manifestly its purpose, the reason of its being in the manufacture of bottle-corks, perfectly illustrates the idea, or that a clerk's ear was made that he might carry a pen in it! And, certainly, in regard to some things adduced by Socrates, the designfulness is but contingent or external, inasmuch as the relation between the terms or factors in the connections alleged are not always seen to depend on qualities of agreement inherent in them. But when Socrates proceeds to refer to thought in man and its necessary exercise, as in discrimination and selection of the beautiful and useful, in the inventing of language, the enacting of laws, the establishing of government, etc., it is possible to demur to as much as that being a matter of mere externality. Nay, when with Aristodemus the little, he goes more into details in this department, as regards the constitution of the human body, say, it seems impossible to maintain that the design he signalizes is only external and extrinsic.

The eyes, ears, nostrils, tongue, the various organs and their uses by no means evidently concern relations of accident. The eyelids that close when necessary, the eyelashes that are as a screen, even the eyebrows that are as caves or copings to ward off the perspiration—I have never been able to persuade myself, as I find some others do, that these, too, involve correlations that are contingent only. In this reference, Bacon, for example, has the following in *The Advancement of Learning* (ii. 7. 7): "The cause rendered, that *the hairs about the eyelids are for the safeguard of the sight*, doth not impugn the cause rendered, that *pilosity is incident to the orifices of moisture: muscosi fontes,*" etc. One is happy to see here that Bacon does still not deny, but admit final causes: "both causes," he expressly says, in the immediate reference are "true and compatible, the one declaring an intention, the other a consequence only." But one does not find it merely self-evident for all that, that eyelids *must* be pilous, even as fountains are mossy. The fountain makes a soil for low germs even out of its stony lip; but the tears can hardly be conceived to do as much by the covered cartilage that borders the eye; while the eyebrow and perspiration bring no analogy. I hold that an eye is immanent in nature, that an eye is a necessity of nature, and that, consequently, all is at first hand complete in that idea,—I hold this, and I am not ignorant of the vast varieties of the vast gradation of eyes which nature shows,—I hold this, and it is to me nothing against it that a lion's eyebrow, or a horse's eyebrow, is not exactly as is a man's eyebrow, or that such and such a tiny insect, microscopic insect if you will, has a score or twice a score of eyes. Nature is externality, nature is boundless external contingency, and the idea can only appear in nature as in externality, as in boundless external contingency.

One hears of "the open secret of the universe:" now the open secret of the universe is just that idea—an idea and a secret, the bearing of which, on design at least, was not hid from Socrates, more than two thousand years ago. He tells Aristodemus that whatever manifests design is a product of thought and not of chance.

He tells him all these things about the eyebrows, and the eyelids, and the eyelashes; and I daresay he could have told Bacon that it is not absolutely necessary for all moist animal orifices to be pilous. Among others, there are the lips, for example; the beard does not exactly grow on the lips; neither is it the moisture of the lips that has anything to do with the pilosity of the beard. Besides what concerns the eye, etc., Socrates refers to the teeth,—the front ones to cut, and the back ones to grind. I mention this as it is insisted on also by Aristotle. Then it is really matter for congratulation to find Socrates dwelling on the *thought* that is present in the general structure of the world. Is it to be supposed, he asks, that it is only we have reason, and that there is none in the whole? It is really wonderful how this man must reflect on everything, and give himself account of everything — the bare-footed, poorly-clad, street wanderer, pot-bellied and Silenus-faced, that was, perhaps, the wisest, best, and bravest man that was then alive. His God—and he was sincerely pious, he worshipped devoutly—His God was the God of the γνώμη, the understanding, the reason, which in admonishing Aristodemus he opposed to the τύχη, the chance, the accident and chance which, at least, as science rules, alone seem worshipped now-a-days. Nor had the pupil Plato missed the lesson; but of this again in our next.

## GIFFORD LECTURE THE SIXTH.

Plato—His position—His prose—Indebted to Socrates—Monotheism—The popular gods—Socrates' one principle—His method—Universalized by Plato—Epinomis—The *Timaeus*—The eyes, etc.—Kant here—Subject and object—Mechanical and final causes—The former only *for* the latter—Identity and difference—Creation, the world—Time and eternity—The Christian Trinity—The two goods—Religion, the *Laws*—Prayer—Superstition—Hume, Dugald Stewart, Samuel Johnson, Buckle—The Platonic duality—Necessity and contingency—Plato's work.

WITH the name of Plato, we feel that we are approaching one of the greatest figures in all time. As a philosopher, the first place, and without a single dissentient voice, was universally accorded him throughout the whole of antiquity. So completely was this the case, that it does not seem for a moment to have been as much as dreamt that even Aristotle could dispute it with him. Nay, it cannot be doubted that, at this very day, were the question put to the world at large as to which of the two philosophers were the greater, an immense majority of votes would be handed in for Plato. The very quality of his writing would, with the general public, readily secure for him this. With an ease and fulness that are natural simplicity merely, there is, as we can only name it, that amenity in the compositions of Plato that constitutes him, unapproachably, the greatest, sweetest, most delicate and delightful master of prose that ever wrote it. One can feel oneself here, then, in such a presence, only with a certain apprehension. What, however, comes to save us from being altogether oppressed at the call to speak on Plato, is the consideration that it is not of the great whole that we are required to give an account, but only of what in it has a bearing historically on the proofs for the Being of a God. And here we can see at once that Plato, as usual, only receives the torch from his master Socrates, not merely to carry it and hand it on to his further fellow, but to make it blaze withal both brighter and wider. That, too, is as much as to say that, said proofs being concerned, we have here, on the part of Socrates and Plato, two degrees in the advance to *monotheism*. What Socrates actually said in this regard comes to us in the course of his conversation, now with Aristodemus, and again with Euthydemus, as respectively recorded in the first and fourth books of the *Memorabilia*. It is as τὸ θεῖον, simply as the Divinity, he characterizes the gods, when he speaks of them to the former as " seeing and hearing all things at once, as being everywhere present, and as equally caring for all things :" while to Euthydemus he names one sovereign god, and others subordinate. " The other gods," he says, " who give us good things do not come before us visibly in so doing, and he who regulates and keeps together the whole world—he is *manifest* as thus effecting what is greatest, but even in such consummation he, too, is invisible to us." There is (no doubt) in such words as these a monotheistic tinge; but it is not yet pure. In that regard, there is a certain advance in Plato; he still makes respectful reference to the popular gods, in whatever has a public bearing, at the same time that, in other circumstances, he reprobates, as in the second book of the *Republic*, the traditional fables about the particular gods almost as though these gods themselves were fabulous.

If we do but consider, however, the scientific principles which dominated the thoughts, whether of Plato or Socrates, we shall not wonder at this. As we have seen, the one great principle of Socrates was the *good*, whether in a moral or a physical regard; for even in the adjustment of the external universe, he took it with enthusiasm from the hand of Anaxagoras that all was for the best, or that everything precisely was where it best should be. Now, there was unity in the very thought here. If all was for a purpose, and if we were all to strive to a single end, there was necessarily a direction given in our thoughts and wills towards a single power. The whole tendency of such teaching could not but be monotheistic—could not but *lead away from* the traditional gods with question and doubt. Plato directly says, "God, least of all, should have many shapes;" and again, "God is what is absolutely simple and true" (*Rep.* 381 B and 382 E).

The mental attitude on the part of Socrates, to which his principle was the vital force, has been made abundantly plain to us both by Xenophon and Plato. Almost any single conversation in the one, or dialogue in the other, will suffice for proof. So far, there is a certain sameness in them all. For example, let us but hear, on the one hand, Socrates ask Hippias what Beauty is; and, on the other hand, Hippias answer Socrates that it is a beautiful maiden,—let us but hear such question and answer, knowing well the retort of Socrates in the end, that he does not want to know what a beautiful person is, but what is Beauty itself, and we are well-nigh admitted to the very heart of the mystery. Beauty itself, courage itself, justice itself—that was the perpetual quest of Socrates. This quest of his, too, was, on the whole, always in a moral direction. It was always, also, by a certain dissection of the very thinking of his respondent, or opposite, that he came to his result. Now, what Plato did was simply to universalize all this. As he deified the man Socrates, so he deified his work. Firstly, to extend the moral quest of Socrates into the whole field of knowledge,—this for Plato was to discover the *Ideas*. Then, again, secondly, the mental dissection of Socrates became for Plato his express *Dialectic*. While, thirdly and lastly, what was an indefinite unity, or "scattering and unsure" unities with Socrates, was carried up by Plato into the single unity of the *Good*—a good that was to Plato more than moral good, more than a summating and consummating goodness—a good that was to Plato God. And all that is in our own direction—all that is towards monotheism—all that is towards Natural Theology—all that is towards realization of the proofs for the Existence and Attributes of God.

Even in that reference, even specially in the matter of design, we may, not altogether wrongly, assume Plato to have still followed his master; but in him we do not find, so easily and so commonly as in Socrates, instances of what we may call particular design. As we saw, indeed, the design instanced by Socrates was not always free from the reproach of externality. For example, we do get many advantages from the animals we have domesticated; but we can hardly intimate, as Socrates would seem to wish, that pigs and poultry were directly made for us. Illustrations in this kind are, perhaps, chiefly or alone to be found in *Plato*, when, as in the *Timaeus*, he is engaged in his fanciful description of the construction of man. There is a passage in the *Epinomis* that refers to the earth producing fruits for us and food for animals, as well as to winds and rains that we see to be seasonable and in measure. The *Epinomis* is denied to Plato, and transferred to Philip of Opuntium. Philip, however, as a pupil of Plato's, may, possibly, in this case, be only repeating his master. The illustration, too, however external on the whole, is not insusceptible of relative application, for I know not that it is unallowable to point to the possibility of human existence as dependent on the totality of influences, though, for the rest, winds certainly do blow as they list, and rains certainly do fall on the barren sea and the unproductive desert. In the *Timaeus* we have (45 E) the eyelids and the hair (76 C and D) of the head spoken of; the former as protective, and the other as a covering, production by intention being assumed in both cases. Plato talks of the flesh simply as clothing, but designedly thin on the joints, not to impede motion (74 E). Had he been more of an anatomist, contracting muscles, with their pointed terminal tendons, would have better suited his purpose. The *Timaeus* dwells (46 E, 47 A) on the wonders of the eyes, too, and on the wonders of what has been submitted to them. But for the eyes, it is said, proof of the universe there would have been found none, since without them we should never have known of either stars, or sun, or heaven; but "now day and night and the changes of the year yield to us the knowledge of time, and the power of investigating the universe;" and "from these we have attained to that thing called philosophy, than which a greater good has not ever come, nor ever will come, a gift from the gods to the race of mortals" (47 B). Here what Plato has in mind is simply the information we attain by sight, simply the intellectual advantage of that information. He has no idea of what the world would be, we may almost say, physically, were there no seeing subject anywhere to be found in it. Such an idea was, of course, impossible to Plato, who knew nothing about the undulations of the aether, etc. Something of the same thought, but more in a moral reference, occurs in Kant. He says in the *Kritik of Judgment* (§ 86), "If the world consisted of beings merely inanimate, or some animate and some inanimate, but the animate still without reason, the existence of such a world would have no worth at all, for there would exist in it no being that possessed the slightest notion of any worth . . . the existence of rational beings under moral laws can alone be thought as final cause of the existence of a world." I may also remind you here of a quotation from Colebrooke which I specially emphasized as of future use. This, namely: "There must be one to enjoy what is formed for enjoyment: a spectator, a witness of it: that spectator is soul." Nature, as I said then, too, is not there independently, self-subsistently, and on its own account: it is there only for a purpose and as a means. Evidently a universe without a spectator to make it his, object without subject, would be a gross self-stultification, a manifest meaninglessness, an idle anomaly, a palpable monstrosity, an arrant cheat.

Proceeding nearer to our main subject of design generally, we may remark that, in the *Timaeus*, Plato is very full and clear on that to us essential interest, final causes, and in their opposition to physical ones. "There are two genera of causes," he says (*Tim.* 68 E), "the one necessary and the other divine." The one cause, that of necessity, being subordinated to that of intellect, and made its minister and servant merely. "The genesis of this world," it is said (48), "has been effected by the conjunction of necessity and intellect;" but necessity is under the rule of intellect. The causes of necessity, in short, are only "the accessory causes which the Deity, in realizing the idea of the possibly best, uses only as hodmen for the work;" adding, however, that that "is not the conception of the most, who hold the causes of things to be cold and heat, solidification and liquefaction, etc.; but both causes ought to be spoken of." We see thus that it is here with Plato just as we saw it was with Socrates in reference to Anaxagoras. Both will insist on final causes as equally present with mechanical ones, but as being, at the same time, the ruling and directing powers of these, which are only the physical materials and mechanical agents in realization, so to speak, of the counsels and will of the causes we call final. This point of view is perfectly plain in Plato. He is perfectly well aware, he says, that there are those who maintain that the causes of necessity are the only causes, and that what are named final causes are merely secondary causes that result from these; that, for example, fire and water, and earth and air, are all of them from nature and chance, and none of them from plan and contrivance—that, in short, chance and physical necessity are to be credited with the production of all things, heaven with all that is in it, the seasons, and earth, and animals, and plants. But he will still believe that earth, and sun, and all the stars, and the seasons so beautifully arranged in years and months, as well as the universal faith of man, whether Greek or barbarian, prove that there are gods. Besides this passage in the *Laws* (886), there is another to a like effect in the *Timaeus*.

There are other two terms very current in Plato, here at once in the *Timaeus*, for example, which involve pretty well the same distinction as the two kinds of causes do. They are identity and difference, for to that meaning the Greek words ταὐτόν and θάτερον amount. These are really, just as in the form of final and physical causes, the warp and woof of the whole divine fabric. The one, the *same* namely, or identity as identity, is the principle of the permanent, of that that eternally is. And that, plainly, is the side of the intellect, the side of thought, the side of the in and in. The other, as the difference, the otherwiseness, is just as it is named, the other as other, the outer. This is the side of the show, of the externalization, the side of the senses, the side of the mutable and transitory. Either, too, is necessary to the other. Identity would be indistinguishable unless *differenced*, differentiated. And what would be a difference that was only difference, and, by consequence, unidentified? The inner must be outered, the outer innered. Whatever *is* must be able to *appear*. The physical cause is but the realization of the final cause. The θάτερον, the other, the difference, is but the realization of the ταὐτόν, of that that is the same, of that that is the identity.

But if there is a side of the intellect, if there is a final cause in the constitution of things, then design is at the heart of them, design is the root and the centre of the universe. And, in fact, it seems the very purpose of the entire dialogue of the *Timaeus* to prove this. That dialogue may be named a teleological exposition throughout. The God, for the sake of what is good only, fabricates, in beauty and harmony, the entire world, and man in particular. The former, indeed, the world, is itself described as a "blessed god," possessed of intelligence, life, and soul. All that is made in it is made after an eternal pattern, the most beautiful of things, and from the most perfect of causes. For the God is good, and there is never any grudge or envy in the good about anything whatever; and he made the world, consequently, to be like unto himself. Thus, then, this world has reason in it, and is truly made by the providence of God. Further, created most beautiful in the perfect image of the most beautiful, it is declared sole and single; for, as is implied, perfection needs no multiple.

It is in this part of the *Timaeus* that Plato comes to the genesis of time. We have seen some of his expressions in that reference already; but it is difficult to follow him here. Difficult, I suppose, the subject itself proved to Plato, and his words are correspondently obscure. The *notion* itself of the Eternal Being that was, and is, and always will be, offered, as a notion, probably no hardship. It is easy to use the words, the predicates that describe what we conceive to be eternal, as, for example, in the terms of Plato, to say that the eternal, "what is always unmoved the same, can become by time neither older nor younger, nor has been made, nor appears now, nor will be in the future, nor can any of those things at all attach to it which mortal birth has grafted on the things of sense;" but how to bring into connection with this everlasting rest the never-resting movement of time —that is the difficulty. Plato seems to say that all the phenomena of sense are nothing but "the forms of time imitating eternity, and moving numerically in its circle." Now, if I read my own notion into these obscure words, perhaps it will help to the formation of no irrelevant idea. Suppose eternity a *continuum*, and time to measure the *discreta* of it,—eternity to be a continuity, and time to enumerate the parts or divisions of it,—eternity to be a completed and an ever-enduring circle, and time to be the counting, the traversing of the dots, the infinite dots, that compose its periphery,—suppose we conceive this, then we may have something of a picture of both the unmoved and the moving, and yet in coherent relation. Now, that may be the truth. Time may be no straight line, as we are apt to figure it, but a curve—a curve that eventually returns into itself. In that way the phenomena of sense will be but as the hands of time externalizing its moments, the moments of time, even as the hands of the clock point out, or externalize, the divisions of the hour.

But, leaving these dark matters, it is in this part of Plato that we find that reflexion of the Christian Trinity which is so often referred to. The words Maker and Father occur about a dozen pages on from the beginning of the *Timaeus*. There it is said: "Of this the All, to find the Maker and Father is difficult, and having found him, it is impossible to declare him to all men." Farther on (37 C) we have this: " When the Father that created it saw it moving and alive, this the created image of the blessed gods, he was well pleased." We have seen this creation itself already called " a blessed god ; " and a few pages earlier than the last quotation (at 31 A and B), unity, εἷς, is not only asserted of this " blessed god," but it is even called μονογενής, a word that in St. John and elsewhere is always translated " only-begotten." This remarkable term, too, is to be found repeated at the very end of the dialogue. Lastly (50 D), we have this that is the " only-begotten " also called " Son." The Greek word is not υἱός, indeed, but still it is ἔκγονος, a word of exactly the same import. On the whole it is not surprising that these expressions in Plato of an only-begotten Son, made in the image of the Father, should, on the part of the Christian world, have attracted so much attention. This passage in Plato probably it was that led the Fathers of the Church, followed by the ecclesiastical majority of the Middle Ages, to represent, as I formerly remarked, the existent world as the Son. The Jew, Philo of Alexandria, it is to be said also, used, in respect of the world, the same expression of Son of God. We may note here, also, that Numenius of Apamea (a Pythagorean philosopher familiar with the writings of Plato, who lived in the second century) has distinct references to the Good as God, and to the world as his only-begotten Son. Philo was still a Jew at least forty years after the death of Christ, so that it is not to be thought that either he or Numenius had a Christian reference in the use of the phrase. Even as regards Plato, the analogy, I doubt not, is only to be characterized as verbal. What, in truth, he means by the two that he names here God and World or Son are simply the two principles which we have so often seen already—identity and difference; the two causes, design and necessity, or the two Goods, as in the *Laws* (631 B), the divine and the human, the latter conditional on the former, so that "if any city receives the greater, it possesses also the less; but if not, it is without either." " It is not possible," says Plato (*Laws*, 967 D), " for any one of mortal men to become permanently pious who accepts not these two affirmations, that the soul, as it is the eldest of all that is created, is immortal, and rules everything corporeal." That is, again, the duality in question, and we see it is made here the condition of piety; for piety is to Plato always the ultimate result. " Whoso, according to the laws, believes that there are gods, he never willingly did a wrong deed nor spoke a wrong word" (*Laws*, 885 B): accordingly Plato is at pains to prove the existence, the power, and the justice of God. The whole of the tenth book of the *Laws* may be regarded as such proof; and a very slight change might make the whole discussion of the religious element there assume quite a modern look. We are not surprised, then, in Plato, to find the first of every inquiry, as in the *Timaeus* (27 C), to be an invocation for the blessing of the God, and a prayer that whatever might be said should be agreeable to his will, and becoming to themselves, the inquirers. And, probably, just such a state of mind is natural to humanity as humanity. I fancy that in front of any serious emergency, of any grave responsibility, invocation rises spontaneously in a man, were he even an atheist. No one to Plato (*Epin.* 989 D) can even teach, unless the God lead. This piety on the part of Plato, as on the part of Socrates his, has been stigmatized as superstition.

Now, there are undoubtedly such things as superstitions, and they may exist in weak minds in such excess as seriously to interfere with the sound and healthy transaction of the business of life. "It is natural," says Hume (*Nat. Hist. of Rel.* iii.), "that superstition should prevail everywhere in barbarous ages." And then he tells us also of the superstition of the educated—of such men as Pompey, and the advanced Cicero, and the wily Augustus. "That great and able emperor," he says of the last, "was extremely uneasy when he happened to change his shoes, and put the right-foot shoe on the left foot." Dugald Stewart also is to be found quoting this same anecdote of Augustus, and reflecting somewhat loftily on superstition occasionally appearing in the most enlightened. In illustration, he quotes a long paragraph from Boswell about Dr. Johnson counting his steps so as to have his left or right foot first in reference to an entrance or an exit, and winds up with this reflection from his Professorial Chair: "They who know the value of a well-regulated and unclouded mind would not incur the weakness and wretchedness exhibited in the foregoing description for all his literary acquirements and literary fame." Dugald Stewart is one of our very best and most elegant writers of philosophical English. Philosophically, he had an excellently well-filled mind too, and seldom writes anything that is not interesting and valuable. Despite a little spoiling, moreover, from a vast success, social and otherwise, he kept, on the whole, as we see in his intercourse with Burns, his manhood by him. Nevertheless, when he prelects in that grandiose fashion on poor Johnson, he can only remind us of the great Mr. Buckle evolving his periods mouthwards like the ribands of a showman from the very drum-head of the Aufklärung. "They who know the value of a well-regulated and unclouded mind," that is the very jargon of the general position, and is not more Dugald Stewart's than it is Thomas Henry Buckle's and a hundred others', David Hume among them. "The weakness and wretchedness exhibited in the foregoing description"—

that means the counting of his steps on the part of Johnson; and, looking at it so, we may fail to see the wretchedness. It does not appear as though Samuel Johnson had, *in the main*, during life been a wretched man. But be it as it may with the wretchedness, perhaps we will allow the "weakness"? Well, truly estimated and appreciated, what underlay and had initiated the habit was certainly a weakness, in the sense that it concerned a *non-ens*; it is quite safe to say that, if Johnson had *not* counted, had not thought of his steps, but had done unconsciously precisely what he consciously did do,—it is quite safe to say that, in that way, no actual circumstance of time and place varying, the events and issue of the day then and thereafter would have been identically the same as they were in fact experienced. But if there was weakness, there was also to some extent strength. Johnson made no attempt in any way at concealment; he did not hide the habit; he practised it *in aperto*. Of course, it may be very naturally suggested that Boswell was but a weak brother, and Johnson might have been careless of his opinion. But, then, in Stewart's very quotation from Boswell, the information is as of a matter within the common knowledge of "his friends." I don't know, therefore, that many of ourselves would have been as bold as Johnson; we might, perhaps, have felt a greater amount of shame and timidity at the idea of exposing ourselves. And yet we may have our own superstitions not less, or not much less, than Johnson. In saying this, I simply go on the broad fact of our common humanity. Man, as man, from the first of days to the last, will always show the cross, the contrarium, the contradiction, the Platonic duality, which forms the frame or groundwork of his nature. Man will never cease to humble himself in heart and soul before the mystic Divinity of this universe; but he will always be found, nevertheless, sneaking towards a Mumbo-Jumbo that he is rather ashamed of. He will always have his luck and his unluck, with the signs and the means to see and foresee, to ward or forward accordingly. I suppose he will always count his sneezes, and wish them to end in an odd one! Such things as amulets, charms, luck-articles of a thousand descriptions, will never die out. Tokens, foretokens, and fortune-telling, Biblical or Vergilian lots—instances of such things will in no time be lost among us. We may depend upon it that our table-turnings, spirit-rappings, spectral apparitions, and what not, will not be without their successors even to the remotest ages. Superstition is the shadow of religion; and they will seldom be found separate,—quite as though there were two authorities, two ruling powers, two dominions: one of the heavens, and another of the earth; one of the light, and another of the dark; one of our hopes, and another of our fears. And so, doubtless, it really is. Here, again, it is but the cross, the contrarium, the contradiction, that crops up to us. Once more, as has been said, we have to look for a rationale to the Platonic duality. Religion shall go with the ταὐτόν, the identity; and superstition with the θάτερον, the difference. Or we may apply in the same way the two genera of causes. He who realizes final causes, and the intellectual side, is necessarily religious; while he who realizes physical causes, and the corporeal side, is necessarily superstitious. And as both causes go together, the same man, as in the case of Johnson, may be at once religious and superstitious; rather, perhaps, it belongs to man, as man, to be at once both. Now of physical causes the outcome is contingency. I know that the opposite of this is generally said. See the waves upon the shore, it is said; there is not one of them that, in its birth and in its end, and in its entire course between, is not the result of necessity. That is true; but it is also true that not one of these waves but is the result of infinite contingency. Every air that blows, every cloud that passes, every stray leaf, or branch, or feather of bird that falls, every contour of the land, every stone or rock in the sea-bottom, almost, we may say, every fish in the element itself, has its own effect; and the various waves, in their form, and size, and velocity, are the conjoint result. That is necessity; but it is also contingency. That is, the serial causal influences *cross* each other, and from their own infinitude, as well as from the infinitude of space and time, in both of which they are, they are utterly incalculable and beyond every ken. That is contingency. There are infinite physical trains in movement. Each taken by itself might be calculable; but these trains cross each other in the infinitude of space and time endlessly; and that is not calculable—the *contingency* of them, the *tingency con*, the touching or falling together of them. This touching together is something utterly unaccountable. The outcome to us in the finite world,—so to speak, in the terminal periphery, can only be that we are submitted to a ceaseless to and fro, to a boundless miscellaneousness, an infinite *pêle-mêle*. But that being, it is with infinite astonishment that I have heard *necessity* thrown at philosophy, as though the belief of philosophy must necessarily be necessity. Plato's intellectual world, the world of the ideas in hypothetical evolution the one from the other, may be a realm of necessity; but such necessity is already contingency the moment that this realm, the ideas themselves, have become externalized—got flung, that is, into otherness as otherness, externality as externality. And thus it is that, in philosophy, contingency is the category of the finite. Every crossing in the infinite *pêle-mêle* may be plain to a spaewife, possibly; but it offers no problem for any reason as reason. It is in this connection, too, that I have heard very competent people speak of the system of philosophy as, of necessity, a system of necessity, moral as well as metaphysical, and not of free will. That, to me, as before, gives again boundless astonishment. Why, it is only in a realm of contingency that there were any scope for free will; it is only against contingencies that free will has to assert itself; it is only in their midst that free will can realize itself.

And here we have come at last, perhaps, to the very angle of the possible rationale of superstition. We have no power ourselves over contingency: it ramps, and frolics, and careers, in its blind way, independent of us. Of course, it is understood that I speak of things as they are open to the reason which is given us: to omniscience and omnipotence, there can be neither contingency nor necessity. But taking it just so as it is to mankind, here, it seems, there were a realm in which chance, and chance alone, ran riot. How, then, propitiate, conciliate, and, so to speak, win the soft side of chance? It is only so that one can explain or excuse the existence of superstition in so powerfully intelligent, and so religiously devout a mind as that of Samuel Johnson. And if we can so speak of the existence of superstition in his mind, we may similarly speak of its existence in those of most others. There is no doubt that Johnson prayed most reverently and fervently—there is no doubt that he trusted himself wholly to God; but yet, for all that, there seem to have been for him as well powers of contingency: he would render *them* favourable, too, and have even chance, luck on his side. The realm of the infinite, the realm of the ταὐτόν, the realm of the final causes, led him to God; but he could not ignore and turn his back upon the realm of the finite, the realm of the θάτερον and difference, the realm of the physical causes. Of course, this also is true: that it is just as the race or

the individual advances in knowledge and in wisdom that
the latter world disappears more and more from our conscience; and the former world alone has place. Far back in
time the race had superstition only, and not religion; but as
regards the individual, it is only some four hundred years
since a king of France, Louis XI., knelt to a leaden image
in his hatband on the ground, and invoked his "gentle
mistress," his "only friend," his "good lady of Clery," to
intercede with God Almighty for the pardon to him of his
many murders, that of his own brother among them! No
man can call that religion. To a Louis XI. heaven was
peopled with contingencies, even as the earth was. To
him final causes there were none; caprice was all. Plato,
in his perception of physical as but the material for final
causes, was quite in another region than the most Christian
king of France. In fact, Plato's whole world view was
that of a single teleological system with the Good alone as
its heart, with the will of God alone as its creator and
soul.

Plato, then, in a way, but carries out and completes
what Socrates began. Socrates was not content with right
action only as action, he must see and know why it was
right; action, as it were, he must convert into knowledge;
that is, for man's action, as a whole, he must find general
principles, and *a general principle*. Now all that involved,
first, a dialectic of search; second, the ideas and the *idea*
as a result; and third, the realization of the State as its
practical application. But that is simply to name the
work of Plato in its three moments. The State was his
one practical result; the ideas and the *idea* the media of
realization; and the dialectic the instrument of their
discovery, limitation, and arrangement. The ideal system,
then, was the centre of the Platonic industry. Sensible
existences, the things of sense, have for Plato no real truth.
All that we see and feel is in perpetual flux, a perpetual

mutation. The ideas alone are the truth of things; and things have truth only in so far as they participate in the ideas. For ideas are the paradeigmata of things, and things are but the sensible representations of these. What the ideas logically are, things ontologically are; but the logical element is alone true; while the ontological element, as representative, is but temporary show only. The only true ontological element, the ὄντως ὄν, is the *Good*. To the Good not only is the knowledge of things due, but it is the Good also that gives them being. It is *for* it, and *because of* it, and *through* it that all things are. It alone is the principle, and the *ratio essendi*, and the foundation of philosophy itself. Man, being in his constitution double, the *truth* of his senses is alone *thought*. The end-aim of everything, and the end-aim of the entire system of everything is thought. That alone is good, and the Good alone is God. And God is the creator of the universe. The Good, design is so absolutely the principle of all things for Plato, that whatever exists, exists just because it is better that it should be than not be. Design, the one principle of design, is the νοῦς itself: ψυχὴ αἴτιον ἁπάντων, the soul is the cause of all things, and that amounts to this, that all things are first of all in the soul, only not externalized. I hope we have some conception of where Plato is historically as regards the proofs required by Natural Theology.

# GIFFORD LECTURE THE SEVENTH.

Sophists—Aufklärung—Disbelief, Simon of Tournay, Amalrich of Bena, David of Dinant—Italian philosophers, Geneva Socinians, Bacon, Hobbes, the Deists, Locke, Descartes, Spinoza—Hume, Gibbon—Germany, Reimarus, etc.—Klopstock, Lavater—Lessing, Hamann, Herder, Jacobi—Goethe, Schiller, Jean Paul—Carlyle—France—Kant and his successors—Necessary end of such movements—Cosmological argument—Locke, Clarke, Leibnitz—Aristotle—Dependency—Potentiality and actuality—A beginning—Aristotle and design—Mr. Darwin's mistake—Empedocles and the survival of the fittest.

ONE can hardly leave Plato without saying a word about the Sophists: it is his handling of some of the most conspicuous Sophists, indeed, that constitutes the special charm of several of his very best dialogues. Amongst the individual Sophists, there are, of course, many characteristic differences; still, when looked at from a certain historical distance, they, so to speak, appear to run into each other, as though but units in a single movement. One general spirit we assume to unite them all, one common atmosphere to breathe around them. In brief, they all step forward as the apostles of the new; and this distinction they all arrogate in one and the same way, by pointing the finger at the old. Suppose the old to be a clothed figure, then one Sophist has the credit of stripping off its gown, another its tunic, a third its *braccae*, and so on. So it is that the whole movement is shut up in a single word now-a-days, the word *Aufklärung*. In the Greek Sophists we have before us the Greek Aufklärung. Aufklärung is Klärung Auf, a clearing up. It means that, as it were, day had dawned, that light had come, that people at last had got their eyes opened to the absurdity of the lies they had hitherto believed in. It was as though they had suddenly turned round upon themselves, and found, strangely, all at once, everything in the clearness of a new revelation. They were all wrong, it seemed: they had been dreadfully stupid. Hitherto they had lived only, and never thought; but now they both saw and thought. This was not true, and that was not true. There was absurdity there, and there was absurdity here. And it was only they were right—only they, the Sophists themselves. They saw how it was with all things, and they could speak of all things. They saw just *so* well, indeed, and had so much power in the seeing, that, on the whole, they could speak of all things pretty well as they pleased. That is very briefly, but not unjustly, to name the Sophists as we see them in Plato. If we but take up into our minds the general characteristics of this movement, then, the movement on the part of these Sophists —if we but take it up into our minds and name it Aufklärung, we shall have some idea of what an Aufklärung means. It was not the Sophists, however, that suggested the word. This, the suggestion, was due, not to an ancient, but to a modern movement—a movement that was, on the whole, more peculiarly French, but still a movement in which England, Germany, Holland, and all the other nations of Europe more or less participated. It was preceded here, in Europe, I mean, by a want. This want was the product of suffering, on the one hand, and of the ordinary human curiosity, or the desire of gain, on the other. Political tyranny and religious corruption had become, on the part of the arbitrators, whether of the State or the Church we may not too incorrectly say, universal. Men grew scandalized, indignant; yearned for delivery from the wrong; and revolted against both—both Church and State. Meantime, too, discoveries in the pursuit of curiosity or gain had been going on. There were discoveries by sea, and there were inventions in the arts. America was discovered, and gunpowder—gunpowder and printing were invented. Greek fugitives had fled into Italy; Protestantism arose. There was but one general result; there was but one desire awakened—the desire to know. And it was the desire to know, conjoined with the political and ecclesiastical wrong, that gave rise to the modern Aufklärung. What concerns religion is, undoubtedly, the most notable phase of the Aufklärung, but it is not the only one. The Aufklärung was a movement of the whole of humanity, and extended into humanity's veriest roots, political, social, educational, and all other. So far as books are concerned, perhaps it is the religious element that shows most. There are not wanting many heretical opinions during the whole history of the Church, some of which were as extreme in their quality as even those of a Hume, or a Voltaire himself. As early as about 1200, there was Simon of Tournay, with his book, *de Tribus Impostoribus*, and, somewhat later, the followers of Amalrich of Bena, and David of Dinant. Considerably later than these still there were the Italian Philosophers of the Transition Period, and the Socinians of Geneva, who, with their questions, harrowed the very soul of Calvin. Bacon, Hobbes, and the English Deists may or may not be reckoned to the movement of the Aufklärung; in strict accuracy, perhaps, they were better named its forerunners; among whom even John Locke is sometimes included, and, if John Locke, then surely also René Descartes. For myself it always appears to me that the *Tractatus Theologico - Politicus* of Spinoza, published perhaps about 1660, may be very fairly accounted *the beginning itself* of the Aufklärung. That work is very much the quarry from which Voltaire drew—very much a source of direction and supply also to the Critics of Germany. In Great Britain we may instance as undoubted members of the Aufklärung such men as David Hume and Edward Gibbon, but only at the head of a cryptic mass. In Germany the movement, as in writers like Nicolai, Mendelssohn, Baumgarten, Semler, Reimarus, and even scores of others, was much milder than elsewhere, if also considerably thinner. In Germany, too, there was speedily a reaction against it, as exemplified in the pious spirit which reigns in the works of its Klopstocks and Lavaters. But what writers put an end to the movement, if not generally, at least in their own country, were Lessing, Herder, Hamann, and Jacobi—four men distinguished (of course, variously among themselves) almost by an *inspiration*, we may say, not less religious than it was philosophical, and not less philosophical than it was religious. There is not one of the four but excellently exemplifies this. Lessing is not an *enormous* genius—he knows himself that he is not a poet, but only a critic. For all that, however, to get the *German spirit* that is peculiar even yet, he is, perhaps, just the very best German writer whom it is possible to choose. As the truth for him was ever the middle between two extremes, so he himself stands there a figure in the middle for ever. Clearness, fairness, equity constitute his quality. Living in the time of the Aufklärung, he, too, would have Aufklärung; but the Aufklärung he would have should not be for his *eyes* only, he would have it for his *soul* as well. It was his heart that would have light—feeling—not mere perception. He was not a man that trusted, like so many other literary men of the day, to himself and his own inspiration. He was a thoroughly educated man, trained in mathematics as well as in philology; and he had read deeply. Even of archaeology, even of Church history, he surprises by his knowledge. Christianity is to him, for all his enlightenment, the religion of our maturer humanity; and he vindicates *for* reason and *by* reason, the very strictest dogmas of the Creed. To him the unity of God and the immortality of the soul are truths *demonstrable*. Yet he prefers the religion of the heart to the religion of the head. He defends the tradition of the Church; and yet he opposes the Christian of feeling to the dogmatist of belief, even as he opposes the spirit to the letter. He clings to the rule of faith—the *regula fidei*; but he would as little sacrifice reason to faith, as he would sacrifice faith to reason. Still his place in theology is only, as he says, that of him who sweeps the dust from the steps of the temple; and his religion proper is rightly to be named, perhaps, only the religion of humanity.

This that I have said of Lessing will dispense me from any similar details as regards the other three. Hamann, with whom I have no great sympathy, is a very peculiar personality, and has left behind him certain pithily far-fetched and peculiar sayings quite currently quoted, while both Herder and Jacobi are eminently noble men, as well as great writers. The specialty that I would attribute to all four of them is, that they correct and complete the Aufklärung by placing side by side with the half on which alone it will look, the failing half on which it has turned its back, and have, in this way, done good work towards the reconstitution and re-establishment of the central catholic and essential truth. Nor has it proved otherwise with German literature in general, and its coryphei in particular. The example of Lessing and the others has proved determinative also for such men as Goethe, and Schiller, and Jean Paul. Neither on their part is there any mockery or disregard of religion as religion. On the contrary, it is approached with sincere feelings by all of them, who know it to be, and never doubt of its being, an essential element in the very construction of man. It is this that is meant when we hear of Thomas Carlyle being directed, at one time of his life, to German literature as likely to supply him with what he wanted, at once in a philosophical and a religious reference. It is this also that he actually did find there. Nothing else than this made Goethe to Carlyle a prophet. Speculating on this relation between two men, in many respects so unlike each other, I had, in my own mind, referred the source of it to that part of *Wilhelm Meister's Travels*, where one of the Heads of an educational institute, conducting Wilhelm from hall to hall, prelects equably on the various religions. To read this was a new experience to Carlyle. As his early letters tell us, the perusal of Gibbon had won him over to the side of heresy; and any further progression in the same direction could only exhibit to him Christianity—in Hume, Voltaire, and the Encyclopedists, say—as an object, not of derision merely, but even of the fiercest hatred and the most virulent abuse. This, then, as on the part of these Germans, was a novel experience to Carlyle,—the dispassionate, open-eyed, significant wisdom of such tolerant and temperate discourse even in respect of the Christian religion; and it was as with the light and the joy of a new revelation that he returned, *at least to all the feeling, and the reverence, and the awe*, that had been *his* in his boyhood under the eye of his father. And so it was that the first aim of Carlyle, as in the *Sartor Resartus*, was the re-establishment, in every earnest, educated, but doubting soul, of the vital reality of true religion. In that work, to such souls, wandering in the dark, the light of Carlyle suddenly strook through the black of night as with the coming of a celestial messenger. "It is the night of the world," they heard, "and still long till it be day: we wander amid the glimmer of smoking ruins, and the sun and the stars of heaven are as blotted out for a season; and two immeasurable phantoms, Hypocrisy and Atheism, with the ghoul, Sensuality, stalk abroad over the earth, and call it theirs: well at ease are the sleepers for whom existence is a shallow dream. But what of the awestruck wakeful?" And thenceforward after this book of Carlyle's it was in the power of any one who at least *would* awake, to lay himself down in the very heart of that awful "Natural Supernaturalism," to see, to wonder, and to worship; while those mysterious "organic filaments" span themselves anew, not in vain for him. That was the *first* mood of Carlyle; and it was his *highest*. He never returned to it. His *Hero-Worship* contains, perhaps, what *feels* nearest to it; and it is significant that Carlyle himself made a common volume of the two works. But history and biography occupy him thenceforth; and in these, unfortunately, so much of the early Gibbonian influence, to call it so, crops out, that Carlyle, on the whole, despite his natural, traditional, and philosophical piety, passes through life for a doubter merely, and is claimed and *beset* by the very men whose vein of shallow but exultant Aufklärung is precisely the object of his sincerest reprobation and uttermost disgust. There is a good deal to confirm as much as this, in his Address as Rector here of this University, especially in his reference to "ten pages, which he would rather have written than all the books that have appeared since he came into the world." These ten pages contain what I have referred to in connection with Goethe's *Wilhelm Meister;* and I was well content to hear from Carlyle's lips on that occasion that I had not speculated badly as to the source of his veneration for a man who, if a prophet to him, might prove, on a closer inspection, perhaps, for all his dispassionate words on religion, somewhat of the earth earthy to us.

All this will, pretty well, have made plain to us what the Aufklärung is. Men, as I have said, instead of simply living blindly straight on, suddenly opened their eyes and turned round to look. What they saw was only the old, and it was not all good—*as how could it be?* They revolted against it; they would not believe a word they had been told; they would see for themselves. Now, naturally what they saw for themselves, what alone they could see for themselves, lay *without*. What was *within* was what they had been told, and they would not have it. The result was that the concrete man was separated into abstract sides; abstract by this, that they were each apart, and not together, as they should be, in a vital *one*. What a man saw and felt, experience, was to be the only truth. All was to be learned and won from the examination of the objects of the external senses. And so, while the outer flourished, the inner perished. The inner was only superstition, prejudice, unenlightened prejudice, and had to be thrown away. But the very best of humanity could not escape from being included in the cast. Religion apart, no one, for example, can read the French writings of the period without disgust at the flippant manner in which the best principles of morality are held up for derision and a sneer — even the principles of the family, say, which are the very foundation of the State and of our social community within it.

Now it was to this movement, certainly to the untrue and shallow extreme of it, that the German writers named put an end. And so it is that the philosophical successors of Kant, all to a man, speak of the Aufklärung as a thing of the past, as a thing that had been examined, seen into, and shelved — shelved as already effete, antiquated, out of date, and done with. This, however, can only be said on the level of true philosophy. It cannot be said at all generally for the mass; the mass at present rather can largely be seen contentedly at feed on the husks and stubble of the Aufklärung, gabbling and cackling sufficiently.

But, in regard to Greece, when we consider that the principle of the Sophists was subjectivity pure and simple, that is, that truth as truth is only whatever one feels, or perceives, or thinks, and only in his own regard for the very moment that he so feels or so perceives or so thinks,—when we consider this, and that the result was only opposition to whatever had been established in law, or morality, or religion, or social life, we must see that the Greek Sophists very fairly represented what is called an Aufklärung.

It is not unimportant withal for us to note that this movement, despite these three greatest and best men and philosophers, — Socrates, Plato, and Aristotle, who, in absolute correction and refutation of it, followed it,— that this movement, despite all, destroyed Greece. Noting this, there may here, I am inclined to say, be a lesson for *us*. What, if all this enlightenment, all this liberation from prejudice, all this stripping bare of everything in heaven and earth, should, despite our telegraphs and telephones, end in the compulsory retreat of the whole of us—men and women of us, after war upon war, and internecine strife, and confusion limitless—into our original woods again! If we will but consider of it, with all that we are taught now to believe of this universe, such a consummation cannot be held to be any longer a matter of mere dream. The subject, however, is inexhaustible; illustrations there are to hand endlessly —in the east, and the west, and the north, and the south, and without one exception of a single human interest.

I must return to our theme—the proofs for the Being of a God. In view of what was currently held in regard to Socrates and the argument from design, I had passed over the claim to priority made by some for the cosmological argument, stating that it had been usually assigned to Aristotle. It is in place now to turn to that argument, seeing that, in our historical survey, it is Aristotle that we have reached. And here I only fear that what presses on us must enforce undue brevity.

A form of the cosmological argument occurs in Locke to this effect: "If we know there is some real being, and that nonentity cannot produce any real being, it is evident demonstration that from eternity there has *been* something, since what was not from eternity had a beginning, and what had a beginning must be produced by something else." That is pretty well the argument of Dr. Samuel Clarke, too. Something is, therefore something has always been, and so on. The proper angle of the cosmological argument, however, is dependence. What we see around us are evident effects; the whole world is but a single scene of change; phenomena follow phenomena. Accordingly, a German writer says: "The teleological view takes not, like the cosmological, its point of departure from the vanity (*Eitelkeit*), but from the grandeur (*Herrlichkeit*) of the world." But that is too much. Dependence is not exactly vanity; and what is called vanity (*Eitelkeit*) in the one argument is really identically the same thing as is called grandeur (*Herrlichkeit*) in the other argument. The grandeur is not vain, though it is dependent. The gardens, pictures, and statuary with which a rich man surrounds himself are dependent, but they are not vain; they are a beauty. The phenomena of the world are dependent—dependent on noumena and a noumenon, and that, on the whole, constitutes the cosmological argument. This argument is often called Leibnitz' argument; but if we call Socrates the originator and founder of the teleological argument, it is Aristotle who is named as the originator and founder of the cosmological argument. And with him this argument turns on motion. Whatever is in motion has had a mover; but we cannot go back from motion to motion, and from mover to mover, endlessly; there must be a final stop at last where motion and mover are one; where what is, is a self-mover, which self-mover evidently also by mere position is infinite and eternal. Motion, mover, that is *causa sui*, cause of itself, that is God. The aim of philosophy, says Aristotle, is to know the truth; but to know the truth of anything, we must know its cause. Then truth in the cause must be eminently what is found in its effects, as fire, being cause of warmth in everything that is near and nearer to it, must *itself* have *most* warmth. The first cause, being from nothing else, and always equal to what it is, must in *its being* be the cause of the *being* of everything else. And that there is a first cause as ultimate principle is evident from this, that there can be no infinite series of causes, whether in a straight line or in natural kind.

"God," says Leibnitz, " is the first cause of things; for all finite things, as all that we see and know, are contingent, and have in themselves nothing that makes their existence necessary, inasmuch as plainly time, space, and matter, each continuously identical with itself and indifferent to all else, might assume quite other movements and forms and another order. We must, therefore, look for the cause of the existence of this world, which is a collection of things merely contingent, only in such substance as has the cause of its existence in its own self, and is therefore eternal and necessary." The angle of this reasoning, whether in the one form or the other, is, as I have said, *dependence*. The contingency of all things which come within our ken in this universe is assumed as of such character that, alone and by itself, it implies a necessary first cause. What is contingent is, as contingent, not something *self*-supported, *self*-subsistent, but presupposes something else that is such, or that is in its own self necessary. But now the world is contingent, for the world is an aggregate of things, all of which are contingent in themselves. Therefore the world presupposes and implies an absolutely necessary being as its substantiating ground or cause.

Not only is this being an absolutely necessary being, but, according to Aristotle, and still cosmologically reasoning, he is an absolutely actual being. And of this reasoning the angle is that what is *potential* only presupposes a preceding *actuality;* for to be potential only is to be such as may quite as well not be as be. In Aristotelian terms, the πρῶτον κινοῦν, what first gives movement to this world, must in itself also be absolute functioning actuality, absolute ἐνέργεια; for were it only potential, only δύναμις, there were no reason, *so far as it was only that*, that it should become actual. What is potential, what is potential only, there is no reason, in such quality, for any step further. There is, then, an actual God. To Aristotle, in fact, there is no beginning. And, for that matter, I know not to what style of thinker there can be a beginning—in the sense, that is, of an absolute beginning, of an absolute first. No theist can assign a first to Deity; and no atheist can assign a first to the system of things in time. But where there is no beginning, there can only be eternity; and that really seems the thought of Aristotle. What is, is not, as it were, a straight line to Aristotle, a virtue, a power, that goes ever out and out, and on and on. Rather, what is, is to him a virtue that returns into itself, a power that returns into itself—so to speak, an eternally circling circle. That *is* eternity; such circle, that ever is, and never was not, and never will not be. Eternity is the self-determining organism that operates, acts, moves out of itself into itself; life that feeds itself, lives into itself; thought that ever thinks, thinks itself into itself.

I omit much here on the cosmological argument, to proceed to what is plainer. Aristotle, it is to be said, is not to be supposed as only limited to the one argument, the cosmological. On the contrary, it may be almost held that, let it be as it may with Socrates and Plato, Aristotle has made the teleological argument expressly and at full his own. In point of fact, design is the central thought of Aristotle in his whole philosophy everywhere. As adaptation of means to ends, it is perhaps seen at its liveliest in the little work of the *Parts of Animals*. The general teaching here is the same as we saw in Plato,—that the element of necessity, physical necessity, concerns alone the external conditions, the materials; while it is the final cause that alone gives meaning to them—alone makes a reality of them—a doctrine—(that the mechanism everywhere existent in the world is at the same time everywhere existent in the world only as the realizing means of final causes)— a doctrine which, after long struggles, was the final conviction of Leibnitz. Perhaps for a distinct, clear, comprehensive statement in both references, that is at the same time brief and succinct, there is no more remarkable chapter in the whole of Aristotle than the eighth of the second book of the *Physics*. All, indeed, is so emphatically plain in that chapter that one can hardly believe in the possibility of any mistake in its regard. It seems, however, from the very first note, almost on the very first page, of the *Origin of Species*, that Mr. Darwin has allowed himself to be misled into a literal inversion of Aristotle's relative meaning. In this note, Mr. Darwin speaks thus: "Aristotle, in his *Physicae Auscultationes* (lib. 2, cap. 8, s. 2), after remarking that rain does not fall in order to make the corn grow, any more than it falls to spoil the farmer's corn when threshed out of doors, applies the same argument to organization; and adds (as translated by Mr. Clair Grece, who first pointed out the passage to me), 'So what hinders the different parts [of the body] from having this merely accidental relation in nature? as the teeth, for example, grow by necessity, the front ones sharp, adapted for dividing, and the grinders flat, and serviceable for masticating the food; since they were not made for the sake of this, but it was the result of accident. And in like manner as to the other parts in which there appears to exist an adaptation to an end. Wheresoever, therefore, all things together (that is, all the parts of one whole) happened like as if they were made for the sake of something, these were preserved, having been appropriately constituted by an internal spontaneity; and whatsoever things were not thus constituted perished, and still perish.' We here see," says Mr. Darwin on this, "the principle of natural selection shadowed forth, but how little Aristotle fully comprehended the principle, is shown by his remarks on the formation of the teeth." This note of Mr. Darwin's is not without value in a reference to his own views. At present, however, I have not to do with that, but only with what interpretation is given to certain declarations of Aristotle in regard to design. And in this reference it will suffice to point out the literal inversion of meaning of which I speak. As is well known, Aristotle is not always easy to translate, nor is his meaning always a clear one. I have no hesitation, however, in saying that, in both references, the particular chapter in question may be quite fairly regarded as an exception. It is at once easy to translate, and clear in its meaning. I cannot afford time to it as a whole now; but I will translate as much of it as is indispensable for our purpose at present. The first words concern the two elements, now familiar to us, which both Plato and Aristotle describe as accompanying each other, and as necessary to each other.

"We have first to tell," says Aristotle here, "how nature exhibits causality on design, and then to speak of the necessary material." In the first reference, for example, he asks, "What hinders nature from acting without design, but just as Jove rains—not, namely, that the corn may grow, but from necessity (the condensed vapour, namely, falling back in rain on the earth, and the corn growing as only *concurrently* receiving the rain)? In the same way, if rain spoils corn on the threshing-floor, it does not rain precisely for this end, that it may spoil the corn: that is only a coexistent incident." Aristotle has thus put the two cases, and he will now bring the truth home by asking how it is that, in regard to living organization, we cannot accept necessity, but must demand design. That is really the single import of the whole of Mr. Darwin's quotation, as a little further translation will at once show. "What then," Aristotle continues, "prevents it from being just so with the parts in nature? What prevents the teeth, for example, from being just *necessarily* constituted so that the front ones would be sharp for cutting, and the back ones broad for grinding the food; which would be, not to be from design, but just to so happen?" What I translate by this last clause, "which would be, not to be from design, but just to so happen," appears in Mr. Darwin's translation, "since they were not made for the sake of this, but it was the result of accident." That is a categorical assertion as on Aristotle's part of the very opposite of what Aristotle has it in mind to say. The Greek, however (ἐπεὶ οὐ τούτου ἕνεκα γενέσθαι, ἀλλὰ συμπεσεῖν), involves no such categorical assertion of an independent fact, but is only an explanatory clause to apply what precedes. So far the whole mind of Aristotle is: Why should we not say that the relative position of the two kinds of teeth, incisors and grinders, is not an affair of necessity; so that it would not take place from design, but only so happen? Even in putting this question the opinion of Empedocles suggests itself, and Aristotle continues illustratively to ask, Why should it not be as Empedocles held it to be? Why should it not be that, in the becoming of things, all such things as, though originating spontaneously, were still found fittingly constituted and, so to speak, undesignedly designful,—why should it not be that these should be preserved, while those that were not so should have perished, and should go on perishing, as is said by Empedocles of his βουγενῆ ἀνδρόπρωρα, his cattle with the faces of men? Now to this question Aristotle's direct answer is, It is impossible that anything such should be—ἀδύνατον δὲ τοῦτον ἔχειν τὸν τρόπον. And why is it impossible that anything such should be? Why is it ἀδύνατον that τοῦτον τρόπον ἔχειν? "Because these and all the things of nature originate, as they do originate, either invariably or all but invariably, but of the things of accident and chance not one." That answer is decisive; but the bulk of this single chapter has still to come with expression upon expression that is confirmatory merely. Referring immediately here, for example, to certain natural processes, his emphatic deduction is, ἔστιν ἄρα τὸ ἕνεκά του ἐν τοῖς φύσει γινομένοις καὶ οὖσιν (there is therefore design in the things that happen and are in nature). "Moreover," he says, "in what things there is something as an end, *for* that end is realized as well what precedes as what follows; as is the action, so is the nature, and as is the nature, so is the action, in each case if nothing obstruct; and as the action is for the sake of the end, so also for the same sake is the nature." Aristotle brings in now illustrations from the intentional works of mankind with the inference that if such works are ἕνεκά του, are from design, it is evident that so also are the works of nature; for both kinds of works are similarly situated as concerns consequents and antecedents in a mutual regard. As illustrations from nature we have now, in animals, the swallow with its nest, and the spider with its web; and in plants (for even in plants Aristotle sees such adaptations), the covering of the fruit by the leaves, and the course downwards, not upwards, of the roots for food. Consequently, says Aristotle, "it is manifest that there is such a cause in the processes and facts of nature; and since nature has two principles, one that is as matter and another that is as form, the latter the end, and the former for the sake of the end, this, the end, must be the determining cause." It may be, Aristotle continues, that nature does not always effect its end; but neither do we always effect our ends. The grammarian does not always spell correctly; nor the doctor always succeed in his potions. And if ever there were those man-faced cattle, it was from some failure of the principle, as may happen now from some failure of the seed. That, then, nature is a cause, and a cause acting on design—"that," says Aristotle, and it is his last word, "is manifest— φανερόν." In short, from its first word to its last, this chapter of Aristotle's has not, and never for a moment has, any aim, any object, any intention, but to demonstrate design in nature and in the works of nature. The next chapter, indeed, only continues the same theme, but with more special attention to the necessity of material conditions in which design may realize itself. How Mr. Darwin should have ever fancied that Aristotle first established necessity as the principle of nature in its action, and then applied that same principle to organization, it is impossible to conceive. Aristotle does ask, Why should we not think of necessity in the arrangement of the teeth? but it is only that he may bring home to our minds the palpable absurdity of the very question. He directly says in the *de Partibus* (iii. 1), "Man has teeth admirably constructed for the use that, in their respect, is common to all animals, the mastication of the food, namely: the front ones sharp to cut, and the back ones blunt to grind." We saw, too, exactly the same reference on the part of Socrates. Indeed, it is difficult to think of any more striking instance of design on the part of nature, or of one in which there could possibly appear less room for the action of mere material necessity. Why, if material necessity were *alone* to act, we might have our molars to the front, and how would it then be with our comfort at our meals, or in speech, or in our mere looks? To find Aristotle suggesting the possibility of a material cause for the arrangement of the teeth, is to find Pythagoras arguing against numbers, Plato against ideas, or Newton against gravitation. But, assuming that, though Aristotle had, in the translated passage, "shadowed forth the principle of natural selection," yet he had also shown, as Mr. Darwin adds, "by his remarks on the formation of the teeth," "how little he fully comprehended the principle"—assuming this, I say, we may resolve the statement, as on Mr. Darwin's part, into a compliment to Aristotle, on the one hand, and into a reproach on the other. The compliment is, that Aristotle was wise enough to see that what was called design was still due to physical necessity. And the reproach, again, is against this, that Aristotle should have applied the necessity just so, *quite unmodified*, to the formation of the teeth. Now, it must be admitted that, if the compliment had been correct, the reproach would have been correct also. Mr. Darwin smiles to himself in superiority over Aristotle, because he (Aristotle) had missed his own (Mr. Darwin's own) little invention, whereby, even on physical necessity, the order of the teeth, designful as it may appear, is and must be precisely as we see it. Justice to that extent must be done Mr. Darwin even here. In Mr. Darwin's scheme there is really supposed a provision for the purpose. Mr. Darwin would have laughed at you, had you objected to him, " Then, in your way of it, the molar teeth might be where the incisors are!" Mr. Darwin would have felt armed against that!

But then, the absurdity of imputing at all to Aristotle the suggestion that organization *was* due, or *might* be due, to physical necessity, no peculiarity of Mr. Grece's translation, not even the questionable clause particularized, will excuse or condone that. Mr. Darwin tells us himself, he had Dr. Ogle's translation of the *de Partibus*, in which a note gives the correct version of the entire passage rendered by Mr. Grece. That note occurs on the very second page of Dr. Ogle's book, and must have been seen by Mr. Darwin. Nay, that very book, the *de Partibus*, and as admirably translated by Dr. Ogle—that very book, just one argument, from end to end, for design, Mr. Darwin has read with so much consequent admiration of Aristotle, that he lauds him *in excelsis* and sets him above the two supreme gods he had previously worshipped—Linnaeus and Cuvier! "Linnaeus and Cuvier have been my two gods," he says, "but they were mere schoolboys to old Aristotle."

I will conclude now by pointing out how it has been

the lot of Empedocles, as early as 444 years before Christ, to anticipate all, every, and any theory that is built on the survival of the fittest. What Empedocles says is in substance this: Nature brought forth and gave existence to every possible animal form; but all such as were incoherently and inconsistently constructed, perished— and the same process continues. That, surely, is to give directest, precisest, and palpablest expression to this, Only the fittest survive! Aristotle slyly remarks here, Then I suppose it was the same with plants: if there were calves of the cow with the countenances of men, there were, doubtless, also scions of the vine with the face of the olive!

# GIFFORD LECTURE THE EIGHTH.

Aristotle and design—Matter and form—Abstraction—Trinity—The ascent—The four causes—A first mover—Lambda of the *Metaphysic*—The hymn of Aristotle—Speculation—Mankind—Erdmann—Theory and practice—Nature—Kant, Byron, Mme. Genlis—Aristotle's ethic and politic—God—Cicero—Time—Design—Hume, Buffon—Plato and Aristotle—Immanent Divinity and transcendent Deity—Schwegler—Bonitz—The soul—Unity—Homer—The Greek movement up to Aristotle, Biese—The Germans and Aristotle—Cuvier, Owen, Franzius, Johann von Müller—Darwin—Aristotle in conclusion.

IN the conclusion of the last lecture we saw that Aristotle, in a chapter in which he was supposed to have shadowed out the modern doctrine of natural selection, had nothing in view but the impossibility of mechanical principles ever explaining the phenomena which seem to bear on their front the relation that is named of final causes. And, in fact, to say it again, the whole philosophy of Aristotle is founded on, and rises out of, the single principle of an object, a purpose, an end that is good, an end that is beneficial, an end that is advantageous. Design animates the whole, but the very breath of this design, the heart that beats in it, the soul that guides it, is the Good—service that is wise. Nature is but a single organic congeries—as it were, a crystallization into externality of internality. There *is* matter; but there is no separate individual entity so named,—cognizable as so named, existent as so named. Conceived as such separate existence, matter is only an abstraction. Objects have matter, but they have also form; and the two elements, the two sides are indissolubly together, though we may *logically* see them apart, and name them apart. That is, we may fix our mind on the material side of some formed object, and, speaking of that side abstractedly, we may name it apart; but it does not exist apart. Conceived apart it is but an abstraction. There is no such thing as matter *qua* matter, any more than there is such a thing as book *qua* book, or paper *qua* paper: there *is* always only such and such *a* book, such and such particular paper. But the other side, already present and immanent in the material side, as it were fused into, integrated and identified with it, is form. An impression in wax, so far, illustrates the idea. There is the wax, and there is the impress: they can be conceived apart, and spoken of apart; but they are practically one. You cannot take the impress into your hand, and leave the wax; and neither can you take the wax into your hand without the impress. Only, in the case of any Aristotelian σύνολον, of any Aristotelian co-integer of form and matter, the one side, without the other, absolutely disappears. Destroy the impress and the wax remains; but destroy form, and with *its* extinction, there is to Aristotle the extinction of matter as well. The form can exist only in matter; the matter can exist only in form. Either of the two sides, as separated and by itself, is abstract, an abstraction; but in the concrete of their coalescence, there is, as it were, a life between them. Even as together, there is always to be conceived a *nisus*, an effort of matter towards form, a hunger of matter for form; and there is no less on the part of form, such *nisus*, or such hunger for realization, substantiation in matter. This is much the same thing as to say: What is, is potentiality that realizes itself into actuality. We may remember now that reference in Plato to a somewhat trinitarian suggestion, where the receiving element was compared to the mother, the formative element to the father, and the formed element between them to the ἔκγονος, the offspring, the son. And we may similarly present here the σύνολον, the co-integer, of Aristotle, and the life at work, as it were, within, even in its elements. There is the matter ὕλη, the form εἶδος or μόρφη, and the σύνολον itself, all three respectively in a sort of relation of mother, father, and son. It is but the same idea, the same life, too, that we see in the further forms of potentiality, energy, and actuality. There is an ἐνέργεια, energy, comparable to the father, that leads δυνάμις, potentiality, comparable to the mother, into ἐντελέχεια, actuality, comparable to the son. This son, too, evidently combines the virtue of both father and mother. The ἐντελέχεια has its own ἐνέργεια in its own δύναμις. It has its own end, τέλος, within itself; it is an end unto itself,—a life that lives into itself, that realizes itself. And there is realization above realization. There is a rise from object to object. The plant is above the stone, and the animal above the plant. But man is the most perfect result. His supremacy is assured. He alone of all living creatures is erect; and he is erect by reason of the divinity within him, whose office it is to know, to think, and to consider. All other animals are but incomplete, imperfect, dwarf, beside man.

Potentiality is realized into form, then, but to effect this, movement is necessary. The realization *is* movement; and the principle of movement is the efficient cause, while of this cause itself the further principle—what gives it meaning and guides it—is the purpose of good, the intention of profit, design to a right and fit end. There are thus, as we saw once before, four causes, and generally co-operant in one and the same subject. There is the material cause, the formal cause, the efficient cause; and there is also the final cause. All four causes may be found apart, as in the building of the house. Here is the matter, say stone, wood, lime, what not; there is the form in the idea of the architect; and there are the efficient causes in the various artizans. But it is the design that sets all the rest in motion; and it is the last to be realized, though also the first of the four that comes into existence; the final cause—namely, the comfort, convenience, pleasure, the shelter and protection which the house is there alone to afford. In such a case, as we see, material, formal, efficient, and final causes are all four apart; but in man, the formal, efficient, and final causes are at once and unitedly the soul—the soul which in its body is the master of matter. But man is still a creature; of all the creatures he is but one. And of all the movements in the universe, and in the things of the universe, he is not the mover. But a mover there must be. In every movement that takes place there are always at once moved and mover; and for the universal series and system of movements there must be an ultimate mover. Further, indeed, there must be an ultimate actuality. Potentiality, were it alone, as has been already said, would remain potentiality. Potentiality presupposes actuality. Were there no actuality already present, neither would there be any movement on the part of potentiality into actuality. There must therefore be a first actuality, and that first actuality must be the first mover, which, unmoved itself, moves all. But that first mover and that first actuality that is required for every other actuality, and requires no other for itself, is God — God eternal, increate, and immaterial. Not throughout never-ending time was there in night and chaos, in darkness and the void, potentiality alone, but what was, was actuality: always, and ever, and everywhere the infinite I AM.

No one, I may venture to say, will read the latter half of

the twelfth book, called by some the eleventh, by all, the Lambda of the *Metaphysic*, and yet feel inclined to reproach me with hebraizing Aristotle here. If we have not in the Greek the direct words of the Hebrew I AM, we have them, every such reader will, I feel sure, readily confess, fully in meaning. When we turn from Plato to Aristotle, it is usually said that we turn from the warmth of feeling to the coldness of the understanding, from the luxuriance of figurative phrase to the dryness of the technical term, from poetry to prose; but to my mind these five chapters of Aristotle are, *at least in their ideas*, more poetical than anything even in Plato. That πρῶτον κινοῦν of Aristotle, let certain critics find what fault they may with it, is as near as possible, as near as possible for a Greek then, the Christian God. And Aristotle *sings* Him, if *less* musically than Milton, still in his own deep way, *musically*, and in a vastly deeper depth *philosophically* than Milton. Especially in the seventh chapter of the twelfth book it is that we find that wonderful concentration and intensity of thought which, deep, dense, metalline-close, glows—unexpectedly and with surprise—glows into song—the psalm, the chant *de profundis*, of an Aristotle. It proceeds somewhat in this way:—

As there comes not possibly anything, or all, out of night and nothingness, there must be the unmoved mover, who, in his eternity, is actual, and substantial, one. Unmoved himself, and without a strain, he is the end-aim of the universe towards which all strain. Even beauty is not moved, but moves; and we move to beauty because it is beauty, not that it is beauty only because we move to it. And the goal, the aim, the end, moves even as beauty moves, or as something that is loved moves. It is thought that has made the beginning. As mere actuality, actuality pure and simple, as that which could not not-be, God knows not possibility, he is before and above and without potentiality, the beginning, the middle, and the end, the first and last, the principle and goal, without peers as without parts, immaterial, imperishable, personal, single, one, eternal and immortal. On him hang the heavens and the earth. And his joy of life is always, as is for brief moments, when at its best, ours. In him indeed is that enduringly so. But it is impossible for us. For joy in him is his actuality,— even as to us the greatest joy is to be awake, to see and feel, to think, and so to revive to ourselves memories and hopes. Thought, intellection is his; and his intellection is the substantial intellection of that which is substantial, the perfect intellection of that which is perfect. Thought as thought, intellection as intellection, knows itself even in apprehension of its object; for holding and knowing this, it is this, and knowing and known are identical. Intellection, indeed, takes up into itself what is to be known, and what substantially is: it acts and is the object in that it has and holds it. What, then, there is of divine in intellection, that is diviner still in its actuality in God; and speculation is what is the highest joy and the best. And if, as with us interruptedly, it is always in felicity so with God, then is there cause for wonder; and for much more wonder if the felicity with God is of a higher order than ever it is with us. But that is so. In him is life; for the actuality of intellection is life, and that actuality is his. Actuality that is absolute—*that*, as life of him, is life best and eternal. So it is we say that God is a living being, perfect and eternal. Life eternal and enduring being belong to God. And God is that.

That is the great passage.

There are many other passages, in several of his works, where Aristotle returns again and again to the bliss of mere thinking, the joy of θεωρία, speculation, contemplation, the joy and the bliss of διαγωγή, of a life that lives on, without a change or a check, in the continuity of mere thinking. That to Aristotle is the enviable beatitude of the Godhead. So we can think of Aristotle as loving to retire from the world, always into the bliss of his own thoughts. There are circumstances in his life, as well as points in his will, that show Aristotle in a very favourable light with regard to integrity, considerateness, and amiability, whether as affectionate father, loving spouse, warm and constant friend, or good master; but, perhaps, experience did not lead him to have any very high opinion of mankind as a whole. In his *Rhetoric* (ii. 5. 7), he speaks of it as a position of fear to be within the power of another, men being mostly bad, timid for themselves, and open to temptations of profit. And the general scope of the observation is not a solitary one. So it is, therefore, that, perhaps latterly at least, his own thoughts in solitude were to Aristotle his own best society.

This is what διαγωγή he assumes always for the Godhead as ἡ ἀρίστη, the best, and the best for us, too, but alas! as he sighs, only μικρὸν χρόνον, only a short time, ἡμῖν, for us—the condition, namely, of contemplative thinking, of inward peace, untroubled from without, where spirit is in the element of spirit, thought in the element of thought, spirit in spirit, thought in thought. This, in his *Ethic* (x. 7. 12), is what he holds to be the true life for us. "It becomes a man," he says there, "not, as some advise, being man to think as a man, or being mortal to think as a mortal, but to be in possibility, immortal (ἐφ' ὅσον ἐνδέχεται, as far as possible, ἀθανατίζειν, to become immortal, make oneself immortal); that is, it becomes a man, as far as possible, to take on, assume immortality. Of course, it has been pointed out that such life of self-absorption may suit the philosopher, but not at all the citizen; and, in the same way, it has been objected that if Aristotle is a theist so far as he assumes or grants an intellectual God, he is not surely such so far as he denies this God the attributes of practical action. And, certainly, it is with accuracy that Erdmann, laying stress on Aristotle bettering Plato so far as reality is concerned, points, nevertheless, to a failure of this practical element in regard to the Godhead; meaning that Aristotle had secluded his God too largely to the region of contemplation. But, says Erdmann, Aristotle "could not have done otherwise, for the time had not yet come when God should be known as the God that took on himself πόνος, labour, without which the life of God were in heartless ease, and troubled with nothing, while with it alone is God love, and with it alone is God the Creator." " It was reserved for the Christian spirit," adds Erdmann, "to see in God at once rest and movement, work and weal." And, no doubt, as I say, that has its own accuracy. But it is to be said also that where there is question of the citizen, Aristotle does *not* confine himself to the joys of contemplation, but has something to say on the duties of action as well. Similarly, then, let Aristotle have expressed himself as he may on the intellectual aspect of the Godhead, it by no means follows that he deserves to be called by such an ugly word as atheist, because, when occupied with one thing, he did not turn his attention to another. It is impossible better to illustrate this than by a reference to the actual fact of Aristotle's practical philosophy. And here the mastery of Aristotle in regard to what is sensible and sound, as well as deep and true, will be more readily apparent, perhaps, than even where it is speculation, theory, that is concerned. I know nothing more complete and cogent than what we have from Aristotle, practically, as regards morals and the State.

Here the question is, How is man to realize his life individually and in association? Man's growth is given to himself to realize. The principle in him is not a mere force which, as in processes of nature, as in plant, as in beast, acts, so to speak, in *his* despite, or without consulting him. Unlike processes of mere nature, unlike plant, unlike beast, man has his own self very much in his own hands. He knows that he is from nature, he knows that nature is in him; but he knows that, if only so, he is evil and the bad. He knows that he must control nature in him; he knows that he must *lift* it, that he must lift sense into reason. Even *externally* he knows that nature is his friend *only if* he harnesses it. He must drive nature out—out into the wilderness, while he remains himself in the cornfield. Nature clamours and brawls and storms around him; but he has made himself a hearth and sits by it. Nature fills the hollows of the earth with poisons, or hangs them on the tree; but man transforms them into health and the means of health. It is somewhat in this way that we may conceive Aristotle to regard *man*, when he approaches him to build man into manhood, and men into humanity—man into manhood being the province of ethics, men into humanity the province of politics. How it is that man stands in need of process and progression in either direction will readily suggest itself by reference to what I have said of an element of nature within him and around him. That element, while it is to be walled out from without, has to be eliminated from within. On both sides it is man's business to convert nature into reason. No doubt, much mistake still obtains here. There are those to whom the prescript, Follow nature, is the open sesame of salvation, and who, hardly opposed by any one in that form, are yet silently controverted by the unceasing industry of millions and millions of hostile life-points—parasites—

without and within them. So far as religion is concerned, indeed, there have always been the two allegations: on the one hand, that man is by nature bad; and, on the other, that man is by nature good. I daresay what has been already said will not be far from suggesting the false abstraction of either phrase. Man, in that he is of sense, falls into the danger of sense; but man, in that he is of reason, rises into the safety and security of reason. But both sense and reason are in the nature of man; and that nature may be named good or bad accordingly. Nevertheless, if either side is to be termed more exclusively nature, surely that side must be sense. It is when we obey sense that we are said to obey nature, and when we obey reason that we are said to rise above sense and, consequently, above nature. Not but that there may be legitimate application enough of the maxim or precept, Follow nature. That nature, however, means an emancipated nature, an enfranchised nature, a moralised nature, a nature that has been lifted from the ground, the blind, confused ground of the particular, and placed on the specular heights of the universal. In regard to clothing, eating, sleeping, drinking, etc., there is much talk about following nature; but if we look close in all such cases, we shall find that to obey nature as it is named, is to disobey nature as it *is*. Nature when she calls to man, with the appetites, vanities, envies, and sloths she has given him, in regard to his eating, drinking, clothing, sleeping, calls to him in general " not wisely, but too well." Immanuel Kant lay down at ten and rose at five; George Noel Gordon, Lord Byron, sat up all night and breakfasted at four in the afternoon; which of these men can be most truly said to have followed nature? Surely it was nature the Lord followed when he yielded to his own inclinations, and surely Kant had put himself in bonds to reason and against nature, when Lampe was obliged to admit that his master had never lain still a moment longer than he was called. Not but that, in its overmuch, it was only a kind of bastard reason that Kant obeyed after all! No doubt, it was only some copyline, "early to bed and early to rise," etc., that Kant followed, as, indeed, such exemplary copy lines were everywhere set by the Aufklärung at that time. It was in deference to some such copy-lines that Madame de Genlis, as governess to a royal family, fed her young princes and princesses on bread and milk, and gave them cow-houses to sleep in.

But what Aristotle would have from or for man was, after all, only his own *happiness*. That was his highest good, he taught him; but, then, it was not from nature that it came, but reason. Not but that it was true still that nothing on earth could be made happy without consultation of its *nature*. To give success to anything, we must give it its own swing; and to effect happiness for man, we must effect the realization of his nature. But that nature, at its truest and best, that nature at its realest, is not mere animal nature; it is, on the contrary, rational nature. And only by being put in accordance with reason is it that nature in man can be realized. Reason is the work of man, and man is to be realized in his work. As it is with the fluteplayer or the statuary, says Aristotle, whose happiness lies in the successful practice of his work, so it is with man generally. He must have the full exercise and complete realization of the ἐνέργεια, the energy that is proper to him. But when a man accomplishes this, he is called virtuous; it is only when he is virtuous that man is able to realize himself; and virtue requires to be developed. All the principles in connection here, Aristotle expounds at full, and in the clearest and most

K

interesting manner, in his *Ethics*, which is essentially a modern book. Curiously analytic and telling, captivating, —*that* is the good sense of the world, one half of the world's historical life back, and it is the good sense of the world still. A like good sense we have in Aristotle's politics. If it is man's virtue to realize emphatically himself, then is that possible for him only in the State. Hence it is ours only to live in the sense, and feeling, and knowledge of what is due to the State. So living, we shall be neither demagogue nor obstructive, not a partizan of self under any name. But it cannot be my intention to enter into the details of either Aristotle's ethics or Aristotle's politics; it is sufficient that I refer to their interest, and their excellence, and their useful application to these our own days and our own experiences. At the same time our main object here was to point out by the example of his practical philosophy as respects man, that, if Aristotle, in one regard, seemed unduly to emphasize the bliss of mere contemplation on the part of Deity, he might not have been without practical ideas in the other regard either. He certainly seems to accentuate mere contemplation as the ultimate good even for man himself; and yet there is that vast and grand practical philosophy of his, both for the individual and the State. So, even in unmoved contemplation, it may be that Aristotle does not conceive the Godhead to be wanting in influence on, and care of, the affairs of mankind. He has such words as these: Poets may lie, but God cannot be envious, and neither is he inactive; for man (*Pol.* vii. 1), if he would be happy, must act, even as God acts, according, namely, to virtue and to wisdom. All things for Aristotle are directed to an end, an end which is good, an end and a good which are ultimate—God. There is but one life, one inspiring principle, one specular example in the whole. All is for God, and from God, and to God. He is the all-comprehending unity, in whose infinite *I am* all things rest; but he is the ἐνέργεια, the actuality, also, that realizes them all from the least to the greatest. Even should we admit, what we do not admit, that contemplation, as conceived by Aristotle, excludes action, we would still point again, in proof of the purity of his theism, to that wonderful hymnic inspiration of his wonderful twelfth book. There is but one idea in the midst of that inspiration; and for the first time to the whole pagan world, for the first time to the whole great historical world, it is the complete idea of a one, supreme, perfect, personal Deity. It is for Greece ultimate and complete monotheism. I cannot conceive how, in any sense, the word atheist, with as much as that before us, can even by mistake be applied to Aristotle. The translator of the *Metaphysic* in Bohn's Classics, however, does so apply it, but in the midst, as one is happy to see, of insoluble inconsistency and contradiction. It is in reference to Aristotle's attitude as regards what are called the moral attributes that the application is made. Nevertheless, in identically the same reference, we can read this: "It is indeed remarkable to find Aristotle thus connecting the moral attributes of the Deity with what we would call God's natural attributes." That is, Aristotle does give God practical or moral attributes. Then elsewhere we have this complete characterization: "The Stagyrite, therefore, beholds in God a Being whose essence is love, manifested in eternal energy; and the final cause of the exercise of his divine perfections is the happiness which He wishes to diffuse amongst all his creatures; and this happiness itself doth He participate in from all eternity. Besides, His existence excludes everything like the notion of potentiality, which would presuppose the possibility of non-existence; and, therefore, God's existence is a necessary existence. Further, also, He is devoid of parts, and, without passions or alterations, possessed of uninterrupted and eternal life, and exercising his functions throughout infinite duration." Now, I think it will be admitted that many of these characters are of a quite Christian quality; they may, for Aristotle, be even a little *too* Christian; so that we may not unnaturally expect excuse for our wonder at association with them of the word atheist.

Cicero has preserved for us a passage from a lost work of Aristotle's which, in its bearing on the proofs for the Godhead, has seldom probably for power and beauty, whether of idea or diction, been either equalled or excelled. It is thus (*d. N. D.* ii. 37) that Aristotle, as Cicero says, *praeclare*, admirably, expresses himself: " Suppose there were a people living under ground, but in splendid domiciles, filled with statues and pictures, and all the beautiful things that constitute in men's minds happiness,—suppose, too, that, though secluded to their subterranean abodes, they had heard of some strange power on the part of some unknown supernatural beings that were named gods,—suppose then that the earth should open to this people, and that they should come forth from their darkness into the light of day,—then, assuredly, we must suppose, when, all of a sudden, they saw the earth, and the sea, and the sky, and the great cloud musters moving in the air, and the mighty sun in the glory and beneficence of his all-pervading brightness, —or when, again, it was night, and they saw the bespangling stars, and the moon that wanes and waxes in her gentleness, and all those movements immutable in their appointed courses from eternity,—then, assuredly, as we must suppose, they would think that there are gods whose handiwork all these wonders were."

Cicero, as we know, speaks of the to us hard, dry

Aristotle being sweetly and exuberantly eloquent. *Flumen orationis aureum fundens*, pouring forth a golden flood of declamation: so it is that he pictures Aristotle to us. And it would seem that Aristotle really had written in that style works which are now lost to us. At all events, it seems true that, let modern scepticism as to the so-called exoteric writings of Aristotle be as well-founded as it may,—it seems true that he did compose, in a popular form, a dialogue on philosophy, from the third book of which Cicero took his extract. And, however all that may be, it is quite certain that, if Aristotle really wrote what Cicero pretends to have extracted from him, then the extravagant terms which have been applied to that golden *oratio* of his are more than justified; for it is impossible to deny that the extract in question is a morsel of genuine eloquence that is at the same time popular. The great Humboldt praises it in his *Kosmos* (ii. 16). "Such argument for the existence of celestial powers," he says, "from the beauty and infinite grandeur of the Creation, stands very much alone in Antiquity." It is indeed magnificent, and reminds us of the inspired Psalmist in his deeper Hebrew grandeur. "The heavens declare the glory of God; and the firmament showeth His handy-work. Day unto day uttereth speech, and night unto night showeth knowledge. . . . He hath set a tabernacle for the sun: which is as a bridegroom coming out of his chamber. . . . His going forth is from the end of the heaven, and his circuit unto the ends of it: and there is nothing hid from the heat thereof." How all that brings home to us at once the grandeur and the stability of the universe! To borrow an earlier illustration. Hundreds of years ago, thousands of years ago, the Hebrew bard, from the streets of Jerusalem, as the Greek philosopher from the streets of Athens, could look up into the night, and see the stars, and the moon, and the clouds, even as we can. Ay, when the first stone of the first pyramid was laid, all was as now, in man, and bird, and beast, and earth, and heaven. For man at least, civilised man, the world is as it was in the beginning. These names and dates by which we would drive God from us, are names and dates, not in time, but eternity. With our scales and weights, and tapes and measuring-rods, we do but deceive ourselves: what is, is dimensionless; the truth is not in time; space is all too short for a ladder to the Throne. And what we say now, was said by Aristotle then. Custom hides it from us; but not one of us can go out into the night and see the heavens, without asking, as Napoleon did, but "Messieurs les philosophes, who made all that?" That is the argument which Aristotle, as reported by Cicero, makes vivid to us—the argument from design, the proof in Natural Theology that there is a Supreme God. So it is that he feigns his underground people coming up to the light of day. And Aristotle has not been left without imitators. "Adam," says David Hume, to whom what was poetry was pretty well starch,—" Adam, rising at once in Paradise, and in the full perfection of his faculties, would naturally, as represented by Milton, be astonished at the glorious appearances of nature, the heavens, the air, the earth, his own organs and members; and would be led to ask, whence this wonderful scene arose?" We have from Hume's contemporary, Buffon, too, an account of the experiences of the first man after his creation: How, "il se souvient de cet instant plein de joie et de trouble où il sentit, pour la première fois, sa singulière existence;" how he, too, was astonished at "la lumière, la voute céleste, la verdure de la terre, le cristal des eaux," etc. One, of course, has little hesitation in finding the original of all that in Cicero's extract, not but that the simple situation might very well have suggested his own picture to Milton. The one idea in all is, how a man should feel when he sees, for the first or the fiftieth time, as a man, the miracle of heaven, and the glory and beauty of the earth. To Aristotle, plainly, it must have brought the certainty and the conviction that it was not from accident it came, not from τύχη, nor yet from τὸ αὐτόματον, the spontaneity of chance. The whole movement and life, on the contrary, must be inscribed with the words, end-aim and design, τέλος and οὗ ἕνεκα. Nature was not to Aristotle, as it was to Plato, the mere μὴ ὄν, the mere region of the false. No, it is to him God's own handiwork, transcendent and alone in beauty, and wisdom, and beneficence. There is nothing in it in vain, nothing humblest but has its own nature to unfold, and its own life to realize. And there is a common striving, as though in mind and will, in all things towards God, who is their exemplar and their home. Each would produce another like itself, says Aristotle, the plant a plant, the animal an animal, in order that, as far as possible, they too may participate in the eternal and divine; for to that all tends. And again, Aristotle directly asks, directly puts the question, How are we to conceive this eternal principle (*Met.* xii. 10)? Does it exist simply as the order of an army exists in the order of an army (which, as the moral order of the universe, was at one time the answer of Fichte)? Or does it exist as the general of the army exists, from whom that order proceeds? Contrary to what some say, Aristotle answers this question quite unequivocally. And I may adduce at once here the authority on the point of the two recognised masters in the *Metaphysic* of Aristotle. Of these, the one, Schwegler, has edited the text of the book, with wonderful power translated it, and, in two volumes, commentated it; while the other, Bonitz, who, for that and much else, is pretty well the acknowledged prince of

Aristotelians, has also edited the text, and, without translating, but, with a perfect insight and marvellous sagacity, in admirable Latin, commentated it. "The answer of Aristotle," it is thus that the former, Schwegler, speaks, " is, that the Good exists in the universe as its designed order and intelligent arrangement; but it exists also, and in a far higher form, *without* the universe as a personal being who is the ground and cause of this designed order and intelligent arrangement: the principle of *immanence* and the principle of *transcendence* are here brought together and combined in one." As for Bonitz, he heads his commentary of the last chapter of the great twelfth book with the words: "How that which is good and beautiful exists in the universe of the world" —and he expresses himself on this question, as I translate his Latin, thus: " In regard to the nature of the supreme principle and its relation to the world, whether that principle as the Good is to be referred to the divine nature of the first substance or to the order of the world itself, Aristotle finds that the Good has place in the world in both ways, the possibility of which he illustrates by the example of an army; for the commander is certainly the prime source of the discipline of the army; but, if he has rightly established that discipline, the individual parts of the army accord together of themselves. In the same way the first cause of that order which we observe in the world is to be assigned to the Supreme Intelligence, but then the parts of the world have been so ordered by him that they are seen to harmonize of their own accord; for all things cohere with all things, and all tend to one." In the presence, then, of both these proofs and these testimonies, we must conclude that the views of Aristotle in the particular reference were very much our own. There was God transcendently existent; but He had created the world in beauty and harmony.

It is in a certain way in agreement with this that we are to understand the soul proper of man to enter into him, as it were, from without. Aristotle's own words are λείπεται τὸν νοῦν μόνον θύραθεν ἐπεισιέναι καὶ θεῖον εἶναι μόνον (d. G. A. ii. 3, med.). "We are left to conclude that the soul alone enters from without, and is alone divine." The word for from without here, θύραθεν, meaning from outside, from out of doors, is too unequivocal for any quillet to be hung upon it. This soul, then, is the self-determinative principle of divine reason in man, and in it is the immortality of man. The two considerations cohere: God, the transcendent Deity as Creator of the universe, and man, in reason, as cope-stone, and key-stone, and end-aim of all. Aristotle is specially emphatic on the unity of God. The universe must have a single head, like any other well-organized community. Polyarchy is anarchy: in monarchy alone is there order and law, and Aristotle winds up with the line from the second *Iliad*: Οὐκ ἀγαθὸν πολυκοιρανίη· εἷς κοίρανος ἔστω. "Many masters are not a good thing, let there be but one."

And it is in this way that " Greek philosophy has in Aristotle completed itself. Up to the time of Anaxagoras," says Biese, " the real characters of objective existence were the business of philosophical inquiry. Through him reason came to be pronounced the principle of the world; whereupon, from Socrates onwards, the development of cognition, as exclusively in the special subjective faculty of thought, occupied philosophy; till at last Plato, through and in the Ideas, returned to the objectivity of cognition, without evincing it, however, as the power and the truth in actuality. Aristotle speculatively resolves the antithesis between reality and ideality, frees the world of sense from the character of mere illusory appearance, and raises it into the position of the genuine reality in which the Idea gives itself form and action. From this high position, to which the philosophical spirit of the Greeks had, in and through its own self, risen, Aristotle considers and examines with interest the manifold forms of reality, and takes up into himself the entire wealth of Greek life, as it has developed itself in science, art, and the State, becoming thereby the substantial channel through which to attain to a view of the Greek world, as well in its various aspects generally, as in regard to the historical development of its philosophy specially."

There are other such testimonies from Germans in regard to Aristotle. In fact, when one considers the enormous development of the study of Aristotle among them which this century exhibits, with the great names that belong to it,— Bekker, Brandis, Biese, Bonitz, Schwegler, Prantl, Trendelenburg, Michelet, Heyder Stahr, Waitz, Zeller, and even a whole host more,—it must be evident that it would quite be possible to fill entire pages in the general reference. Even in a special regard, as concerns matters of fact in science, there are great names in all the countries that bear their emphatic testimony to the ability, compass, and exactitude of Aristotle. Thus Cuvier, for example, "lavishes unstinted praise" on much that concerns Birds; while both Cuvier and Owen regard as "truly astonishing" the fulness and accuracy of his details in respect to the Cephalopods. Franzius, in that connection, and otherwise, alludes to the "surprising result that, in many references, Aristotle possessed a far more extensive and intimate knowledge than we." The celebrated Johann von Müller expresses himself in this way: "Aristotle was the clearest head that ever enlightened the world; he possessed the eloquence of a great, all-penetrating understanding, supported on the direct observation of experience: he is astonishingly learned, and, in natural history, compared with Buffon, has led me into remarkable thoughts." Even, as we saw, Mr. Darwin himself, who is recent enough, and, certainly, a special expert enough, when he reads *Aristotle on the Parts of Animals* in the admirable translation which, with its valuable notes, had been executed and forwarded to him by his friend Dr. Ogle, is obliged to cry out in his letter of acknowledgment by return : " I had not the most remote notion what a wonderful man he (Aristotle) was : Linnaeus and Cuvier have been my two gods, though in very different ways; but they were mere schoolboys to old Aristotle." Aristotle, however, is no mere specialist : he is as wide as the circumference, and as the centre deep. The old idea of him is that he is cold and dry, technical, practical, and of the earth earthy only. But this is not the case. Aristotle is even a deeper mind than Plato. He may take up things as he finds them, or as they come to him ; but he never lets them go till he has wrung from them their very inmost and utmost. We have to bear in mind, too, that we have lost five-sixths of his writings, while the best of the sixth we have has suffered lamentably. For myself here, I feel in this way, that, if I were condemned to solitary confinement for the rest of my life, and no book allowed me but an edition of Aristotle, I should not, as a student, conceive myself ill-served. Perhaps, indeed, looking round me to think, I know only three other collective writings which, in such circumstances, I should wish added to those of Aristotle; but these I shall leave to your own conjectures.

Professor Blackie, after hearing the foregoing lecture, was kind enough further to honour it by publishing (as dated) the following obliging note and admirable verses :—

### ARISTOTLE.

(*Lines written after hearing the masterly discourse on the Philosophy and Theology of Aristotle by Dr. Hutchison Stirling, in the University of Edinburgh, on Saturday, 23rd March.*)

    Well said and wisely ! Who would measure take
      Of his true stature, let him choose the tall :
    We all are kin with giants when we make
      Ourselves the big yoke-fellows of the small.
    Give me no peeping scientist, if I
      Shall judge God's grandly-ordered world aright ;
    But give, to plant my cosmic survey high,
      The wisest of wise Greeks, the Stagirite.
    Not beetles he alone and grubs might ken,
      Narrow to know, and curious to dissect,
    But with a broad outlook he stood erect,
    And gauged the planful ways and works of men,
      And owned the God who rules both great and small,
      The soul, and strength, and shaping power of all.

                                JOHN STUART BLACKIE.

THE SCOTSMAN, *Tuesday, March 26*, 1889.

# GIFFORD LECTURE THE NINTH.

The Sects—The Skeptics—The Epicureans—Epicurus—Leucippus and Democritus—Aristotle, Plato—Stoics, Pantheism—Chrysippus—Origin of evil—Antithesis—Negation—Epictetus—The Neo-Platonists—Important six hundred years—Course of history—Reflection at last—Aufklärung, Revolution—Rome—The atom, the Cæsar—The despair of the old, the hope of the new—Paganism, Christianity—The State—The temple—Asceticism—Philosophy, the East, Alexandria—The Neo-Platonists—Ecstasy—Cicero—Paley and the others all in him—All probably due to Aristotle—Sextus—Philo Judaeus—Minucius Felix—Cicero now as to Dr. Alexander Thomson and the Germans—A word in defence.

WHAT, for philosophical consideration, follows Aristotle, are what are called the Sects—the Stoics, the Epicureans, and the Skeptics. Our subject, however, relates only to the proofs for the existence of God; and we shall have to do with the Sects, consequently, only so far as they have any bearing on those proofs: it is not the history of philosophy that we are engaged on. Now, in regard to that bearing, the very *name* of the Sect may here, in a case or two, be determinative and decisive. Of them all, in fact, it is only among the doctrines of the Stoics that we shall find anything that bears on our business. The Skeptics, for example, knew nothing—neither a καλόν nor an αἰσχρόν, neither a δίκαιον nor an ἄδικον, neither a good nor a bad, neither a right nor a wrong. They knew not at all that *this* is more than it is *that;* that anything, in truth, *is;* that, in fact, anything *is,* any more than that it *is not.* Their standpoint was ἐποχή:

they would not speak; or it was ἀκαταληψία, and they did not understand; or it was ἀταραξία, and they would not be troubled. It is in vain to seek for any argument on their part in reference to the existence of the Godhead. The very best and most advanced of them admitted, in regard to anything, only a more or less of *perhaps*.

Nor with the Epicureans are we one whit better placed. They believe in no reality but that of the body: they have no test for that reality but touch, or sight, or hearing—the ear, or the eye, or the fingers; and the transcendent object we would prove is within the reach of no sense. As it is written: "Eye hath not seen, nor ear heard." In fact, Epicurus directly tells us that we are not to believe in design, but only in the movements proper of mere nature. We are not to suppose, he says, the order of the universe to result from the ministration or regulation of any blessed god, but that, to the original consequences of the whirlings together at the birth of the world are due the necessary courses of movement (*Diog. L.* 24, 76). In short, in all such matters we are to see only a physical operation (*ib.* 78). *Why* Epicurus will have all from natural causes, and *not* from any influence of beings supernatural *is*, that belief in the latter would be the occasion of *fear*. Very evidently, Epicurus has been an exceedingly sensitive person. For him the best thing from within is calm enjoyment, and the worst thing from without *fear*. All is useless and superfluous that does not promote the one and prevent the other. So it is that it is quite idle to have knowledge, as knowledge of astronomical phenomena, say, since those who have it are not led thereby to happiness; but, on the contrary, have rather more fears; for such is the effect of belief in the action of superterrestrial powers. But all accounts of such powers are only fables. Undisturbed assurance—

that is the only end (*ib.* 85). " Our life," he says, " has need, not of ideology and empty opinion, but of untroubled tranquillity" (*ib.* 87). "As for the size of the sun and the stars, it is, as regards us, just such as it seems " (*ib.* 91). " With contradiction of our senses there can never be true tranquillity" (*ib.* 96). " If no meteorological apprehensions, and none about death, disturbed us, we should have no need of physiology" (*ib.* 142). But "death is nothing to us, for what is dissolved feels not, and what is not felt is for us nothing " (*ib.* 139). These notices will be sufficient to show the absolutely materialistic nature of Epicureanism, and how it rejected everything like teleological agency, or explanation, and referred all to the mechanical movements of mere corporeal particles. In short, what we have from Epicurus is but a repetition of the atoms of Democritus and Leucippus, of whom Aristotle (*d. G. A.* v. 18) said that " they rejected design, and referred all to necessity." It seems to be they also whom Plato (*Soph.* 246 A, and *Theaet*, 155 E) has in his eye when he speaks of "those who pull all things down to earth from heaven and the unseen, stubbornly maintaining, with their insensate fingers on rocks and oak trees, that only what they touch *is*, and that body and being are the same thing, while of things that are incorporeal they will not hear a word." Neither Skeptics nor Epicureans, then, are here anything for us.

The religion of the Stoics, so far as they had a religion, consisted probably, on the whole, in a sort of clumsy and crude material pantheism. Nevertheless, unlike both Skeptics and Epicureans, they *did* point to the nature of this universe — its contingency and design—as demonstrative of its origin in a divine and intelligent causality. This causality is to them a conscious God, creative of the world through his own will, but, according to the necessity of law, in beauty and in order ever—and as much as that, in its terms at least, must be confessed to be theistic rather than pantheistic. The argument of Socrates is put by them: Can we fancy that there is consciousness in us—the parts, only—and not also, and much more, in the All from which we come. Aulus Gellius (vii. 1) testifies to the cogency with which the celebrated Stoic, Chrysippus, redargued the reasonings in denial of a Providence, because of the evils in the world,—the reasonings, namely, that if Providence were, evil were not; but evil is, therefore Providence is not. "Nothing can be more absurd," says Chrysippus, "than to suppose that there could be good, if there were not evil. Without correspondent and opposing contrary, contrary at all there could be none. How could there be a sense of justice, unless there were a sense of injustice? How possibly understand bravery, unless from the opposition of cowardice? or temperance, unless from that of intemperance? prudence, from imprudence, etc.? Men might as well require," he cries, "that there should be truth and not falsehood. There are together in a single relation, good and evil, happiness and unhappiness, pleasure and pain. They are bound together, the one to the other, as Plato says, with opposing heads; if you take the one, you withdraw both (*si tuleris unum, abstuleris utrumque*)." On similar grounds Chrysippus vindicates or explains the fact of man suffering from disease. That is not something, he would seem to say, ordered, express, and on its own account. It is only there κατὰ παρακολούθησιν, as it were by way of sequela and secondary consequence. The greater *in*trinsic good is necessarily attended by the lesser *ex*trinsic evil. If you make the bones of the head delicate and fine for the business of thought *within*, you only expose it the more to blows and injuries from without.

"In the same way diseases also and sicknesses enter, while it is for *health* that the *provision is made*. And so, by Hercules, while by the counsel of nature there springs in men virtue, faults at the very same moment by a contrary affinity are born." In this way the Stoics have put hand on a most important and cardinal truth—this truth, namely, that discernibleness involves negation. We should not know what warmth is, were there no cold; nor light, were there not twin with it darkness. Everything that is, is what it is, as much by what it is not, as by what it is. The chair is *not* a table; the table is *not* a chair. Negation, nevertheless, is no infringement on affirmation: evil *may* be without prejudice to the perfection of the world. Evil in the creation of the universe was not the design: it is but the necessary shadow of the good, as the dark of light. "Just as little," says Epictetus (*Enchirid.* c. 27), "as there is a target set up *not* to be hit, is there in the world a nature of the bad"—an independent bad. "In partial natures and partial movements, stops and hindrances there may be many, but in the relation of the wholes, none" (Plut. *ref. St.* 35).

The Neo-Platonists belong to a much later period than the principal Stoics; but, being Greek, we may refer to them here—not that we can illustrate the arguments for the existence of God technically from their writings, or at all further from them themselves, than by their devotion to God, a devotion which manifested itself in the form of what has been named *ecstasy*. This phase of humanity, however, or of philosophy, is to be better understood by reference to the historical period at which it appeared.

From the death of Aristotle in 322 B.C. to the conversion of Constantine, or say, to the date, more memorial as a date, of the Council of Nice in 325 A.D., there is an interval of some six hundred and more years. Now these six hundred years belong to that period in the history of the world when it is probable that a greater number of civilised men were intellectually interested, occupied, and active than ever before or since. The cause of this was, so far, politics without, and religion within.

The general course in the common life of mankind seems to be this: men are at first hunters, passing gradually, perhaps, into nomads; and intellect can assert itself for many many years only in wild warfare, crude art, superstition rather than religion, and a dawning literature that is, for the most part, exclamation or song. By and by the wanderers settle themselves, and take to agriculture. Agriculture necessitates dwelling-places and implements — quite an assemblage of coverings and shelters, of goods and chattels. This assemblage necessitates the artizan to make them and mend them; and the artizan, to be paid and to buy, necessitates exchange. Then exchange itself necessitates, or, in fact, is trade; while trade, again, necessitates the town. Now, in this settled life, what men are to become the leaders? Not any longer, as was formerly the case, necessarily the young, the strong, and the bold. What is required now is, so to speak, counsel, advice, direction in practical conduct: and counsel, advice, direction—direction in practical conduct—belongs to him who is tempered, chastened, matured by experience; enlarged, enlightened, and enriched, made wise by actually living life's many and multiform eventualities. The calm hearts and grey heads are now the guides, and this their guidance naturally, in expression, takes the form of proverbs. Practical sagacity is the crown of life. But the faculty thus brought into action is the intellect. Insight into results and the means of results, the causes of results, is now the life of the matured brain. Every event is canvassed, every proposal is canvassed, with all that appertains to it, in the new light that now is ever spreading, and ever clearing around them. But in the midst of all this science is seen to have taken birth, and to grow. Step by step man learns to harness to his own ends the very powers that were his fears; and step by step he becomes presumptuous, contemptuous. What he feared is weak, he finds; and he that feared is now strong. There are cobwebs all round about him from that old past; he laughs as he thinks of them, and will scatter them to the winds. Betimes it is an age of scepticism; and bit by bit, politically, socially, religiously, the whole furniture of humanity is drawn into examination and doubt. And the more they examine, and ever the more they doubt, the more their rebellion at the old grows. Not a man but issues from his old wont as from a bondage and darkness in which he has been wronged. He is bitter as he thinks of what is and of what was. They are all bitter as they think of what is and of what was. They are in their *Aufklärung*, and their *Revolution* must come—has come. They rush with a cry from their corners; and, all together, like a flood, they lay flat the walls and the roof that had sheltered and saved them. For a time all is joy, happiness, delight, action, in the new light and the fresh air. But presently the mood is changed, and they wander disconsolate amid the ruins. They have nothing now to come to them and lift them into a life that is common; they have nothing to believe in. They are together; but they are single, each man by himself. Had they been scattered down from a pepper-box, they could not be more disjunct.

This is the condition of the Sects and of the atoms around them; for we are still in the ancient world —the ancient world at its close. Everywhere, at that time, there was the reality of political, social, religious revolution, if not the madness and violence, if not the blood, with which it has been convulsed and disfigured into hideousness and horror here in Europe within a century. And what, generally over the known world, saved them from as much as that then was the shadow of a vast vulture in the air that had not even yet filled its all-devouring maw, and that, making their hearts beat, suddenly darkened and terrified them into the silence and stillness of an awaited doom. That vulture was Rome. Her prey was helpless, and she had but to seize. Any and everywhere she could stoop; and any and everywhere she could seize. The entire world, within all its bounds, was her booty. And with this her booty at her feet, the insatiable maw was at length glutted, but not, even so, the fierce heart stilled. Even so, the fierce heart could not be stilled. The one vulture became a crowd of vultures. Each in the fierceness of its own heart—each in its own pain, turned and tore at the other; and it was a distracted universe in fight, until at length and finally, utterly worn out, exhausted to the dregs, they sank in apathy at the feet of *one*, a single one of themselves, *who*, all too soon, drunk with solitude —the solitude of power and of place—reeled into the imbecility and delirium of the irresponsible, abstract, absolute self that knows not what to do with itself, nor any more what *not* to do—the realized Cæsar!

What I endeavour to picture thus in these brief terms is the condition of the whole world during the greater part of the six hundred years which I have signalized.

The fall of the old world, which was at once political, religious, and philosophical, was characterized by a universal atomism. *Politically*, the individual, as an atom, found himself alone, without a country, hardly with a home. *Religiously*, the individual, as an atom, has lost his God; he looks up into an empty heaven; his heart is broken, and he is hopeless, helpless, hapless in despair.

*Philosophically*, all is contradiction; there is no longer any knowledge he can trust. What this world is he knows not at all. He knows not at all what he himself is. Of what he is here for, of what it is all about, he is in the profoundest doubt, despondency, and darkness. Politically, religiously, and philosophically, thus empty and alone, it is only of himself that the individual can think; it is only for himself that the individual must care. There is not a single need left him now—he has not a single thought in his heart—but εὖ πράττειν, his own welfare. How he can best take care of himself, provide for his own comfort, or as the word was then, and, in like circumstances, still is, secure his own *tranquillity*,— effect it that *that*, his *tranquillity*, shall be undisturbed,— this now is the sole consideration. He becomes an Epicurean, and lives to sense. He lets his beard grow, and, as a Stoic, is a king in rags. Or he is the jeering Skeptic, and laughs at both at the same time that his own heart is but a piece of white ash. As one sees, it is an age of what is called particularism, subjectivity. Nothing is real now but what is particular, and particular for the particular subject. Universal there is none. A universal is logical, a thing of the intellect; and things of the intellect are no longer anything to anybody. A universal there is none; in that sense—in the philosophical sense of permanent, guiding, and abiding principle, *object* there is none. That is, there is no longer any common object for all men certainly to know, for all men certainly to believe in, for all men certainly to strive to. This that is now before us is about the most important lesson that philosophy can bring to us—the lesson that lies in the antithesis of universal and particular, of objectivity and subjectivity—a lesson that will be found more or less fully suggested, but only suggested, in the *Note on the Sophists* in the English Schwegler. It is such a time as what is now before us that best illustrates this lesson—a time when the old and the new are to be seen in the deadliest grips of internecine battle. The phoenix is being burned; the phoenix is being born. To the dying spasms of paganism the birth throes of Christianity oppose themselves; and the hope of the new cannot but exasperate the despair of the old. There is, in fact, so far as the prevailing externality is concerned, but a heaving welter of misery everywhere. The State has perished; and its organic cells, its magistracies, namely, and other offices, are dens and holes, mainly, for fox or wolf, for snake or worm. The gods have fled; and in their temples there is only an empty echo of departing footfalls. The world is struck asunder and disintegrated into a mere infinitude of disjunct selves—selves that must in the wildest orgies rage, or, in the most prostrate asceticism, crouch. The West, in this its utter bankruptcy—religious, social, political,—if it looked around for help, could only look to the East. There, at least, there were still tales of religious communication, religious acceptance, religious grace. The darkening mundane of the West would turn to what gleam there was of a still shining *supra*-mundane in the East. If philosophy, that had still words for the individual, was dumb in regard to all that was universal, theosophy still spoke. And Alexander, too, had flung down the barriers that, on this side and on that, had excluded union. He had, as it were, built a bridge between them; he had founded a city, and given it his name—a city that, as common to orient and to occident, became for both the centre of a new life. Here, in Alexandria, it was that occidentals, on the one hand, were orientalized into a theosophizing philosophy; and orientals, on the other hand, were occidentalized into a philosophizing theosophy. The conditioning elements, Eastern, were Indian, Persian, but especially Jewish;

while, Western, they were the doctrines of Plato, Aristotle, and perhaps, above all, Pythagoras; and, as the one tendency led to the Gnostics, so we can say that the other terminated in the Neo-Platonists. And, beside both, there were the so-called Egyptian Therapeutae, who, under Parsee, Buddhist, Pythagorean influences, largely drew, probably as well, from the ascetic mysticism and cabbalistic doctrines of the Jewish Essenes. If Rome had been a colluvies of outcast and fugitive particulars, surely Alexandria was a conflux, from the very ends of the earth, of streaming universals.

As regards the Neo-Platonists, then, with whom we are more particularly interested, we can see how much they are conditioned by the historical influences that precede and surround their rise. They, too, like the Skeptics, the Epicureans, and the Stoics, would save the individual from the misery and unhappiness of the centreless, dispersed, and mutually self-repellent life that alone now is. But this they would effect by ecstasy. We are miserable, one may conceive them to feel, we are wretched, we are lost in this world, which has nowhere a refuge for us, which has nowhere a rest for our very feet. What signifies the indifference of the Stoic, who would conceal the serpent that still gnaws beneath his rags? What signifies the complacency of the Epicurean, whose aching void within no sensuality can fill? What signifies the jeer that covers the white ash of the Skeptic? Security so, salvation so, there is none for us. This wild soul of ours that would know all, this wild heart of ours that would have and hold all —ah! *we* would leap to God; only with Him, on His bosom, in absorption into His essence, can there be satisfaction, consummation, peace for *us!* This is the sort of rationale of the ecstasy by and in which Plotinus and the other Neo-Platonists would obtain entrance to the very presence of God—communion, as it were, with His very being. In them, too, we see the same loneliness, the same atomism, as in all the rest. They, too, have turned themselves away from the world. They are without, any longer, a nationality. Native country they have, any longer, none. Almost any longer they are without a home—without family, children, wife. All that remains to them still human, though they say themselves they are ashamed of their very bodies, and would gladly part with them, is the amiable vanity that meekly suffers—these disciples who *will* come to them !

Leaving the Greeks for the Romans now, it is Cicero that will interest us most in regard to the arguments for the existence of the Godhead. It is impossible for us here to do any justice to the length of treatment which Cicero, in his *de Natura Deorum*, bestows in particular, for example, on the argument from design; he returns to it *there* a score of times, and it reappears again and again in his other philosophical works. In fact, it would almost seem as though even a Paley had but few supports to add to those already supplied by Cicero, and as though what the former had mainly to do was simply to elaborate the latter. Cicero follows design from the heavens to the earth and to the creatures of earth; and Paley does no more. The sun, how it fills the world with its *larga luce*, its large light ! Should we, for the first time, suddenly see the light, what a *species caeli*, what a presence the heavens would be for us ! It is only the custom of our eyes that stifles inquiry into the wonder of such things. But that any one should persuade himself that this most beautiful and magnificent world has been produced by a fortuitous concourse of atoms ! As well might innumerable scattered alphabets, thrown down, take shape before our eyes as the annals of Ennius. Who would call him a man who, seeing the assured movements of the heavens, the marshalled ranks of the stars, the harmony of all things mutually apt, should yet deny that he saw reason in them, and assign to chance the regulations of so great a wisdom, and a wisdom so impossible to be reached by any wisdom of ours? He himself, certainly, is without a mind, who regards all that as without the guidance of a mind—all that which could not only not be made without reason, but which cannot possibly be understood without the highest reason. From things celestial Cicero passes to things terrestrial, and asks what is there in these in which the reflection of an intelligent nature does not appear? There are the plants with their roots, their rinds, their tendrils, etc. There is the infinite variety of animals with their hides, fleeces, bristles, scales, feathers, horns, wings, and what not. All of them have their food provided for them; and Cicero refers to the admirable manner in which their frames are adapted for the seizure and utilization of their food. All within them is so skilfully created and so subtly placed, that there is nothing superfluous, nothing that is not necessary for the conservation of life. The progression of animals, the adaptation of their construction to their habits of life, their means of defence, beak, tooth, tusk, claw, etc.; the trunk of the elephant, the cunning and artifices of various animals, as of spiders, certain shell-fish, certain sea birds, cranes, crocodiles, serpents, frogs, kites, crows, etc. etc.—I only name these things to suggest how much what we have been accustomed to read in Paley and the *Bridgewater Treatises* is largely, or for the most part almost universally, indeed, already represented in Cicero. Even the calculated contrivances found within the animal, in its anatomical and physiological system, are gone into by Cicero at very considerable length and in particular detail. In short, the second book of the *de Natura Deorum* of Cicero may itself be regarded as, in preliminary sketch or previous outline, already a sort of Paley's *Natural Theology* or *Bridgewater Treatise*. In so early a work that would base itself on natural science, blunders, of course, there must be; and they are there for the enemy to make his own use of them; nevertheless, I will venture to say that whoever reads this book impartially and without prepossession will find himself under a necessity, willingly and generously, to express his admiration and surprise. In fact, from various accidental vestiges, it may even be that a suspicion will grow that here, too, in the main, it is still Aristotle that we have before us. The *de Mundo* wholly apart, it is quite possible that, in his lost work or works *de Philosophia*, Aristotle really did include such embryo Natural Theology that acted as suggestive exemplar to Cicero. It does seem that there are some slight hints to that effect in the references to, or the actual quotations from, Aristotle, which are to be found in other writers.

In Cicero, for example, there occur, not once or twice, but several times, eloquent passages that lay stress on the analogy between this furnished and inhabited universe and a furnished and inhabited house, or an adorned and decorated temple of the gods. "As," he says (second book, chap. 5), "any one coming into a house, or school, or forum, and seeing the design, discipline, method of all things, cannot judge them to be without a cause, but perceives at once that there must be some one who presides over it and whom it obeys; so, much more in such vast motions and such vast revolutions, orders of so many and so great things, in which immense and infinite time has found no falsity, he must conclude that such mighty movements of nature are governed by a mind." In the next chapter he says again, "If you should see a large and fine house, you cannot be brought to believe, even if you should see no master, that it was built for mice and weasels." Twice afterwards, also in the same work, there is allusion to this comparison of the world to a fine house built for a master, and not for mice.

Now there actually are some signs in existence to suggest that it was Aristotle who was the original of this illustration, and even of its extension generally. Cicero himself, for example, in the thirteenth chapter of his second book, *de Finibus*, has this: "They did not see that as the horse is born for the race, the ox for the plough, the dog for the chase, so man (*ut ait Aristoteles*) is born, *quasi mortalem deum*, as though a mortal god, for two things, *ad intelligendum*, namely, *et agendum*." In a similar passage in the *de Natura Deorum* where, instead of Aristotle, Chrysippus is the authority, the two things appear as *ad mundum contemplandum et imitandum*. Born for thought and action before, man is now born for contemplation and imitation of the world. It is evident, however, that if the former words were those of Aristotle and the latter those of Chrysippus, these latter have only been borrowed from those former. But Cleanthes, as his master, preceded Chrysippus in the Stoic school; and Cleanthes shows traces of Aristotle as the original quarry in these or similar references. Cicero, for example, twice over refers to a fourfold origin for the notion of Deity as—1. Presentiments or divinations natural to the mind itself; 2. Destructive movements of nature, storms, thunder, and lightning, etc.; 3. Provision and supply of all things necessary for us; 4. The constant order of the celestial phenomena—twice over, as I say, Cicero refers to this fourfold origin of our belief in Deity, and twice over he refers it to Cleanthes. Now the inference is that Cleanthes again got this from Aristotle. There is more than one passage in Sextus Empiricus, namely (see *Fragmenta Heitz*, p. 35), in which it is directly attributed to Aristotle that he said the notion of a God arose in us from the phenomena in the heavens and the experiences of our own minds through the communications of dreams or prophetic vision just before death. There is the remarkable passage we cannot forget in regard to the feelings of a subterranean race of mortals if suddenly brought into the light of day or the beauty of the night; and again also there is in the tenth chapter of the twelfth book of the *Metaphysic* that comparison of the order and its Commander in the world with the discipline and general of an army, followed up as it is there by a similarly constituted reference to a house with its planned and regulated household. The illustration of the army will be found carried out at full length in Sextus, who figures a spectator to look down from the Trojan Ida, and observe the army of the Greeks variously marshalled, "the horsemen first with their horses and their chariots, and behind them the infantry," as Homer is quoted to say.

Generally in this reference it is certain that Philo Judaeus did adopt the illustration of the house, carrying it out, too, into considerable detail. Of course Philo Judaeus was born some fourscore years after Cicero, and might very well have borrowed from him; but being the accomplished Grecian he was, and writing in Greek, it is quite probable that he took the illustration from a Greek rather than a Roman source. It is in this way he speaks: "Those before us inquired how it was we assumed the Godhead, and those who were considered the best of them, said that from the world and its parts, from the excellences that were in these, we formed an inference to the cause of the world; for as, should any one see a house skilfully constructed with forecourts, porticoes, and all the various chambers for the various persons and purposes, he would conclude to its builder, — for not without art and an artist would he suppose the house to have been completed; and in the same way as regards a city, or a ship, or any other lesser or greater production; so now, also, any one coming into this vastest house or city—the world—and beholding the revolution of the heavens, and the planets, and the stars, and the earth, and then the animals and plants, assuredly he would reason that these things had not been constructed without a consummate skill, but that the creator of all this is God." There are other passages also in which Philo serves himself with the same illustration. We find it repeated by others after him, as, in a remarkable manner, by Minucius Felix.

It is now in place to say that, so far, we have seen but the two arguments—that known as the teleological, and that other which has been named cosmological. We have still to see the rise of the third and, to us, concluding argument. This, the ontological argument or proof, unlike the others, has a Christian origin, in that, as an invention or device, it is due, namely, to Anselm, who died Archbishop of Canterbury in the year 1109. That is more than a millennium after Cicero. But it is to be borne in mind that, without any other exception than this of Anselm's, already, as Cicero presents it, the general argumentation was complete. Paley and the *Bridgewater Treatises*, though writing it, so to speak, into modern instances, really added to the teleological argument—generally as an argument—nothing whatever else. That argument, as it appears in the *de Natura Deorum*, may be left on the whole as pretty well finished.

I take it, we may suppose Cicero's to be good hands to leave it in. Dr. Alexander Thomson published in 1796 a translation of Suetonius; but his principal object in so doing, it seems, was to give him an opportunity of perorating in his own way on Roman literature in general.

In the course of that peroration he has this emphatic affirmation, "The most illustrious prose writer of this or any other age is M. Tullius Cicero." But, alas! even as Dr. Alexander Thomson was writing, the Germans were bent on altering all that. For many years back there has come only one note from Germany as regards Cicero. The vanity and vacillation of the man, together with the interminable wordiness of the writer, seem to have set everybody there against him—except the philologists, who will have no Latinity absolutely classical except pretty well only that of Cicero and Caesar. I could quote largely from the Germans themselves in support of what I say. But a sentence or two from Prantl, whose word, in consequence of his *Riesenarbeit*, his giant labour on logic, is pretty well authoritative now—a sentence or two from Prantl, by way of specimen, will probably suffice. Prantl, indeed, seems unable even to speak the name Cicero without disgust. Cicero, he says, can certainly *Schwätzen*, that is, jabber or jaw. Then he speaks of his "entire impotence," and "equally disgusting verbiage:" "Cicero, in fact," he says again, "is either so ignorant or possessed of such frivolous levity that he, the boundless babbler that he is, has the conceit to think that, in his three books, '*De Oratore*,' he has brought together the Rhetoric of Aristotle and that of Isocrates, although it is notorious that in very principle there is an utter difference between the two." In a note here also, he has this: "Just generally, wherever Cicero names the name of Aristotle, the effrontery is revolting with which, without the slightest capability of an understanding, he presumes to enter a judgment either for praise or blame." These expressions will seem so extravagant as to defeat themselves. Nevertheless, the present sentence of philosophical Germany lies not obscurely at the bottom of them. I fear we must admit the vanity, the vacillation, the verbiage, and the want of either accuracy or depth; but still one would like to say something for Cicero. As regards the Catiline conspiracy, for example, it was, to be sure, tremulously, but still it was truly, persistently, and successfully that he broke its neck. There are a considerable number of jokes too current in his name, as of the Roman Vatinius, who had been consul only for a few days, that his consulship had been a most remarkable one, that there had neither been winter, spring, summer, nor autumn during the whole of it; or of that other consulship which had been of only seven hours' duration, that they had then a consul so vigilant that during his whole consulship he had never seen sleep. These and other such jokes attributed to Cicero are to be found in Macrobius; and I, for one, cannot believe that a man with humour in him wanted, like a pedant or a craven, either reality in his soul or substance on his ribs. Rather I will give him credit for both, sincerely thanking him, as well, for his three books, *de Natura Deorum*.

---

The lecturer has again gratefully to acknowledge the honouring obligation of Professor Blackie's felicitous verses on occasion of the foregoing:—

### ATHEISM AND AGNOSTICISM.

(*Lines written after hearing the Gifford Lecture by Dr. Hutchison Stirling on the Theism and Theology of the Stoics, Cicero, and the Neo-Platonists, last Saturday in the University.*)

    All hail, once more! when nonsense walks abroad,
        A word of sense is music to the ear
    Vexed with the jar of fools who find no God
        In all the starry scutcheon of the sphere
    Outside their peeping view and fingering pains,
        And with the measure of their crude conceit
    Would span the Infinite. Where such doctrine reigns
        Let blind men ride blind horses through the street:

I'll none of it. Give me the good old Psalm [1]
King David sang, and held it deadly sin
To doubt the working of the great I AM
In Heaven above, and voice of law within.
Where'er we turn, from earth, and sea, and sky,
God's glory streams to stir the seeing eye.

JOHN STUART BLACKIE.

[1] Psalm xix., which subsumes under one category of intelligent reverence the physical law without, and the moral law within, and thus avoids the error of certain modern specialists, who see only what can can be seen in the limited field of their occupation.

J. S. B.

THE SCOTSMAN, *Friday, April 5, 1889.*

# GIFFORD LECTURE THE TENTH.

Cicero—To Anselm—The Fathers—Seneca, Pliny, Tacitus—God to the early Fathers—Common consent in the individual and the race—Cicero—Irenaeus, Tertullian, Chrysostom, Arnobius, Clement of Alexandria, Lactantius, Cyril of Alexandria, Julian, Gregory of Nyssa, and others, Athanasius—Reid, religion, superstition—The Bible—F. C. Baur—Anselm—His argument—The College Essay of 1838—Dr. Fleming—Illustrations from the essay—Gaunilo—Mr. Lewes—Ueberweg, Erdmann, Hegel—The Monologium—Augustine and Boethius—The Proslogium—Finite and infinite—What the argument really means—Descartes—Knowledge and belief.

WITH Cicero we reached in our course a most important and critical halting-place. As we have seen, he is even to be regarded as constituting, in respect of the older proofs, the quarry for the argumentation of the future. Henceforth, his works, indeed, are a perfect *vallée de la Somme*, not for celts, flint-axes, but for topics of discourse. We have still, in the general reference otherwise, to wait those thousand years yet before Anselm shall arrive with what is to be named the new proof, the proof ontological, and during the entire interval it is the Fathers of the Church and their immediate followers who, in repetition of the old, or suggestion of the new, connect thinker with thinker, philosopher with philosopher, pagan with Christian. Before coming to Anselm, then, it is to the Fathers that we must interimistically pass. A word or two may be found in some few intervening writers, as Seneca, perhaps, or Pliny, or even Tacitus; but the respective relevancy is unimportant.

M

Seneca is a specious writer, with a certain inviting ease, as well as a certain attractive modernness of moral and religious tone about him, all of which probably he has to thank for the favour that made him an authoritative teacher during many centuries. But his lesson is seen pretty well now to be merely skin deep, and he is, accordingly, I suppose on the whole, for the most part neglected. Dr. Thomas Brown, I fancy, is about the last writer of repute that takes much note of him. Brown, *ore rotundo*, does indeed declaim, at considerable length too, in Seneca's glib, loose Latin, from his very first lecture even to his very last; but then we must consider the temptation, as well of the convenience, it may be, as of the ornament. Aulus Gellius assigns to Seneca a diction that is only vulgar and trivial, and a *judicium* that is but *leve* and *futile*. He is in place here only in consequence of the frequency with which he recurs to the idea of God: "Prope a te Deus est, tecum est, intus est; Deus ad homines venit; immo, quod propius est, *in homines.*" That is not badly said, but is it more than *said?* One reflects on Seneca's *laeta paupertas* of speech while in midst of the luxury of fact, and on the consequent meek self-sacrifice with which he expatiates on the *posse pati divitias!* The elder Pliny is, as his time is, quite philosophical in regard to the gods; but he is evidently deeply impressed by the spectacle of the universe, of which there can be but one God, he thinks; who is "all sense, all sight, all hearing, all life, all mind, and all within himself," and that, in terms at least, is the One, Personal, Omniscient, and Omnipotent Deity, whom we ourselves think. Tacitus is later than Pliny, and his judgment is in uncertainty, he admits, whether the affairs of mortals are under the determination of a Providence or at the disposal of chance. The chapter, the 22nd of the sixth book of the *Annals*, is a remarkable one.

What strikes us first in the early Christian writers in this reference is the frequency with which they employ that argument that is known as the *Consensus Gentium*. Nor is this strange. There came to these pagans with Christianity *then* the awful form of the majestic Jehovah, I Am that I Am, whom German and French writers have taken of late, degradingly, I suppose, familiarizingly, to call Jahve. But under whatever name, He came for the first time then to those we call the ancients, as the Almighty God of this vast universe, the Creator, Maker, Sustainer, and Preserver; the power that is for ever present with us, to note and know, to bless or to punish. This was the one great mightiness, the mystic, here and now present awfulness with whom, to overwhelm, to crush, and destroy, the early Christians confronted the loose rabble of the polytheistic deities, the abstract null of Neo-Platonic emanation, and the gloomy daemons of the wildly heretical Gnosis. This was He of whom Job spoke, of whom the Psalmist sung, with whose wrath the Prophets thunderstruck the sinner. That this God was, that this God alone was, there was, on the part of the Fathers, a universal appeal, as well to the common experience of the nations historically, as to the very heart and inmost conscience of the natural man. Cicero was quoted in many texts, as that, among men, there is no nation so *immansueta* and so *fera* as not to know that there is a God. This is a truth which seems to have been insisted on by all the Fathers, from the first to the last. Man, they say, is in his nature endowed by the Creator with such capabilities and powers that, as soon as he attains to the use of reason, he, of himself, and without instruction, recognises the truth of a God, and divine things, and moral action. That is the true light, which lighteth every man that cometh into the world (John i. 9). "All know this," says Irenaeus, "that there is one God, the Lord of all; for reason, that dwells in the spirit, reveals it." Tertullian has a remarkable work named *De testimonio animae naturaliter Christianae* (Of the testimony of the soul as naturally Christian), in which there occur many striking passages in regard to the testimony of the soul itself, as, even from the first, and by mere nature, Christian. He calls it "an original testimony, more familiar than all writing, more current than all doctrine, wider spread than every communication, greater than the whole man. . . . The conscience of the soul is from the beginning a gift of God," and that there is a God is a "teaching of nature silently committed to the conscience, that is born with, and born in us." God from the beginning laid in man the natural law, says Chrysostom. Arnobius asks, "What man is there who has not begun the first day of his nativity with this principle; in whom it is not inborn, fixed, almost even impressed upon him, implanted in him while still in the bosom of his mother?" "Among all mankind," says Clement of Alexandria, "Greek or barbarian, there are none anywhere upon the earth, neither of those who wander, nor of those who are settled, that are not pre-impressed with the conviction of a supreme being. And so it is that every nation, whether in the east, or opposite in the west, in the north, or in the south, has one and the same belief, from the beginning in the sovereignty of Him who has created this world; the very utmost of whose power extends equally everywhere within it." "Man cannot divest himself of the idea of God," is the averment of Lactantius; "his spontaneous turning to Him in every need, his involuntary exclamations, prove it:—the truth, on compulsion of nature, bursts from his bosom in its own despite." To Cyril of Alexandria τὸ εἰδέναι θεόν, the knowing of God, is ἀδίδακτόν τι χρῆμα καὶ αὐτομαθές, an untaught thing, and self-acquired; and he even quotes the Apostate Julian to the effect that the proof of this is the fact that "to all mankind, as well in public as in private life, to single individuals as to entire peoples, the feeling for divine things is universal; for even without teaching we all believe in a Supreme Being." Gregory of Nyssa, Eusebius of Caesarea, John of Damascus, Jerome—in short, it is the common doctrine of the Fathers of the Church and their followers, that belief in the existence of God is in man innate; and, among them, Athanasius, in so many words, directly declares that for the idea of God "we have no need of anything but ourselves." So far, then, I think we may admit that we have sufficient illustration of the argument for the existence of God—it can hardly be called *proof*—that depends on the common agreement of mankind, nationally and individually, and is frequently expressed by the Latin brocard: *Quod semper, quod ubique, quod ab omnibus.* It is hardly a proof, as I say; but, as an argument, it has its own weight; and, as Reid says, "A consent of ages and nations, of the learned and the vulgar, ought, at least, to have great authority, unless we can show some prejudice as universal as that consent is, which might be the cause of it." And here, of course, the tendency to a belief in the supernatural on the part of mankind may be adduced as precisely such a prejudice; but the question remains, is not such tendency precisely the innate idea—only, perhaps, not always in the highest of its forms? That, as an argument, it should have possessed the full acceptance of the Fathers, is only natural; for there in their reading it was ever before them: the intense Godwards of the Bible as on every page of it. For that, indeed, is it estimable: *that*, to all mankind, is its fascination and its irresistible and overpowering charm. But, be it as it may with the argument from the *consensus omnium* as being the *vox naturae*, if it was from the Bible that the Fathers were led to it, there was about equal reason for their being led, by the same authority, to the *other* arguments; as that from design especially. Why, to that, innumerable passages of the grandest inspiration were perpetually before their eyes or ringing in their ears. It were out of place to quote such passages at any length here; but I may remind you of such exclamations in the Psalms, as: "How manifold are Thy works! in wisdom hast Thou made them all: the earth is full of Thy riches: who coverest Thyself with light as with a garment; who stretchest out the heavens like a curtain; who maketh the clouds Thy chariot; who walketh upon the wings of the wind." "Whereupon are the foundations of the earth fastened? or who laid the corner-stone thereof, when the morning stars sang together, and all the sons of God shouted for joy?" With such expressions as these before their eyes, as I say, or ringing in their ears, it was impossible but that the Fathers of the Church should think of the wonders of the creation. Ferdinand Christian Baur points out, as though, indeed, they (these proofs) were but beginning *then*, that in many the usual expressions of the Fathers, elements may be seen to show themselves towards the development of both arguments, the cosmological as well as the teleological. And he directly quotes, in evidence, passages from Tertullian, Irenaeus, Theophilus, Minucius Felix, Athenagoras, Lactantius, and others. But there are a great many other ecclesiastical writers than those mentioned by Baur, who give their testimony to the arguments for the existence of God. One might quote at great length in this reference, but time fails, and I must pass on.

Though it is perhaps possible to find matter of suggestion elsewhere, especially in Augustine, I proceed then, at once to Anselm of Canterbury as alone responsible for the proof that bears his name. This, the ontological proof, as it appears in Anselm's own Latin, I translate thus:—

"That there is in the understanding something good, than which a greater cannot be thought—this, when heard, is understood; and whatever is understood is in the understanding. But assuredly that than which a greater cannot be thought, cannot be in the understanding alone: for if that than which no greater can be thought were in the understanding alone, then plainly than that (than which a greater cannot be thought), a greater *can* be thought—that, namely, which is such also in reality. Beyond doubt there exists, then, something, than which a greater cannot be thought, both in the understanding and in reality."

I hold in my hand a little essay of my own, entitled, "An estimate of the value of the *argument à priori*," a little optional essay it was, written for, and read in, the Moral Philosophy Class, Glasgow University, in the winter of 1838. Dr. Fleming, the Ethical Professor at that time, was not a man of large culture, either ancient or modern; and with the literature of this present century, chiefly poetry and romance as at first it was, he was on the whole, perhaps, not specially sympathetic. *His* literature rather, as I think we may say, was Pope and Goldsmith, Hume and Robertson; Samuel Johnson and Dr. Hugh Blair; and his philosophy, in the main, that of Reid, Stewart, and Brown, at the same time that his favourite writer of all, perhaps, philosophical or other, was David Hume. Dr. Fleming was a very acceptable professor, a man of eloquence, judgment, and taste, and taught well; but, somehow, one did not expect to hear of Anselm at his hands. His *Student's Manual of Moral Philosophy* shows, however, that the notice of Anselm was no peculiarity of the one session, but belonged, in all probability, more or less, to all. In that particular session, the form in which it was given to us appears to have been this: "Our notion of God is that of a Being than whom nothing can be greater; but if His existence be only in our intellect, there is room for the existence of a Being greater (by the addition of reality) than the One of whom we have the notion that He is infinitely great; which is absurd. God has therefore a real existence." That, indeed, comes pretty well to the same meaning as what I have translated. The essayist remarks of it: "With respect to Anselm's argument, it is indisputably a mere sophism, a cunningly-entangled net, but still one which it is possible to break through." And then he continues : "But, though its nature be such, it may not be altogether useless to be able to expose its fallacy. Let us try, for example, if we cannot concoct an argument in appearance just as conclusive as Anselm's, and yet evidently absurd. When Milton attempted to describe the Garden of Eden, he attempted to portray the most perfect paradise his mind could conceive. Milton's notion, then, of Eden, is that of a garden than which nothing can be more perfect; but if the existence of Eden be only in Milton's intellect, there is room for the existence of a garden more perfect than that of which Milton has the conception; which is absurd. Milton's Eden has therefore a real existence. Again, when Thomson conceived his Castle of Indolence, his conception was that of a scene than which nothing could be more lazy, languid, and indolent; but if the existence of this scene be confined to his intellect, there would be room for a scene still more lazy, languid, and indolent (as it might have a real existence) than that of which he has the notion; which is absurd. Therefore there is a Castle of Indolence." "The fallacy lies in the forming the conception of something superlative, and yet leaving out one of the notions necessary to render it superlative." I quote this for the purpose of showing that if I now view Anselm's argument somewhat otherwise than I did then, it cannot be for any want of the usual and reputed common-sense and correct understanding in its regard There is no book *now*, which tells us anything of Anselm, but tells us as well of Gaunilo or Gaunilon. "Gaunilon," says Mr. Lewes, "pointed out the fundamental error of Anselm in concluding that whatever was true of ideas, must be true of realities." This, indeed, was so clearly the whole state of the case to Mr. Lewes, that that remark appears enough to him, and he does not condescend to repeat Anselm's argument at all. Prantl, too, seems very much of the same mind as Mr. Lewes. In a note he does, indeed, give the argument; but he adds, "and so on in a current, crude confusion of thought and being;" while in the text, he writes of it thus: "It exhibits to us only the spectacle of the grossest self-contradiction, made possible by the attempt to prove precisely subjectively, the most perfect objectivity. But the absurdity of the enterprise was quite clearly seen into by Gaunilo, who alleged that the proof was equally applicable to the existence of an absolutely perfect island." Gaunilo was a certain Count de Montigni, who had retired, late in life, and disgusted by feudal failures, into the convent of Marmoutier, near Tours. Every reader of philosophy knows about Gaunilo and his island now. It is certain, however, that the essayist who opposed Milton's Eden, and Thomson's Castle of Indolence, to the argumentation of Anselm, had still many years to wait before he should know that there had been any such man as Gaunilo. Indeed, I am very much inclined to believe that Gaunilo was at that time a perfectly unknown name almost to everybody, perhaps to the professor himself.

Ueberweg seems to be of the same opinion in regard to the entire argument of Anselm. "The notion of God," he says, "which, in the Monologium, Anselm arrives at cosmologically by a logical ascent from the particular to the universal, he endeavours to make objectively valid in the Proslogium ontologically by mere development of the notion, thereby demonstrating the existence of God from the simple idea of God; for he was dissatisfied that, as in the method of the Monologium, the proof of the existence of the absolute should appear dependent on the existence of the relative." As is easy to understand, Ueberweg has little favour for the idea of actually extricating real existence out of ideal existence, things there without out of mere thoughts here within: he sees very clearly the absurdity of sacrificing one alleged maximum to another alleged maximum *because*, after all, the allegation is false, and what is alleged in the one case is not a maximum. His words are: "The absurdity of comparing together two entities, one of which shall, not exist, but only be thought, while the other shall both be thought *and* exist, and so inferring that this latter, as greatest, must not only exist in thought, but also in reality!" Generally, is Ueberweg's perfectly cogent remark here: "Every inference from *definition* is only hypothetically true, with presupposition, that is, of the actual existence of the subject."

There cannot be a doubt, then, of the correctness of all these views in their hostility to the argument of Anselm. It is hard to believe, however, that any mere absurdity, and for nothing but the curiosity of it, should have been distinguished beyond all others such by the unexampled honour of such enormous reference. Accordingly, as Erdmann puts it, there is already a turn given to it towards a more respectable significance. Alluding to the Monologium as preliminary to the Proslogium, and to the cosmological result of the former as preliminary to the ontological operation of the latter, Erdmann writes thus: "The resultant notion of God is now applied by Anselm in behoof of the ontological proof for the existence of God, which he has developed in his Proslogium, the further title of which is *Fides quaerens intellectum*, faith in search of an understanding for itself. Referring to the first words of the 14th Psalm, he would prove to the fool who says in his heart, There is no God, that he contradicts himself. He assumes for this only the single presupposition that the denier of God knows what he says, and does not give vent to mere meaningless terms. Assuming him to understand by God that than which nothing can be thought greater, and assuming him also to admit that to be both in the intellect and in fact, is greater than to be in the intellect only, then he must likewise admit that God cannot be thought *not to* BE, and that he has therefore only thoughtlessly babbled. And just so also is Anselm perfectly in the right when he replied to the objection of Gaunilo, in his illustration of the island, namely, that what he (Anselm) started from was not something that *is* greater than all, but something than which nothing can be *thought* greater, and that he had thereby brought the fool into the necessity of admitting either that he thinks God as actually existent, or that what he *says* he does not *think*." If this account of the matter be followed out, I doubt not most people will feel inclined to allow Anselm a greater amount of sense than in this particular instance he has hitherto got the credit of. His reply, in fact, in that sense, is utterly irresistible. You say there is no God; but if you think what you say, then God *is*. If you *think* God necessarily as that than which nothing can be greater, then God is: God *is*, a God thought *not to* BE were no God: give such an import to it, then the notion of God were no notion of God. It is very probable that Erdmann has touched the very kernel of the nut here. Kant does not come into consideration at present, as his place is among the opponents of the proofs, and characterization in his case is still distant. As for Hegel, Anselm's argument comes to be mentioned by him a great many times, and always with the greatest respect. He actually says at page 547 of the second volume of his *Philosophy of Religion:*

"This argument has been found out only first in Christendom, by Anselm of Canterbury, namely; but since then it has been brought forward by all other later philosophers, as Descartes, Leibnitz, Wolff, always, however, *with the other proofs, though it alone is the true one.*" This, nevertheless, is not, as one knows, the common opinion; as, indeed, I find not badly put in this little old essay of fifty years ago, the concluding words of which are these :—" Such, then, is our estimate. And we think ourselves entitled to conclude, that the value of the *à priori* argument is, in comparison with that of the *à posteriori*, insignificant. It is needless to make use of a weak evidence, when we can get a stronger. Why should we attempt to read by the light of a candle, when we may open our shutters to the sun?" Evidently, therefore, it will require us to look at Anselm's argument in a very peculiar manner before we shall be able, in opposition to the current opinion, to endorse that of Hegel. Hegel, in fact, will not satisfy many readers in these proofs of his for the existence of God. They seem so diffuse, so vague, so indefinite; even to abound so in repetitions, in circumlocutions, in strange clauses out of place, or insusceptible of any meaning *in* their place— in short, so confused, dry, colourless, and uninteresting, that one wonders if it be possible that there ever was found a class of young men able to listen to them. I do not suppose it can be denied, indeed, that it is impossible to find in all Hegel more slovenly writing than in these *Beweise* that constitute pretty well the latter half of the second volume of the *Lectures on the Philosophy of Religion*. Words seem thrown down again and again just at a venture: as they came they were taken, no matter that they looked more or less ineffectual perhaps. We seem to have before us, in fact, a marksman who has indeed a mark in his view, but who fires at it always carelessly, and often almost as though intentionally widely. Nevertheless, ever here and there, grains are to be found by an eye that shall look long enough and deep enough; and they are not wanting in what concerns Anselm.

But in the method of Anselm an essential preliminary to the Proslogium is the Monologium; the reasoning of which is, in a certain modified way, cosmological. The fulcrum of it lies in what the act of predication is found to involve. Things similar have a common predicate, which common predicate obtains less or more according to the individual condition of each. Each, as participant, then, in what is common to them all, presupposes that in which it is participant. What is good presupposes the Good; what great, the Great; what true, the True; what beautiful, the Beautiful, etc. But all things also are: they all participate in Being; and they, therefore, all presuppose Being. Being as Being, highest Being, truest Being, best Being, supreme Being, perfect Being, absolute Being is the one universal presupposition. *Relatives* only prove an *absolute*. All that relatively is, only is through that which absolutely is—which withdrawn, all falls, all disappears. This is the teaching of Augustine as well; and Anselm exclaims, it must be "most certain and clear to all who are only willing to see." Further, there cannot be a plurality of absolute beings; for even if there were many, they must all participate in a common absolute Being, which is, therefore, one and single, and alone by itself. "This highest nature," says Anselm is "*per se ipsam et ex se ipsa:* all other things are not through themselves, but through it, and not from themselves, but from it. . . . Then, since it were wickedness to think that the substance of the most perfect nature is something than which something else were in any way better, that most perfect substance must itself *be*." In this way, evidently, we have a complete introduction to what is regarded as the proper argument of Anselm. We have here, that is, completely formed, what that argument starts with as the *notion* of God, the notion, namely, of that, than which there cannot possibly be a greater. In the Monologium, Anselm puts the case at full length; but the same strain is to be found in Boethius as well as in Augustine. Boethius held, namely, that negation as such equally presupposes affirmation as such; and that, consequently, imperfect things being, there must of necessity be a highest perfect; and in such wise that the perfection were no mere predicate, but the very essence, substance, and nature. Anselm, then, having made good in the Monologium this notion of a most perfect being, as in Augustine and Boethius, proceeds somewhat thus in the Proslogium to secure his notion reality. "Thinking of my opusculum, the Monologium," he says, "which I had put forth as an example of meditation on the reason of faith, and considering that it was made up of a concatenation of many arguments, I began to ask myself if it were by chance possible to invent a single argument, which to prove itself should stand in need of no other, and which alone should suffice, etc. etc., I have written this little book which I have named Proslogium, that is, *alloquium Dei.*" He then begins his book by an actual prayer to God in its reference, and in the same way, at the conclusion of his argument, he gives " thanks to Thee, because what, by Thy gift, I first believed, I now, by Thy illumination, so understand that if I were unwilling to believe I should not be able not to perceive." In fact, Anselm, it appears, had long anxiety and no rest day or night for the thought of proving, by a simple argument, that whom we believe, exists, fearing for long that it was mere temptation of the devil to propose to establish by reason the things of faith, but rejoicing at length in his success through the grace of God. We cannot but see, then, that this was a most serious matter to Anselm, and that he conceived himself in the end to have accomplished only what was a true and genuine work under the approbation and through the inspiration of the Deity Himself. His reply to Gaunilo, indeed, makes all this only the plainer; and it, too, must be pronounced in its own way, and in what it aims at, not only genuine, but successful. Anselm needed no Gaunilo to tell him the difference between ideality and reality. His own words are these: "It is one thing, that there is something in the intellect and another thing to perceive that it *is*. For when a painter prefigures in thought the image of what he is to do, he has indeed that image already in intellect, but he does not yet perceive that it really is, because he has not yet made it; but when he has painted it, then he both has in the intellect, and perceives as existent, what he has done." That Anselm was broad awake, then, to the usual distinction, must be held as a matter absolutely beyond doubt; and there can, consequently, be no means of saving his intelligence in the matter of his argument, but by the supposition that he assumed the distinction in question to be plainly inapplicable to God, who was a Being, not finite as an island, or a garden, or a castle— but infinite. God was no object for the senses, like the picture of the painter: God was the infinite substance that *is* of all that *is*. That, indeed, is the burden of his argument. At the same time, it is certain that, as a formal syllogism, it is faulty and inadequate. The major premiss, in fact, already, by presupposition, contains within it the whole case. Its subject is that which is reallest, that which is most perfect; but that subject cannot be reallest or most perfect unless it *is*. To compare a part of the notion with the whole notion cannot possibly *give* the real existence which the notion, by presupposition, already has. At best, considered as a syllogism, it has all the cogency it can have when put as Erdmann puts it, who expressly says, "Precisely by the quite subjective turn which Anselm gives his proof, is its value greater than in the later forms of Wolff and others." That word "subjective" here is the *merit* of Erdmann. Anselm is supposed to speak to the fool who says in his heart, There is no God, and twits him with self-contradiction. When you say God, you name that than which nothing can be thought greater: you understand as much; but you still say, it has no existence; but if it has not existence, it is not greatest, and you have contradicted yourself. That is the truth of the matter, then. To think God—truly to think God, we must think Him to exist. Existence is an element in the very notion of God; or with God notion and existence are inseparable. Existence is involved in the very thought of God—flows and follows from His very nature and essence. That is the very idea of God,—viz. *that He is*. We cannot think God, unless we think Him to be. To say it is only an idea, contradicts the very idea that it is, for that idea is that God is. The idea of what is most perfect, of what is reallest, is the idea of God, take that idea as a rule, and compare with it what shall be thought, but not be, why, plainly, as much as this is not enough; it falls short and fails. Or, to say the same thing otherwise, we admit the notion of God, the idea of God, to be the highest possible notion, the highest possible idea; but if it is the highest, then it *is*. Examine ourselves as we may, *that* we find to be our own actual subjective condition: our own actual subjective condition is precisely that notion, precisely that conviction. The syllogism of Anselm, then, is but an explication, an analysis of our own state of mind: it is there simply to bring home to us what our own thought amounts to.

In a word, God is not something that can be *thought*, and yet thought *not* to BE. That is a contradiction—that is a contradiction of thought itself; and that really is the thought of Anselm. That is the sublimest thought of Descartes also, and that is the very first word of modern philosophy—this, namely: God is that whose nature cannot be conceived unless as existent: the very *notion* of God includes and implies the *being* of God: *Deus causa sui est*—God is His own cause. It has been objected in blame to Anselm that, as regards the two polar elements, Knowledge and Belief, he has given the precedency to the latter, to belief; but we may remind ourselves that, "As the earth must be loosened for the reception of the seed, so must the heart be softened (by Belief) for reception of the truth (in Knowledge)." . And, really, there is, after all, no harder heart than that of your sceptic—no shallower soul than that of him whose enlightenment is a sneer. That, as it is the lesson of Augustine, so it is the lesson of Anselm, to whom the *thought* of God means the *being* of God. And with that word in our ears, we may well conclude this part of the course.[1]

[1] "The fallacy lies in the forming the conception of something superlative, and yet leaving out one of the notions necessary to render it superlative." These words of the little Essay (p. 184), may be interpreted as unwittingly telling precisely in the opposite sense. That is, it is the "fallacy," we may say, not of Anselm, but precisely of the fool, so to leave out! To *say* God and *unsay* existence, is to say and unsay at once. If God is a necessary thought, then as sure as His thought is, He is. But God *is* a necessary thought, therefore, etc.

# THE SECOND COURSE OF LECTURES:
## THE NEGATIVE.

1890.

# GIFFORD LECTURE THE ELEVENTH.

Lectures by Lord Gifford—By whom edited—Germane to, and illustrative of, natural theology—Number and nature—Their literary excellence—Even poetical—*Der laute Lärm des Tages*—On attention—On St. Bernard of Clairvaux—(Luther, Gibbon)—What Lord Gifford admires—The spirit of religion—The Trinity—Emerson, Spinoza—Substance—Brahmanism—Religion—Understanding and reason—Metaphysical terms—Materialism—Literary enthusiasm—Technical shortcomings—Emerson and Carlyle—Social intercourse—Humanity—Liberality and tolerance—Faith—Mesmerism—Ebenezer Elliott—An open sense to evidence.

I BEG to express to you, in the first place, the pleasure which it gives me to meet once again an assembly like the present, in the interest of these lectures on the Lord Gifford Bequest. Then, in the reference that seems naturally next, as regards an introductory discourse, namely, perhaps I may be allowed to say that I might excusably hold no such preliminary to be expected from me on this occasion, when what we begin is but the *half* of a whole that had abundantly its preparatory explanations at first. So far one may incline to accept that, probably, as a very reasonable view. Still, I know not that I can proceed to act on it with any grace, in face of the fact of this little book. As one sees, it is a handsome little volume; and it came to me, bound as it is, unexpectedly and with surprise, from Frankfort-on-the-Main. It has, somehow, a singularly simple, pure, and taking title-page, the words on which are these: " Lectures Delivered on Various Occasions by Adam Gifford, one of the Senators of the College of Justice, Scotland." This title-page is followed by a perfectly correspondent modest little note, to the effect, that the lectures concerned are " a selection from a miscellaneous number of others given from time to time by request, on very various occasions, and to greatly differing audiences, the preparation of which was a great pleasure to the lecturer," and, if " of necessity sometimes hurried, never careless." " They were in no case," it is added, " meant for publication, and we print a few of them now only for his friends." The signatures to that note—the " we "—are Alice Raleigh and Herbert James Gifford; the one the niece, so long, in loving attention, associated with Lord Gifford, and the other his son. The lectures themselves, as we see, are not to be regarded as published; and that I should speak of them here, consequently, may seem to border on impropriety. But, as we see also, they are printed for his friends; and I know not that I speak to others than the friends of Lord Gifford when I speak to this audience. I am very certain of this, too, that I can adduce nothing from these lectures that will not prove admirably illustrative and confirmatory of the express terms in which, in the Trust-Disposition and Settlement, directions are given with respect to the duties necessarily incumbent on the holders of this chair. It is *in* that light and *for* that light, that, precisely to me at all events, these lectures of Lord Gifford's own are very specially welcome. And if now, by quotation, comment, or remark, I proceed to make as much as that good to you also, I have the hope that the result will prove constitutive, as well, of a lecture in place, a lecture in just such a course as this is, a lecture on the subject of Natural Theology, and a lecture, too, even in a way, almost at the very hands of the founder himself of this chair itself. There are seven of these lectures of Lord Gifford's, and they are respectively named as they come: 1. Ralph Waldo Emerson; 2. Attention as an Instrument of Self-Culture; 3. Saint Bernard of Clairvaux; 4. Substance: A Metaphysical Thought; 5. Law a Schoolmaster, or the Educational Function of Jurisprudence; 6. The Ten Avatars of Vishnu; and 7. The Two Fountains of Jurisprudence. Only two of them, then, so far as the titles would seem to suggest, belong to the writer's own profession of law, while the rest are literary, philosophical, or even metaphysical. Three of them in spirit, and even more or less in matter, might not unreasonably be held to have a direct bearing on the very subject which it has been his will that the four universities of Scotland should be bound in perpetuity expressly to discuss.

What strikes one at first in these lectures, and from the very face of them, is the constant vivid writing, the literary accomplishment that everywhere obtains in them. He says once, for example, " If first principles have not been carried out, if on the firm foundations the walls have not risen rightly, by truest plummet perpendicular towards heaven, and by bedded block parallel to the horizon; then be sure that sooner or later we must begin again, for Nature will find out our failure, and *with her there is no forgiveness.*" Surely that last is what is usually described as a *fine thought;* and there is concrete reflection throughout, as well as felicitous phrase. It is in the same way that he says once: " The prophet can *tell* his vision, but he cannot give his own *anointed* eye." What we may almost call technical literary balance is perpetual with him, as when he says: " Hinduism offers culture to the educated and wisdom to the wise, while with equal hand she gives superstitions and charms to the ignorant and to the foolish;" or when he holds of Emerson that " Many of his essays are refined and elevated poems, and some of his poems are really very abstruse and difficult essays." Genius "takes its own way," he tells us once; "it comes in its own air-borne chariot; it is bound by no forms, tied and swaddled in no etiquette of costume. In the rudest garb it enters the dress circle or the robed conclave, and white neckcloths and square caps reverently make room for it." Similar examples of expression are these: " He (Emerson) is not covered over and covered up, swathed and swaddled in his learning, like some learned mummies, but he wears it like a dress. He possesses it, and not it him. He bears it with him like an atmosphere and an aroma, not like a burden upon his back. It is used naturally and spontaneously. It flows like a fountain or exhales like a perfume; never forced, never artificial, never added for show or effect.—Let no one despise learning, true learning, the lessons of experience or the words of ancient wisdom, but remember that the greenness of earth's latest beauty rests on the rocks and the ashes which it took millenniums to form." Lord Gifford displays always a like literary talent when the occasion calls on him to be descriptive, and often then there are tones and accents of even a very veritable poesy, as when he says once: " If you will go up with me step by step, I think we may hope to reach the mount of Transfiguration and almost to see the glory! If you will only give me your strength and strive upwards with me, I think I can almost promise you that, even within our hour, we shall enter the white cloud that rests upon the summit, and feel the dazzling of the light that is ineffable!" Of the Middle Ages he says: " It was a fierce world. No wonder gentle natures were glad to quit it; and when we think of it and realize it, we cease to be surprised that dukes and princes, peasants and paupers, are ready to leave their luxury or their misery and to seek a haven of shelter, where during this short life they may say their prayers, and then lie down in peace to sleep, in death." "The Middle Ages!" he cries, "what strange scenes and pictures do not the words recall! The fortalice of the half-savage baron and the mean huts of his degraded serfs. The proud pomp and spiritual power of the haughty churchman, before which the strength of kings and the might of feudalism were fain to kneel. The chivalry of Europe drained time after time to furnish forth the armies of the Crusaders. Religious excitements and revivals passing like prairie-fires over Europe, and compared with which modern revivals, even the wildest, seem but the coldest marsh gleams. Strange and terrible diseases and epidemics, and plagues both bodily and mental, that mowed down millions as with the scythe of destruction. The spotted plague, and the black death, and the sweating sickness. The dancing mania, the barking mania. The were-wolf and the ghoul. Strange mystical schools of philosophy exciting popular admiration and enthusiasm to us unexampled and inexplicable. And below all, the swelling and the heaving of the slow but advancing tide, which even yet is bearing us upon its crest." In all that, there is no want of effective description everywhere; but, surely, the last sentence is, in a way, sublime! What is loudest in the day, what is most visible, what attracts the attention and excites the voices of the crowd, is not always to us admirable, is not always to us cheering, is not always to us hopeful; oftentimes it is disappointing, dispiriting, disheartening; sometimes it seems degrading, or is even at times sickening. And then it is that we are glad to think in the strain of that last sentence of Lord Gifford's. That, that —on the top—before our eyes—is degrading, beastly, disgusting; but "below all" there is "the swelling and the heaving of the slow but advancing tide" that, "bearing us too on its crest," flows on ever, heedless of the temporalities of earth, on and on to the perpetuities of heaven.

Of the seven lectures in the little book, there are specially three which are more particularly in *our* way: they are Ralph Waldo Emerson; Substance: a metaphysical thought; and the Ten Avatars of Vishnu. Of the two others which are more or less assonant to the interests that engage us, the lecture on Attention as an Instrument of Self-culture may be recommended as, in the midst of its excellent general advice, containing many useful hints for practical service; while that on Saint Bernard of Clairvaux, taking moral and religious occasion from the peculiarities of the theme, is an interesting narrative. We may regard it as, to some extent, a proof of Lord Gifford's glowing sympathy with whatever was heroically moral and religious, that he should have given himself so much trouble with, and bestowed so much care on, the career of the young man of twenty-two who, as he says, " renounced his inheritance and fortune, renounced his nobility of birth and every title of distinction, and stood penniless and barefoot, a candidate for admission at the gate of the monastery of Citeaux." He certainly became a great power in Christendom, this young man, perhaps the greatest of his time; but it was neither for worldly honours nor for bodily comforts. Every preferment was at once rejected by him—him whom Luther " holds alone to be much higher than all the monks and popes on the entire surface of the earth;" while Gibbon says of him, he " was content till the hour of his death with the humble station of abbot of his own community." The *life* in that community, again, Lord Gifford depicts to us thus: " They (the monks) were aroused every morning at two o'clock by the convent bell, and they immediately hastened along the dark, cold passages and cloisters to the church, which was lighted by a single lamp. After private prayer they engaged in the first service of the day, ' *matins*,' which lasted *two hours.* The next service was '*Lauds,*' which was always at daybreak. Lauds was followed almost without intermission by other religious exercises till about nine, when the monks went, without any breakfast other than a cup of water, to labour in the fields or in the necessary work of the house, and this continued till two o'clock. At two o'clock the famished monk was allowed to *dine,* as it was grimly called: and this was the only meal in the twenty-four hours. The dinner consisted almost always of a pottage made of peas, lentils, or barley, sometimes with the addition of a little milk, but oftener not. No Cistercian monk under Bernard's rule ever tasted *meat, fish, butter, grease,* or *eggs.* On this one meal the monk had to subsist till the same hour came round another day—retiring to his hard pallet about nine o'clock to be roused to the same daily round at two o'clock next morning." This day's "*darg*" was worse than a Scotch ploughman's yet; and we are not surprised to hear that Bernard was as thin as a skeleton, and that "physicians wondered he could live at all." Still we have to see all this has a charm for Lord Gifford. "All through these frightful austerities," he says, "it is not possible to withhold our tribute of admiration; here at least is a man who believes in the unseen, and acts out his belief unflinchingly." That, then, is what Lord Gifford admires—belief in the unseen, and the sacrifice of a life to it. But all through these essays, the mood, in the main, is not a different one. Lord Gifford, however it be with the *letter* of his creed, is always *spiritually* religious. Religious feeling is his blood; and his sympathy is with the Christian. "Uneventful lives are often the most influential," he says; "it is thought, not action, that ultimately moves the universe.—The ink in the inkstand of a quiet thinker of Kirk Caldy (Adam Smith) now floats the commercial navy of the world; and (to take with reverence the highest of all instances) a few spoken and unwritten words of a young carpenter of Nazareth,— words dropped by the waysides and in the fields of Galilee,—have regenerated mankind and given His name, 'Christianity,' to half the globe." And not here only, but elsewhere also, he would seem to testify almost even to the life of the very letter that is spoken by the Church. Of incarnations, he says: "Ever and again man's spirit tells him—'The gods are come down to us in the likeness of men,' in the crowd or in the solitude, by night or by day, ever still the heavens are opened, the dazzling smites us to the ground, and deep calleth unto deep." "God's revelations are not over, are not completed. We have not yet heard His last word, we shall never do so. We look for His *coming* still." "May we not all unite in the wish, which is the prayer, Thy kingdom come!" "I find the great central doctrine of Christianity, that on which all its other doctrines turn and revolve as on a pivot, to be an impressive, most mighty, and most magnificent Avatar—*God manifest in the flesh!*" It is in reference to Hindu ideas that Lord Gifford is speaking when he is moved to say, "God is manifested in the Trinity! Three essences in one God! Three aspects of the Infinite." And I may stop here to remark how deeply philosophical Lord Gifford would seem to be in his sense of a doctrine that has proved a stumbling-block and a stone of offence, perhaps to hundreds and to thousands within the bounds of Christendom. If what we can number one, two, three, mean, and must mean, three individual things, essentially separate and disjunct, then unity in trinity is an expression that can have, not possibly, any concrete interpretation. I have a vague recollection of having read somewhere of Carlyle that he once somewhat disparagingly illustrated the Trinity by a man, in a gig, drawn by a horse. The gig was a unit, the horse was a unit, and the man was a unit: how could these three units be different, yet the same; three, yet one! If this is true of Carlyle, I should be very much inclined to hold that, in this instance at all events, Lord Gifford was the deeper philosopher. Three aspects of one *Infinity*, says Lord Gifford; while Carlyle refers to three units that are palpably quite as many *finites*. Carlyle, had he wished to illustrate an *essential trinity*, need not have wandered out of his own self. That body of his, as he walked about, was Carlyle; and that thinking in his head, as he wrote his book, was Carlyle; and that ego—that I or Me—that was one and the same identical ego all through his body and all through his thinking, was Carlyle; and body, thinking, and ego were three, at the same time that body, thinking, and ego were one: the three were one! Had Carlyle remained within himself, and eschewed the gig, he might have found an illustration for the Trinity that was, to some extent, essential, and not numerical only. There cannot be any doubt that Lord Gifford, for his part, at all events, was perfectly open to the distinction, and quite beyond the hazard of confounding concretion with abstraction. Philosophically he knew that there might be three aspects of the one Infinite; and, as a student of the Middle Ages, he was perfectly aware of the historical position of the idea ecclesiastically. Lord Gifford terms it "a doctrine of our own Church, I mean of Christianity, known as the Eternal Procession of the Son and of the Holy Ghost from the Father, a doctrine which in scholastic times engaged the learning of the Church, and helped to clothe the walls of its spacious libraries." And perhaps some of us, indeed, may not have yet forgotten a precisely similar mention, in our course last year, with regard to the early Church, modern German philosophy, and the relation of the Son to the world. Another casual allusion of last year's may also be within our recollection, which was to an apparent assonance to pantheism in certain expressions of the Bequest. In the religious reference, it is in place to say now that some such assonances reappear here in the little book that at present claims us. I daresay we are not unprepared for this when we consider that one lecture is on Ralph Waldo Emerson, another on Substance, and a third on what concerns Hinduism. Of Emerson, Lord Gifford remarks that he "inclines to the higher or subjective pantheism; but he (Emerson) will not limit, and he cannot define. Before all such questions he stands uncovered and reverently silent. No proud denial, no cynic scoff, no heartless sneer escapes him; and without a theory of the universe he clings to its moral meaning." This is certainly well said as regards Emerson; and it certainly names a very admirable catholic attitude as regards religion, which attitude, not by any means necessarily pantheistic, would do honour to any man, Lord Gifford, Emerson, or another. In the lecture on Substance, naturally, we are in presence of the arch-pantheist, named and described by Lord Gifford as "Benedictus de Spinoza, one of the most eminent of the philosophers who have treated of substance." Of him, one cannot fail to see, on the part of Lord Gifford, an even familiar knowledge. If *substance* was to Spinoza God, it is no less divine to Lord Gifford; for to him God is the all-pervading substantiality and the single soul that is alone present everywhere. Of animals, he says, "Their mainspring is the Eternal, and every wheel and every pinion is guided by the Infinite—and there can be but *one Infinite*—this is the root-thought of the fetichism of the Indian or of the Hottentot; and this is what the Egyptian felt when he saw sacredness in the crocodile, in the ibis, or in the beetle. Said I not"

(Lord Gifford exclaims)—"said I not that the word *substance* was perhaps the grandest word in any language? There can be none grander. It is the true name of *God*. Do you not feel with me that it is almost profane to apply the word *Substance* to anything short of God? God must be the very substance and essence of the *human soul*. The human soul is neither self-derived nor self-subsisting. It did not make itself. It cannot exist alone. It is but a manifestation, a phenomenon. It would vanish if it had not a substance, and its substance is God. But if God be the *substance* of all forces and powers and of all beings, then He must be the only substance in the universe or in all possible universes. This is the grand truth on which the system of Spinoza is founded, and his whole works are simply drawing deductions therefrom." These are very trenchant expressions; and their full import cannot be mistaken. As a single sample in the Indian pantheistic reference, I may quote this: "Whatever Hinduism, or Brahmanism, may have latterly or in its bulk become, still in its purest and highest essence it was (indeed I think it still is, and I am glad to think so) a monism, a monotheism, and in one aspect a pantheism of a pure and noble kind. Pure Brahmanism knows only one God, indeed only one Being, in the universe, in whom all things consist and exist."

Now, whatever pantheism may be, and however we may be disposed to regard it, surely we cannot revolve in mind these various deliverances of Lord Gifford's without feeling that we can apply to him his own words in regard of Emerson: "Emerson," he says, "is not distinctively a religious writer; that is to say, he does not profess to teach or to enforce religion, but his tone is eminently religious." And then he goes on to say that, do as we may, "religion will not be separated from anything whatever: you cannot produce and you cannot maintain a religious vacuum, and if you could, even secularism would die in it." That is particularly well said, and is surely a great truth. We are too apt, each of us, to concentrate ourselves into our own abstractions. If we are mathematicians, we will be mathematicians only, or, similarly, chemists only, physiologists only, botanists only, and so on. Whereas there is a single concrete for which all abstractions should unite, to which they should all tend, and in which they should all terminate. And that is religion, not religion as it is a dry bone of divinity, but religion as it is the vital breath of humanity. You might as well expect digestion in independence of the heart-beat, as foison for humanity, or any department of humanity, in independence of religion. That is the truth of the matter, and what Lord Gifford says is the very word for it: Let Secularism, once for all, *effect* its religious vacuum, and Secularism itself will die in it! Man doth not live by bread alone; and neither will humanity advance on the understanding only. Above the understanding there is reason. The understanding distinguishes, and divides, and makes clear the many; but it is reason that, in vision and in love, makes us all one soul, while only in the element of religion does the soul find breath. "There is," says Lord Gifford—"there is an eternal and unchangeable system and scheme of morality and ethics, founded not on the will, or on the devices, or in the ingenuity of man, but on the nature and essence of the unchangeable God. The individual man, Lord Gifford intimates, may worship "the phenomenon, the appearance; but the noumenon, the substance" still is, and still is the truth: "it is a high strain of Christianity to worship only the eternal, the immortal, and the invisible." In these and other expressions of Lord Gifford's, we have observed the occurrence of terms which are strictly and technically philosophical. He opposes, for instance, phenomenon to noumenon, and appearance to substance. "Without the true doctrine of substance and of cause," he says once, "philosophy would be a delusion and religion a dream, for true philosophy and true religion must stand or fall together;" but of both we are to understand "*substance*" to be "the very foundation-stone." There is a "force behind and in all forces," an "energy of all energies." "Nature! 'Tis but the name of an effect. The cause is God!" These and such like expressions occur again and again in the little book; and, "if all this be a part of metaphysics," Lord Gifford declares, then "metaphysics can be no empty and barren science." Accordingly, we find no sympathy here with the mere materialistic views and tendencies of the present day. "There are some who say and think"—we may quote by way of example —"there are some who say and think that they could find in the grey matter of the brain the very essence of the soul—to such materialists the proper answer is to be found in the truths of ultimate metaphysics. Only go deep enough, and the most obstinate materialist may be made to see that matter is not *all* the universe. Mind is not the outcome of trembling or rotating atoms."—"The substance and essence of a man is his *reasonable* and *intelligent soul*."—"The substance of all forms, of all phenomena, of all manifestations, is God."

I have spoken of literature in connection with Lord Gifford; and there are many keen expressions to bear out the implication, some already seen—such phrases, namely, as "anointed eyes," or "shining countenances;" or "to mete with the measure of the upper sanctuary;" or decisions "straight as the rays that issue from the throne of God;" or his words when he admonishes his brothers of the Law, ever, in the first place, to ascend and meditate on the "moral heights," whence descending, he assures them, "their pleading robes, in the Courts of Jurisprudence, will shine with light as from the Mount of Transfiguration." I have spoken also of philosophy in connection with Lord Gifford, and certainly we have seen much that is not alone an acknowledgment of philosophy, but is itself philosophy. Still it is not to be understood that I would wish to represent Lord Gifford, whether in literature or philosophy, as precisely professional. *For* both he has splendid endowments: *in* both he has splendid accomplishments. One almost fancies that it was as a literary man he began—witness, as he expresses it, the "fresh and startled admiration," the "overflowing enthusiasm" with which he read Emerson. "That enthusiasm," he exclaims, "ladies and gentlemen, *I still feel.* I rejoice to think that my early admiration was not misplaced. Time with his ruthless mace has shattered many idols of a fond but false worship. But let us thank God if we were not wholly idolators, if any of our youthful delights are delightful still, if some of the morning colours are unfaded, and part of its fine gold undimmed." To doubt or deny the full liberty of the guild in the teeth of such expressions as these, which syllable the very vernacular of the precincts, trenches very closely on the mere invidious, and pretty well reduces to foolishness what laudation we have already expended. Still, with all natural endowment and all acquired accomplishment, we fancy we catch, here and there, a note at times that betrays the Gentile, the Ephraimite, the visitant, rather than the brother. Lord Gifford tells us once, for example, "of sleight-of-hand, of *cheiromancy,* as it is called;" or, again, we hear of Henry VI., "that drum-and-trumpet thing," which Shakespeare had, probably, little to do with, as being yet a "whole drama grandly original!" We saw, some time ago, too, the phrase, "the higher or subjective pantheism." Knowing that it is from his perusal of Spinoza that Lord Gifford has derived his idea of pantheism, one has difficulty in associating "*subjective*" with it. One thinks that a subjective pantheism would be, properly, theism, and not pantheism at all; at the same time that one knows withal that there is no more familiar commonplace in philosophy, than the fact that what the system of Spinoza lacks is precisely subjectivity. Familiar acquaintance with, is not, in truth, exactly technical knowledge of, Spinoza. We are accustomed to this. Statements of theories by admirers of their authors, which said authors would, it may be, have been somewhat gratefully perplexed with; finding in them, perhaps, such partial accentuations or partial extensions, as, with similar partial limitations or omissions, made their own work (so called) strange to them. Such will not prove to readers by any means an uncommon experience. In the immediate reference, we can certainly say this, that the God of Lord Gifford, much as he venerates *substance*, is only very questionably the God of Spinoza, and that Lord Gifford, had he been familiar with what we may call the accepted statistical or historical *return* of Spinoza, would have written of him from considerably different findings.

But "*subjective*" is not only objectionably associated with pantheism by Lord Gifford, we see also a similar association of it on his part with the word "*higher*." "The higher or subjective pantheism," it is said. But, philosophically,—of any philosophical system, that is,— the association of "higher" with "subjective" is an association that, more than any other, perhaps, in these days, *grates*. It is the objective *idealism*, for example, that, to all metaphysical ambition, is the higher, and not the subjective. To Professor Ferrier it was little short of a personal insult to call *his* idealism subjective!

Another point in this connection is that Lord Gifford signalizes, and dwells very specially on the "*learning*" of Emerson. Now, I do not think that any one, formally and fairly a member of the guild, however much he might admire Mr. Emerson, would feel prompted to call him *learnëd*—if learnëd, that is, means erudite, technically and scholastically erudite. Miscellaneously, no doubt, Mr. Emerson was an excellent reader. He read many books, and he meditated on them. But he also walked in the woods, and meditated there. What he read, too, was mostly in English. He tells us himself he never read an alien original if he could at all compass a translation of it. Mr. Emerson nowise suggests himself to us in his books as a professed expert in languages, whether ancient or modern. Neither are we apt to think of him as a student, properly, of the sciences, or of any science. Even of philosophy, so to speak, he was no *entered* student,—into what deeps and distances soever, and by what means soever, his intellectual curiosity may have relatively carried him!

Further, in regard to learning, when I am told by Lord Gifford this: "He (Mr. Emerson) has edited Greek plays —he has edited several Greek standard authors!" I confess I am astonished at my own ignorance! (He did write a preface to a translation of Plutarch's *Morals*.)

This is to be said in the end, however: That, with whatever discount, Lord Gifford is literary and philosophical, even as Mr. Emerson was literary and philosophical. In fact, in reading these lectures of Lord Gifford's, we are constantly *reminded* of Emerson. Lord Gifford would seem to have remained so persistently by Emerson, that we may be pardoned if we conceive him to have fallen, at times, into Emerson's very attitude, and almost taken on Emerson's very shape. Again and again in Lord Gifford it is as though we heard the very words of Emerson, and in their own peculiarity of cadence, rhythm, or even music. Lord Gifford, at one time, must have been inflamed for Carlyle. Nevertheless, he has dwelt so long in mildness at the side of Emerson that the passionate voice of Carlyle, at the last, hurts him. So it is that he says, " In Emerson is no savage and vindictive hatred; no yells for the extermination of the wicked and of folly." We see thus that gentleness is more to Lord Gifford than force. *That*, in fact, is the grain of his character; and it comes out again and again in this little book. How he rejoices that intercourse with his fellows, for example, and the friction of a formed society had, as regards himself, made " an humbler and more modest man of him than he had been before." A test *that* of the amount and quality of the original substance; for it is precisely such a situation and precisely such influences that make the shallow man shallower. It is characteristic of this sound humanity in Lord Gifford that he would have us " regard our neighbour's joy and sorrow," even " his wealth and rank," " in precisely the same way as if they were *our own*." That is an admirable touch, the *wealth and rank!* It is a fact that the man who looks through the palings need not envy the man on the other side of them. The scenery, the woods, the hills, the stately architecture, are as much his as they are their owner's, and in a free transparency of mind unsmutched by a single care. " Every sky," says Lord Gifford, and there is his heart's love to nature in the word, " gleams, morning and evening, with loveliness upon us, if we but lift our eye to it, *even from the city lanes.*" So it is that his fellow is the core always of the thought of Lord Gifford. He rejoices in " the prophecy of the future," " in every high and holy aspiration," and sympathizes " in every effort to elevate the character and improve the condition of man." Lord Gifford is himself (in a slightly different sense) manly withal. " I am here to-night," he says to his audience on one occasion, " freely and frankly to talk with you, man to man, as friend with friend;" and there is even humour in him. " An old Scottish lawyer," he remarks, " quaintly said, ' You cannot *poind* for charity,' and so you cannot, by any form of diligence, compel kindness, or consideration, or courtesy." As is only to be expected, a wise, an open, and a liberal tolerance is another characteristic of the humanity of Lord Gifford. He will not have us forget that " The Church was the last bulwark of humanity in the Dark Ages," that " the Church, and the Church alone, was the home of learning and the guardian of letters," and that she took always " the poor and forsaken to her bosom." " To the everlasting praise of the Catholic Church be it said," he cries, " she never knew any difference between rich and poor, between the nobly born and the lowly born, but welcomed all alike to her loving though somewhat rigid arms: to her every one *born at all* was well born." Yet it is with comment on the bigotry and persecutions of this same Church and of his favourite St. Bernard that he says, " Truth passes like morning from land to land, and those who have sat all night by the candle of tradition cannot exclude the light which streams through every crevice of window or of wall." It gladdens him, even in the same mood of enlightenment, to see " some old prejudice given way, some new view got of the perfect and the fair." That is enlightenment akin to the Aufklärung, to the enlightenment of name, which, of course, is good so far as it *is* enlightened; but *here* is the substantial enlightenment. " A few words now," says Lord Gifford, " on the miracles of Saint Bernard. For [in strong italics] *he did work miracles*—attested by scores of eye-witnesses, whose testimony nothing but judicial blindness can withstand." How explain them? "The Talisman is [in small capitals] FAITH!" "All things are possible to him that believeth!" But then, adds Lord Gifford: All " is closely connected with the modern phenomena of mesmerism," etc. It is, perhaps, too late in the day for any one to dispute or deny certain contraventions of *the usual* on the part of mesmerism; but this was not so at first. The ordinary routine of common sense, which alone was philosophy to the *Aufgeklärter*, the man of enlightenment then,—in his freedom from prejudice and his hatred of the lie,—the ordinary routine of common sense could not be said to be interrupted without a pang to the heart of this Aufgeklärter in the beginning, at the stupidity of the vulgar, caught ever by some new trick! It is told of Ebenezer Elliott, the Corn Law Rhymer,—a warm-hearted, honest, able, perfectly admirable man in his day, but still something of that day's Philistine, or something of that day's Aufgeklärter,—that he was loud in his denunciations of mesmerism as mere " collusion and quackery," but that he unwarily undertook to stake the question on trial of himself. " Accordingly the poet," says the narrator and the operator, a man whom I personally knew, " sat down in his chair, and the moment my hand came in contact with his head, he shrunk as if struck by a voltaic pile, uttered a deep sigh, fell back upon his chair, and all consciousness fled from him." We are not surprised to hear, nevertheless, that the poet (Elliott himself), alone of the whole company, remained unconvinced: he only " rubbed his eyes," and " would have it that he had fallen asleep from exhaustion." Lord Gifford, then, has still the substantial enlightenment that is open to all evidence, and will not reject, because of physical facts, others which happen to be psychical.

And with this I will conclude the picture, trusting that you will find it only natural and sufficiently in place that, with this little book before me—and the information it extended—I conceived an introductory lecture on the Founder of this Chair only my duty, and the rather that it necessarily involved much of the matter of Natural Theology.

# GIFFORD LECTURE THE TWELFTH.

A settlement for faith Lord Gifford's object—Of our single theme the negative half now—Objections to, or refutations of, the proofs—Negative not necessarily or predominatingly modern, Kant, Darwin—The ancient negative, the Greeks, Pythagoreans, Ionics, Eleatics, Heraclitus, Empedocles, Democritus, (Bacon), Anaxagoras, Socrates, Sophists, Diagoras, Aristotle, Aristoxenus, Dicaearchus, Strato, (Hume, Cudworth), Aristophanes, etc.,— Rome—Modern Europe, France, Hume and the seventeen atheists—Epochs of atheism—David Hume, his influence—To many a passion and a prejudice—Brougham, Buckle–Style!— Taste!—Blair—Hume's taste, Pope, Shakespeare, John Home —*Othello*—The French to Hume—Mr. Pope!—Some bygone *littérateurs*— Personality and character of Hume — Jokes, stories, Kant, Aristotle—The Scotch—The *Epigoniad*—America —Germany—Generosity, affection, friendship, hospitality— Smollett—Burke—but Hume, honest, genuine, and even religious and pious.

WE must now address ourselves to the business proper of the course. I think our shortest statement of the general object of Lord Gifford at any time during last session was this: "Faith, belief,—the production of a living principle *that*, giving us God in the heart, should, in this world of ours, guide us in peace." I probably did enough then, by way of general explanation and illustrative detail, to enforce and give its own due proportions to this object and this theme, constitutive, as I take it of the entire burden of the bequest itself. But, had I failed in this, had my statement of that object—had my representation of the *spirit* of Lord Gifford in setting up the exposition of that object as the single and sole duty of a special chair—had statement and representation been insufficient and incomplete, we should have had to acknowledge ample compensation and satisfactory relief in what we saw, in our last lecture, of expressions of Lord Gifford's own. Be the language of the Bequest what it may, that little book, with its seven lectures, as we may say, on law, ethics, and religion, presents us with the full length Lord Gifford, and dispenses us from any relative doubt.

Further, then, now, as regards our treatment of the theme prescribed to us. I also explained last session that I took the theme itself precisely as it *was* prescribed. That theme, I said, is "Natural Theology and the proofs for the Being of a God. These proofs I follow historically, while the reflection at the same time that we have still before us what Lord Gifford calls the only science, the science of infinite being, may bring with it a certain (complementary) breadth and filling." "This is one half of my enterprise. The other half, the negative half, shall concern the denial of the proofs. This session (I said then), I confine myself to the affirmative. Next session, I shall conclude with what concerns the negative. In this way we shall have two correspondent and complementary halves: one irenical, and the other polemical; one with the ancients, and the other with the moderns. For I shall bring the affirmative half historically down only "—only, in fact, to within sight again of Raymund of Sabunde.

We have to understand, therefore, that we have now seen the affirmative of our whole theme—the rise, namely, and progress of the proofs or arguments for the being of God as they are thetically presentant in history; and what remains for us at present is the exposition and discussion of the negative. We have to see, that is, what objections or refutations have been brought forward in regard of the proofs; and we have to consider as well what weight attaches to these objections, or what cogency follows these refutations. It appears also that we are now to find ourselves only in the modern world. This does not mean, however, that we are to regard the modern world as only negative in respect of the being of a God, and never affirmative. That would be a singular result of monotheism, universal now, as opposed to polytheism, all but universal then. The reverse is the truth. Up to within a score of years or so we may say that modern writers on religion, while countless in numbers, were, with but few exceptions, affirmative to a man. And this we feel we can hold to in spite of Kant and his *Kritik* of 1781; for Kant, whatever his negative may be, has his own affirmative at last. It is only since Mr. Darwin that, as the phrase goes, atheism has set in like a flood. It was not, then, because of relative numbers that we made the ancients affirmative and the moderns negative in regard to the belief in a God. The principle of determination did not lie there at all. What alone was considered in the laying out of our theme was the historical course and fortune of the proofs themselves.

And if the modern world is not for a moment to be considered exclusively or predominatingly negative; so neither is the ancient world to be any more considered exclusively or predominantly affirmative. There were atheists then quite as well as now. I suppose, indeed, to the bulk of the Grecian public, every philosopher before Socrates was an atheist, not even excepting the Pythagoreans. Thales and the other Ionics are, as Hylozoists, nothing but atheists; while to call the Eleatics and Heraclitus pantheists is tantamount, for all that, to an admission, as their doctrines were, that they were atheists. Empedocles was no better. Democritus could point to the superhuman powers he believed in, as it were in the air; but still a nature built up by atoms was his God, no matter that, as Bacon maintains, the atoms of the atomists were so very immaterial that an actual atom no one had ever seen—no one ever could see. Then Anaxagoras with the principal Sophists, even Socrates himself, had been publicly arraigned as atheists. Diagoras, in the time of Aristotle, became an atheist in consequence of a real or supposed wrong unretributed by the gods, and was known and named, and is still familiar to us in our books, as Diagoras the atheist. Aristotle himself hardly escaped a similar imputation; which, besides, his own school in the end would only have justified; for almost every member of it, at least in the second generation, gave more and more breadth to what naturalistic doctrine had taken birth in it. Aristoxenus, for example, held that "the soul was but a certain tension or intension of the body itself, like what is called music on the part of strung cords;" while Dicaearchus, another Aristotelian, declared the soul to be "only an idle name and nothing but the body, which, one, single and simple, acts and feels by organization of nature." Later than these, too, there was, above all, Strato, surnamed Physicus, and physicus is really equivalent to materialist or atheist, not but that two of our modern authorities in this reference differ, Hume declaring "Strato's atheism the most dangerous of the ancient," and Cudworth maintaining atheism at all to be no necessity of the position; a view, however, to which he has been simply won over by persuading himself that what unconscious spontaneity Strato ascribes to matter is no more than his own "plastic nature," and only saves God, as is the very intention of that plastic nature, from any derogation of direct intromission with the inquination of sense. But Cudworth's view is no more the view of the ancients than it is that of Hume; for if we look to Cicero and Plutarch alone, we shall be satisfied that

Strato had no God or principle of design in his belief, but referred all in nature to mere mechanical movement, to accident and chance. Strato, according to Diogenes Laertius, became so thin in the end that he slipped away into death quite insensibly—truly a *tenuitas mira*, as is the Latin of it!

It is evident from all this that a negative in regard to the existence of God is by no means to be conceived as confined to the modern world. Among the Greeks, at all events, in the ancient world it existed in an undeniable plenitude. Nor is the reason of this remote or hidden from us. Polytheism was dying out; the popular religion had ceased to be believed in. And Aristophanes, who was even intolerant and a bigot in his tenacity for the old, is as much a proof of the fact as the very Diagoras to whose atheism he alludes, and whom, as proclaimed by law, he names. Nothing can exceed the derogatory familiarity of tone with which, at all times, he treats the very gods in whom he would believe, and on whom he would depend. After Pericles, indeed, irreligion and atheism become in Greece rampant; nor there alone. Later, it is a like manifestation we witness in Rome on the fall of the republic. And, later still, we have similar characteristics in Europe, especially France, before the outbreak of the revolution. David Hume, who, in his inmost soul thought nothing greater than a named writer —David Hume, in Paris, to his own admiration, sitting radiant, at table, among the foremost bookmen in the whole world then, could not help letting slip his innocent belief that there were no such things as atheists, that he had never met any—how he must have been astounded at the reply—that he must have been very unfortunate so long, for he was at that moment in the midst of seventeen of them!

Whether in Greece or in Rome, then, whether in the

ancient or the modern world, there are epochs of atheism, and always from similar causes. In Greece, as I have said, the popular religion had, among many, ceased to be believed in; and with religious disbelief, political and social corruption went hand in hand. Even Sparta, which was the manly heart of Greece, under such influences, fell away into individual greed and personal selfishness. The spot of earth from which Leonidas and his three hundred marched to their deaths is hardly known now. As it was in Greece, so was it in Rome, in modern Europe, France—religious disbelief, political equivocation, social laxity, portend historical ruin. With all that can be said, however, of irreligion in ancient as well as in modern times, it is still specially to these latter that we turn for our negative; and for the reason that in them only is it first fairly formulated to our present ideas. The same reason leads us to begin with Hume.

David Hume stands out historically as one of the most interesting and influential figures of modern times. In the philosophical reference, he constitutes for the various views a veritable rendezvous, a veritable meeting-place, if only variously, for the start apart again. He is a knot-point, as it were a ganglion in philosophy, *into* which all *converge, from* which all *diverge* into the wide historical radiation that even now is. Scotch philosophy, and French philosophy, and German philosophy, all are in connection with him. Under the teaching especially of John Stuart Mill, he is at this moment English philosophy. From him come Adam Smith, and Ricardo, and whatever their names involve. Hume is the guide of the politician; through the economists he is the spirit of our trade and commerce, and I know not but, in what are called *advanced views*, he lies at this moment very near even the heart of the Church. At all events, he is to the mass of the *enlightened*, the *Auf-*

*geklärt*, their high priest still; his books are their Bible. It is really surprising to how many Hume is, or has been, a passion and a prejudice almost in their very hearts. You will find articles in the Reviews, especially of some years back,—in the *Westminster* perhaps,—that talk with baited breath of Hume as though he were divine. I recollect of one in particular that, engaged in running down George IV., compared that monarchical imposition with sundry celebrities near his own time, and ended with a reference in that sense to Hume, a reference that seemed simply lost in its mocking feeling of an utter contrast. The article, indeed, might have been written by Lord Brougham himself, who, from what we know, alone of all mankind, possibly could have conjoined the worship of Hume with the application of as much in reduction of Gentleman George. Mill, and Mackintosh, and Macaulay, and William Gifford, and Francis Jeffrey, were all intense admirers of Hume; but I question if any one of them would not have felt lost in his wits for a moment at so grotesque and absurd a proposition as the bringing together of two such disparates! I know only one man since Brougham who could have united with him as well in the prostration of the worship as in the loftiness of the parallel. It is possible to find no pair or peer to Lord Brougham here but Thomas Henry Buckle. I do believe he, too, in his big way, might have thought it apt—might have risen into the moral sublime even—indignantly to remark on the mockery and degradation in the comparison of George IV. with Hume!

But, further, of this prejudice or passion for David Hume, it used to be a common experience to find enthusiastic examples of it, not only among the specially learned, but even among those of our men of business who knew what a book was. Sir Daniel Sandford, in certain Dissertations of his, at one time popularly publishing in parts, spoke of "the spotless style of Hume;" and just for the word, many scores of delighted *Aufgeklärters* would have been ready to die for him (Sandford). Style, in fact, was for long, and very much owing to David, the single thought that was present to every man the moment he took a book in hand. Addison's style was, of course, the *ne plus ultra*. But there was the delightful style of Goldsmith, too, and the excellent style of Robertson. There were the stilts of Johnson, and the wood of Adam Smith. There was the easy, lax, complacent style of Fielding, and the pointed style of Smollett. There was the finical style of Blair, and the measured style of Gibbon—but, oh, the style of Hume, "the spotless style of Hume!" And so style was the one consideration: style was the watchword. We read for the style, and it was by the style we judged. We were not at all exigent about the matter, if the form, the style, the words but—as we said, indeed—*flowed*. That *flow* was enough for us, provided, as the master insisted, it were but "smooth" enough, "harmonious" enough, "correct" enough, "perspicuous" enough. It was to enjoy that flow mainly that, business apart, we took up a book at all. Of course we expected some matter in a book, something of information, say. Still, if with that, with something pleasing, that ran along in the telling, there was but style—style and the certainty of the writer's *enlightenment*—we sought for nothing more. We sought for nothing more—that is, as pupils of Hume— than pleasing information, antireligious enlightenment, and literary style. And I should just like to ask Mr. Huxley if, with his will, there should be anything else than that still.

It is in this way we see how much, in the time of Hume, and after him, depended on taste. Almost it seemed as though, did we but cultivate taste, the world would be well. But *what* taste was it that *was* to be cultivated? There are certain formal essays of Hume, there are certain little *propos* of Hume, scattered everywhere, that can leave us no difficulty in that regard. And were there any difficulty, there is Dr. Hugh Blair with his *Lectures on Rhetoric and the Belles Lettres*, to settle it. Dr. Hugh Blair is a kind of henchman to Hume; and he has formally set himself to the business of formally teaching the principles of Hume, and even of formally representing them,—I mean on Taste, leaving his clerical principles completely under shelter. To that latter effect, indeed, Blair can produce a certificate under the hand of even Hume himself. "This city,"[1] meaning Edinburgh, says Hume, "can justly boast of other signal characters, whom learning and piety, taste and devotion, philosophy and faith, joined to the severest morals and most irreproachable conduct, concur to embellish. One in particular, with the same hand by which he turns over the sublime pages of Homer and Virgil, Demosthenes and Cicero, is not ashamed to open with reverence the sacred volumes; and with the same voice by which, from the pulpit, he strikes vice with consternation, he deigns to dictate to his pupils the most useful lessons of rhetoric, poetry, and polite literature." This, as we see, is *prettily* comprehensive; and Hume must have plumed himself on his success in having touched up in it a sufficiently good character for Dr. Blair — even of a Sunday. But still, I doubt not, "polite literature" forms the keynote in the combination to Hume. Polite literature, taste: it is probable that David Hume, superstition apart, thought of nothing more constantly. I do not know, however, that we now-a-days would quite approve of what was to him polite literature, of what

[1] Burton, ii. 470.

to him was taste. In these respects Hume, like most of his contemporaries in truth, was completely French. Polish was the word; human nature in the raw was simply barbarous: beards were remnants from the woods —and even the hair on our heads was a growth. We could not be shaved close enough, and wigs were indispensable; wigs were civilisation—wigs and ruffles! *So*, the words from our lips, from our pens, would be smooth, correct, perspicuous. This was the very *proper* way in which Hume felt. He was, in a literary regard, not what *we* call a Philistine, a man of the outside, who knows prose only, but what the Germans call a *Philister*, a narrowly fastidious, airily-refined formalist. To him Mr. Pope, as a poet, had carried polish to its uttermost limit, and Shakespeare was a barbarian. *Apropos* of Mr. John Home and his tragedy of *Agis* (how many of us know that there was ever any such tragedy in existence; for practically it is very certainly out of existence now?)—of this *Agis*, Hume writes from Ninewells, on the 18th of February 1751: "'Tis very likely to meet with success, and not to deserve it; for the author tells me he is a great admirer of Shakespeare, and never read Racine!" Some three or four years later he writes again: "As you are a lover of letters, I shall inform you of a piece of news, which will be agreeable to you—*We may hope to see good tragedies in the English language*. A young man called Hume (Home was so pronounced then), a clergyman of this country, discovers a very fine genius for that species of composition. Some years ago he wrote a tragedy called *Agis*, which some of the best judges, such as the Duke of Argyle, Sir George Lyttleton, Mr. Pitt, very much approved of. I own, though I could perceive fine strokes in that tragedy, I never could in general bring myself to like it; the author, I thought, had corrupted his taste by the imitation of Shakespeare.

But the same author has composed a new tragedy (*Douglas*); and here he appears a true disciple of Sophocles and Racine. I hope in time he will vindicate the English stage from the reproach of barbarism" (Burton, i. 392). Then, some three years later still, he writes to Adam Smith: "I can now give you the satisfaction of hearing that the play (*Douglas*), though not near so well acted in Covent Garden as in this place, is likely to be very successful. Its great intrinsic merit breaks through all obstacles. When it shall be printed, I am persuaded it will be esteemed the best and, by French critics, the only tragedy of our language." The letter winds up with—"I have just now received a copy of *Douglas* from London; it will instantly be put in the press" (Burton, ii. 17). No doubt, many contradictions and absurdities that have happened in this world may well be wondered at; but surely a greater contradiction and absurdity than this at the hands of Hume—precisely the one man in this world who was well assured that it was perfectly impossible for him (above all, in any such matters) to commit or perpetuate any such thing as a contradiction and absurdity—surely, just this, for all that, is the very greatest contradiction and absurdity that ever was wondered at, or that ever can be wondered at. When we examine the volume, or volumes, called Essays of Hume, we shall find that of the thirty-seven dramatic pieces commonly printed as Shakespeare's, only three ever occur to be referred to there. They are *Pericles*, *Othello*, and *Julius Caesar*; and of these the second is actually mentioned twice. In the essay "Of Tragedy" Hume moralizes in this way: "Had you any intention to move a person extremely by the narration of any event, the best method of increasing its effect would be artfully to delay informing him of it, and first excite his curiosity and impatience before you let him into the secret. This is the artifice practised by Iago in the famous scene of Shakespeare; and every spectator is sensible that Othello's jealousy acquires additional force from his preceding impatience, and that the subordinate passion is here readily transformed into the predominant." In the essay named "Of the Rise and Progress of the Arts and Sciences," again, near its close, remarking on the encouragement given to young authors in their first attempts, as leading in the end to their later mature and perfect ones, Hume declares, "The ignorance of the age alone could have given admission to the *Prince of Tyre;* but 'tis to that we owe 'the Moor.'" Besides four lines quoted from *Julius Caesar* without direct name, that is all that I find of any reference to Shakespeare in the whole of Hume's *Essays*. Of the doubts subsequently thrown on the amount of Shakespeare's authorship in the *Prince of Tyre*, Hume, of course, could know nothing: what alone he had in mind when he wrote, probably, was the line from Dryden, "Shakespeare's own muse his *Pericles* first bore." Inferentially, then, we have, on the part of Hume, so far gratitude to Shakespeare, and the praise of maturity to the *Othello*. Shakespeare, too, must be allowed to be indebted to Hume for a certain amount of approbation in regard to what is called his "famous scene." Hume says "the famous scene of Shakespeare," as though, of all the scenes of Shakespeare, it was *the* "famous" one; and we have thus, and generally, on his part testimony to the great popularity of Shakespeare even in his day. Of course it is utterly impossible to say too much of the scene in question; but I know not that in all we say it is still the praise of "*artfulness*" that we must alone mean. Artfulness there is—on the part of Iago enormous artfulness; and impatience that what is hinted at be got to, must be conceded, as at least one element in that appalling convulsion of all terrific elements that is then the mind, and alone the mind, of the perfectly colossal Othello. What we have before us are not the mere miseries and suspicions in the awakening of a small human thing called jealousy. What we have before us are the throes of a volcano—the confusion, anguish, and bewilderment of a vast nature, a gigantic soul, that in itself was too mighty, too grand and great ever to have a doubt—of one, as it is said, "not easily jealous, but being wrought, perplexed in the extreme!" It is the perplexity of this great nature that we are to see, and not the puling pains of a predominant jealousy only philosophically increased by the artful excitation of a subordinate and preceding impatience. In fact, what we are to wonder at is not art, but the marvellous *nature*, which alone we are to see breathing, living, moving throughout the scene.

As for the four lines from *Julius Caesar*, they occur in section 7 of the *Enquiry concerning the Principles of Morals*: "Few men would envy," says Hume there, "the character which Caesar gives of Cassius—

"He loves no plays,
As thou dost, Antony; he hears no music:
Seldom he smiles; and smiles in such a sort,
As if he mocked himself, and scorned his spirit
That could be moved to smile at anything."

Now, is it not monstrous that any man, especially that any man pretending to education and taste, above all, that any man bearing himself, as Hume always emphatically did, to be the very Aristarchus, the very Simon Pure of critical taste and judgment, should have been so absolutely blind to what lay there, in all its reality of power, immediately before his very eyes? Hume had seen, and we may say, read *Othello*, the very highest height in that kind, it may be, ever by mortal man reached yet; a composition in its very *nature* supernatural; and his whole soul is not seized, and entranced, and wonder-stricken by what he sees! No; very far from that, he is rejoiced that, after the author of *Agis*, we may hope at last to see good tragedies in the English language; we may hope at last to see the English stage vindicated from the reproach of barbarism! we may hope at last to have acquired in the *Douglas* of John Home what he is persuaded will be esteemed the best, and, by the sole true critics, the only tragedy in our language! *Othello* lies before David Hume, and yet *Douglas* is to be the best and only tragedy in our language! How any man could write down even these four lines from the *Julius Caesar*, and yet not know that he had in them a communication from the depths, but should turn from them to refresh his ear (say) with the tinkling, ten-syllabled couplets that give us the usual see-saw of purling streams, and enamelled meads, and warbling choristers, is a mystery to me! Hume knew something even of the Elizabethan drama generally; he speaks of the *Volpone* of Ben Jonson, and of how *Every Man in his Humour* was but a preliminary essay towards it.— " Had *Every Man in his Humour* been rejected," he says, " we had never seen *Volpone* "—and yet in his essay of " Civil Liberty " he writes thus: " The French are the only people, except the Greeks, who have been at once philosophers, poets, orators, historians, painters, architects, sculptors, and musicians: with regard to the stage, they have excelled even the Greeks, who have far excelled the English!" What strange infatuation! Shakespeare is so alone in mere dramatic quality, the breadth and depth of his matchless humanity apart, that there is not in all ancient times, there is not in all modern times, one solitary individual that we can set beside him.—I heard a German once in Paris tell a

professor there, who was vaunting his Corneilles and
Racines, that their entire French literature put into the
scale were all too light perceptibly to lift a Shakespeare
from the spot; and yet, according to Hume, the French
drama far surpasses the Greek, and the Greek far
surpasses the English! What a height of superiority
Hume must have feigned for the Racines and Corneilles
over Shakespeare! All this, however, is of a piece with
the general literary judgment of the period in which
Hume lived, at the same time that Hume must be seen
to constitute in himself the very extract, and summary,
and personification of that judgment. "A hundred
cabinetmakers in London can work a table or a chair
equally well," says Hume, in his essay " Of Eloquence,"
" but no one poet can write verses with such spirit and
elegance as Mr. Pope." Mr. Pope! Mr. Pope is very
often on the lips of David Hume, and seldom absent,
very possibly, from his mind. "England," it seems,
according to him, "must pass through a long gradation
of its Spensers, Johnsons,[1] Wallers, Drydens, before it
arise at an Addison or a Pope!" At Spensers and
Jonsons in this rise, one wonders a little; and one is
pleased to see no Shakespeares or Miltons in it; but
why no Chaucers? He, at least, had the ten-syllabled
clinks! Well, very possibly, if Shakespeare was barbarous to Hume, Chaucer was worse—very possibly he
was to Hume both barbarous and unintelligible. Then
the rise from Spensers, Jonsons, Drydens to Addison!
Why Addison's verse—and it is only verse—is now
absolutely unknown. One thing one wonders at in
Hume is the respect with which, when named, he seems
always to have for Milton. Some time ago at least, I
do not think any true follower of Hume, any genuine
aufgeklärt *epigon* of his, was apt to imitate his master in

[1] By that "Johnson," Hume must mean Ben Jonson.

this. Late genuine Aufgeklärters of the Hume stamp, for the most part, coupled Milton with Shakespeare—in their aversion. Aufgeklärt, as they were, enlightened, and with a perfect hatred in their hearts at that lie, the Bible, they did not relish the subjects and the beliefs of Milton; and they disliked blank verse! These were the men who owned no music in verse, who could not read any verse, unless it murmured on in regular ten-syllabled clinking couplets without a break. Any break, even in these, was a horror to them; and doubly so, therefore, any measure else; for any measure else was but too often broken into pauses, and was without that charming, close-recurrent, heroic clink—was, to the ear, in fact, no better than without clink at all. So it was, in the main, that these men knew only two poets, Pope and Goldsmith; for even Dryden, in his "incorrectness," they said, did not satisfy them. What alone satisfied them was "a good author," whom they could take up (as recommended by Blair) at any interval of leisure, to beguile them by the murmur of the manner into oblivion of the matter, whether in verse or prose. I am picturing a class of men that are not so common now. They were all what is called well-informed men, and had a taste for the reading of books. With individual differences, they were, in literary taste, very much as I say; and they were, in religious enlightenment, or anti-religious enlightenment, still more as I say. After these characteristics, the most notable remaining one was their freedom from prejudice! They had not a prejudice, these men; they were above every one of the prejudices that we, common men, their weaker brothers, truckled to, as in regard to—religion in the first place—but then also in regard to place of birth, or country, or kindred, or the wise saws of our grandmothers about "green Yules," etc. And yet these all opened, these calm, free, dispassionate minds were the least calm, the least free, the least dispassionate — the most narrow and the most narrowly intolerant minds that could well be found in the whole gradation of humanity. Now of these men Hume was the originating prototype. Of course, he was much larger than they. Whatever he was, he was in that, prime, original, sole and single, himself. He was a most taking mass of good nature, too, and was capable of generosity, —generosity with forethought, generosity with prudence.

Kant was surprised that Hume—to him "the fine and gentle Hume"—should have been "a great four-square man." Caulfield, Lord Charlemont, speaks of "the unmeaning features of his visage: his face broad and fat, his mouth wide, and without any other expression than that of imbecility, his eyes vacant and spiritless." In person, too, he was so remarkably huge and corpulent that he says himself, his "companions," when he and they were backing from the imperial presence at the Vienna Court, "were desperately afraid of his falling on them and crushing them"— a perfect Gulliver among the Lilliputians! Then we are to fancy that prodigious corporeity of a man bashful as a boy, rustic-looking, uncouth, as shapeless and awkward in his military uniform as a train-band grocer, speaking his English ridiculously "in the broadest Scotch accent, and his French, if possible, still more laughably," and that, too, in "a creeping voice" that piped a weak falsetto! It will only complete the picture if we fancy such a figure as this of Hume at the opera in Paris,— his "broad unmeaning visage" "usually rising," as it is said, *entre deux jolis minois* (between two piquant female faces),—or better still, if we fancy him, in the Tableau of the Salon of a night, as the sultan between the two sultanas, sorely put to it as to what to say to them, but desperately ejaculating, "There you are, ladies! there you are!" and yet, more desperately thumping his stomach or his knees, for a quarter of an hour continuously, till one of his sultanas jumps up impatiently, muttering, "I did just expect as much—the man is only fit to eat a veal!" It was in this way that his philosophic dignity suffered at Paris; but it is characteristic of the man that he rather liked it; he himself "seemed to be quite pleased," it is said, "with this way of living." He was particularly simple and soft in fact; his own mother used to say of him, "Oor Davie's a fine guid-natured crater, but uncommon wake-minded." It is really extraordinary that, in the midst of this mass of simplicity, goodnature, and, if I may say so, blubber, there should have been found the subtlest analytic intellect that was then, probably, in existence—almost as though it were itself the paradox that it alone loved. That perfect refinement of written speech, too; we might as well expect Daniel Lambert to have the lightest foot in the dance! How it is such refinement, indeed, that he would wish to have before him always! It is a perfect joy for him to say to himself, Virgil and Racine and Mr. Pope! One is almost tempted to think that David Hume would have been contented to pass his life with no more than a schedule before his eyes of all the great classical names in literature. He is quite happy to see them, one after the other, named in his pages. "Of all the great poets," he says, " Virgil and Racine, in my opinion, lie nearest the centre." " 'Tis sufficient to run over Cowley once, but Parnell, after the fiftieth reading, is as fresh as at first." "Seneca abounds with agreeable faults, says Quintilian, *abundat dulcibus vitiis*." "Terence is a modest and bashful beauty." "Each line, each word in Catullus[1] has its merit; and I am never tired with the perusal of him."

[1] It says something for Hume that he could see that perfect *diction* in Catullus.

Ah! how such studies "give a certain elegance of sentiment to which the rest of mankind are strangers!" How they "produce an agreeable melancholy," and how "the emotions which they excite are soft and tender!" Ah! "such a superiority do the pursuits of literature possess above every other occupation, that even he who attains but a mediocrity in them, merits the pre-eminence above those that excel the most in the common and vulgar professions!" Then he laments how far the English are still behind in such politeness and elegance! He even fears that they are "relapsing fast into the deepest stupidity and ignorance" (Burton, ii. 268); "their comic poets, to move them, must have recourse to obscenity; their tragic poets to blood and slaughter." "Elegance and propriety of style have been neglected;" "the first polite prose they have was wrote by a man who is still alive (Dr. Swift)." And what a very limited improvement that was to Hume, we can see from a letter of his to Robertson (Burton, ii. 413). Remonstrating with Robertson in regard to certain usages in style on his part, he says, "I know your affection for *wherewith* proceeds from your partiality to Dean Swift, whom I can often laugh with, whose style I can even approve, but surely can never admire.—Were not the literature of the English still in a somewhat barbarous state, that author's place would not be so high among their classics." Then, again, in the same letter, "But you tell me that Swift does otherwise. To be sure, there is no reply to that; and we must swallow your *hath*, too, upon the same authority. I will see you d——d sooner." It looks odd,—it is the custom of even swearing gentlemen to respect clergymen,—but Hume, for his part, seems to reserve himself in that way just for his clerical friends! In a letter of about the same date to Blair, when praising Robertson for his second historical work, the *Charles V.*, he says, playfully enough and good-naturedly enough, for it concerns the rival whom the public begin to place above himself: "I hope, for a certain reason, which I keep to myself, that he does not intend, in his third work, to go beyond his second, though I am damnably afraid he will!" It is really very odd. I have read all the letters in Burton's two volumes, and I positively do not believe Hume ever to swear in the whole of them, except once to each of these two clergymen! Of course on both occasions it is what is dearest to him, literature, that is concerned, and as we forgive the Englishman who, in his delight, d—d the Swiss Engadine, I suppose, for some such reason, we may also excuse Hume. "A celebrated French author, M. Fontenelle," says Hume, and it is evidently a sweet morsel in his mouth, but why it should be so, it is difficult to see; for Fontenelle is no more than a name now, even to his countrymen, who have forgotten all he ever in such quantities wrote. Hume, however, actually quotes Fontenelle three times oftener than any other French writer; while Molière he only once just names! Of the Italians, he refers to Tasso and Ariosto, but never to Dante. I suppose, however, that, for him, a philosopher by profession, his very greatest blunder is that about Aristotle. "The fame of Cicero flourishes at present," he remarks, "but that of Aristotle is utterly decayed." But Hume's studies, as we saw formerly, were not at all deep in his own business—metaphysic. His ambition went out of that, it would seem, into literature as literature, polite literature. With what unction he allows himself to cry, "At twenty Ovid may be the favourite author; Horace at forty; and perhaps Tacitus at fifty!" But, at any age, when he says, "Virgil and Racine," "Mr. Pope and Lucretius," he puffs his breath, and actually rises two inches higher!

With all that, undoubtedly, and just with all that, and

despite his stupidity of face and mere corpulence of body, Hume was, in heart and soul, a man of even rare sensibility. It is hardly possible to imagine greater pain, greater mortification than his was at the failure of his first literary ventures. He never recovered perfectly from the prostration of his early unsuccess. It was in vain for his publisher Millar, somewhat later, to write him of the sale of his books, of the remarks upon them, of new editions, etc.; it was impossible to console him for that first insult. Even at Paris, in 1764, at the very moment when he seemed to be worshipped as the very greatest of living literary celebrities, he writes (as though from a mind still humiliated and sore under the recollection of unmerited rebuff and disgust), " I have been accustomed to meet with nothing but insults and indignities from my native country, but if it continue so, *ingrata patria, ne ossa quidem habebis:* ungrateful native country mine, thou shalt not even have my bones!" Some little time before that, too, he had said to the same correspondent, " As to the approbation or esteem of those blockheads who call themselves the public, I do most heartily despise it." And yet Hume, in that great carcase of his, like Falstaff, perhaps, was not without humour. " Is not this delicious revenge?" he writes once to a friend; "it brings to my mind the story of the Italian, who, reading that passage of Scripture, 'Vengeance is mine, saith the Lord,' burst forth, 'Ay, to be sure; it is too sweet for any mortal.'" He was once asked, " What has put you into this good humour, Hume?" and answered, " Why, man, I have just had the best thing said to me I ever heard." Hume had been complaining, it seems, that having written so many volumes unreprehended, it was hard and unreasonable that he should be abused and torn to pieces for the matter of a page or two. " You put me in mind," said one of the company, " of an acquaintance of mine, a notary public, who having been condemned to be hanged for forgery, lamented the hardship of his case; that after having written so many thousand inoffensive sheets he should be hanged for one line!" Hume enjoyed jokes even against himself, though not always it would seem. On one occasion, remarking on the moral problem of a certain respectable Edinburgh banker eloping with a considerable sum of money, he was replied to by John Home, "That he could easily account for it from the nature of his studies and the kind of books he read." "What were they?" said Hume. "Boston's *Fourfold State*," rejoined Home, "and Hume's *Essays*." It is said David, for a little, did not quite see the joke.

Kant, as we know, tells some wonderful stories that seem no better than jokes, as that certain mineral waters, already hot, come much slower a-boil than ordinary water, etc. etc.; and we are tempted to fancy that here, too, as usual, Kant has been under the influence of Hume, who records it as a fact that, "Hot mineral waters come not a-boiling sooner than cold water," as also that "Hot iron put into cold water soon cools, but becomes hot again." Kant, however, could not have seen these notes, which are from a memorandum book of Hume's, first published by Burton, I suppose, in 1846. If the θαυμάσια ἀκούσματα are really Aristotle's, one might think that both moderns were vying with their ancient master, who has whole scores of such wonders as that, "In the Tigris there is found a stone such that whoever has it will never be harmed by wild beasts;" or that, "In the Ascanian lake the water itself cleans clothes;" or that "there is a stone like a bean in the Nile, which if dogs see, they do not bark." But it is not certain that the studies of either Kant or Hume had gone so deep in Aristotle! It is to the advantage of Aristotle, too, that, in his case, the stories are, in all probability, spurious; while for Kant and Hume, they are beyond a doubt. Physical science is apt to be "enlightened" now-a-days, and to revere Hume as a priest of "enlightenment;" but, it would seem, Hume himself does not like physical science; he has this memorandum here: "A proof that natural philosophy has no truth in it is, that it has only succeeded in things remote, as the heavenly bodies; or minute, as light!"

It is supposed that Kant was rather proud of his Scottish origin; but it will be difficult to match the satisfaction of Hume at times in the literary, and, consequently to him, general superiority of his countrymen. He opines that we, the Scotch, are "really the people most distinguished for literature in Europe!" (Hear that, Mr. Buckle!) He asks with indignation on one occasion later, Do not the English "treat with hatred our just pretensions to surpass and govern them"? And it is in consequence of the same conceptions that nothing can exceed his exultation, or his assurance, that, in the *Epigoniad* of Wilkie, the Scotch have produced one of the world's great epics. It was in the heroic ten-syllabled tink-a-tink, and it read like Pope's *Homer*. So it was that it took David. He just raved about it, and he actually got seven hundred and fifty copies sold of it; but, with all that he raved about it, and all he did for it, it died. I suppose nobody alive now has ever seen it; but no doubt it was as foolish a sham as ever impotence produced, or honesty believed in. It never served any purpose in existence, but to show, in the case of Hume, on what mere rot-stone a literary taste might be founded. The extravagant language of Hume here, if humiliating for him, is specially instructive for us. The *Epigoniad* is for David "the second epic poem in our language:" "it is certainly a most singular production, full of sublimity and genius, adorned by a noble, harmonious, forcible, and even correct versification:" its author, "relying on his sublime imagination, and his nervous and harmonious expression, has ventured to present to his reader the naked beauties of nature!" And so one sees that it was not in David's eyes that the *Epigoniad* was a mere teased-up, tricked-out counterfeit to be taken to pieces in a day: it was impossible for him to get beyond what for him had "even correct versification"—a harmony quite possibly, so far as he could judge, like that of Mr. Pope! The letters of Hume, in which these things appear, are always, nevertheless, very interesting, and not without hits at times of rare sagacity, as when he asks Gibbon, why he composes in French, and tells him that "America promises a superior stability and duration to the English language;" or when, from his own observations, he expresses it as his opinion of Germany that, "were it united, it would be the greatest power that ever was in the world." One learns, too, from these letters, and, generally, from Burton's Life of him, many earnest things of Hume. He was a warm and active friend, without a vestige of a grudge in him. How generous he was to Robertson, urging him to write, negociating for him with publishers, pushing his books, and praising them to everybody! And as he was to Robertson, so was he to every other possible rival—to Ferguson, to Henry, to Gibbon. To Adam Smith he had been so kind, and good, and helpful, that Smith, like the affectionate, simple creature he was, veritably worshipped Hume. Hume's friends indeed were a host, and not one of them but loved him. He had old mutton and old claret for them, and was very hospitable to them. He was a most zealous and affectionate uncle and brother; and did his best, simply for everybody, related or unrelated. One might, perhaps, except a little in the case of Smollett, whom, as a be-puffed rival, he had evidently viewed with impatience, and spoken somewhat disparagingly of in the character of a historian. That was not quite just. Smollett wrote his History for bread; but he wrote it well; with admirable style in the main, and he broke his constitution in its service. It was when so worn and exhausted that Smollett made an application to Hume, who was at that time a Secretary of State. Hume's answer, that he had spoken for him, but could give him no hope of a consulship, is cool business, and no more. A year later, Smollett, on the eve of starting, as he says, for his "perpetual exile," writes again to Hume, not for himself this time, however, but for a certain neglected, though deserving, Captain Robert Stobo. Hume, on this occasion, writes warmly in return; but what contributes, perhaps, to move him now is the opinion, expressed by Smollett, that he (Hume) is "undoubtedly the best writer of the age." David cannot resist that compliment; it goes to his heart; and he "accepts" that "great partiality" of "good opinion" on the part of Smollett, "as a pledge of his goodwill and friendship!" Edmund Burke is said to have affirmed of Hume, that "in manners he was an easy unaffected man previous to going to Paris; but that he returned a literary coxcomb." There does not appear to have been really any such change in Hume, so far as we are to accept the testimony of his friends at home. It would have been very strange, at the same time, if all his varied circumstances of life had left behind them no traces on his character. Such flatteries as that of Gibbon, who offers to *burn* a work if Hume says so, though he would "make so unlimited a sacrifice to no man in Europe but to Mr. Hume," or that of Smollett, which we have just seen, must have been not rare in the end; and they were precisely the incense that would intoxicate a Hume, if, in such a subject, intoxication were possible at all. But, really, after everything, his experiences at the hands of the public and at those even of his friends, his experiences at Paris, his experiences as a Minister of State, he could not have been any longer the mere floundering youngling in the dark; but must, in thought, speech, and action, have borne himself with the crest and confidence of a grown man that knew his own support in the trainings and trials within him. Hume was too genuine a man to be carried, so to speak, out of himself—to fall away into the insolence and conceit of the shallow. It might have been of him that Dr. Young said: "Himself too much he prizes to be proud." I think we shall see reason, too, when we specially come to that, not to be so very hard and harsh on Hume in the matter of religion. He hated superstition; but no thought lay nearer his heart all his life than the thought of God. He meditated nothing more deeply, more reverently, more anxiously, than the secret source of this great universe. Walking home with his friend Ferguson, one clear and beautiful night, "Oh, Adam!" he cried, looking up, "can any one contemplate the wonders of that firmament, and not believe that there is a God?" On the death of his mother, too, whom he loved always with the most constant affection and the sincerest veneration, a friend found him "in the deepest affliction and in a flood of grief:" to this friend, then taking occasion to suggest certain improving religious reflections, David answered through his tears, "Though I throw out my speculations to entertain the learned and metaphysical, yet, in other things, I do not think so differently from the rest of the world as you imagine."

We are now prepared to advance to our conclusion in these matters, as I shall hope to accomplish in our next lecture.

# GIFFORD LECTURE THE THIRTEENTH.

The Dialogues concerning Natural Religion—Long consideration and repeated revision of them—Their publication, Hume's anxiety for, his friends' difficulties with—Style, Cicero—Words and things, Quintilian—Styles, old and new—The earlier works—The *Treatise*—The *Enquiry*, Rosenkranz—Hume's provision—Locke, Berkeley—Ideas—Connection in them—Applied to the question of a Deity—Of a Particular Providence—Extension of the cause inferred to be proportioned only to that of the given effect—Applied to the cause of the world—Natural theology to Hume—Chrysippus in Plutarch—Greek—The order of argumentation—The ontological—Matter the necessary existence—The cosmological answers that—Infinite contingencies insufficient for one necessity—The teleological — Analogy inapplicable—Hume's own example.

IN passing now to those works of Hume which more especially regard our precise subject, we are naturally led, in so far as literary considerations still influence us, to the Dialogues concerning Natural Religion. At the time of his death, these Dialogues, it seems, had been under their author's hands for no less than twenty-seven years—exactly the judicial nine years three times over! —twenty-seven years, during which they had been the subjects of innumerable revisions, corrections, alterations, emendations, and modifications of all kinds. I daresay we do not doubt now that what was principally concerned in these was the matter of style. "*Stylus est optimus magister eloquentiae*, style is the supreme master of eloquence," a quotation of his own from Quintilian, seems to have been ever present to Hume's mind as his constant guide in writing. So it is we find that these

twenty-seven years have eventuated in effecting for the
Dialogues in question a perfect finish and a polish ultimate. Doubtless, it is in his belief of this that their
author manifests so much anxiety in regard to their
posthumous publication. In his will, he leaves his
manuscripts to the care of Adam Smith, with power to
judge in respect of the whole of them, the Dialogues concerning Natural Religion alone excepted : these Dialogues
are to be published absolutely. It would appear now
that, in Hume's circle, these dispositions of his will
leaked out somehow and became known ; for already
before his death there is question of these Dialogues
between Hume and his friends. His biographer, Burton
(ii. 491), says, " Elliot was opposed to the publication
of this work ; Blair pleaded strongly for its suppression ;
and Smith, who had made up his mind that he would not
edit the work, seems to have desired that the testamentary
injunction laid on him might be revoked." Hume was
not to be baulked. He becomes sensitive on this subject
of his Dialogues: " If I live a few years longer, I shall
publish them myself," he says ; and, after various rejected propositions, losing patience even with Smith, he,
by a codicil to his will, retracts his previous destinations,
and leaves his " manuscripts to the care of Mr. William
Strahan of London," with the express condition that the
Dialogues on Religion shall be " printed and published any
time within two years after his death." But the anxieties
of Hume, even after signature of this codicil, were not
yet at an end. He is found to have returned to it, and
to have tacked on to it a paragraph—to the effect that,
if his Dialogues were not published within two years and
a half after his death, he " ordained" the property to
return to his " nephew David, whose duty in publishing
them, as the last request of his uncle, must be approved
of by all the world." And this David it was who did,

in the end, publish the work; for Strahan, too, had found it prudent to flinch. After so much gingerliness on the part of so many of the dearest friends of Hume, one expects to find something very dreadful in the book. So far, however, as I may judge, Hume, to use the phrase, had written much more dreadfully on the same subject before. The essay Of a Particular Providence in the *Enquiry*, for example, certainly seems to me to have left the Dialogues, relatively, nothing of any importance to add.

What strikes us at once in these is, as I have said, the style. One would think that Hume, in his admiration of Cicero, whether in point of matter or in point of form, had taken Cicero's various dialogues, mostly written in his own academic spirit, into serious study and emulation; and had pleased himself with the idea that, as *he* resorted to the Latin of Cicero, so, in a far distant future, with deaths of nations, perhaps, men would resort to his English—for a like *enlightenment* of opinion, and even purity of prose! For, indeed, it is Cicero that is the model to these writings of Hume, and not Plato; though the simplicity of the latter may seem to have no less place in them than the ineffaceable labour of the former. It is really as Cicero has his Cotta and his Velleius, his Varro and his Atticus, and not as Plato has his Socrates, and his Hippias, and the rest, that Hume has his young man Pamphilus, writing didactically to his young friend Hermippus of what Philo, and Demea, and his guardian, Cleanthes, said to each other in the library of the last. "My youth rendered me a mere auditor of their disputes," says Pamphilus; "and that curiosity, natural to the early season of life, has so deeply imprinted in my memory the whole chain and connection of their arguments, that, I hope, I shall not omit or confound any considerable part of them in the recital." That sentence, in a way, is a specimen of the whole; every word in it has been anxiously chosen; and every clause has received its place from a sufficient trial of the ear. The actual dialogue proceeds altogether as the circumstances suggest: we are in the society of the refined, of the polite, who are perfect in their consideration each of the other, and whose lips drop pearls. All here, indeed, is so very fine that every the least particular of it seems to have been cut by hand,—to have been pared, polished, trimmed,—nay, actually, to have been smoothed and finished off with morsels of window-glass and relays of sand-paper. But it remains a question whether Hume has not precisely made a mistake in what was so very dear to him. Even Lord Brougham, who was the last man, I suppose, that wrote such things, dropped the Hermippus's and the Pamphilus's, and took to the Althorps, the Greys, and others the like around him. It is to be feared that Hume here, and elsewhere indeed, has, in despite of his well-thumbed Quintilian, sinned precisely in the way which Quintilian reprobates—maintaining this, namely, that, insist on words as you may, you must not, in the first place, for all that, neglect *things*, which are as the *nerves* in causes, verbal eloquence being a very good thing, certainly, in the second place, " but only when it comes naturally, and is not affected " (Quintil. viii., Introd. 18). It is to be feared, I say, that Hume has not been sufficiently on his guard in this respect; for all here is all too fine; all here is truly so very fine that it largely fails to impress. They will always, no doubt, maintain their historical place and importance; but I know not that there are many, in these days, who make much case of these Dialogues. The Ciceronian *set* of them—the turns, " Said Cleanthes with a smile," or " Here Philo was a little embarrassed, but Demea broke in upon the discourse, and saved his countenance,"—I know not that any one, since Lord Brougham, has cared for that kind of thing. The names Cleanthes, Philo, Demea, etc., are no longer to our taste. Now-a-days, it is, on the whole, the material contribution, what Quintilian means as the " things," the " nerves," and not the mere verbal form, that is the main desideratum. For that part, indeed, after the more pointed, forceful, pictorial, less intentional and laboured style, to which we have been accustomed by our later writers of all kinds, novelists, historians, critics, publicists, the older, so very smoothly flowing, well-balanced style rather affects us as opaque. We lose ourselves, as it were, in the murmur of it. In Hume, too, the well-bred Philister, in his super-refinement of craze, is too constantly betrayed to us. "The book," he tells us with such a proper air, " carries us, in a manner, into company, and unites the two greatest and purest pleasures of human life, study and society!" One could hope, for Hume's sake, that all would turn out to his wish to leave something classical behind him that, as such, would be cherished by posterity, and ever by the young as standard consulted. But it is time to refer to the " nerves," the matter of the book. Profitably to do this, however, it appears to me necessary that we should first know something of this matter in the form it took in its author's earlier works.

The *Treatise of Human Nature* is a work in three volumes, of which the first and second, when first published in 1739, fell, its author avows, " dead-born from the press." Hume, however, pocketed fifty guineas for these two volumes; and it is pretty certain he would not have pocketed fifty shillings for them had his publisher then been as most publishers now. As for the third volume, we learn that it *was* published, a year later, by another publisher; and that is all! *At present*, I do not think it is ever read. There are some readable passages in it on political subjects; but as for the general text on morals, one reads and reads—at least I read and read, and wonder what it is all about—wonder is there any meaning in that cheerful, endless, prolixity that will not enter one's mind, and give itself a place there! Indeed, if others are as I am, then I fear the second volume may not generally interest more than the third. But with the first volume it is altogether otherwise. That volume, with its Book on the Understanding, is full of interest, and will always command the attention of the philosophical student. Here Hume is really in earnest, and always saying something, unless, perhaps, in the mathematical part, where, indeed, his ideas—crude, callow, wild — fall, on the whole, hopelessly wide. Hume's style is always excellent where he has, as generally in this Book, business before him. Where that is the case — business, reality — Hume discards all unnecessary *ambages;* the softness, looseness of uncertainty disappears, and, in its place, we have the force and the stroke and the feeling of decision. No publicist now could write a better style than the young Hume then. Every word is clear, flexible in shape to the meaning and the mood. I am not sure but that it is a better style than when in his *Essays*, a year or two later, he adds to these qualities—by express effort adds to these qualities, what is to him *elegance;* and I am quite sure that when, some six years later still, judging that his unsuccess in the *Treatise* had, as he says, "proceeded more from the manner than the matter," he "cast the first part of that work anew," and published it as the *Enquiry*—I am quite sure that then, in contradiction of himself, it was not the manner but the matter he improved. The new manner, in fact, strikes as something *dis*improved; as something that has been artificially taken in hand, and only unsuccessfully re-made; as something

externally introduced, and that seems affected. It is
certainly that that has been in the mind of Rosenkranz
when he had to apply the term "*redselige*" to
these essays—dub them, that is, "talkative," or, as we
might say, verbose. In matter, however, the later work
really is an improvement on the earlier, which, with its
ability of any kind, always suggested the idea *young!*
At the same time it is to be said, mainly of Hume's
specially metaphysical efforts, and in his own words to
Francis Hutcheson at the very time he published the
*Treatise*, that his "reasonings will be more useful by
furnishing hints and exciting people's curiosity, than as
containing any principles that will augment the stock of
knowledge." How accurately Hume judged of himself
then, we are only getting more and more clearly to understand now, after a hundred and fifty years! Hume was
original on a very small provision—from without, namely.
In effect, it appears to have been the fashion then to read
beforehand little more than contemporaries. It would go
hard to tell what John Locke had read before he wrote
his Essay. With all his Greek *in the end*, too, Berkeley
seems only to have read Locke *at first*. Now, these two
writers are really library enough for all Hume's metaphysics. Rather we may say that, in that reference, it
was with what he took from Berkeley that Hume started
as his whole stock-in-trade. Not but that, again and
again, we may read Locke as Hume, and Hume as Locke.
Berkeley conceived all to consist of two sorts of spirits,
with what he called ideas between them. To finite
spirits an infinite spirit gave ideas; and these were the
universe. The ideas between the two spirits constituted
the universe. Hume, now, was completely taken by this
thought; he was absorbed into it. And he issued from
this absorption with his own rearrangements. It
appeared to him, in the end, that the *ideas* were the only

facts; that so they were evidence for themselves, but for nothing further. The spirit that gave, the spirit that received: the one as well as the other was a gratuitous hypothesis. The sole evidence that could be alleged for either was the ideas themselves. But that the ideas were, and were together, was no reason for assuming quite another and peculiar entity in which they were; and if we were to start with a presupposition, we might as well start with the ideas at first hand as with only a presupposed presupposition at second hand. No doubt, said Hume, *to* that presupposed presupposition, *to* the infinite Spirit, *to* God, it was what was called *reasoned, from* the ideas, and, specially, from the *connection* of the ideas. But had they, then, this connection, these ideas? This was the question Hume here put to himself; and into that question, pretty well, his whole metaphysic summed itself. It is not necessary that we should enter at full into the resultant theory of cause and effect. One can see at once, from the materials as put, how it would all go. There were the ideas; and they were said to be connected; but what did that mean? They certainly came in conjunctions; but if we examined them the one with the other individually, even as in conjunction, not one of them showed a reason, a tie, that bound it to the other. They *were* associated; no doubt that was the fact; but we knew no more than that. We found the associations to be such and such; and just so we expected them as such and such. Even by the habit of the association, the one member of it suggested the other; and that alone was the connection, that alone was the reason, the sole tie that bound them together. There was no ground for the necessity, under the name of power even, which we feigned or believed to exist in the association, but, as now fully explained, habit, custom. There were certainly two kinds of ideas. There were ideas mediate, and there were ideas immediate; the latter in two distinctions, the former only in one. The double distinction was named of externality and internality. Internal immediate ideas were all our feelings within as at first hand, or directly experienced; while external immediate ideas were what come before us, as the world of objects perceived, of things seen. Both classes of immediate ideas, whether within or without, were naturally to be named *impressions;* while the single class of mediate ideas were, just as commonly regarded, *ideas*— ideas proper. They were but reflections or copies of the impressions. What is, then, as it all lies there now before the eye of Hume, may be pictured as an infinitely minute but sole-existent prism, the light on one side of which shall represent the impressions, as the resultant colours on the other shall be surrogates of the ideas. Ideas and impressions are but the same thing twice. With Locke and Berkeley, therefore, they may be all called *ideas;* and there seems no reason for making a separate entity of the spot, the personality, the mere *locus,* in which they meet. That they meet is the sole fact; nor has the meeting-point any substantiality further. Ideas, and ideas alone, constitute the universe. This is what Hume has made of the stock of thought he received from Berkeley, and he is wholly dominated by it; he implicitly believes in it; it constitutes truth for him— *philosophical* truth, that is; for Hume makes the distinction between *natural* and *philosophical, instinct* and *reason.* As David Hume, his mother's son, he is quite as you or I; sees all things around him just as we do; and has no doubt whatever but that there is *that* in the cause—an agency, an efficacy, a power—which by very nature necessitates the effect; but, as a philosopher, he challenges you and me and all mankind *if* an intellectual reason—an insight, an understanding, not a mere instinct, not a mere blind, unintelligible, mechanical force—*if* an intellectual reason can be given for the necessity of the effect ensuing on the cause, he challenges you and me and all mankind to produce it—" show," he says, " one instance of a cause where we discover the power or operating principle."

We have probably as much of Hume's reasonings before us now as is necessary, and may proceed to apply it to the question of a God. In this he takes full advantage of our demonstrated inability, as he thinks, to give a philosophical reason for the admitted necessity of cause and effect. He thinks he has proved to a certainty *that*, as he says, " the supposition of an efficacy in any of the known qualities of matter is entirely without foundation ; " *that* " all objects which are found to be *constantly conjoined* are *upon that account only* to be regarded as causes and effects ; " *that* " as all objects which are not contrary are susceptible of a constant conjunction, and as no real objects are contrary, it follows that, for aught we can determine by the mere ideas, anything may be the cause or effect of anything ; " " creation, annihilation, motion, reason, volition—all these may arise from one another, or from any other object we can imagine ; " *that* " the necessity of the cause to its effect is but the determination of the mind by custom ; " *that* this necessity, therefore, is something that exists in the mind, and not in the objects ; " *that* " the connection between cause and effect, the tie or energy by which the cause operates its effect, lies merely in ourselves, and is nothing but the determination of the mind from one object to another object acquired by custom." Hume, now, in the light of these conclusions, has as little difficulty in emptying God of all efficacy as any the most common and everyday agent, fire and water, or earth and air; for, as he says, " anything may be cause or effect of anything!" "Thought is in no case any more active (operative) than matter;" "we have no idea of a Being endowed with any power, much less of one endowed with infinite power;" so far as "our idea of that supreme Being is derived from particular impressions, none of which contain any efficacy, there is no such thing in the universe as a cause or productive principle, not even the Deity Himself." If any one will take the trouble to read parts three and four of the first book of the *Treatise*, he will find such phrases as these that I have quoted without difficulty almost upon every page. In these respects the *Enquiry*, if more measured and somewhat less direct, is on the whole fuller and quite as explicit; and our reference in it, apart from the express consideration of causality, is the section Of a Particular Providence. There he puts the argument, which he engages to refute, thus: " From the order of the work you infer that there must have been project and forethought in the workman;" "the argument for a divine existence is derived from the order of nature, the marks of intelligence and design in it;" "this is an argument drawn from effects to causes." Now, that being so, says Hume, "we must proportion the one to the other; we can never be allowed to ascribe to the cause any qualities but what are exactly sufficient to produce the effect." And that is the single fulcrum on which the entire course of the subsequent argumentation rests. That argumentation we must see; but may we not say at once that, on Hume's own premises, any such argumentation must find itself in the air, for he himself has already withdrawn beforehand its single basis of support? The one absolute fulcrum is to be an equality of qualities in the two terms of the relation; the qualities in the cause must be proportional to the qualities in the effect; we must ascribe to the cause only such qualities as are sufficient to account for the qualities in the effect. I daresay we are all directly not a little surprised at this. Qualities! qualities that have efficacy! we think to ourselves — why, Hume has just told us that in the matter of causation we must not think of qualities at all! "The supposition of an efficacy in any of the known qualities of matter is entirely without foundation!" And that means, though he says, "known qualities," *any* qualities, as implied by his own expressions now. That means, too, not "matter" alone, but anything whatever; for he has already said that, so far as qualities are concerned, anything may be the cause of anything. We can only secure to Hume some measure of consistency here, in his demand to proportionate the qualities in the cause to those in the effect, by regarding the qualities as themselves objects, by assuming out of the plurality of qualities in the cause and in the effect one quality in the one, to have always been respectively conjoined with a correspondent quality in the other—a plurality and an assumption, plainly, which will still bring Hume each its own difficulties. But that apart, what of the subsequent argumentation? Now that still depends on the presupposed fulcrum, the intention of which we must see to have been this: In reasoning from the world to God, and so reaching God, we must not proceed to dwell on the idea reached, and so expand it in our imaginations beyond what constituted it *as* reached and *when* reached. Really in that lies the whole subsequent argumentation itself, just as in what was said of proportionate qualities in the cause and the effect, we saw the one fulcrum in support of such argumentation. "The same rule holds," Hume says, "whether the cause assigned be brute unconscious matter or a rational intelligent being: if the cause be known only by the effect, we never ought to assign to it any qualities beyond what are precisely requisite to produce the effect; nor can we, by any rules of just reasoning, return back from the cause and infer other effects from it beyond those by which alone it is known to us." And this here evidently means that if the order in nature entitles us to infer an artificer of great power and great wisdom, it is inadequate to the conclusion of almighty power and almighty wisdom, and may not improbably suggest other very different attributes from those of all-justice and all-goodness. In point of fact, it is precisely of such *propos* on the part of Hume that the whole subsequent argumentation consists. It seems to have been summed up by some writers in this way, that they supposed Hume to say that the world was a "singular effect." That is true, however, only in so far as singular shall be allowed to be equal to particular, so that we are to infer a particular cause from the particular effect that the world is. If Hume uses singular of the world, the word does not mean for him, then, unexampled, unprecedented, incommensurable, transcendent beyond all relation or comparison, but simply, as I have said, and in the sense I have said, *particular*. Even when a doubt is expressed whether it be possible for a cause to be known "*only by* (that is, *only so far as*) its effect, or to be of so singular and particular a nature as to have no parallel and no similarity with any other cause or object that has ever fallen under our observation," what is really meant is precisely what I mean by particular: the effect of the doubt is to a singularity or particularity that would bind down the reasoning to itself alone, which doubt, moreover, is put into the mouth of the opponent to the argument, who, however, is represented to acknowledge in the end that the previous reasonings on the supposition of a singular effect warranting no more than an equally singular cause, "seem at least to merit our attention. There is, I own" (he concludes), "some difficulty how we can ever return from the cause to the effect, and reasoning from our ideas of the former, infer any alteration on the latter or any addition to it;" and these are the very last words of the whole section. To say then that Hume calls the world a "singular" effect, means only, Hume holds the world to be a particular effect, referring only to a proportionately particular cause.

We have now seen as much as I think it was necessary to see of the *Treatise* and the *Enquiry*, and I return to the consideration of the *Dialogues*. They are laid out into twelve parts, but one cannot say that so much externality has any bearing on the internality of the development and exposition of the subject. While the ontological and cosmological arguments, if touched at all, are no more than touched, the teleological argument is, on its side, only most inefficiently and disappointingly scattered, in a mere miscellany of remark, over the whole dozen dialogues, or so-called parts. This argument, though all but exclusively the single subject of consideration, is indeed most confusedly presented to us, and in a mass, simply, of unmethodized objections. Not but that Hume has, in his secret self, all his life dwelt on the question of a God, and gives here now most respectful voice to his estimation of it. "What truth," he says (and these are about his first words)—"what truth so important as this (the Being of a God, namely), which is the ground of all our hopes, the surest foundation of morality, the firmest support of society, and the only principle which ought never to be a moment absent from our thoughts and meditations?" Why, that is a sentence which Lord Gifford himself might have included without a jar among his own so very similar sentences in the body of his Bequest. And in regard to the subject itself, even as *named*, Natural Theology, Hume speaks always not less with the most impressive respect. It is "the saying of an ancient," he remarks, not far from the sentence quoted, "'That students of philosophy ought first to learn Logics, then Ethics, next Physics, last of all the Nature of the Gods.' This science of Natural Theology, according to him, being the most profound and abstruse of any, required the maturest judgment in its students, and none but a mind enriched with all the other sciences can safely be entrusted with it." This position assigned to our subject, Natural Theology, is probably no more than in itself it deserves; but it is not so certain that Hume is correct in his interpretation of the authority he quotes. That authority he names Chrysippus in a certain passage of Plutarch's. Hume now, in his Autobiography, takes credit to himself, as we know, for having recovered, while living with his mother and brother in the country, "the knowledge of the Greek language, which he had too much neglected in his early youth." David's Greek, I fear, might have stood a little more recovery. In his own editions of his books it has mostly a very shabby look; and certainly here, so far as the translation goes, it does not come well to proof. Hume does not give the original, but I have looked up the Greek and transcribed it here (πρῶτον μὲν οὖν δοκεῖ μοι κατὰ τὰ ὀρθῶς ὑπὸ τῶν ἀρχαίων εἰρημένα τρία γένη τῶν τοῦ φιλοσόφου θεωρημάτων εἶναι· τὰ μὲν λογικά, τὰ δὲ ἠθικά, τὰ δὲ φυσικά· τῶν δὲ φυσικῶν ἔσχατον εἶναι τὸν περὶ τῶν θεῶν λόγον). Literally translated, it runs thus: "First then, it seems to me, as was rightly said by the ancients, that there are three kinds of theorizings of the philosopher, Logics, Ethics, Physics, and that of Physics the last part is that concerning the Gods." We have thus three sciences, and in a certain succession, but it is not intimated that they are to be so studied, and still less that what concerns the Gods is a fourth study, and one which is to be taken alone after the other three.

On the contrary, what concerns the Gods is only termed the last part of *physics*. Nay, if the good David had only read further, he would have found the Greek going on to speak of physics, and specially that last part of physics, not as dependent on and following ethics, but as precedent to and conditioning ethics (Plut. *de repug. Stoicorum*, or *de stoic. paradox*, *Opp.* i. p. 1035 A). And it stands to reason that the practical moral should postulate beforehand all that can be theoretically known. The passage, however, gives certainly an eminent place to what concerns the Gods; and Hume, let his Greek be what it may, is to be justified in referring to it in support of the supremacy as a study of Natural Theology. It is not a little to his praise, indeed, that, after Paris, and D'Holbach, and the seventeen atheists who surrounded him,—after these experiences, and no less than twenty-seven years of labour and reflection, he should so unequivocally declare himself.

If, as regards the Dialogues, we take Hume's immethodical miscellany interrogatively in hand, and introduce such order and arrangement into it as shall enable us with confidence and ease to grasp its reasonings, we shall find these susceptible of falling into such a scheme as this:—Taking advantage of expressions of Hume's own, we may say that the arguments in question are, first of all, either *à priori* or *à posteriori*; and then, that while, in the latter class, the teleological stands alone, both the ontological and the cosmological are, by Hume, conjoined in the former. It cannot be said, however, that the cosmological argument is strictly or purely *à priori*; for, in reality, it involves an empirical fulcrum, an empirical basis of support. Nevertheless, as, *any further*, it may be named *abstract* only, the cosmological argument may be regarded as constituting, from its peculiarity, an exact mean between the two other arguments.

Taking the ontological argument first, then, we find that it can hardly be more perfectly and concisely expressed than by Hume himself. In an early memorandum book of his, copied out by Burton, it appears thus: "The idea of infinite perfection *implies* that of actual existence." Of the very idea of God, namely, existence is a necessary complement. Hume, in his Dialogues, quotes Malebranche to the effect that Being simply, Being, existence, is the very nature of God—" His true name is, *He that is*, or in other words, Being without restriction, All Being, the Being infinite and universal." In Part IX., however, where the *à priori* argument is expressly placed, Hume has already dismissed this idea of Malebranche from his mind, and perhaps quite forgotten his own early statement. There his statement now of the ontological argument is that it regards God as the "necessarily existent Being, who carries the reason of His existence in Himself, and who cannot be supposed not to exist without an express contradiction;" but of "this metaphysical reasoning," as he names it, Hume, who characterizes it also as obviously ill-grounded and of "little consequence," will show, he says, the "weakness" and the "fallacy." "I shall begin with observing," he declares, "that there is an evident absurdity in pretending to demonstrate a matter of fact." "Nothing is demonstrable, unless the contrary implies a contradiction. Nothing that is distinctly conceivable implies a contradiction. Whatever we conceive as existent we can also conceive as non-existent. There is no being, therefore, whose non-existence implies a contradiction. Consequently there is no being whose existence is demonstrable. I propose this argument as entirely decisive, and am willing to rest the whole controversy upon it." The reply to this, of course, is, that God, as the Infinite Being, is above and beyond all such reasoning, limited and restricted, as it is, only to what is finite. God, as the Infinite Being implies existence: to deny His existence, negates his very idea, and is a direct self-contradiction. But we have to see more of this later when we come to Kant.

Hume continues, "Why may not the material universe be the necessarily-existent Being?" "It may contain some qualities which would make its non-existence appear as great a contradiction as that twice two is five." "No reason can be assigned why these qualities may not belong to matter; as they are altogether unknown and inconceivable, they can never be proved incompatible with it." I fancy we will all allow the irrefragableness of that reasoning: it would be a hard matter for any of us to prove that whatever is utterly unknown and inconceivable is incompatible with anything whatever! To talk of the inconceivable as a possible fulcrum of proof is surely peculiar to Hume. He says himself that "to establish one hypothesis upon another is building entirely in the air:" to build upon the inconceivable is hardly different or better. But why the material universe may not be the necessarily-existent Being is precisely the cosmological argument which comes now in its turn. Hume himself mentions this argument as "derived from the contingency both of the matter and the form of the world;" nevertheless, as he seems to found his notion of contingency only on Dr. Clarke's representation that "any particle of matter may be *conceived* to be annihilated, and any form may be *conceived* to be altered," we cannot feel sure that what he has got hold of is the quite adequate notion. That notion, however, is simply to the effect that contingent existence, by very name, means what is, what exists, simply as supported, and as unsupported, sinks, falls,—must sink, must fall, and drop out of being. That is the contingent; while *e contrario*, the necessary is the self-supported, the self-subsistent, or the self-existent, the complete in itself and sufficient of itself. By very definition, then, or by very nature, it follows that the former implies the latter. The contingent infers the necessary, the accidental the substantial, by which or in which it is. That simple notion, now, is the fulcrum of the cosmological argument; yet, simple as it is, Hume, on the whole, does not quite seem at home in it. While it is his single purpose in Part IX., for example, to dispute, controvert, and refute it; he had already passed his own deep imprimatur upon it in the second part, when he said, " nothing exists without a cause; and the original cause of this universe we call God : Whoever scruples this fundamental truth, deserves every punishment," etc. But as much as this, it is not difficult to see, constitutes the whole cosmological argument, for it simply refers what is contingent, what is insufficient of itself to God, to that cause which is alone necessary, alone ultimate and final in itself. In Part IX., however, somewhat contradictorily, Hume argues against this reasoning in some such strain as follows:—

He starts, as already referred to, with the question, "Why may not the material universe be the necessarily-existent Being?" and when he is answered by the cosmological argument which rests on the necessity of a regress through a whole possible chain of contingent causes back to a single absolute cause, he rejoins: " In such a chain, each part is caused by that which preceded it, and causes that which succeeds it—where, then, is the difficulty? But the whole, you say, wants a cause. I answer—this is sufficiently explained in explaining the cause of the parts—add to this, that in tracing an eternal succession of objects, it seems absurd to ask for a general cause or first author." That, as one sees, is not profound argumentation; and it will be sufficient to remark for the present that no multiplication of parts will make a whole potent if each part is impotent. You will hardly reach a valid conclusion where your every step is invalid. Will you ever fill one full with nothing but empties, or put together a single significant figure with a million millions of ciphers? It will be in vain to extract one necessity out of a whole infinitude of contingencies. Nor is it at all possible for such infinitude of contingencies to be even conceivable of reason. If each link of the chain hangs on another, the whole will *hang*, and only *hang* even in eternity, unsupported, like some stark serpent—unless you find a hook for it. Add weakness to weakness, in any quantity, you will never make strength; if you totter already, the tottering against you of ever so many totterers will only floor you.

But, on the whole, Hume may be said only to mention, and not seriously to meet, what are to him the *à priori* arguments. On the *à posteriori* argument it is that he puts forth all his strength. Even here, however, his strength is but a sceptical play; for it is at least as a sincere *Deist* that he takes up his position before the curtain in the end. Nevertheless, when one considers how Adam Smith and the rest were glad to escape any responsibility here, our curiosity is roused, and we would fain see for ourselves the terrible argumentation that had so frightened them. Allowing for the ninth part, which we have just seen, for the first and last parts as only the one introductory and the other concluding, and for two other parts which are taken up with little more than tirades on the evils of existence, there remain seven parts in which the strict teleological argument is alone considered. As I have said, the conduct of the dialogue is so miscellaneous in these parts that, for one's ease, even for one's intelligence, one is glad to turn to some principle of arrangement. Now what is considered here is God on one side and man on the other, with the analogy of design between them; and it is with such scheme we may conceive Hume to open. Accordingly, the omnipotence of God, even as in supposition, is described at great length on the one side, as the impotence of man at equal length on the other, and it is asked, Can there be any analogy between them? Man's *sentiments* are "calculated for promoting the activity and preserving the existence" of such a finite being; his *ideas*, "derived from the senses, are confusedly (confessedly?) false and illusive;" and as these "compose the whole furniture of the human understanding," how can such *materials* be "in any respect similar in the human and in the divine intelligence"? Are we not "guilty of the grossest and most narrow partiality, when we make ourselves the model of the whole universe"? Of course, the reply to such objections is obvious. In arguing from design we simply use the reason which is our very power and our very selves; and in which, with whatever accidents, we have all history and all science to support and encourage our trust. Nor do we desire in the smallest degree to push our reason beyond what bounds it can itself realize. We may presume that reply sufficient for Hume himself even on his own principles; for he will be found to grant us the right of speculation and inquiry to any extent, and into any region which the desire of knowledge, the love of truth, or even mere human curiosity may suggest. To as much as that, indeed, his own example would warrant, not only liberty, but one might even say, licence. We turn now, then, to the third consideration which we have indicated here, the middle that lies between the two extremes of God on the one side and man on the other, the argument from design itself. That we shall see again. Meantime, I may seem, so far, to have been only cursory

—to have remarked little, and to have quoted less. But I have really given all that there is in Hume as regards either the ontological or the cosmological argument; and, perhaps in other respects, I shall be found in the end even to have hit the truth of the position which conditions Hume's whole way of looking.

# GIFFORD LECTURE THE FOURTEENTH.

The teleological argument--Two moments—First, the alleged necessity of thought—It has itself no end—So matter enough—Thought itself only a part, limited, imperfect, and in want of explanation—Thought as thought common to us all, Grote, Hume, Erigena, Heraclitus—The sole necessity—Second, the analogy—The supreme cause not situated as other causes—Other principles, vegetation, generation—The world an animal—The Empedoclean expedient—The effect only warrants great power, not Almighty power—Evil—Free opinion—Hume's friends — Epicurus's dilemma — Superstition results — Four suggestions—No pain—Special volitions—Greater strength—Extremes banished from the world—Creation on general principles—Erasmus Darwin—Mr. Froude, Carlyle—Finitude as such, externality as such—Antithesis—Charles V.—Abdalrahman III. — Septimius Severus — Johnson — *Per contra*—Wordsworth, Gibbon, Hume—Work, Carlyle—The trades—Comparison — Self-contradiction — Identity—Hegel — "As regards Protoplasm"—The Hindoos—Burton on cause—Sir John Herschel — Brown, Dugald Stewart — Spinoza — Erdmann — Notions and things, Erigena—Rabelais—Form and matter—Hume in conclusion.

HUME'S discussion, in his Dialogues, of the teleological argument, the argument from design, random as it runs, requires, in the first place, such arrangement as shall extend to us the ease of intelligence which is so necessary here—such arrangement as has been already referred to. The entire scattered discussion, then, we reduce to, and consider in, the following order, an order suggested by the single argument itself, which this discussion would overthrow. That single argument is this. The design which is admitted to exist in the world infers—by the necessity of thought, according to the principle of analogy—the existence also, or coexistence, of a designer. Now, here it is only the *inference* that is denied, and not the design it founds on: the design itself is admitted to exist. But that inference can be opposed only in one or other of its two moments. Either its first moment (A), the alleged necessity of thought, or its second moment (B), the alleged analogy, is the subject of denial and dispute. On the first head, (A) it is first (1) argued, that, granting the necessity of thought, it is not completed or concluded by the inference, but continues to be equally valid further. If a material world, or universe of objects, be such as to require a cause for the arrangement in it; not less will a mental world, or universe of ideas, to which as cause the arrangement has only been transferred, require for itself a cause—a cause of its own. God Himself, that is, if offered as cause for the one world, would constitute in Himself just such other mental world, and would equally stand in need of just such another cause. The explanation is only shifted one step back, thinks Hume; but why stop at the first remove? "If we stop, and go no farther," he says, "why go so far?" "Why not stop at the *material* world?" "If the material world rests upon a similar ideal world, this ideal world must rest upon some other; and so on, without end." "That the parts of the material world fall into order of themselves" is "as intelligible as that the ideas of the Supreme Being fall into order of themselves." And that being so, "we really assert the material world to be God; and the sooner we arrive at that Divine Being, so much the better." These are Hume's own words; and it is really sufficient reply, so far, to say: There is no principle in matter itself to explain the design it exhibits; only a Designer can explain that. So far we believe our argument valid;

and so far we challenge disproof. To ask a second question is not to dispose of the first. (2) A second objection to the necessity of thought is: That it does not apply: we are but a part—our thought is but the part of a part; and it is in vain to apply a part in explanation of the whole. Nay, (3) in the third place, our thought, even as in us, requires an explanation; at the same time that, (4) in the fourth place, it is so limited and imperfect that we can place no dependence upon it. I think, however, it will be plain that these are cavils, so far, rather than arguments. It is not true that thought can be characterized as only a part in reference to the whole; nor do we apply it, or wish to apply it, otherwise than as it justifies itself. It may, in individuals, and at times, err indeed; but it is caricature to throw it out of count, because, as Hume says, "we never find two persons who think exactly alike, nor does the same person think exactly alike at any two different periods of time." Mr. Grote borrows these words, and relying upon them, cannot help exclaiming in perfect astonishment, "Can it really be necessary to repeat that the reason of one man differs most materially from that of another?" To which, in the very intensity of its shallow conviction, I reply, "Can it really be necessary to repeat that the reason of one man *does not* differ most materially from that of another; but, on the contrary, the reason of one man is essentially identical with that of another?" Here, in fact, Grote has not only forgot Hume, but Hume has forgot himself; asserting, as he does elsewhere, that "there is a great uniformity among men in all nations and ages, and human nature remains still the same." That is to the effect that there is but one reason, which is the truth and the cosmical fact, though we had to go further back for it than the *intellectus* of Scotus Erigena, or even the λόγος ξυνός of Heraclitus. Thought is the one generality, the one universality, the one general solvent, the one universal solvent, which nothing may resist. "And what wonder!" says Scotus Erigena, "what wonder if the notion of things which the human mind possesses, concreated with itself, is found to be the true substance of the things themselves of which it is the notion?" The universal, as the universal, is its own principle and its own basis of support. Thought, even as thought, accounts for its own self, if not in the finitude of man, then in the infinitude of God. There it is the one ἀνάγκη, the sole necessity, that that could not not-be!

And with this we may suppose sufficiently met and discussed all that Hume has objected to the necessity of thought. Matter cannot account for its own arrangement; a part *may* apply to the whole, if that part is thought; which again, as in the race, is not incomplete and partial, but, as primal entity, as sole and primal ἀνάγκη is, with God, the reason for itself. In fact, in the whole of the relative reasoning, there is not one reasonable word why man may not *think* the design which is as undeniable in his own self as everywhere around him.

The second object of the attack of Hume is (B) the analogy. Man, as a thinking being, recognises in nature such adjustment of means to ends as is in perfect analogy with what he knows to be the product and result of design in the experiences and proceedings of his natural life in common with his fellows upon earth. Now, Hume's objections here may be arranged according as they seem to concern more especially the cause, or more especially the effect.

In the first place, on the first head, he intimates that the cause is not placed as it is placed in the other cases to which we are accustomed. In these, we have usually experience of both terms. If we infer the step of a man from a footprint in the sand, say, the cause is already known to us from a great number of other effects, and the inference, consequently, does not really depend on the single experience. And then, in point of fact, what we see in matter may depend on principles of its own. We cannot say that motion, or other arrangement, is not native to it: we have never assisted at the origination of worlds; we have not, as elsewhere, any custom, any to and fro of effect to cause, or of cause to effect; we have no experience of the divine. Nay, in the second place, if the design be not original to matter, it may be due to other principles than to the principle of thought, as to vegetation, for example, or to generation. We really do see such principles operative in matter. There *is* motion in it; not one particle of matter, probably, ever is at rest. Then we do see vegetation and generation both spontaneously operative. The world may be as a tree that sheds its seed; or, as an animal that lays its eggs. A comet may be a seed—a germ, which, ripened from system to system, may itself become further in the inane a system of its own. And so it may have been with this our world, which, in point of fact, exhibits the traces of innumerable changes before it settled down into the orderly arrangement of the present. Indeed, in the third place, the whole world may be just one animal —an animal with a body, and an animal with a soul. This was an idea familiar to the ancients, who could not conceive, as we do, of souls purely as such—of souls without a body. The world has really much more analogy with an organized body than with a mechanical contrivance. " A continual circulation of matter in it produces no disorder; a continual waste in every part is incessantly repaired; the closest sympathy is perceived throughout the entire system; and each part or member, in performing its proper offices, operates both to its own preservation and to that of the whole." Or, in the fourth place, returning to the idea of innate material arrangement, Hume has recourse to what I may call the Empedoclean expedient. We may remember Empedocles to have feigned the present orderly organic world to be due to the survival of the fittest, in this way, that the earth gave birth at first to all possible organisms, so to speak, pêle mêle. There were bull-headed men, and olive-leaved vines; but in that heterogeneous form they could not survive. What could alone survive was the homogeneous: there were no stable or persistent forms till only, at long and last, when what was homogeneous took its turn. It is absolutely the like suggestion that Hume now makes for matter. The particles of matter are all in motion; and they have been in motion in the infinitude of time. But, so, they must have undergone an infinitude of revolution—an infinitude of vicissitude and change; or, the complexions they formed must have passed through infinite successions until, I suppose, as mathematically demonstrable, the present complexion emerged, which, being orderly, is more or less permanent. And hence the appearance of design.

On the second head, as concerns the effect, Hume maintains, in the first place, that the world as an effect only warrants the inference to *great*, but not to *perfect* power; while, in the second place, the existence of evil in the world puts us in no very hopeful situation as regards the moral attributes of the Deity. It was here, perhaps, that Hume's friends, one and all of them, took fright at these Dialogues, and positively fled from any connection with the publication of them. Here, indeed, Hume is so very free in his objections and suggestions to the Almighty, that almost in these more audacious days they may shock even us. Hume himself, possibly, had a consciousness of something of this; for these words of his at the end of the work read to us at once as an apology and a defence, quite as though it was to these very friends he spoke. "It is contrary to common sense," he says, "to entertain apprehensions or terrors upon account of any opinion whatsoever, or to imagine that we run any risk hereafter by the freest use of our reason." And surely it will appear to every one that, as we are sent here to think, as to think is our vocation, we shall hardly be held responsible for the expression of our thought, provided only that both thought and expression are serious and in earnest. Hume, doubtless, must have considered himself sufficiently within these bounds, and must have been both vexed and surprised at the scruples of Smith and the rest, especially in view of his having, by express name, mentioned and met the very apprehension under which, it could not but seem, they laboured. Nevertheless, it is quite certain that Hume, in all conscience, is not at any loss for boldness here. It is scarcely credible that the evils of this life were ever more glaringly painted, or the emendations of them ever more unmisgivingly proposed. But, after all, it comes, on the one head, to the usual tirades about misery and pain, and, on the other, to the customary remonstrances with the Deity for failure on His part either in will or in power. "Epicurus's old questions are yet unanswered," says Hume, "Is God willing to prevent evil, but not able? then is He impotent. Is He able, but not willing? then is He malevolent. Is He both able and willing? whence then is evil?" "Why is there any misery at all in the world?" And human life is human misery within and without. It is in the sense of his own imbecility to meet these evils, which come upon him from a power above him, that man grovels to that power, and would fain conciliate to himself its good-will by flatteries and gifts. Hume has four suggestions of remedy in these respects. Like Alfonzo of Castile, had he been present, in the beginning of creation, at the counsels of the Almighty, some few things, he thinks, would have been better and more orderly arranged. He would, in the first place, have made all living creatures incapable of pain: they should have been impelled to the necessary action only by the diminution of pleasure. In the second place, he would have remedied all impending inconveniences by particular volitions: he would have given the dram to his brain that would have made Caligula a Trajan, and he would have taken care to save the Roman republic by swelling, a foot or two, the sea that threatened Caesar. Thirdly, he would have endowed all animals with a much more satisfactory stock of strength. And fourthly, he would have given an amended constitution to the universe at large: the wind should never be allowed to become a storm, the heat a drought, or the rain a deluge. "So many ills in the universe," says Hume, "and these ills, so far as human understanding can be permitted to judge, might so easily have been remedied." Why, all is owing simply to "excess or defect" in consequence of "inaccurate workmanship!" These are but a word or two from the pages of the original; but they may serve to suggest the never-doubting openness of Hume in the story he tells and the propositions he makes. Perhaps of all these propositions, the most surprising, as on the part of Hume, is that of a particular providence that would be on its guard always, and take all necessary precautions against accidental inconveniences, such as a Caligula or a Caesar. It is certain that in another work (*Enquiry*, vii. 1), after long consideration and careful revision, too, Hume holds it to argue "more wisdom in the Deity" to contrive a creation on general principles from the first, and "more power" to delegate authority to these principles "than to operate everything by His own immediate volition." Erasmus Darwin, too, will be found to express himself strongly to the same effect. But it would seem that others later incline to Hume's later view, and would like a God that prevents rain at harvest, and would cut in pieces beforehand the murderers of a Princesse de Lamballe. Mr. Froude, in his *Life of Carlyle* (ii. 260), writes: "I once said to him (Carlyle) not long before his death, that I could only believe in a God who *did* something. With a cry of pain, which I shall never forget, he (Carlyle) said, 'He does nothing!'" One may be permitted to express one's surprise here at such crude doctrine under whatever or whichever name. It is altogether to mistake the very possibility of a universe to hang a God over it, like a big man in the air, to overlook, and interfere, and see that our children do not burn themselves. There is the fang of the serpent and the claw of the tiger—I suppose these gentlemen would have God draw both; and we must not be incommoded in summer with midges on the Clyde. A creation is, by the very terms of it, the finite as the finite, externality as externality. Now, finitude as finitude, externality as externality, brings with it its own conditions just as surely as the triangle involves its own necessity of two right angles, or parallel lines, theirs never to meet. To have light you must put up with shade, and to have warmth you must submit to cold; you cannot have a right hand unless you have a left. All in the phenomenon is contradiction, and it cannot be otherwise if there is to be a phenomenon at all. The same stress that would take us to the sun baulks for ever our approach to it. If you draw close to me, I embrace you as my friend; but if you draw closer still, I repel you as my enemy. Were attraction

S

alone in this universe, things would be reduced to a mathematical point; and were repulsion all, there would be nothing but a blank. There cannot be union without disunion, nor this without that. These and other such-like contrarieties, infinitely, are the terms on which you have a finite universe, and alone the terms on which you possibly can have it. If you will be, then you must be in the stress of adversatives. The single necessity of the necessity to be is its own opposite—contingency. And what does that amount to? It amounts to this: Destroy evil and you are straightway *felo de se*, you have committed suicide; or, what is the same thing, abolish contingency, which is at once the sole source of evil and the secret of the universe—abolish contingency and you abolish existence, you destroy what it is to exist. When all is considered, I fancy we have but little business to set so much store by all these "racking pains," which Hume enumerates, of "gouts, gravels, megrims, toothaches, rheumatisms." The toothache alone is certainly bad enough; but I do not see that we have any right to make such a noise about toothache, were it only for our friends, the dentists! I suppose Hume here would say, as he literally does say, " If you feel not human misery yourself, I congratulate you on so happy a singularity. Others, seemingly the most prosperous, have not been ashamed to vent their complaints in the most melancholy strains. Let us attend to the great, the fortunate Emperor Charles V., when, tired with human grandeur, he resigned all his extensive dominions into the hands of his son. In the last harangue which he made on that memorable occasion, he publicly avowed, *that the greatest prosperities which he had ever enjoyed had been mixed with so many adversities that he might truly say he had never enjoyed any satisfaction or contentment.* But did the retired life, in which he sought for shelter, afford him any greater happiness? If we may credit his son's account, his repentance commenced the very day of his resignation." Gibbon, too, would seem to join his master here, and only repeat the story. He transcribes "an authentic memorial which was found in the closet of the deceased caliph," the great and glorious Abdalrahman III.: " I have now reigned above fifty years in victory or peace; beloved by my subjects, dreaded by my enemies, and respected by my allies. Riches and honours, power and pleasure, have waited on my call; nor does any earthly blessing appear to have been wanting to my felicity. In this situation I have diligently numbered the days of pure and genuine happiness which have fallen to my lot: they amount to fourteen. O man, place not thy confidence in this present world!" Nor are these all. Septimius Severus was certainly one of the most successful Roman emperors, and even he sighs out, " Omnia fui et nihil expedit!"

These are what are called the lessons of history; and Samuel Johnson, in his *Seyhed, Emperor of Ethiopia*, and his *Rasselas, Prince of Abyssinia*, drives them well home. But it seems to me that if these mighty sovereigns had been content with health, and not perpetually longed for honey, " the mere sweetness in the mouth "—if they had counted the days in which they were absorbed in human action, which is alone The Good, they might have found their " fourteen days " sufficient to eke out the full sum of their miseries. I, for my part, when tired of all these tears and groans, and this litany of woes, am apt to cry, Let me get out of this eternal whine, which, the brave Wordsworth tells us—

" Erebus disdains;
Calm pleasures there abide—majestic pains!"

Gibbon is honest enough, in the end, to speak in this same sense. " If I may speak of myself," he owns, " *my* happy hours have far exceeded, and far exceed, the scanty numbers of the caliph of Spain." And even Hume, in the person of Cleanthes, who certainly speaks then as Hume the man, is obliged to say, "I can observe something like what you mention of misery in some others; but, I confess, I feel little or nothing of it in myself, and hope that it is not so common as you represent it." And it is not so common! The misery that is, is largely on the part of people who have nothing to do. He who has work mostly never whines; though I admit that sometimes Thomas Carlyle unduly whines over his. Consider the population as a whole! Surely the bulk of it cannot be called unhappy! The carpenter, the joiner, or other such under his paper cap, his feet in dry shavings, a roof overhead, and his body warm, spends the day to the whistle of his plane and the jokes of his comrades. The shoemakers, how they prattle in a semicircle to the tap-tap of their hammers, as the tailors on their shop boards to the snore of their needles! If you walk out some country road, say at four o'clock of the dawn, you will find the weaver in his village, pipe in cheek, pacing cheerfully before his door, and snuffing up the morning air with uncommon satisfaction. Just so, and so early, in a street at Paris, I have seen the chiffonier, chief of the proletariate, him, too, with his pipe in the morning air, quite gaily whip up, with his hook, over his shoulder, into the basket on his back, some rag from the dust-heap before him. At their work they are all quite cheerful— workman of the proletariate or workman of the trade. What a strong, healthy fellow is the navigator on the line, picking with pick, or shovelling with shovel, always effectively, but always, too, with a stroke so tempered and temperate, that it never moves a pulse! There are spells of danger and difficulty to some; but if a man in a state of nature is a hunter or fisher, and so, as it were, at play, most of the employments of the population have still the interest of nature in them, and many of them its romance. It does not belong to riches, nor to honours, nor to titles to give happiness. Happiness is in the mind; and it will come more readily into the mind of a rag-picker than into the mind of a lord at a horse race. Happiness, at least the possibility of happiness, so far as it depends on the mind, is, there may be reason to think, not so unequally meted to the most part of mankind, and for the most part of their lives. People are apt to mistake what, in regard to happiness, another can do for us. "She's gi'en me meat, she's gi'en me claes," says the "young thing" in the song; and that is about the total or the staple, the main and marrow, of what can be done for us from the outside by anybody. If any of us will look to the substance of our lives, we shall find that that staple contains all the realities and strict matters of fact either possible or necessary for our existence here. Whatever drawback may appear, we shall find that it comes from our own trick of comparison. If we would only look to ourselves and our own means of enjoyment, we would be contented enough; but, unfortunately, we must look to others; and that is the shadow that falls for us with a blight on all we have, let it be in itself what bounty soever. I have been accustomed to think that a capable handicraftman who comes home of an evening, pleased with his day's work, to a tidy wife and tidy children, and a cosy meal, by a cosy fire, in his room and kitchen, or two rooms and kitchen, with a chest of drawers and an eight-day clock, and a book to read, need not envy any prince in the land, and still less any lord at a racecourse,—were it not for comparison. Nature is there ready at any moment to spread all her beauty before his eyes, all her wealth of hill, and dale, and champaign. There is music in the air; there is glory in the heavens; and every tiniest shell upon the shore has its own charm of a loveliness of form that was never due to sexual selection. Of course, I do not deny that sex enters in some way there too; but I am quite sure that never mollusc female loved mollusc male, or mollusc male, mollusc female, for the beauty of his or her shell, in the same way as a woman may fall in love with a man for the beauty of his coat, or he with her for the beauty of her habit. I suppose it never occurred to Mr. Darwin that the tailor might have something to do with sexual selection, at least so far as *some* anthropoids are concerned!

So it is on the whole, then, with the question of evil in the world. In short, let Hume harangue as he may, in his Parts X. and XI. of these Dialogues, piling pain upon pain, and black upon black, human life remains for all that, even to the individual, a possession that pleases. Human life, of course, is but another name for work; but that is not a fault; that is rather a laud; for the subject has the right of satisfaction in his work, and, according to philosophy, it is the quality of the universe to realize no less.

Then as regards the complaints or objections about design itself, several of which it has been enough only to exhibit, it really does not appear in the end that Hume in his ninety pages of the Dialogues has added any strength to the argument of his nine pages of the Essays. That argument generally rested on the single idea that, in ascending from the world to God, we have no right to descend from God to the world with more than we took up. The inference to the cause lies in the effect alone; or the argument from design gives the cause as equal to the effect, and we have no warrant to make it more. Of course, the reply is, just *look* to the effect. Can such effect as that, the universe namely, not warrant every supremacy that we name God? But what dominates Hume are his own peculiar ideas—the very peculiar ideas which he has himself come to in regard to cause and effect. In the first place, Hume, as he says himself (Burton, i. 97), "never asserted so absurd a proposition as that anything might arise without a cause;" still he did assert that, as regards any insight of reason, we have no warrant for connecting the effect with its cause, but our habitual experience of their customary conjunction; and that, consequently, so far as we see, anything may be the cause of anything ("the falling of a pebble may, for aught we know, extinguish the sun, or the wish of a man control the planets in their orbits"). That, no doubt, is Hume's contention so far; for these are his own words. In the second place, however, Hume, in his reasoning against design, simply contradicts himself, and unconsciously implies what principle of connection really exists between the cause and its effect. That is, he will allow in the cause which we infer, only such qualities as are contained in the effect. Say it is $x$ we find in the effect, then, says Hume, it is just that $x$, and no more than that $x$, that you are to find in the cause.

It is really very odd; but Hume is never for a brief instant aware that in that he has answered his own cardinal, crucial, and climacteric question. The immediate nexus, the express bond, the very tie, which he challenged you, and me, and the whole world to produce, he actually at that very moment produces himself, holds up in his hand even, openly shows, expressly names, and emphatically insists upon! That tie is identity. When Hume will allow no qualities in the cause but those that are found in the effect, that amounts to saying the $x$ that virtually is the cause is the same $x$ that virtually is the effect. And what is that but the assertion of a relation of identity between the cause and the effect? Now, indeed, that as much as that is manifest, explicit, and express, you will be astonished how often it has been said—almost in terms, if unconsciously—positively by every philosophical writer you can possibly take up. Nevertheless, so far as I know, it was only first consciously said in Europe by George William Frederick Hegel, and first consciously repeated in English, and for the first time of all as consciously directed to the problem of Hume, in the little essay named *As Regards Protoplasm*. And I suppose we owe it all only to the Hindoos. Hegel was well acquainted with the writings of Colebrooke, and in his pages he found the Hindoos to say: "The nature of cause and effect is the same:" "a piece of cloth does not essentially differ from the yarn of which it is wove; barley, not rice or peas, grows out of barley-corns; rice is in the husk before it is peeled; milk is in the udder before it is drawn; and milk, not water, is taken to make curds," etc. etc. For I might quote much more from the same author to the same effect. And, in reality, is it not precisely the same import when Hume says, and when it is commonly said, like effects prove like causes? The wonder is that Hume, in spite of this natural conviction, existent in all of us, of "a more real and intimate connection between the cause and its effect than habitual sequence," to use the words of Sir John Herschel—the wonder is that Hume brought over so many to his way of thinking, that to him was sport only. Burton in his Life of Hume (i. 82), as late as 1846, has these astounding words in a note: "This refers to the notion, which now may be termed obsolete, at least in philosophy, of an inherent power in the cause to produce the effect!" There is no power in the cause to produce the effect—there was no power in God to create the world! Hume could be consistent in his *theories*, whatever his *conviction*. Burton himself points out that it was only consistency led Hume to "the annihilation of the notion of power," as well in the immaterial as in the material world (i. 275). "As we cannot find in physical causes any power to produce their effect, so when a man moves his arm to strike, we have no notion of any *power* being exercised!" There is such a thing as compression, surely; and it is a force, a power: if we compress a full sponge we drive the water out; and this compression involves in the body compressing, here the hand, a certain strain or stress, which we feel, and which, consequently, we indentify with power. Prick a blown bladder, and the fluent air, under pressure of the elastic membrane (as of a hand), escapes. There is a rationale in the whole process. Surely there is a reason why a garter supports a stocking, or a button fastens a coat! To say that the hammer that knocks a nail in to the head can be reasonably regarded, not as a force, but only as an antecedent! It is really wonderful how Brown, and so many others, could accommodate themselves to such extravagant ideas. Why, even Dugald Stewart, despite his master Reid, must go over to Hume, and very glaringly stultify himself. Burton quotes (89) him to the effect that Hume's theory "lays the axe to the very root from which Spinozism springs," and this because "physical causes and effects are known to us merely as *antecedents* and *consequents*," and "the word *necessity* is altogether unmeaning." Stewart thus intimates that Spinoza's system is, as he says further, "nothing better than a rope of sand," and for the single reason that it is founded on the necessity of cause and effect. Now-a-days, in the words of Erdmann (ii. 49), the opinion of philosophy is, that Spinoza "knows not any actual causal connection, but only conditionedness in consequence of a Vorbegriff," a pre-notion; and surely that is absolutely Hume on both of his sides, at once as negative of causal power and as affirmative, instead of the relation only of antecedent and consequent. Dugald Stewart has not been quite happy here. And, in general, it was sufficiently simple on his part, after all that Reid had said, seriously to adopt, almost as a philosophical truism, what Hume himself, who proposed it, had really only sceptically played with, certainly at last, and for little else than the sceptical conclusion that, viewing our limited faculties in that and other respects, it is in vain to expect "ever to satisfy ourselves concerning any determinations which we may form with regard to the origin of worlds, and the situation of nature from and to eternity" (*Enquiry*, xii., iii.). It was on the eve of his death, and in allusion to his own health, that Hume himself said, "A wind, though it extinguishes a candle, blows up a fire;" and that contains the whole case. So much power has this effect: so much more, that. It is decidedly in contradiction of his own propos that "anything may be the cause or the effect of anything," that Hume, against design, asserts it as a fact that thought follows matter, but not matter thought: "we see every day," he says, "the latter arise from the former, never the former from the latter;" "ideas are copied from real objects, and are ectypal, not archetypal." That is a vast matter that is involved, a question of questions, and goes far beyond the ideas of Hume. In the meantime, we may be reminded of Erigena's ruling, that it is the notion that is the original of things, and not things of the notion. Of course that is not the doctrine we are accustomed to of late. What we hear now, rather, is much rotund oratory about the physical basis, that there is an original matter. Well, perhaps there is, though I cannot say it has ever been held up to me or anybody else. But this I can say, that, hold up an original matter when you may, you will never hold it up without an original form; which original form, too, is the original first and furrow of the whole business. I get it from Rabelais even that, *forma mutata, mutatur substantia*, the substance itself is dependent on its form. It is the form, namely, and not the matter, that is the valuable element. Why, we know that even land, which, surely, is material enough, has its value in its *form*, the form which the hand of labour has impressed upon it. At all events, we are evidently under no necessity to conclude with Hume or his belated followers, that matter is, in any respect, earlier than form. But, in fact, as is customary with Hume, it would seem in the end that he has been only at play. The very Philo in the Dialogues who makes all the sceptical objections, comes out at last with such an acknowledgment as this: "The beauty and fitness of final causes strike us with such irresistible force that all objections appear (what I believe they really are) mere cavils and sophisms . . . the Atheist, I assert, is only nominally so, and can never possibly be in earnest." And Cleanthes had already said before him: "The order and arrangement of nature, the curious adjustment of final causes, the plain use and intention of every part and organ,—all these bespeak in the clearest language an intelligent cause or author. The heavens and the earth join in the same testimony: the whole chorus of nature raises one hymn to the praises of its Creator." Would you not say here that David had suddenly grown poetic? Even speaking in his own name and character, he is quite as explicit, and not much less eloquent. "The whole frame of nature," he says in his *Nat. Hist. of Religion*, "bespeaks an intelligent author— one single being who bestowed existence and order on this vast machine, and adjusted all its parts, according to one regular plan or connected system." "Look out for a people entirely void of religion," he concludes, and "if you find them at all, be assured that they are but few degrees removed from brutes!"

In fact, there can be no doubt that it was only superstition Hume hated, and not religion: "You, Cleanthes, are sensible that, notwithstanding the freedom of my conversation, and my love of singular arguments, no one has a deeper sense of religion impressed on his mind." And when this is said for Philo, it is said for Hume himself. His reverence of true religion, indeed, he has not been slow, again and again in his own person, to express. There was nothing covert in the man: much obloquy he might easily have escaped by simple silence, or by speech more guarded; but he was a big man, and he spoke free: he scorned to be seen of men otherwise than with face to the front. He was loyal in his nature, generous. Almost as much as in his own, he rejoiced in the fame that competed with it. Letters were his only weakness. When he ought to have been "poring over Voet and Vinnius, Cicero and Virgil were the authors he was secretly devouring." He was still a boy when he wrote, "I could not quit my pretensions in learning but with my last breath." It is a satisfaction to know that, naturally, such zeal and devotion cannot be without their reward. Hume is a peer only to the highest of his people, to Scott, and Burns, and Carlyle. His best works will endure. For perspicuity and ease of flow, his history is as yet unsurpassed in the language. Its "careless, inimitable beauties of style" made Gibbon, when he read, lay down the book in despair. One cannot but hope that its author, wherever he is, has the satisfaction of reflecting that not a single Scoticism more remains for the weeding. Though so eager to be an Englishman in his writing, what a Scot of the Scots he was in his speech, looks, person, and the pride of his heart! He was simply so common Scotch, indeed, that, when the servant girl breathlessly broke in upon him to say, Somebody had chalked St. David Street upon his house, he could only ejaculate, "Never mind, lassie, many a better man has been made a saint of before!" And if we cannot discover much point in the phrase, we can all recognise how like it is to the great, stout, simple sort of Dandy Dinmont Scotchman that he was! And I hope now you will go and look at that house, the old-fashioned one at the corner of St. Andrew Square, that, in St. David Street, stood alone at first. Hume himself had it built, and he lived in it the last five or six years of his life. Go and look at it, and, as you look, believe that, whatever his shortcomings and deficiencies, it is still with love, and respect, and gratitude that we ought to think always and at any time of the "good David."

# GIFFORD LECTURE THE FIFTEENTH.

Transition, Hume to Kant—Effect of Kant on natural theology—
The centre of Kant's thought—Hume led to this—Causal
necessity—That necessity objective—Still in matters of fact—
Relations of ideas—Hume on one side, Kant on the other, of
the dilemma—Hume quite as Reid, on natural necessity—
But what the explanation to intellectual insight — Synthetic
addition—Analytic implication—Change—Kant's explanation
is, There are *à priori* syntheses native to the mind—The whole
Kantian machinery in a sentence—Time and space—The twelve
categories and the three ideas — A toy house — A peculiar
magic lantern—A psychology—A metaphysic—Analysis of
the syllogism for the ideas—Simple apprehension missed—An
idea—The ideal—The teleological proof.

THERE can be no straighter or nearer transition than from David Hume to Immanuel Kant. The latter does himself claim the former as his direct and immediate predecessor. This is true, too, not only in the reference, generally, to philosophy, but in that, particularly, to the special subject presently before us. Perhaps not in English, but certainly in translations, Kant (very evidently) is perfectly familiar with Hume's main doctrines in regard to the existence of a God; nor do his own results differ much from those of his forerunner, otherwise than in weight and authority. It was principally because of these results, namely, that the *Alleszermalmender*, the everything-to-pieces-pounding Kant, received his title. Kant's countrymen, unlike their neighbours, the French, are not reputed to be particularly versatile; nevertheless it seems certain that, not long after reading his three chapters on the impossibility of each of the three proofs for the existence of God, most of them who were at least of the same guild with Kant, suddenly ceased, or were even ashamed, to mention the subject. For them the whole science of Natural Theology had, in a moment, passed silently into the limbo of the lost. And so it is that it is of greater importance for us to put to scrutiny the relative views of Kant than even those of Hume. At all to effect this with any satisfaction, however, requires that we should preliminarily know at least the spirit of the system from which these views naturally take origin. That may sound ominous; but I do not know that what is concerned may not be put simply and intelligibly enough.

The centre of Kant is, to say so, the *à priori*—those elements of knowledge, those elements of the ordinary perception of things, that are native and proper to the mind itself, even before, or independently and in anticipation of, any actual experience of these things. That is what is meant by pure reason. Our minds shall be at birth, not, as with Locke, so many *tabulae rasae*, so many mere blank sheets for things to write themselves into, so many empty bags or sacks for things to occupy; but, on the contrary, they shall be, already, beforehand, rich quarries, filled, as it were, with the needful handles and cues of all things. What led Kant to this was Hume. Hume, as we know, took the cause as one thing and the effect as another; and holding them out so, apart, challenged any man to show any principle of union between them. Without experience of the fact, it is impossible to tell that gunpowder will explode, or a loadstone attract. Consequently it is only by the custom of experience that we know the effect of the one on iron, or the consequence on the other of a spark. Kant was deeply impressed by such examples and the general challenge of Hume. He admits himself that he brooded over the problem concerned for "at least twelve years;" and of that brooding I think it is possible to detect traces as early as the year 1766, or fifteen years before the publication of his *Kritik of Pure Reason*. What, in the end, prevented Kant from agreeing with Hume in his rationale custom, was perception of the nature of the necessity which was involved in the problem. That necessity Kant saw was not a subjective, but an objective necessity. The necessity by which, when I think A, I cannot help thinking also B, C, D; or when I think 1, then also 2, 3, 4—that necessity, as being only one of habitual association in me, is a subjective necessity. But, when I think of an eclipse of the sun as following the intervention of the moon, I do not think of a necessity subjective, a necessity for no other reason than habitual association of my own. On the contrary, I think of a necessity objective, of a necessity that exists independently of me, and without any reference to me or my feelings in any way. In short, I know that the moon, coming between me and the light, casts its shadow upon me, and must cast its shadow upon me; which is an event and an entire resultant necessity, utterly independent of me, and of any way in which I may be pleased to regard it. In the same way, when I see a bridge overthrown by a river in flood, it is impossible for me to think the necessity involved to proceed from custom—to depend on the influence of custom. I cannot think that necessity a subjective necessity in me, but, on the contrary, an objective necessity in the facts themselves. This, then, is what occurred to Kant in face of the contention of Hume. But then he was obliged to admit at the same time that Hume was right in pointing out that all examples of causality were but matters of fact, in regard to which, as matters of fact, we know that they *are*, or are as they are, but not that they *must be*. Cork floats, coal burns, etc. etc.; we know the fact or the event; but we did not know the fact or the event in any case until we tried it; then and then only we knew that the propositions, cork floats, coal burns, were true; but we did not know, and we know not now, that they must be true. Cork might not float, coal might not burn: we see no necessity for cork to float or for coal to burn. But all examples of causality are just such facts as the matters of fact that cork floats or coal burns; and yet the proposition concerned in every one single example of causality is as necessary, as apodictically necessary, as any proposition dependent on what are called relations of ideas, and which, accordingly, is intuitively *known* to carry or involve the necessity in question. It was precisely this peculiarity that struck both Hume and Kant. Both saw that all examples of causality were only known by experience; and both saw that they all brought with them a suggestion of necessity. Both, then, further, immediately asked how was this? for both knew that experience was only competent to say this thing or that thing *is* so, not this thing or that thing *must be* so. But both, putting the same question, in the same circumstances, and with the same knowledge, came to an answer, each, which was the contradictory of the other. Hume said, As it is an affair of experience alone, it can be no affair of necessity. On the contrary, said Kant, As it is an affair of necessity, it can be no affair of experience *alone*. Hume had no objection whatever to the necessity in question being regarded by us as a natural necessity. He did himself regard it as a natural necessity. Neither did he object to the reference of it, as a natural necessity, to instinct. On the contrary, as a natural necessity, he did himself so refer it. And Reid, consequently, in the case, might

T

have profitably spared himself much gratuitous excitement. All that Hume insisted on was that, putting aside instinct and asking for an explanation, an intelligible reason, of the necessity we felt in the inference from the effect to the cause, or from the cause to the effect, he, for his part, could discover or detect none but the constant previous conjunction, nevertheless, that he was quite open to the better explanation and the better reason which another man, abler than himself, or more fortunate than himself, might have succeeded to obtain. That for Hume is his whole relative position; and that for Hume is the whole relative position that remained the same till the end of his life. Not, indeed, till some five years after the death of Hume was there heard in reply to his challenge the answer of Kant. That answer, as we have seen (Hume, of the two elements concerned, having chosen *experience* for his fulcrum of support), took up its position *ex adverso* on the ground left to it of *necessity;* where the first movement of Kant was to point to this necessity as objective, not subjective, and withal as in its matter synthetic and not analytic. When you say, Every change has its cause, you feel that you say something that is as absolutely and necessarily true as when you say that a straight line between any two points is the shortest line. You feel also that you say something that is true, not for the same reason that it is true that All windows let in light, or that all peninsulas are almost islands. It is the very meaning of a window that it lets in light, and it is the very meaning of a peninsula that it is almost an island. These last are analytic propositions, for what you allege of the notion, the window, or the peninsula, is involved in the very notion itself—in what it directly means, namely. But the notion cause is not in the same way involved in the notion change. A change has a cause; but a change is something on its own account, and does not mean a cause in the same way that a window means admission of light or a peninsula approach to an island. The proposition of change, therefore, is no mere analytic or tautological proposition; and its truth, while as certain as that of any such, is as certain also as the truth of any non-tautological or synthetic proposition, an example of which was the truth that, between any two points the straight line is the shortest. Straight is not short; a straight line may be anything but short. The two things are perfectly different; nevertheless the proposition brings them together into a certain identity. So two angles called right are not the same as the three angles of any triangle; just as the two squares on the two sides are not the square on the third side of a certain triangle, and the parallelism of two lines is not their continuation into infinity. Nevertheless, the two notions respectively concerned in these three examples *can* be brought, however different they are each by itself, into a certain common identity. That now is the case with the proposition of causality, That every effect, or change, has its cause. The change is not the cause, and the cause is not the change. I may show you a lobster black, and, leaving the room, may return with it red. You see the change, then—a thing quite by itself; but, even if there be a cause, as you will certainly surmise, you do not yet know it. I may have plunged the lobster in a bath of acids, or I may have boiled it, or I may have done some quite other unknown something to it. In a word, the change is one thing and the cause another, and to bring them together into a relation of identity is an act of synthesis, an act that involves a synthetic process or a synthetic proposition.

Here now, then, we stand before Kant's problem. We may even assume Hume himself to be present, and to admit now that his answer was no answer to the necessity concerned, and that he is eager to hear Kant's answer.

Well, says Kant, I have got to find the source of a *necessary* truth that is not analytic, but synthetic, and that at the same time is not due to experience. What not due to experience means has been already explained. There is no particular causation, no particular example of causality that is not due to experience. The indentation of a cushion by a bullet is an example of causality, but it is known only by experience. So it is with all other examples, as the drifting of a ship in a stream, or the warming of a stone by the sun. All such things are just *seen;* they are facts of experience—they are affairs of perception. Nay, the universal of causality, the universal proposition of causality, does itself involve eyesight, does itself involve experience, does itself involve perception. Every change has its cause: it is impossible that we should have any knowledge of what a change is, unless we had experience of it. There are certainly intellectual changes, changes in the process of the understanding, changes in the process of reason, changes in belief, etc.; but any change, even any such change, is always known to us as an alteration, substantially, of consciousness, and an alteration of consciousness is just another word for experience. We *can* have an experience only when we have an alteration of consciousness: an experience is that—an alteration of consciousness. Even the universal of causation, then, every change has its cause, is a proposition that involves experience, is a proposition *à posteriori*—at least so far. But so far only. Otherwise, it is, in its vital force and virtue, a proposition *à priori*. That is the contention of Kant. A change *must* have a cause. This is a truth which, though synthetic, is also apodictic — necessary and universal namely.

But, says Kant, *necessity* and *universality* are "sure criteria of *à priori* cognition." The proposition of causality, therefore, must be, as said, at least in its *virtue*, of an *à priori* place. The synthesis it implies, the synthesis of the two notions, of *change* on the one hand and of *cause* on the other, is not a result of experience, is not a result *à posteriori;* for, in that case, the truth of it would not be apodictic, would not be universal and necessary, but a truth only as for the moment *found*,—a truth only probable, then, and a mere matter of fact.

The question for Kant, now, then, plainly is—How is this? How *can* the causal proposition be possibly *à priori?* How can its validity be a product of mind, and wholly independent of any experience *à posteriori?* It was this single question that led Kant in the end to his whole cumbrous, extraordinary, and incredible system. Simply to explain causality by innate principles of reason, native and original to the mind itself, Kant invented that whole prodigious machinery—merely for such explanation, Kant forced into the geometrical point of his own consciousness the infinitude of space and the infinitude of time, but grasped, throughout their whole infinitude, together both, by the tree of the categories, the enchanted and enchanting Yggdrasil, whose branches reduced the infinitude in which they spread into the very finite net of the schematism that held to our ears, and eyes, and fingers, nostrils, and palate their own sensations always. That was the monstrous birth to which Kant came at last after his fifteen years' sitting on the simple egg of Hume. And, all the time, we may fancy our Indian fellow-Aryans laughing at them both, and pointing, as seen, to nothing but identity!

That, then, was the course of Kant. The proposition of causality was to be placed within us, and made into a principle of the very mind. Strangely, somehow, the first step in this operation was the internalization of space and time. We may think, if we like, space a boundless vacancy without us, and time a mighty throb which is ever at once throughout the whole of the boundlessness; but we are only all wrong—we are only the victims of our own magical privilege and miraculous endowment. Newton himself might see "the floor of heaven thick-studded with patines of bright gold," and, in rapture of his awe, murmur to himself, " Since every particle of space is *always*, and every indivisible moment of time is *everywhere*, assuredly the Fabricator and Lord of all things will not be *never* and *nowhere ;* " but he, too, would only deceive himself and stray. The truth is that all these unfathomable depths and illimitable spheres, with all their rich contents, are not without at all, are not in a heaven at all, but only in me. That, as I say, was the first step of Kant. Time and space were only forms of *general* sense really within, which still, at touch upon *particular* (*special*) sense, were thrown as mirages *apparently* without. Then all these touches of special sense—sensations namely—received into these mirages, were wrought up into perceptions, objects—the things of this external universe—and associated into rule and system by the twelve *categories* and the three *ideas.* To arrive at such results as these was a work of a long brooding—a fabrication of multiform piecing on the part of Kant. There, however, in the end it is, and all for no other purpose than to demonstrate that the necessity, which we all feel and know to lie in the connection of the cause with its effect, was not, as Hume mischievously argued, subjective and *à posteriori*, but, on the contrary, objective and *à priori.* To effect this, time and space were both retracted within us, and, while there, were acted upon in the peculiar succession of their parts by the function of judgment, named antecedent and consequent, till there issued, in category and schema, the full formed *à priori* machinery of cause and effect. Fancy it all—it is like a toy-house, which children take piecemeal out of a box, and put together in play. There are first the two long and broad bits, time and space, folded together, but expansible, at once an indivisible centre and a boundless circumference. These are then fitted into another piece which is called *productive imagination*—productive, as so contrived, that is, that, motive *of* and *in* them, it can expand the sort of collapsed wings, the long and broad bits of time and space, at the same time that it receives into them the sensations which, come from where they may, gave it the hint. But, after all, our toy materials do not seem, on the whole, so very well adapted for the construction of a house. Let us conceive rather that we put them together into a magic lantern—a peculiar, a very peculiar magic lantern. Well, the pieces called time and space shall be the slides, and imagination shall be the containing case of the lantern. Now, to complete this case, with the slides in it, we make an addition from within to its top. And the piece which we fix there is the most curious piece of all. It is a sort of cone—in shape, let us say, something like an extinguisher, but as suited to a magic lantern, a very magical extinguisher. The little round top of the extinguisher, now itself at top of the whole case, shall be the reuniting unity and unit, as it were, of the entire contrivance. Fancy it the light— the illuminating light of the whole arrangement—or fancy it rather—this little round top—the eye that sees into the whole internality of the machine, and, as it were, throws its light down into it. Well, suppose this extinguisher in place as the lantern's top: the eye, that is placed there—a mere bead—throws its glance, its light, down into the sensations, the figures on the slides, or, what is the same thing, receives the light from them up into itself—*but through lenses.* Round the circle at the wide end of the extinguisher, as fixed in place, there are twelve lenses; and these are the *categories!* They are the functions of judgment, which is the hollow of the extinguisher, and collects and concentrates all into the eye, or the mere bead at top. This eye, this bead at top, is the Pure, Primary, or Original Apperception, or, as it is otherwise called, the Synthetic Unity of Apperception. Now, then, that is the way Kant fancies us to perceive this universe—that is the Transcendental Deduction of the Categories. Sensations, we know not how, but feigned to be due to things in themselves,—which things in themselves, whether as *what*, or as *where*, are utterly unknown to us, —sensations, I say, so due, appear, we know not how, on the slides of time and space in the material of the imagination; and, carried up thence by judgment, through its twelve lenses of the categories, into the unity of apperception, into the unity of self-consciousness, suddenly stand around us infinite, as this whole huge formed, ruled, and regulated universe! To that grand finale and consummation, at least, Kant only adds three toy pieces further. They are what he calls the Ideas: the Psychological Idea, the Cosmological Idea, and the Theological Idea. They may be conceived—the three ideas may be conceived as three lenses, beyond the twelve categorical lenses, and fitted into apperception, the eye (I), or bead itself at top. There now, that is the whole, and that is not, after all, merely a deduction, the transcendental deduction—that is really the way in which Kant *creates*—positively *makes* for us this actual universe! Kant, to construct this universe, takes absolutely nothing *from* the universe, but all from himself. The sensations are his, the imagination is his, the categories are his, the Ideas are his, the Apperception is his—what is not his are alone, the unknown ghosts, the Things-in-themselves; and for them he has not a vestige of a warrant: to his own self they are, by his own self, admitted and declared to be absolutely unknown ciphers, nonentities, which nowhere exist, or which exist, as idle suppositions, only in name. Nor is Kant less autocratic in his further and final step as concerns the Ideas—God, that is, and our own soul, are *only* ideas, without correspondent objects or with correspondent objects only feigned—again ciphers, then!—Not but that, in a practical point of view, we may grant them to be— what?—postulates! And that only means that, as moral beings, we are under a necessity to—*suppose* them!

In the prosecution now of our own immediate theme, it is to these three Ideas that we must turn at last for a more particular relative inquiry; and, in the first place, we are to understand that their function is not *constitutive*, but only *regulative*. This world, as we have seen, according to Kant, is only an affair of our own subjective affections, and our own subjective actions. Our own categories, acting on our own forms of space and time, and, through these, on our own sensations, bring all into our own unity; and all so far is *constitutive*. It is the Ideas now come in as *regulative*; for their action has no part in the *formation* of things. To the formation of things there go only the sensations; the spectra of space and time that receive the sensations; and the categories which, under the unity of apperception, order, arrange, condense, and work up the sensations into the perceived objects of the perceived world in time and space around us. All these materials, then, are *constitutive*; and, in discussing them, we have realised a Psychology, a Philosophy of the Mind, an *Erkenntnisstheorie*. It has been left for the *Ideas*, especially in their moral reference, to realize a Metaphysic, the interests of which are God, the Soul, and the Freedom of the Will; but all here is only *regulative*. If the categories give unity to things, the Ideas, on their side, give only a further degree of unity to the categories themselves, and are of no objective, but only of a subjective or internal application for the mind's own wants of order, arrangement, simplification, and unity. So far as they seem to effect more than that indeed, they are the sources of a necessary, natural, and unavoidable *illusion*. But we shall understand better what Kant means by that, if we refer, in the first place, to the peculiar means and method by which he describes himself to attain to these ideas.

It was by a fortunate recollection of the doctrine of Judgment in ordinary school logic that Kant, after long meditation, examination, and trial, came to his categories in correspondence with the subordinate three moments under each of the four common and familiar rubrics of Quantity, Quality, Relation, and Modality. It was only by an extension, as it were, of this hint, that Kant passed from the section of the Judgment to the section of the Syllogism; and from its three forms, Categorical, Hypothetical, and Disjunctive, extricated, at least to his own satisfaction, the three Ideas. The three parts of Logic, as we know, are Simple Apprehension, Judgment, and Reason; and it is probable that it was only by an unfortunate oversight that Kant, in passing forward, from Judgment (that first occurred to him) to Reason (or the Syllogism) did not also pass backward to Simple Apprehension. If he had done so, he would have made good for himself the whole of Logic. As Reason seemed to yield and legalize the Ideas, Judgment the Categories; so from Simple Apprehension he might have drawn an equal warrant and authority for his Pure Perceptions, Time and Space. In that case the system would have had the security of an entire science as basis of support, and not the insecurity and unsatisfactoriness, instead, of a mere incomplete and partial reference. What immediately concerns us here, however, is only the Ideas. How Kant came to his pure perceptions, his Æsthetic namely, such as at is, or how, in his Analytic, he extricated from Judgment his Categories—all that we leave on one side or behind us; we have only to do with his Dialectic, and with the manner in which he there extricates from the three forms of the Syllogism his three Ideas. This, as only technical and dry, I pass. Kant, in fact, may be said here to *extricate* only what he wants, and that, too, only by the most arbitrary and absurd *torture* for his own convenience.

It is sufficient for us to understand at present that all such proceedings here of Kant are but respective preliminaries to the destruction of the proofs for the existence of God. And that they can be nothing else appears at once from the very definition of an Idea. "I understand by Idea," says Kant, "a necessary notion of reason, to which there can be given no congruent object in the senses." That is, though necessary notions of reason, the Ideas are objectively *transcendent*, or they suggest objects that have no existence in *rerum natura*; and are only subjectively *transcendental*—there, namely, with a calculated function of regulating the interests of the understanding into ultimate unity and totality: they apply a collective, systematizing, or synthesizing condition to experience as a whole; but are no more than mental principles only illusively conceived respectively to denote things. Now, what is called the Transcendental Ideal, or God, can be no exception here; and we see at once that, with such presupposition, Kant can only declare all the proofs which have so long occupied us, merely null and void. In this declaration, however, he extends to us a scaffolding of demonstration, which we have now to see. We begin, as has been our way hitherto, with the teleological argument, the proof from design. And here Kant is at once profuse in compliments. He acknowledges that "This world opens to us an immeasurable spectacle of variety, order, designfulness, and beauty;" that the consequent proof "has its existence from the study of nature, and takes thence ever new force; that, accordingly, "it raises our belief in a Supreme Originator up to an irresistible conviction;" and that "it would be wholly in vain to seek to withdraw anything from its credit"—"one glance at the miracle of nature and the majesty of the All rescues reason from every too nice doubt, as from a dream." He had already praised Plato in the same reference, for that he, namely, "rightly saw in nature clear proofs of its origin from thoughts—plant, animal, the order of nature, and the plan of the whole cogently evincing that they were only possible on thoughts;" and he goes on to exalt these ideas of the philosopher above the copy-like procedure of the physicist. In fact, in Kant's latest Kritik, that of Judgment, the lapse of years has only led to the recording, if possible, of still stronger expressions of consideration and respect for the argument from design. One would like to say, indeed, that Kant is only half-hearted in his opposition to it, and that he is only reluctantly compelled to the course he takes by the exigencies of his system. It is the very essence of that system, namely, that all objects are only formations of our own within us, to which design, consequently, as a modifying principle from without or from elsewhere, would seem not possibly to apply. Kant, *on his system*, can allow no source for the notion of design, but a subjective harmony, or a subjective "*as if*," a subjective maxim, that is within us, and not from without at all.

Hence one is apt to be persuaded that, but for his system, Kant would be himself the most enthusiastic of Teleologists. And so, consequently, only to his system is it to be imputed that he brings himself to make the objections which we have now to consider. It is from the standing-ground of the system that he remarks first, The question here can be readily brought to a conclusive answer at once, "For how can an experience ever be given, which were adequate to an Idea? Why, an Idea, (that is one of Kant's peculiar three), is just that that has nothing empirical correspondent to it." And we are reminded of his earlier words: "The Ideas (his Ideas, namely) are sophistications of reason's own: the wisest of men, even when aware and on their guard against it, can never wholly escape the illusion which is always there to mislead and mock them." "A necessary all-sufficient God is a Transcendental Idea so boundlessly great, so exaltedly high above everything empirical, that never in all experience were it possible to beat up matter for the filling of it." To seek in the conditioned for the unconditioned were in vain and without a clue; for were it found, even as found, it would be itself conditioned. And it is only in the conditioned that any such search can be made; for the instrument of such a search is but the principle of cause and effect, a principle which is only in place in possible experience, and has no application beyond it. If even, then, what is sought is out from, and beyond, the conditioned, where find a possible bridge to it, since for all and any new acquisition of knowledge, we can only be referred to experience and the law of cause and effect that obtains in it?

It is here now that Kant, passing from his own peculiar views, enunciates that respect for the teleological argument which we have already seen; but, even while commending it and bidding it God-speed, he cannot

accept its claims — the claims of this argument to apodictic certainty: he will attemper and rebate these claims to a proper moderation and modesty. And he begins by stating it in what to him are its four moments :—
1. "Everywhere in the world there are to be found evident signs of an arrangement on express intention, carried out with great wisdom and in a whole of indescribable variety of content, as well as of unlimited magnitude of extent. 2. This designful order is quite adventitious to the things of this world, and attaches to them only extrinsically. 3. There exists, therefore, a wise and high being who, as an intelligence, must, with free-will, be cause of this world. 4. The unity of this cause may be inferred from the unity of the world in the reciprocal relation of its parts." That must be admitted, on the part of Kant, to be only fair statement. He then alludes to the possibility of a cavil in respect of natural reason when, from the mere analogy of certain productions of nature with those of man, in houses, ships, watches, etc., we conclude to just such a causality for these natural productions as well—a will and understanding, namely; thus referring to another cause the inner possibility of "free-working nature itself (which perhaps alone gives possibility to all art and even reason)." With no more than allusion here, and just the hint that, peradventure, his own transcendental critique might, if it chose, subvert all such reasoning, he passes on to his own formal objections to the main argument itself. And of these the first concerns form as distinguished from matter. The argument from design, that is, founds wholly on the form, which seems to have been added to, or infused into things, so that, as means to ends, they appear to constitute a single series and system of final causes. That form, these connections seem independent of the things themselves: they (the latter) themselves,

and in themselves, are not such that were they not members, native members, essential members of the series and system we see, they would contradict themselves. The contrivance, that is, the designfulness, does not depend on things in their matter, but only in their form. What agency seems to be operative, consequently, is that of an architect or artificer who may be responsible for the form, the adaptation, which has been given to things, but not as Creator from whom derives the very matter of which they, individually, or as a whole, consist. His second objection, Kant's second objection in the same reference, is that, if you infer a cause from an effect, the former must be proportioned to the latter: you cannot impute to the cause more than the effect allows you. Now, who knows this world in its infinitude? So far as the knowledge of any of us goes, the world is still limited, and we have no authority from our own knowledge of the world to infer the omnipotent, omniscient, all-sufficient God whom we are all forward to assert. Accordingly, says Kant, it is not from the teleological argument that we come to that immeasurable conclusion of a God, but from an unconscious and involuntary shift —resort on our part to the cosmological and ontological arguments. The design of the teleological argument is the contingency of the cosmological argument; and it is from that contingency we infer the existence of an absolutely necessary being, while it is from the influence of the considerations under the ontological argument that we come to the idea of an *ens realissimum*, of a being that is in himself limitless and the sum of all realities.

And now we have before us the entire course of reasoning which Kant has instituted against the teleological argument, partly from the point of view of the peculiarity of his own system, and partly from considerations which at least take on a more general aspect. The latter alone call for any special remark from us at present. In that reference, we may say of the objection in regard to form and matter, that Kant has forgot his own relative, or at least relevant, metaphysic. Notion without perception is empty: perception without notion is blind. This he said once, and it is identically the same principle that is potent and at work when we say, Form without Matter is empty, Matter without Form is blind. A matterless form would vanish, and a formless matter never even be. Either, in fact, is but an element of the other. Both together are the concrete truth; as much as an inside AND an outside. Then as regards the objection that we can infer no more than an architect or an artificer, and that, too, only in the relative proportion, I fancy the answer will be in every mouth, It is precisely an architect or an artificer that we do infer, and precisely also in proportion of the work; but just in proportion of the work, that architect and that artificer must be, and can only be, He that is; and whom there is none other beside, Alpha and Omega, the first and the last, the beginning and the end.

# GIFFORD LECTURE THE SIXTEENTH.

The cosmological proof—Contingency—*Ab alio esse* and *esse a se*—The special contingency an actual fact in experience — This Kant would put out of sight—Jehovah—Two elements in the argument, experience and ideas — The generality of the experience — Also of the idea — Contingency *is* a particular empirical fact—*Ens realissimum*—Only the ontological argument in disguise—Logical inference—But just generally the all-necessary being of such a world—Hume anticipated Kant—Why force analogy—Why transcend nature—No experience of such cause which must not exceed the effect—Hume's early memoranda—The "nest"—All Kant dependent on his own constant sense of school-distinctions—His entire world—The system being true, *what* is true?—The ontological argument — No thinking a thing will bring it to be—What it all comes to, the single threefold wave—Hegel—Middle Age view from Augustine to Tauler—Meister Eckhart—Misunderstanding of mere understanding — The wickedest then a possible divine reservoir — Adam Smith and the chest of drawers — Absurd for Kant to make reason proper the "*transcendent shine*"—The Twelfth Night cake, but the *ehrliche* Kant.

THE last lecture concerned the proof from design; we come now to the other two, and first to that which is named Cosmological. As is known, the fulcrum of this proof is the peculiarity of existence as existence. Existence, that is, as existence, is contingent. But this word has so many meanings, important meanings,—even, in philosophical application, crucial meanings,—that a little preliminary explanation in its regard may seem called for, and may prove useful. In a former part of the course we had a contingency of things which almost meant chance. It is common knowledge that events

U

happen, which might have been foreseen and calculated; and it is equally common knowledge that other events happen which no faculty of vision or power of reason, omniscience apart, could either have foreseen or calculated. Now, philosophically, that to me is, as proper quality and fundamental condition of things, the *main* contingency. I may walk the streets with whatever care I may; but I may for all that slip on a bit of orange peel, and fracture a limb or dislocate a joint. Such contingency as that is our very element; we pass our lives in it, and are never safe. The powers of nature threaten us from all sides, and we must wall them out. As I have already explained, this is the necessary and unavoidable result of externality as externality. Then in passing from the one argument to the other, design was spoken of as contingency. This, however, is a use of the word not quite common in English, and was suggested for the moment to meet the language of Kant. Kant, that is, in order to reduce the teleological argument to the ontological, through and by means of the cosmological, characterized the design which we see in things as *zufällig* to them, contingent to them. And by this he meant that this ordering of things which we call design is not inherent in the things themselves, but something added to them as though from without. Contingency, in this sense, is inessentiality, adventitiousness, extrinsicality. It is easy to understand that the order of the things on a dinner table is such inessentiality, adventitiousness, extrinsicality, contingency; it is not inherent in these things; it is something given to them — something *zufällig*. And we see *so* that at least the German word may, naturally and legitimately enough, be used in such sense and with such application. As for the English word contingent, if similarly used, the shade of meaning implied will not really be found unintelligible or unconformable and misplaced. A third sense of contingent is proper to the cosmological argument which we have now in hand. The very fulcrum of that argument, in fact, lies in the word. Because all the things of this world are capable of being characterized as effects, we infer a cause for them. If no more than effects, they are unsupported in themselves, and seem bodily and miscellaneously to fall. That is, they are contingent. So it is that, in the very word, there lies the call for the argument in question. The contingent, as an *ab alio esse*, necessarily refers to an *esse* that is *a se*; what depends only must depend on something else. The cosmological, like the teleological argument, proceeds, therefore, from a fact in experience. Design is such fact, and so also is contingency—contingency in the sense of the unsupportedness, the powerlessness of things in themselves. In the three arguments for the being of a God, we proceed either from the fact to the idea, or from the idea to the fact. In the ontological argument, namely, we reason from the idea of God to the fact of His existence, while in the cosmological and the teleological arguments, we reason from the facts of existence to the idea of God. What Kant misses in the ontological argument is the element of reality, existence, fact, or the element that depends on experience. It is in vain to look for such element, he avers, in mere ideas. His action with the two other arguments, again, is, so to speak, reverse-wise—*to put aside* this element—the element of actual fact, on which they, both of them, found. It is Kant's general object, that is, in regard to the reasoning for the existence of God, to reduce the teleological to the cosmological argument and both to the ontological, which, as dependent on mere notions, he thinks that he will be at little pains to destroy.

Kant himself states the cosmological argument thus:—

"If something exists, then an absolutely necessary being must also exist; but at least I myself exist: therefore there exists an absolutely necessary being." My existence, namely, is contingent. It is no existence complete in itself and sufficient of itself; it is only a derivative existence, and an existence in many ways dependent. Whether as derivative or dependent, it has its support elsewhere. It is unsupported in itself, powerless in itself, a house on the fall, a very terminable security. But I am no solitary case, I am no exception; others are as I, and there is not a single thing in this universe that is not as the others. All are contingent, all are derivative, all are dependent; they are all such that you postulate an originating and sustaining cause for them; but any such cause—any terminal, final, and ultimate cause, it is impossible in the whole series of causes *in* the universe anywhere to find. Trace causes as you may, you must end always with an effect. Now, it is taking our stand on these facts that we involuntarily conclude to the existence of an absolutely necessary being that is the reason at once of the existence and support of all these things—of all these things which are so utterly unsupported and powerless in themselves. And so it is that the cosmological argument has been specially put in connection wtth the religion of power. Power, indeed, must have been one of the earliest feelings that, in view of this great universe of effects, surged up in the human breast. In the Hebrew Scriptures, for example, what an attribute is power! Hence that sublimity in which the earth, the ball of the universe, is but as the footstool of Him who says, I Am that I Am. We have only to think of this to have it very vividly realized to us that the cosmological argument is founded in the depths of man's own soul. It is not an argument forced, scholastic, artificial,—it is not a thing of words; it is religion to the peoples. That whole image of Jehovah and the footstool of the universe is but the cosmological argument itself in its sublimest and most natural form. The contingent universe is but the footstool to the absolute necessity of God.

We must turn now, however, and see how Kant would deprive us of this rationality that we have, to say so, almost in our very blood.

The cosmological argument, we may take it, stands at this moment before us thus :— Inasmuch as *something* exists and *contingently* exists, there must exist also something that is absolutely necessary. Of this argument Kant admits: *That* "it is based on experience;" *that* "it is not led altogether *à priori*;" *that* it is called the cosmological proof, for this reason, that the world, from which it takes its name and on which it founds, "is the object of all possible experience." Nevertheless, it is precisely this ground of experience which Kant would remove from it; this, in his desire to establish it as a mere matter of void ideas only. There are thus in the argument two interests against both of which Kant turns. First, namely, there is the question of the experience; and, second, there is that of the ideas. On the first question Kant, as I have said, would put out of sight the experience; and, on the second, he would have us regard the necessary being that is concluded to, as a mere idea, and as a mere idea, further, that is only illicitly converted into the other idea of the *ens realissimum*, or God. Of these two operations Kant himself gives the description thus: "In this cosmological argument there come together so many sophistical propositions that speculative reason seems to have exerted here all its dialectical skill in order to effect the greatest possible transcendental false show;" but he (Kant) will "expose a trick on its part,

—the trick to set up, in a masked form, an old argument for a new one, as though with appeal to the agreement of two witnesses, one, namely, of reason, and the other of experience, while all the time it is only the former that is present, having simply changed its clothes and its voice in order to pass for the latter as well." That on the part of Kant, plainly, is to the effect that the cosmological argument is but the ontological argument in disguise. What is alone concerned in it is the inference from mere ideas, while the reference to experience is but an idle trick and an unfounded show. With that, I think, we may assume as substantiated what has been said in the assignment to Kant of two relative operations. So, now, of these in their order.

Collecting, connecting, and reducing the various relative clauses, we may take Kant's first objection to run somewhat in this manner :—The cosmological argument professes to take its ground on experience. This experience, however, is indefinitely general : it proceeds from no single definite existence whatever ; and it attains to no single definite existence whatever. Kant's actuating motive in such propositions is, probably, again to be found only in his system. Nevertheless, he begins with a certain show of general argumentation ; and it is this we have first to see.

So far as the indefinite generality is concerned, Kant's expressions are that the proof in question is only "referent to an existence given by empirical consciousness in general," and it "avails itself of this experience only to take a *single* step, namely, to the existence of a necessary being in general." One, of course, cannot well understand how a step, as a step, should be objected to because it is single. A single step may be true enough ; a step—any step—is not necessarily false because it is single. But the expression, probably, is merely incidental on the part of Kant, who has in his eye, at the moment, only the immediate object of the step, "the existence, namely, of a necessary being in general;" and has no thought, perhaps, but of the *generality* involved. It may be asked, however, Are we the least bit worse off because the experience is a general experience? The fact and basis of experience, it at least allows, in common with the other phrases which have been already quoted; and the generality of an experience is not seen at once to be tantamount to its extinction. Surely, on the contrary, it is on its side the advantage lies; surely it is a great thing to say that we shall reach the same conclusion if you give us anything at all. You are only asked to allow the fact that *something* exists; it is enough that you grant us any experience whatever; we are not particular what experience; just give us an experience of any kind—experience absolutely general if you like. The objection withdraws nothing from the argument; rather, indeed, it only adds to it. Nay, what does Kant himself say? "It is something very remarkable," he naively admits, "that if it is presupposed that something, anything, exists, the conclusion cannot be escaped that something also *necessarily* exists." After all, then, generality as a drawback does not seem to hold even in Kant's own eyes.

But there is another side to the generality—this, namely, that the necessary being inferred is also a generality. The alleged experience, Kant says, is only a step to "the existence of a necessary being in general," "but not demonstrating this necessity in regard of any particular thing"; "what sort of Eigenschaften, what sort of properties or qualities, the necessary being possesses, the empirical ground of proof is incompetent to declare." It must be some importation from his own system that Kant has in mind here when he objects to the argument as not leading to a one empirical object. Otherwise, surely, of all philosophers, Kant is the only one who has complained that he cannot clap an actual hand or eye on God! How could God possibly be any particular experience? The infinite is not the finite. But to take Kant as he speaks, he would seem to be unhappy and out of heart because, in reasoning to God, he fails to get in touch with some one empirical object, or the actual properties of some one empirical object. Are we to give up or despair of God, then, because He is not the Pillars of Hercules or the Gates of Gaza?

But, in the reference to generality, if it is not to be objected that we do not come *to* some particular, so neither is it to be objected that we do not start *from* some particular. Nay, if the experience we start from is in a certain way general, it is also, after all, in a certain way particular. That is, it is not from mere indefiniteness, from mere experience in name, that we start, but from an actual fact, and actually definite *in* and *of* experience. We start from—the cosmological argument rests on—an actual, particular, empirical fact. Contingency is a fact; contingency is particular; contingency is empirical; contingency is actual; and it is from contingency that all our reasoning starts, and on contingency that all our reasoning rests. Kant has been no more able to quash or put out of sight contingency as a fact of experience in the cosmological argument, than he was able to quash or put out of sight design as a fact of experience in the teleological argument. And so long as such facts remain, the ontological argument, which rests wholly on ideas, cannot be used as a lever for the destruction of its cosmological and teleological fellows.

But, now, to turn to Kant's second objection to the cosmological argument—that, namely, it was still only a trick when, in intromission with mere ideas, it converted the necessary being of the first part of the supposed proof into the *ens realissimum*, or supreme being, of the second part. Arrived once for all at the notion of the necessary being, Kant intimates, we only look about us for what other desirable qualities we suppose such a being must have, in order to arrive at its own complete and perfect substantiation. These qualities are supposed to be found in the idea of supreme reality alone; and so the necessary being at first hand is converted into the supremely real being at second hand. Kant goes on at great length in the discussion of this matter. The better to expose the fallacy, he is even at pains to put the whole reasoning, as he alleges, in the technical syllogistic form. "All blind show is most readily detected," he says, "if we set it down before us in a scholastically correct shape." With all, however, sentence after sentence, phrase upon phrase, word upon word, and all the technical processes of the dryest school logic, it comes to this that the cosmological argument, having only pretended to reason from a ground of experience, has intromitted with ideas only, and has simply converted, fallaciously, the mere idea of a necessary being into the further idea of the all-reallest being; in short, as has been already said, the cosmological argument is no more and no less than the ontological argument in disguise. In Kant's own words, what the cosmological argument maintains is this: "The notion of the all-reallest being is the only notion whereby a necessary being can be thought; that is, there necessarily exists a supreme being;" and that is to Kant an *ignoratio elenchi*. We commit no fallacy, however, no *ignoratio elenchi*, if from one logically established proposition we only logically deduce another. Probably most people would be quite content with the one proposition, and would give themselves little concern about the other. All-necessary, they might say, and all-reallest come pretty well to the same thing; it is positively enough that it should be either. But there is no difficulty in even logically deducing the one from the other. What has its necessity within itself is sufficient for itself, and is without dependence on another. That is, it is without dependence for its reality on anything else; it is without any negation to its reality: it is the all-reallest! The one proposition is simply contained in the other; and we have no call to go to experience in search of it. Kant has simply forgot his own doctrine of analytic propositions. As certain as (Kant's own example) the proposition—all bodies are extended—is an analytic proposition, the truth of which requires analysis only, and no resort to actual experience, so certain is it that the proposition—the all-necessary being is the all-reallest being—is no less an analytic proposition that, as such and so far, is independent of experience. The cosmological argument is sufficient within itself, and neither requires nor takes support from any other. But, in a general way, we are situated here just as we were with the teleological argument. Let the teleological argument prove only a former of the world, then we say the former of such a world must have been its Creator. And let the cosmological argument prove only the all-necessary being of the world, then we say, the all-necessary being of all that contingency of the world must be, and can only be, what is reallest in the world; and that, namely, is the Most High God.

It would be unjust to Hume not to remark here that, though the German words and ways seem so very unlike, Kant, when he wrote, must have had before him all the three relative writings of the good David: the essay, namely, Of a Particular Providence and of a Future State, The Natural History of Religion, and the Dialogues concerning Natural Religion. Much of what the German says had, in his own way, been already said by the Scot. Thus Hume talks also of houses and ships, and conceives it only to force analogy to transfer it from things finite to such an unexampled infinite: it may be that for such powers and quality, says Hume too, we need not go beyond nature or even matter itself. We can only reason from experience, and experience has no *locus standi* on such an elevation. Then Hume's objection of the universe being a singular effect, that is, that we can only credit the cause with no more than we find in the effect; and that we cannot return from the cause as with new data to extended inference,—all that is precisely what Kant means by the translating of absolute necessity into absolute reality. The young Hume in the early memorandum book referred to by Burton (i. 135) has (as we partly know) some excellent expressions in regard to the three proofs of the existence of a God, which Kant, of course, had no opportunity of seeing, but which have their interest here. The first of these proofs runs, "There is something necessarily existent, and what is so is infinitely perfect;" and the third, "The idea of infinite perfection implies that of actual existence." It is really very strange, but these two propositions suggest, not too imperfectly on the whole, Kant's entire relative action, which is the complaint that the cosmological argument converts, first, necessary existence into infinite perfection, and, second, infinite perfection into necessary existence, thus placing itself at last only on the ontological argument.

Kant follows up his general argumentation by indicating and shortly refuting what he calls "an entire nest of dialectical assumptions that is concealed in the cosmological proof." The entire "nest," however, may be said to be a construction of his peculiar system. Kant says, for example, that causality and the other principles of reasoning employed in the argument concern only the world of the senses and have no meaning out of it; and, in each of the four heads which he enumerates, there appears nothing whatever else. That just amounts to the one averment peculiar to the system, that whatever, namely, is incapable of being actually experienced is nothing but a *Hirngespinnst*, a cobweb of the brain. As regards God, it is valid reasoning to Kant that in this world as he (Kant) has constituted it, there cannot be an actual object of the senses, named God; and so God can only be an Idea, an idea of *our* own, and useful for us in giving a sort of convenient unity and arrangement to the house we live in. God is precisely that to Kant, and He is nothing more.

All these wonderful constructions of Kant, toys of his own gluing, all spring from the constant sense of distinctions that is the single life within him. Every reader of Kant, even the least familiar, must have memory of this. There is probably not a page of Kant in which he does not split up something into two distinctions—distinctions to which he is apt to give contrasting Latin names, as the *quid facti*, and the *quid juris*, and actually thousands of others. Kant, in fact, is a very schoolmaster. He is constantly laying down the law—a law that concerns verbalisms only. If Kant is ever real, it is where, as in his *Practical Kritik*, he is occupied with Morals; and even there I honestly believe that it would be quite possible to show that his very best findings are but artificial results of his pedagogic distinctions. Distinctions and artificiality are certainly both the levers and the materials of his theoretic system. Time and space are both within us, and *in them* there are our own sensations: these are the materials, and the only materials of perceptive knowledge; and they become such by being in a twelvefold manner categorized into our self-consciousness. There are further, three Ideas, to be sure, but they are only ideas—only ideas of order and arrangement for our own private use. Now that is really the entire world to Kant, and he has made it wholly and solely out of distinctions in his own vitals. Does it give more reality to this soap-bubble of a universe that it hangs between two absolutely unknown *x*'s, mere algebraical *x*'s, that are only supposed, only feigned, though *named* things in themselves; the one on this side for sensation, and the other on that side for belief? Never was the world so befooled by a system as it has been befooled by the system of Kant; and the world has no excuse for itself, but that Kant had, with such perfect conviction, with such luminous and voluminous detail, fooled himself into it. What, according to this system, are we to suppose truth to be? If *it* (the system) is, *what* is there that is true? The sensations are not true. Their truth is only unknown points in an unknown dark. Time and space are not true: they are only figments of my imagination. The categories are not true: they come from a tree, an Yggdrasil that has no roots, but again in me. The Ideas have no truth: they are mere illusions. And this me itself: it is but a logical breathing, a logical dot on a logical *i*. Where, according to this system, is there a single truth in the whole huge universe?

But we must come to an end with our consideration of Kant: we must turn at last to our final interest here: we must now see how Kant disposes of the ontological argument. The form given to that argument, which we have seen from the early memorandum book of Hume, is, perhaps, as simple and short, and as good as any. "The idea of infinite perfection implies that of actual existence." Really the young Hume has put what is concerned there in its very best form. If you say you have the idea of infinite perfection, and yet that actual existence is not thought of in that idea, then you only contradict yourself.

It would be a very strange all-perfection that yet was not. Kant, of course, has a good deal to say in the reference; but I know not that all he has got to say amounts to more than the objection that comes to every one. We can think what we like, but no thinking of ours will make a thing to be! It would be a fine thing if, only by thinking of the "dollars," in Kant's well-known illustration, we could have them; but— We can all readily understand as much as that, and Anselm himself told us, It was one thing for a painter to think his picture and another thing to make it. So always when we think these easy thoughts in regard to this argument, we are thrown back to the question, Is it, then, a self-contradiction to think God as non-existent; and for the reason that He is infinite, and not like a perfect island, or a perfect garden, etc., which, with whatever perfection, are still things finite? Is God such and so different from all else, that if we think Him, that is, truly *think— Him*—then we will see that He *is?* Perhaps to put the questions in that manner is to put them rightly. But if so, then the conclusion is—that we are all referred to ourselves. What we are asked to do is to *think* God; but if it is only in the actual *thinking* that the truth emerges, then each of us must do that for himself; not one of us can do that for another. Of course, Anselm develops the matter in a formal syllogism, and into a self-contradiction on the negative side. But, so put, we cannot help suspecting that we have to do with words only, and we remain unmoved. We still ask how *thinking*—which will assure us of the existence of nothing else—will yet assure us of the existence of God? That is the question; and we see that Kant's objections—*all* summed up in the illustration of the dollars—are beside the point, are out of place. The whole matter is for us to *think* God. But what is God?—what is this that we are to think? Now, in attempting to answer that question, we do think God—we just do what is required. And what do we find for result? We find that we have thought this universe into its source—we find that we have realized *to thought, as* a necessity *of* thought, the single necessity of a one eternal, all-enduring principle which is the root, and the basis, and the original of all that is. In fact, we may say that when this task of thought is put upon us, we just think, in a moment, and at once, and altogether, the teleological argument, and the cosmological argument, and the ontological argument, each and all, summarily, into God. And with that acknowledgment we have the reality and the substantiation of Natural Theology: our whole task is accomplished—the whole Gifford problem solved—in a turn of the hand! What, in effect, are the three arguments in proof of the existence of God? There is a triplet of perpetual appearance and reappearance in the ancient Fathers of the Church. It is *esse, vivere, intelligere;* and these are but three successive stages of the world itself. *To live* is to be above *to be,* and *to think* is to be above *to live.* All three are at once in the world; and though they offer hands, as it were, each to the other, each is for itself. So it is that the Three Proofs are but the single wave in the rise of the soul, through the Trinity of the Universe, up to the unity of God. And, with such thoughts before us, it will be found that the ontological proof will assume something of reality, and will cease to be a mere matter of words. The very *thought of God* is of that *which is, and cannot not-be.*

It is undoubtedly with such thoughts in his mind that Hegel declares the ontological proof to be alone the proof. To him, manifestly, it was not an affair of *Barbara, Celarent, Baroko, Bokardo,* and the rest in mere words: it was an actual mood of mind, a veritable process of the soul, a movement of spirit to spirit, and a revelation of God to man. We might almost say that this alone is the *meaning* of the work of Hegel—that in this alone he is in earnest —that, in philosophy and in religion, *as struggling to this*, he would present himself almost literally on every page. He complains that recent theology speaks rather of religion than of God; whereas, in the Middle Ages, the whole interest was to know God. What is now only a matter of subjective information was then objectively *lived*. The true relation is that of spirit to spirit. The finite spirit, in separating itself from the mundane, or in gathering up the whole mundane into its essential reality and truth, rises into unity and community with the infinite spirit, and knower and known are one. In that one intensity, where difference is at once identity and identity at once difference, man is conscious of himself in God, God is conscious of Himself in man. That really is what the ontological proof is to Hegel. Spirit gives testimony of itself *to* spirit; and this testimony is the true inner nature *of* spirit. " God," says Hegel, " is essentially self-consciousness;" and it is only when man has realized himself into union with God, *only then* also has he realized his *true free* will. Readers of the history of philosophy know that Hegel is by no means singular in these views: they are common and current in the Middle Ages from Augustine to Tauler. Meister Eckhart alone has passage after passage which, in intensity and ecstasy, leaves nothing for Hegel. " The eye," he cries, " with which God sees me, is the eye with which I see Him; my eye and His eye are one; in righteousness, I am cradled in God, and He in me. If God were not, I were not; if I were not, He were not; but there is no need to know this; for these are things easy to be misunderstood, and which are only to be comprehended in the spirit." As to this of misunderstanding, Hegel, too, says, at least in effect: If you speak such things in the terms of the understanding, you will look in vain to find them again: If you make an ordinary generalization of such doctrine, and describe it in common words as the tenet of the knowing of Man in God and of God in Man, you have shut yourself out from it; you are on the outside, and have closed the door on yourself. These things are only in the inmost being of a man to be struggled and worked up to. Another ready objection is—*pantheism*. But if there is an assertion of God in the relation, there is also no denial of man. My own objection is that it at least seems to trench on a degradation of God: the very wickedest and least considerable of human beings may represent himself as a sort of reservoir from which at any moment he can draw on God, have God on tap. Of course, it may be answered that, in the relation, take it as it is, there is no room for any moment of compulsion —it is not a case of mere ancient theurgy, black art, magic; the divine approach will come at its own good time—free; and not any one human being that so tempers himself is *then* either wickedest or least considerable. Nay, in humanity, is it so certain that the least and the greatest, the best and the worst, have any such mighty difference between them? May not even the least and the worst cry, And we then—are not we, too, made in the image of God?

With all this that concerns a living ontological proof, these external manœuvres and contrivances of Kant are strangely in contrast. To him it is quite clear that as he can reasonably think a hundred dollars not to exist, he can equally think God not to exist, but to be a mere idea of our own respondent to our own human desire for order. Adam Smith, in reply to the Doctrine of Utility, was surprised if " we have no other reason for praising a man than that for which we commend a chest of drawers."

x

What, then, should be our surprise if, in Kant's reclamation for order, we have no other reason for the production of a God than that we have for the production of a chest of drawers — convenience, namely! God is but an illusion or delusion caused by the false light of sense misleading our judgment. This light Kant calls the "transcendental shine," and he is very proud of it. He is wonderfully contented with what he thinks his discovery of these three false lights of the Ideas. But if any one will just look for himself, his wonder will be —where they come from? When we reason from the contingency of all things, as it were, to the linch-pin of all things—when we reason from design to a designer— even when we reason from a certain notion to the existence of the object of that notion—in a word, in reasoning towards God, whether from existence to idea or from idea to existence, we think we have been only *reasoning;* but, no, says Kant, you have been only led by a natural *ignis fatuus*, which you cannot turn your back upon, even when you know it.

This system of Kant is but a Twelfth Night cake of his own manufacture, wonderfully be-decked and be-dizzened, be-queened and be-kinged, be-flagged and be-turreted; but, for all that, it is no more than a thing of sugar and crumb of bread. Nay, even for the quantity of the bread and the quality of the sugar that are in it, we cannot but thank Kant, naming him even there*for*, the *ehrliche* Kant, the plain, honest, honourable Kant.

# GIFFORD LECTURE THE SEVENTEENTH.

The three degrees, positive, comparative, superlative in negation of the proofs, or Hume, Kant, Darwin—*The Life and Letters of Charles Darwin*, chapter viii. of the first volume—Darwin one of the best of men—Design—Uniformity and law—Darwin's own words—He himself always gentle—But resolute to win—— Concessiveness—Religious sentiment—Disbelief—Jokes—Natural selection being, materialism is true, and ideas are only derivative — The theory — A species what — Sterility—What suggested natural selection to Darwin—Bakewell's achievements as a breeder—Darwin will substitute nature for Bakewell, to the production, not of new breeds, but, absolutely, of new species—His lever to this, change by natural accident and chance : such *necessarily* proving either advantageous, disadvantageous, or indifferent—*Advantage* securing in the struggle for life survival of the fittest, *disadvantage* entailing death and destruction, *indifference* being out of count—The woodpecker, the misletoe—But mere variation the very fulcrum—Variation *must* be, and consequences to the organism *must* be : hence the whole — But never design, only a mechanical pullulation of differences by chance that simply *prove* advantageous or disadvantageous, etc.—Conditions—Mr. Huxley—Effect of the announcements of Sir Joseph Hooker and Sir Charles Lyell—Mr. Darwin insists on his originality—His difficulties in winning his way—Even those who agree with him, as Lyell, Hooker, and others, he demurs to their expressions : they fail to understand—Mr. Darwin's own qualms—" What makes a tuft of feathers come on a cock's head, or moss on a moss-rose ?"—That the question—Still spontaneous variation both universal and constant.

IN regard to the *negative* on the question of the proofs for the being of a God, having now passed through what we name the *positive* and *comparative* degrees of it as found respectively in the writings of David Hume and Immanuel Kant, we have reached at length the similarly conditioned *superlative* degree in so far as it is represented, on the whole, that is, by the views of the celebrated Charles Darwin. In chapter viii. of the first volume of *The Life and Letters of Charles Darwin*, a chapter which bears to inform us in regard to the religious views of Mr. Darwin, and which is actually entitled " Religion," I think we shall easily find abundant evidence to prove that this distinguished naturalist, especially in the latter part of his life, came greatly to doubt of the existence of a God at all. I should not find it difficult in this reference, then, to paint a picture which should exhibit the original of it in a form and colouring still very odious to the great majority of the English-speaking populations anywhere. His absolute want of sympathy at last with all in nature and in art which we are in the habit of regarding as appealing to what is highest, or to what is deepest and divinest in the soul of man—that might be taken advantage of, and, according to ability, worked up into a representation, or misrepresentation, which should actually revolt. But I, for my part, have not the slightest inclination for the daubing—it would be only that—of any such caricature. I know that, if a man has long accustomed his thoughts exclusively to run in a single, special, and peculiar groove—I know, I say, that then all other grooves become distasteful to him. In many such grooves—*for* many such grooves, he may have been enthusiastic once. He does not value them the less now; but, in the intensity of his devotion to the one, he has ceased to be susceptible of the interest which it surprises, disappoints, disturbs him to find he no longer possesses for the others. This is a state of mind which, in regard of intellectual working, we may expect to meet, after a time, even in the best of men. And Charles

Darwin *was* one of the best of men. As son, brother, husband, father, friend, as servant or master, as simple citizen, that man was, as is well possible here, perfect. It is to be understood, then, that, if I have to refer at any time to Mr. Darwin's religious opinions, I do so only in the regard that my subject compels. That subject at present is, specially, the negative of the proofs for the being of a God, and in Mr. Darwin's reference, that negative is secluded and confined to the argument from design. To this argument his peculiar theory is fatal; and Mr. Darwin himself is not only aware of this, but in express terms acknowledges it. And that for me is enough, that for me is all. I have to do with Mr. Darwin in this respect alone. I know that in regard to the theory in question—Natural Selection—there are in existence all manner of views—I know that there are those to whom this theory has extended the satisfaction and consolation of universal uniformity and enlightened law ; but with these views or representations of views, I have, in any way whatever, no call to intromit. In fact, I may say at once in regard to uniformity, that it is not its presence, but its absence, that I find in the theory of Mr. Darwin. He who does not see—who does not know and proclaim that this world is dependent on ideas, is hung on ideas, is instinct with ideas—he to me has no true word to say for uniformity. I refuse to acknowledge uniformity in mere *matter* that is figured in mere *mechanical* play from beyond the Magellan clouds to within the indivisible unit of every living soul. My uniformity is the uniformity, not of matter, but of mind ; and that is the uniformity which I precisely fail to find in the theory of Mr. Darwin. He himself, as I say, acknowledges this. He doubts the existence of God ; he denies design. What I have first to do here, then, is to lead evidence in proof of the allegations made. So far as these allegations concern design, *that* is the direct interest; in other respects they concern only an indirect implication in consequence of necessary quotation. I desire Mr. Darwin to be regarded only with respect—or, in truth and sincerity, only with love. It was in this spirit that, in the first place here, I contemplated a psychological inquiry, not only into the life and character of Mr. Darwin himself, but into those of his father, and specially of his grandfather, the celebrated Dr. Erasmus Darwin of *Zoonomia* and the *Botanic Garden*. In these references I collected largely. I ransacked the two lives of Dr. Erasmus, that of Miss Seward and that of Ernst Krause, as also that remarkable book of Miss Meteyard's, *A Group of Englishmen*, in which we are introduced to the enormous bulk of Mr. Darwin's father, "the largest man whom" the son "ever saw," "about six feet two inches in height, with broad shoulders and very corpulent," "twenty-four stone in weight, when last weighed, but afterwards much heavier," a man represented by Miss Meteyard as "eating a goose for his dinner as easily as other men do a partridge." Charles denies this: we must be cautious in receiving such reports: others, he says, "describe his father as eating remarkably little." Evidently that goose is not to the stomach of the family. I read and made large extracts also from the various works of Dr. Erasmus, from the *Zoonomia* and the *Botanic Garden*. And it is possible that were I to apply all the material collected, I might be able to realize some not altogether uninteresting psychological characterization which might even have its bearing on the peculiar theories of the son and grandson; but this would lead me much too far at present, and I am reluctantly compelled to turn to what my space alone allows me, the theory itself of Charles Darwin, and in so far as it concerns design.

On that last head, design, we have it in our power to

adduce in evidence a great variety of expressions of Mr. Darwin's own. Such expressions are principally to be found in the letters to Mr. Asa Gray, and in the chapter entitled "Religion," which occur in the work already referred to. From the latter, the eighth chapter, namely, of the first volume, I quote, for example, this: "The old argument from design in Nature . . . fails, now that the law of natural selection has been discovered. . . . There seems to be no more design in the variability of organic beings . . . than in the course which the wind blows." Now, these are only a few words; but they are unmistakable. They are crucial as to this, *That*, to Mr. Darwin, there is no more design in organic variation, than in the course of the wind, *That*, consequently, the argument from design fails, and *That* this failure of said argument is to be attributed to the law of natural selection. By implication we see that Mr. Darwin's general doctrine is this, The varied organizations in nature are due, not to design, but to natural selection; or, as we may put it reverse-wise, natural selection accounts for all organic variation in nature, and any reference to a so-called principle of design is unwarranted, groundless, and gratuitous. Of course it cannot be said that Mr. Darwin exactly triumphs in this supposed destruction of the argument from design. Mr. Darwin is a most amiable man. He was ever courteous in expression—whether by letter or by word of mouth—almost to a fault; "he naturally shrank," as his son says, "from wounding the sensibilities of others in religious matters." So it is that in his letters to Asa Gray—an earnest-minded man—all that he has to say on design is mitigated ever by gentle words in regard to theology. With respect "to the theological view of the question. This," he says, "is always painful to me. I am bewildered. I had no intention to write atheistically.

"But I own that I cannot see as plainly as others do, and as I should wish to do, evidence of design and beneficence on all sides of us. . . . I am inclined to look at everything as resulting from designed laws,[1] with the details, whether good or bad, left to the working out of what we may call chance." It is ever thus in meek conciliant vein he writes concessively to all his intimate friends,— even to Hooker and to Lyell, who were his most intimate. An element in this was, of course, the desire that was ever present to him of winning his way for his theory into the conviction of his correspondents, and of softening the opposition which he constantly encountered from them. It is rather amusing to watch his shrewd manœuvres in this reference both with Hooker and Lyell, especially the latter, whom he is always reminding of his own eminence and of his own teaching in his geology! At times he even gets humorously cross with his own self when consciousness of this his concessive attitude has come upon him, as in reference to his having "put in the possibility of the Galapagos having been *continuously* joined to America," though, "in fact convinced, more than in any other case of other islands, that the Galapagos had never been so joined." At such instance of concessiveness as this, I say, he gets humorously cross with himself, and exclaims, "It was mere base subservience and terror of Hooker & Co." With all softness of expression, however, Mr. Darwin's candour is never for a moment in doubt. He says himself that he "does not think that the religious sentiment

---

[1] "Designed laws:" Mr. Darwin has just denied design; there is no law for Mr. Darwin, but natural law, as of "the course of the wind,"—natural mechanics! The "working out" of the law, "good or bad," is left indifferently to "*chance*." The word is the inadvertence for the moment of unpremeditated writing;—or is Mr. Darwin in it only conciliant to Mr. Asa Gray?

was ever strongly developed in him;" and he writes with perfectly conscious unreserve of his unbelief in a revelation whether *of* or *by* God,—writes quite jokingly at times, indeed, with reference to articles of faith and the priests that teach them. But it is only in what regards design that there is any interest in Mr. Darwin for us at present; and we are happily spared here, consequently, all citation and any further reference to the subject of religion, so far as Mr. Darwin is concerned.

The result before which we stand now, then, is this: If natural selection is true, design is false. That, at least, is the conclusion of Mr. Darwin; and Mr. Darwin it was who, in regard to natural selection, first made current the phrase and held valid the doctrine. Evidently, then, Mr. Darwin being right, our whole enterprise is brought to a very short issue. There is an end to the whole interest of Natural Theology—an end to all our relative declamation—an end to all our arguments for the existence of God, in so far, namely, as, to the general belief of the modern world, all these arguments concentrate themselves in design. Design, namely, is the product of ideas; but there can be no ideas to begin with on the footing of natural selection. Natural selection being true, ideas are not producers, but produced. What alone results in that case is that materialism is all, and that ideas only issue from the order and arrangement which things themselves simply fall into. The immediate question that presses on us, consequently, is, What is natural selection? And for an answer to this question I confine myself to the same work already spoken of— *The Life and Letters*. I am not unacquainted with the other relative writings of Mr. Darwin; but I find no answers to all my questions in these references so simple and direct as those suggested in the three volumes of the book I have named

Now, to say it all in a word, the theory is this: Every organism has varieties; of which varieties certain examples being selected, settle into longevity, as it were or into quasi-permanence as species. Species, so far, are but long-lived varieties; and the question is, To constitute a species, is that enough—is longevity enough ? What, in fact, is it that does constitute a species, or what is the ensemble of qualities that is proper to, and distinctive of, a species; what is the definition of a species ? Now here, according to Mr. Darwin (ii. 88), "it is really laughable to see what different ideas are prominent in various naturalists' minds when they speak of species; in some, resemblance is everything, and descent of little weight; in some, resemblance seems to go for nothing, and creation the reigning idea ; in some, descent is the key; in some, sterility an unfailing test; with others, it is not worth a farthing. It all comes, I believe, from trying to define the undefinable." A species, then, would appear from this to be undefinable to Mr. Darwin ; so much so that he can afford to laugh at his coadjutors and fellow-workers. When we turn in upon him, however, actually engaged in the work of determining for himself a species, we find Mr. Darwin not by any means in a laughing humour. He tells his friend Hooker (ii. 40) that, "after describing a set of forms as distinct species, tearing up my MS., and making them one species ; tearing that up, and making them separate ; and then making them one again (which has happened to me), I have gnashed my teeth, cursed species, and asked what sin I had committed to be so punished !" Plainly, if we have first of all to make out for ourselves what the thing that is to originate *is*, we have our own difficulties before us. Nevertheless, from the various definers laughed at by Mr. Darwin, we may gather a list of what qualities are, on the whole, considered as more or less specific ; and they are these—Resemblance, Descent,

Creation, and Sterility. Creation we may dismiss as almost constituting precisely the single point that happens to be in question; Mr. Darwin, that is, holds species not to be created, but to develop the one from the other. Of the other characters named, we may assume Mr. Darwin to allow resemblance and to accentuate descent, but to deny sterility. Of this last—sterility—Mr. Darwin holds that neither sterility nor fertility affords any certain distinction between species and varieties (*Origin*, 237). I fancy, however, on this head, that we shall very probably hit the truth should we say that sterility is, after all, the rule, and that Mr. Darwin's conclusion, being in his own favour otherwise, is only plausibly supported on mere exceptions and consequent superficial discrepancies (somewhat exaggerated) between authorities. What I mean by the accentuated descent is Mr. Darwin's peculiarity— the peculiarity of opinion, namely, that there is descent from species, not only of separate individuals and separate varieties, but also of other and separate species. That is what is meant by the "Origin of Species by means of Natural Selection." How Mr. Darwin was led to his peculiarity in this respect he tells us again and again himself. "All my notions," he says (ii. 79), "about *how* species change are derived from long-continued study of the works of (and converse with) agriculturists and horticulturists; and I believe I see my way pretty clearly on the means used by Nature to change her species and *adapt* them to the wondrous and exquisitely beautiful contingencies to which every living being is exposed." Of what is meant by the "change" referred to here, as concerns first its artificial side (the action of the breeders), he speaks elsewhere (ii. 122) thus: "Man, by this power of accumulating variations, adapts living beings to his wants; he *may be said* to make the wool of one sheep good for carpets and another for cloth," etc. It is the celebrated Robert Bakewell of Dishley, and the means by which he arrived at his wonderfully improved breeds of domestic animals—sheep, oxen, horses—that are here specially in allusion. Having observed that the young of animals are almost quite like their parents in qualities, he was led to infer that, if care were taken only suitably to pair, the result would be a breed uniting in itself whatever qualities should be the most desirable. Accordingly, it was in this way that he came to effect all those modifications in the families of the domestic animals which are now so well known. Mr. Darwin, then, intimates further here, on the natural side, that he himself, by example of Bakewell, was led to place, instead of Bakewell, *nature as a breeder*,[1] with the result that he names natural selection. For the genesis of the idea in the mind of Mr. Darwin, that is the important point; and this genesis will be full and complete if we only add two other less important and subordinate points. These are—1. the Galapagos Archipelago, and, 2. the book of Malthus on population. In those altogether lonely, singular, and peculiar Galapagos Islands, namely, he thought he had caught nature in the very act of originating species; and by Malthus there was suggested to him the Struggle for Existence. This phrase, we may add, afterwards led of itself to the further phrase Survival of the Fittest. So far, then, we see that Mr. Darwin was minded to discover in nature such operations upon animals as were exemplified by man in his artificial breeds; and that he had accordingly come to see that the means to these operations was the Struggle for Life that eventuated in the Survival of the Fittest. *How* the struggle acted was his ultimate con-

---

[1] To Mr. Darwin, however, nature simply *reverses* Bakewell. He exaggerates similarity; she exaggerates difference—literally that! Neither is there any "struggle" to Bakewell, but again the reverse. Man's operations, then, and those of nature are *not* "exemplified" the one in the other. One would like to see nature *pairing* for *improvement* of *breed!*

sideration; and the agent in result was variously named by him divergence, difference, modification, variation, etc. It was on this difference, or through this difference, that Nature operated her selection. Rather, in fact, it was the difference operated the selection on nature, and not nature on the difference. When advantageous, that is, the difference did itself enable the organism to take a new departure in nature, to rise a step, to seize itself of a new and higher level in existence, a new and better habitat, a new and better food, a new and better attack, a new and better defence, etc. All this is precisely what is meant by Mr. Darwin when he says (i. 84): "The modified offspring of all dominant and increasing forms tend to become adapted to many and highly-diversified places in the economy of nature." To the same effect Mr. Darwin says more fully elsewhere (ii. 124): "I cannot doubt that during millions of generations individuals of a species will be born with some slight variation profitable to some part of its economy. Such will have a better chance of surviving, propagating this variation, which, again, will be slowly increased by the accumulative action of natural selection; and the variety thus formed will either coexist with or, more commonly, will extirpate its parent form. An organic being like the woodpecker or the mistletoe may thus come to be adapted to a score of contingencies, natural selection accumulating those slight variations in all parts of its structure which are in any way useful to it during any part of its life." These are Mr. Darwin's own words; and his scheme is really at full and entire in them. Still it may be brought considerably more clearly home to us, if we will but pay a little separate attention to its constitutive parts. The one great point in the whole, however, is the variation. That is the single hinge on which the entire fabric turns. That is the cue for natural selection to interfere; that, and that alone, is the source of the material that enables natural selection to succeed. Now that is a very simple affair; there is neither complication nor mystery in it. All organisms are variable; and all organisms do vary. The interest is therefore that into which at any time the variation is made. That may be a mere slight increase of something already there; some mere slight change of shape; some mere slight change of direction even. Or it may be some initial new streak, some initial new caruncle, nodule, tubercle, alto relievo or basso relievo, some mere dimple or some mere lip, some mere initial crease, fold, pucker—some mere stain even. But whatever it be, there are necessarily the rudiments of advantage or disadvantage in it; and whatever it be, there is a tendency for it to be propagated. It is inherited by the progeny of whatever organism we may suppose to have been suscipient (sufferer or beneficiary) of the change; nay, not only inherited, but inherited with increase and with tendency of increase. Should it be a dimple, a *basso* relievo, for example, it may grow into a hollow that should hold water, and as joint on the stem of a plant prevent the ascent of the insect that would plunder its nectary. Or should it be a tubercle, a nodule, an *alto* relievo, it may become in the end a new fibril, a new tentacle, a new tendril, an actual new organ to increase of the security, to increase of the nourishment and support of the plant. I say in the end; and that end may be reached only by a long gradation, only by an accumulation of slowly successive, almost insensible steps—*really* insensible, if only looked at from day to day. What is alone concerned is this, that there shall be a change, and that that change shall tell upon the life of the organism. If it tell at all, then, through propagation, it can only tell with increase. But, with such telling gradation of change fairly conceived, we can be at no loss to conceive also the process carried out on this side and on that into organisms eventually so changed, that, compared with their antecedents or originals, they cannot be denied to be new species. Assume the change to be one of advantage, then the accumulation of necessarily increasing differences can only end in the production of a new creature. Mr. Darwin is resolute in his adherence to this, that there shall be no design from elsewhere —that the whole appearance of contrivance and construction shall be due to nothing else whatever than, so to speak, to this mechanical pullulation of differences, that can only end in such mechanical accumulation as can be only tantamount to a new species. Of course, it is plant *life*, animal *life*, that so pullulates or develops; and it is not denied that life may be more than mechanism. But still, as in life, the process here can only be called mechanical. We only assume it to be certain that organisms do vary, and quite as certain that any variation they present is in the first instance no more than an accident—a simple appearance of chance. Even the influence of conditions is not to be taken into account: the same organism may exist under any conditions whatever, from the north to the south, or from the east to the west. Conditions or no conditions, it is the appearance of difference alone that is crucial—difference into advantage, and accumulation of difference into advantage, until by mere process of natural eventuation of steps the old has become new—out of one species another has been evolved. This, whatever may be said, is the genuine Darwin. Mr. Darwin has been much impressed by the progress of physical science —by the enormous revolution in it which the discovery of one law—the attraction of gravity—has accomplished, and it would rejoice his heart to introduce a like natural simplification into the process of organic change. As primal condition of the realization of this process, Mr. Darwin expressly excludes (ii. 176 s.) any necessity to presuppose an aboriginal "power of adaptation" or "principle of improvement;" it is enough that there be granted "only diversified variability." And "so," he says, "under nature any slight modification which *chances* to arise, and is useful to any creature, is selected or preserved in the struggle for life." To Mr. Darwin, the slight modification only "*chances*" to arise—chances in italics! This one passage is decisive; but there are many such. He says once to Lyell, for instance: "No change will ever be effected till a variation in the habits or structure, or of both, *chance* to occur in the right direction, so as to give the organism in question an advantage over other already established occupants of land or water; and this may be, in any particular case, indefinitely long." And the word *chance* is again underlined. To Hooker, too, he speaks in the same conviction. "The formation of a strong variety, or species," he says (ii. 87), "I look at as almost wholly due to the selection of what may be incorrectly called *chance* variations or variability;" and again he italicizes *chance*. The adverb "incorrectly," namely, is only added under the influence of common parlance.[1] The physical, natural changes, that are the groundwork of the theory, are to him—as physical, natural—results of mere mechanical play that may be named chance, or, as he says elsewhere, *accident*. His one desire, indeed, is to keep this chance, this accident, pure. Under it alone he would see a difference arise for a consequent series of differences, by propagation, heredity, to accumulate. So it is that he manifests most unmistakably, and almost everywhere, a rooted disinclination to consider any diversity in organisms as the result of an alteration in external conditions. Courtesy was the very nature of Mr. Darwin; and under its leading he goes always so far as ever he can in agreement with his

[1] "Incorrectly" here is pretty well as "designed" on p. 328— see note.

various correspondents. In a letter to Herr Moritz Wagner, for example, who seems to have accentuated conditions, "I wish I could believe," he says with all gentleness,—"I wish I could believe in this doctrine (the agency of changed conditions), as it removes many difficulties." Even here, however, his wish for, is followed by his objections to. No doubt, Herr Wagner is not the only correspondent to whom there may be some polite expression of favour, more or less, for conditions; but even within a year of his death, in writing to Professor Semper with reference to Professor Hoffmann's experiments in discredit of conditions, he ventures to tell the former, —" I thought you attributed too much weight to the *direct* action of the environment;—changed conditions act, *in most cases*, in a very indirect manner." Elsewhere in these letters, when he judges his correspondent to be with him, there is to be found quite a superfluity of expressions unexceptively averse to the belief in conditions. To Hooker, for example, he says once, "The conclusion I have come to . . . is that external conditions (to which naturalists so often appeal) do by themselves *very little ;* " and this very little is an italicized very little. On another occasion he finds " the common notion absurd that climate, food, etc., should make a pediculus formed to climb hair, or woodpecker to climb trees." " I quite agree with what you say about the little direct influence of climate," he seems quite glad to tell Hooker at another time. To Thomas Davidson, again, he courteously and concessively admits, " I oscillate much on this head ;" still he takes heart to intimate that he " generally returns to his belief that the direct action of the conditions of life has not been great." To Lyell, he throws off every rag of reserve, and actually swears. " I feel inclined to swear at climate " (ii. 174), he says ; " no error is more mischievous than this" (ii. 169); and again, " It has taken me so many years to disabuse my mind of the *too* great importance of climate that I am inclined to swear at the North Pole, and, as Sydney Smith said, 'even to speak disrespectfully of the Equator;'" and then he bids Lyell reflect how "readily acclimatization is effected under nature"—how "thousands of plants can perfectly well withstand a little more heat and cold, a little more damp and dry," etc. As all inorganic phenomena are under the law of physical gravitation, so Mr. Darwin would wish all organic phenomena to prove under the law of mere physical variation. So it is that he dislikes all reference to conditions. It is very natural that one, for a time, should fail to see this in Mr. Darwin; for the influence of conditions is so glaringly conspicuous, so palpably indispensable indeed, that it takes long to be prepared for their denial. Nevertheless, it is obvious from these quotations—and they might be largely augmented—that he who insists on conditions as elements in the construction of an organism, cannot be in agreement with, but is in opposition to, Mr. Darwin. And it is here that Mr. Huxley puts us to some difficulty—not for his opinions, but only in his use of the phrase "external conditions." As regards the 1844 Essay, for example, he points out to Mr. Darwin's son that in it "much more weight is attached to the influence of external conditions in producing variation, and to the inheritance of acquired habits, than in the *Origin;*" while to Mr. Darwin himself he had, after reading his book in 1859, remarked,—and the remark is the second of the only two objections that have occurred to him,—"it is not clear to me why, if continual physical conditions are of so little moment as you suppose, variation should occur at all" (ii. 231). Mr. Huxley, from these quotations, had evidently observed that Mr. Darwin put little moment on physical conditions, and that this tendency on his part was stronger on a later occasion than on an earlier. Evidently, also, Mr. Huxley was so far in disagreement with Mr. Darwin. It cannot be so far, then, that we mean Mr. Huxley to have put us to any relative difficulty. No; the reference in that case is to a passage in Mr. Huxley's writing, just of the other day, which (*Life and Letters of Charles Darwin*, vol. ii. p. 195) runs thus: "The suggestion that new species may result from the selective action of external conditions upon the variations from their specific type which individuals present—and which we call 'spontaneous,' because we are ignorant of their causation—that suggestion is the central idea of the *Origin of Species*, and contains the quintessence of Darwinism." Here "external conditions," as we see, have become the very motor, and agent, and source, and spring of Darwinism; and they do give difficulty, if they are to be supposed the same as before. But they are not to be so supposed —they are not the same as before. No, very far from that! The conditions then were supposed to precede the variation: the conditions now are supposed to follow it. Or, while the former were the conditions that brought about the variation, the latter, again, are those that only take advantage of it. The first set of conditions were those of climate,—heat and cold, damp and dry,—food, etc. What the second set refers to—quite otherwise—are the increased means of nourishment, support, shelter, security, which have been already described as the advantages on the part of nature, pictured in the theory, to be consequent upon the variation. As was said then: It is on the variation that Nature operates her selection; or, as it may be otherwise conceived, the selection is operated on nature by the variation. Now, that is the whole meaning of Mr. Huxley in the apparently discrepant usage of the phrase " external conditions," in his respective passage that has just been quoted. Further, as we may allow ourselves to note, when, in the same passage, Mr. Huxley calls the variation "spontaneous," there can be no hesitation in acknowledging that he is absolutely correct in asserting the single suggestion he has in view to be the central idea, and to constitute the quintessence of Darwinism : the suggestion, namely, that new species may result from such and such selective action on such and such individual variation. *A* variation occurs spontaneously in an organism ; and it is followed up by a selective action on (or through) the conditions in its environment. These are the conditions Mr. Huxley means now ; and that to him, as it is to us, is the whole idea of Darwinism—the quintessence of Darwinism— the centre, and the soul, and the very self of Darwinism. For the sake of clearness, I may just point out here a third set of external conditions. The "attraction of gravity," namely, " light," etc., which Mr. Darwin names in connection with the "power of movement" in plants, are quite entitled to the same designation ; but, however relevant as referred to, they are not to be regarded as elements in the Darwinian *construction.*

We may return now to this, that, in their first sense, Mr. Huxley disagreed with Mr. Darwin as to the action of external conditions in respect of variations in individual organisms—disagreed so widely, indeed, that it was not clear to him (Huxley) "how, without continual physical conditions, variation should occur at all." Confusion in regard to the various sets of conditions is not to be thought of when these words were written. There must, at that time, have been points of serious disagreement on the part of Mr. Huxley with the views of Mr. Darwin. It is Mr. Darwin himself who writes to Mr. Huxley in 1860 (ii. 354) : "This makes me feel a little disappointed that you are not inclined to think the general view in some slight degree more probable than you did at first. This I consider rather ominous. I entirely agree with you that the difficulties on my notions are terrific." Nor, if it was so with Mr Huxley, was it in any respect better—rather, was it not worse?—with Sir Joseph Hooker and Sir Charles Lyell, who, as the confidants of Mr. Darwin, had, on various public occasions, been the means of trumpeting the story of our long-tailed or four-footed ancestors to an astonished world, which could but breathlessly rush to see and to know? Mr. Darwin will have it (i. 87), that it was not, "as it has been sometimes said, that the success of the *Origin* proved 'that the subject was in the air,' or 'that men's minds were prepared for it.' I do not think that this is strictly true," he says, "for I occasionally sounded not a few naturalists, and never happened to come across a single one who seemed to doubt about the permanence of species. Even Lyell and Hooker, though they would listen with interest to me, never seemed to agree." Of Lyell he had already written to Dr. Asa Gray in 1863, "You speak of Lyell as a judge; now what I complain of is that he declines to be a judge. I have sometimes almost wished that Lyell had pronounced against me." To Lyell himself, too, he writes (ii. 300), "It is a great blow to me that you cannot admit the potency of natural selection;" and again, "I grieve to see you hint at the creation of distinct successive types, as well as of distinct aboriginal types." To the same Gray he avows also, "You never say a word or use an epithet which does not express fully my meaning. Now Lyell, Hooker, and others, who perfectly understand my book, yet sometimes use expressions to which I demur." It is to be feared that even this Dr. Asa Gray, who never said a discrepant word, was pretty much, for all that, in the same state of mind as Hooker and Lyell. Mr. Darwin, himself, in the very next paragraph of the very same letter, can only say of him, "I yet hope, and almost believe, that the time will come when you will go farther, in believing a very large amount of modification of species, than you did at first, or do now. Can you tell me whether you believe further, or more firmly, than you did at first?" It is quite touchingly suggestive of the situation, and quite pathetic, to hear Mr. Darwin, so painfully, simply in earnest, follow up his question by, "I should really like to know this!" Mr. Darwin, indeed, must have occasionally suffered dreadfully at this time from distrust, and mistrust, and want of confidence in the soundness and cogency of what he had so much his heart in. He tells Asa Gray of the thought of the eye making him "cold all over." Nay, he says, "the sight of a feather in a peacock's tail, whenever I gaze at it, makes me sick!" It is in much the same mood of mind, or with the same problem before him, that he cries out once to Huxley, "If, as I must think, external conditions produce little *direct* effect, what the devil determines each particular variation? What makes a tuft of feathers come on a cock's head, or moss on a moss-rose?"

For us, from such expressions as these, we are brought very close to the question as Mr. Darwin sees it. There is no formed difference that he would not like to account for; and he does not always see his way to this in a start from certain rudimentary or initial spontaneous differences, which his theory obliges him to assume. "I believe," he says, "most beings vary at all times enough for selection to act on,"—that is, he means, as it were, and as Mr. Huxley directly says, "spontaneously" vary. Hence advantage and disadvantage in the struggle for life, with the necessary survival of the fittest.

We have thus broken ground on the views of Mr. Darwin, and will be already able to judge, in some degree, of the relation which, according to Mr. Darwin himself, these views bear to the argument from design; and that alone is the consideration which interests us here. We must continue the subject with, I hope, a closer approach in our next.

# GIFFORD LECTURE THE EIGHTEENTH.

The theory—Individual variation—Darwin early looked for natural explanation of design—Creation, its senses—Antisthenes, Colebrooke, Cudworth — Creative ideas—Anaxagoras—Aristotle—Mr. Clair Grece and Darwin—For design Mr. Darwin offers a mechanical pullulation of individual difference through chance, but with consequent results that as advantageous or disadvantageous *seem* concerted—The Fathers—Nature the phenomenon of the noumenon, a boundless externality of contingency that still is a life—Nature, the object will only *be* when it reaches the subject—That object be, or subject be, *both* must be—Even the crassest material particle is already both elementarily—As it were, even inorganic matter possesses instincts—Aristotle, design and necessity—Internalization—Time space, motion, matter—The world — Contingency — A perspective of pictures — The *Vestiges* and evolution — Darwin deprecates genealogies, but returns to them—The mud-fish—Initial proteine—There are so many mouths to eat it up now—Darwin recants his pentateuchal concession to creation—Depends on "fanciers and breeders"—The infinitudes of transition just taken by Mr. Darwin in a step—Hypothesis—Illustration at random—Difference would go on to difference, not return to the identity—Mr. Lewes and Dr. Erasmus—The grandfather's filament—Seals—The bear and the whale—Dr. Erasmus on the imagination, on weeping, on fear, on the tadpole's tail, on the rationale of strabismus.

WE have now reached something of an insight into the theorem or theory of Mr. Darwin. I know not that it can be better put than as we have seen it put, in his own clear way, by Mr. Huxley. "The suggestion," he says, "that new species may result from the selective action of external conditions upon the variations from their specific type which individuals present, and which we call 'spontaneous,' because we are ignorant of their causation — that suggestion is the central idea of the *Origin of Species*, and contains the quintessence of Darwinism." Perhaps we might object to the phrase "variations from their specific type" as insufficiently exact. Variation from specific type, we might say, has already achieved the whole problem—at a word! If there *is* spontaneous variation from the specific type— if that is a fact, then "the selective action of external conditions" seems supererogatory, seems to have nothing left for it to do: what was wanted is already accomplished. A variation from the specific type, a new creature, is already there; and we are just simply ignorant of its causation. Mr. Darwin himself does not conceive the first variation to be more than an individual variation (children only *individually* vary from their parents)—he does not conceive it to be by any means a *specific* variation—a variation at once into a new creature. Specific variation, a new creature, is to Mr. Darwin only the result — perhaps after millions of generations—of the eventual accumulation, by inheritance, of an indefinite—almost of an infinite—number of individual differences. So much importance, indeed, does Mr. Darwin attach to the first individual difference, to the very first initial modification as the absolutely first step in the process, and the consequent divergence of character from the gradual accumulation of steps, modifications, that he would almost consent to withdraw the phrase natural selection. "Compared to the question of Creation *or* Modification," he says (ii. 371), "Natural Selection seems to me utterly unimportant." And that brings us to the question that is between Mr. Darwin and ourselves—the question of design, namely. Early in life Mr. Darwin's father "proposed that he should become a clergyman," and he himself in the first instance was nothing loath. He was "heartily laughed at too," he says, "by several of the officers of the *Beagle* for quoting the Bible." Nevertheless, he seems, still early in life, to have taken an antipathy to *creation* as the explanation of the adaptations and contrivances he saw in organic life. How was the woodpecker, for instance, so wonderfully formed for the climbing of trees, he asked himself; and he could not at all quiet himself by the answer, it has been just so made. That was a supernatural explanation, and he for his part could only be satisfied with a natural one. If all that is *in*organic is absolutely determined by natural law, why should not all that is *organic* be similarly determined? And so, as I have just quoted, he came to his idea of "modification," on which as a principle of explanation he took his stand, in opposition to, and supersedure of, "creation." That was the colour he definitely nailed to his mast— "Creation *or* Modification." And his *or* here is an italicized *or;* for to Mr. Darwin there could be no other *or*. In fact, to the general crowd of naturalists at this moment it would appear that there can be—rather that there is, no other *or*, no other alternative whatever, than "creation *or* modification." A good deal depends here, however, on what sense is to be given to "creation." Antisthenes must have believed snails and locusts to have been mere products of the earth; for Diogenes Laertius reports him to have called the Athenians no better than such low spawn when they bragged of being earth-born. The Indian philosophers, too, according to Colebrooke, held the "spontaneous generation of worms, nits, maggots, gnats, and other vermin." Then Ralph Cudworth was undoubtedly a most devout, sincere, and pious Christian; but he seems to have felt it such an indignity to God to hold that "God Himself doth all immediately; and, as it were, with His own hands form the body of every gnat and fly, insect and mite," that he invented, and extended as medium between God and the world, what is known to all students as his "Plastic Nature." This Cudworth describes, not as "the divine, not archetypal, but only ectypal," as "reason immersed and plunged into matter, and, as it were, fuddled in it and confounded with it." We see, then, from this what sense Ralph Cudworth gave to creation. And I at least am so far of his mind that I as little believe God to have put hand to gnat or fly, insect or mite, as I believe Him to have manufactured, quarried, or mason-like made, the little bare rock on the top of Arthur's Seat. But, again, in the other direction, I am absolutely of the same mind with Cudworth in regard to ideas. To him "knowledge is older than all sensible things; νοῦς, *nous* is senior to the world, and the architect thereof." Since Anaxagoras, it will be within recollection, that is the view that has been argued in these lectures; and since Aristotle design has been the name of our conviction. "It is better to be than not to be," says Aristotle, "and nature always strives to the better" (336b); "it is not the wood that makes the bed, but the skill; and it is not water itself that makes out of itself an animal, but nature" (335). Anaxagoras was, as we know, nicknamed νοῦς; and with quite as much reason the boys and girls of Athens might have cried after Aristotle, ἕνεκα οὗ, ἕνεκά του, τέλος, τέλος, all of which words mean design. Mr. Darwin, I repeat, never made a greater mistake in his life than when he allowed Mr. Clair Grece's translation to make him believe that Aristotle, like himself, was above design and all for natural necessity or chance. As I say, Aristotle might have been as appropriately called Design, as Anaxagoras was called Mind; and even much more appropriately, for Aristotle, unlike Anaxagoras, was true to his principles throughout; design was his first word and his last. Now, it is in consequence of just such a belief in design that it is impossible for me to accept the theory which Mr. Darwin offers us in lieu of it. Mr. Darwin, for his part, has no such belief, and he offers us, instead, a mechanical pullulation of individual difference which is to eventuate in all the beautiful and complicated forms, whether of plant or animal, which we see around us. We have seen that it was the alternative of "creation" or "modification" that determined him to this. Others, might call in the supernatural, the god from the machine, if they liked; he, for his part, would only have the *usual* at work. He would see all these fine adaptations just naturally *inflect* themselves. He had only one sense for "creation," and apparently it was only the crass, common, literal one of a workman turning something out of hand. As we have seen also, Cudworth, to say nothing of Antisthenes and the Indians, could not away with this conception, but felt under a necessity to interpose a plastic nature between God and the world. For their parts, the most and greatest of the Fathers, Clement of Alexandria, Origen, Athanasius, Basil, Hilary, and especially Augustine, believed that the world was called into existence even as by a wish; and in this way, handiwork there was none. To a certain extent that illustrates what we may call perhaps the true or correct idea in the immediate reference. Nature is but the phenomenon of the noumenon, the many of the one, the externale of the internale, thrown down from the unity of reasoned co-articulation and connectedness—thrown down and abroad into the infinitude of a disunited, disconnected, and disarticulated inorganic chaos, which, however, turns upon itself—turns upon itself for restoration and return to the image from which it fell. Nature is not dead, nature is a life, and, if all unconsciously to itself, it has still an aim in view. "It is better to be than not to be," says

Aristotle; and so, as I take it, *it is*, that what is, is. And if it is for the better that what is, is, so it is that this same better is never lost sight of. "We say that nature," as is the expression of this same Aristotle, "always in all things strives — ὀρέγεσθαι — reaches, stretches out hands to the better." In a word, nature would articulate itself, nature would see, nature would be seen —nay, at the last, nature would see its own self. Nature with all its rocks and seas and mountains, with all its suns and moons and planets, with all its vast star-systems and all its immensity of space and all its infinitude of time, would be—if only that — no more than the blackness and silence of a point—no more than the blackness and silence of an all-indefinite point. But nature would not remain that—nature would *be*—nature would be a universe—a marvellous crystal universe, with an eye to see it, and an ear to hear it. The object would be the subject; and then only, first of all, would itself *be* — then only first of all would the object be the object—then only first of all would it be even *an* object. Nature must have a man to make it even nature—object must have subject to make it even object. Alone, unseen, the Bayadere of the universe will not even dance. Now the subject is what hears and sees and thinks, while the object is what is heard and seen and thought; and that there *be*, just that anything be—that there be anything, both must be. But it is not to be supposed that there is only such union to be found when we come to find ourselves, when we come to find a man. The mud of the river, the sand by the sea, the very dust beneath our feet, is at once both. Were it not so, it would be naught, nothing; it would disappear—it would be incognizable of us. That it is cognizable of us depends upon this, that it is already a concretion of categories, a complexion of thoughts. As you may wash away all colour from a clot of blood, and be left at last with a pure transparent ultimate, a pure transparent web which held the colour, so you may discharge materiature from any particle of dust, or sand, or mud, and be left at last with a pure diamond of fibres intellectual. No particle of dust, or sand, or mud but is there in *quantity*, and *quality*, and *measure*, in *substance* and *accident*, in *matter* and *form*, and in quite a congeries of many other categories. In this way one can see that it may be said that even inorganic matter possesses instincts. Not dog alone, or rat or cat, or bee or swallow, is endowed with instinct, but even the rocks, and stones, and all the materials around them. The lower animals to Mr. Darwin, as he says, "seem to have the very same attributes in a much lower stage of perfection than the lowest savage" (ii. 211). To him, that is, there is an intellectual gradation from the lowest animal to the highest man. *Still* he calls it "a strange view of instinct, and wholly false," that would "regard intelligence as a developed instinct." That, however, must arise from Mr. Darwin's peculiarity to look upon instinct as only an inherited habit. Most people mean by instinct the whole thinking faculty of an animal, so far as it has a thinking faculty at all. It is in the same way that Aristotle, though he says that "God and nature do nothing in vain," yet assigns to nature no *divine* quality, but only one that is *dæmonic*, acting on unconscious motive, even as we might conceive wood to act, did it make out of itself a boat or a bed; for nature's ends are wrought out blindly and without reflection. Nevertheless, even so working, nature, continues Aristotle, 645a, affords inexpressible delight to those who are able to discover causes, and are philosophers by nature;" not but that, as he says elsewhere, 677a16—, "design is not always to be looked for, inasmuch as, certain things being such as they are, many others follow from them through necessity." This operation of necessity, as we see, is what Mr. Darwin alone trusts to, and under its iron feet, unlike Aristotle, he would annihilate design. But alone the consideration gives pause to that—the consideration, what would the whole universe be, did it not attain to an eye that would look at it, to an ear that would listen to it? To that co-articulation of mutual necessities it is impossible for any thinking being to conceive of chance as the cause. As we saw, it is better to be than not to be, and so there *is;* but if there *is*, then there is both object *and* subject. Either without the other were a blank; either without the other were in vain. In order that anything be, there must both be. No one can look at nature, even as it is there before our eyes, without acknowledging that what it shows everywhere is the rise from lowest object up to highest subject. Science has already divided this rise, and made of it a succession of terraces, of which any one is already more reasonable than its predecessor. To take this succession and progression from below upwards is, as it were, a reversal of emanation, a sort of retrograde emanation, and the only truth, perhaps, of that whole doctrine. We have first utmost *space* and furthest *time*, and then *motion* and the *moved* merely—the *moved* merely, matter, namely, that, as space is externality outwards, has already commenced to be externality inwards, and so approached the subject, as it were, individually and from within; while motion, that has thrown the whole into the unity of law and system—astral system—is the same approach, as it were, universally and from without. Nay, earlier still, we may place the beginning of the approach. Space in itself is manifestly the externale as the externale; it is externality pure and simple, externality as such; it is always out and out endlessly, it is never in and in. And it lies there motionless, a motionless, infinite *Out*. There seems no pure internal framework there as in the clot of blood, no hidden categorical nucleolus of ideas as in material particles. Yet, even as these particles have categories, space has, as its soul, time. Space is in the clutch of time: in each moment of time the whole infinitude of space at once is: no moment of time but is at once everywhere. Is it not strange just to think of that— that even the perishable moment of time is, as everywhere in space, at once infinite! And yet for us to count the infinitude of space, we should require the eternity of time. Evidently, whatever they are, they must both go together; time and space are a concrete, of which the one is the discretion and the other the continuity. But the universe, in that it holds of the infinite and absolute, is independent of either. No one can say *where* the world exists, nor *when*—it is above any where or any when: it is its own there and then, and everywhere, and at once, and always. As we have said, it is the phenomenon of the noumenon; and as everywhere the turn and return of the out to the in, it makes confession of its origin. Even in the finite there is rise of the object into the subject, and science tells us of it—in astronomy, and geology, and botany, and zoology, and man. The whole effort of nature in its zoology is to get to man; and it is a long ascent to get to him, through sponge and mollusc, fish and reptile, bird and beast. Nature, all the time, is in no hurry or haste, however, but spreads itself out, in its contingency, in millions and millions of indifferent shapes which, nevertheless, collect and gather themselves in their contingency to the rounds and rungs of their ladder in its rise. Nature scatters its living products abroad, as the sea its shells upon the strand. Contingency is the word; he that cannot put himself at home with contingency as philosophically understood, will never philosophize this world. Mr. Darwin's inherited individual differences will never prove a match for the contingency that *is*. Mr. Darwin had the richest memory of anecdotes in nature of any man that ever lived, and, with an even infinite conjectural ingenuity, he carried every anecdote to its purpose in the march. But what these anecdotes were to illustrate or establish was, in the first instance, this. Mr. Darwin said to himself, Children resemble their parents; but they also differ from them. Evidently, therefore, they are as likely to propagate differences as to propagate resemblances; for the fact of propagation, the fact of inheritance, is to be admitted, is simply to be named. Now, any given difference may be an advantage, or it may be a disadvantage. That is, the animal, by reason of the difference propagated and inherited, may be obstructed in the exercise of its functions and the use of its conditions; or, in all these respects, it may be furthered. The ultimate of obstruction can only be extinction. But, in the case of furtherance, inasmuch as furtherance only encourages furtherance, ever the more and the more, say for incalculable periods, the ultimate can only be something perfectly new—can only be a new organism, in fact, that is tantamount to a new species. Now observe how, all this time, and even as I have been using the words—observe how we have all passed through a long, fascinating, and most natural-seeming perspective. We have all, in imagination, quite pleasedly, and without a rub or a check, assisted actually at a new birth. We could not help ourselves. Seeing that inherited difference going incalculably on and on, we felt involuntarily minded to admit any intermediate metamorphosis with any terminal result whatever. We heard words which gave us a picture in imagination; and we submitted to them. Nothing can be more plausible than an incalculable time; nothing can be more plausible than an infinite series of infinitely small numbers—here of infinitely small differences that gradually pass into one another. It belongs to the human mind to picture an endless time,—an endless continuity,—and then break it up into an endless number of points—an endless number of discretes. We yield to the plausibility of all this, then, I say; we yield and—we are lost. But, consider, is it a fact that length of time will of itself account for anything? Is it a fact that we must allow the capability of insensible degrees to account for any change whatever? Given a thing that is granted to vary, surely we may see it in imagination vary into anything whatever—should there further be granted any number of insensible degrees and any length of time we may wish. Such conditions must prove irresistible to any imagination that has not prepared and fortified itself for opposition in advance. Our possible mental pictures have really a most potent effect upon us, but a new species, made by man, or made by nature, has it been ever *proved?* Followers of Mr. Darwin have been asked, Is it at all conceivable that any length of time, or that any insensible degrees, would ever convert a canary into an elephant, or a bee into a bull? And followers of Mr. Darwin have always turned upon the questioner with contempt for his ignorance, and indignation for his injustice. Did he not know that Mr. Darwin ever poured scorn on all such questions? Even in the case of a man so eminent as Dr. Robert Chambers, and of a book so justly authoritative as the *Vestiges,* did not Mr. Darwin find "the idea of a fish passing into a reptile, monstrous"? Did not such things amuse him in the great geologist Sir Roderick Impey Murchison? and did it not give him "a cold shudder (ii. 334) to hear of any one"—Professor Parsons it was—"speculating about a true crustacean giving birth to a true fish? How very different his own ideas of genealogy were, we may understand from this. "We might give to a bird the habits of a mammal," he says (ii. 335), "but inheritance would retain almost for eternity some of the bird-like structure, and prevent a new creature ranking as a mammal." That is, a bird, even though it had already the *habits* of a mammal, would remain bird-like, and never, in all eternity, rise to the *rank* of a mammal. Fish, amphibians, reptiles, birds, mammals, must have had, for each of them as a class, their one "necessary and peculiar progenitor, having a character like the embryo" of an individual of each of them. It is Mr. Darwin's own declaration always, " We must imagine "— he does not say *discover*—" we must imagine some form as intermediate—I cannot conceive (ii. 335) any existing reptile being converted into a mammal." It is gross ignorance, then, to hear enemies of Mr. Darwin courageously maintain that they, for their parts, had never come from a cow, just as though Mr. Darwin had ever said that! This is something like those enemies of Berkleianism who attribute to Berkeley the direct communication on the part of God to man of every possible absurd particular, whereas Berkeley has no thought in his mind but of communication on the part of God to man of this whole orderly, law-regulated, systematized universe. Such caricaturists in objections are to be found in opposition to every new truth. As there were those who told Berkeley to knock his head against a lamp-post, so there are those who tell Mr. Darwin they did not come from a cow! Well, then, I suppose we may grant that, as on the part of the friends of Mr. Darwin, to be all right. It *is* gross ignorance to say that Mr. Darwin ever holds us to come from a cow, or can be construed into so holding. When Mr. Darwin called "the idea of a fish passing into a reptile, monstrous," he also expressly declared, as for his own part, "*I* will not specify any genealogies—much too little known at present." We see, however, that Mr. Darwin's knowledge must have very sensibly increased, for we are in his debt in the end for several genealogies. He is quite confident at last, for example, that the early progenitor of man was a catarhine monkey covered with hair, its ears pointed and capable of movement, its foot prehensile, its body provided with a tail, and it habits arboreal (*Descent of Man*, 155-60). At an earlier period he says, "*Our* ancestor was an animal which breathed water, had a swim bladder, a great swimming tail, an imperfect skull, and undoubtedly was a hermaphrodite!" (ii. 266). Mr. Darwin is so sure of his affair here that he can say "undoubtedly." Of course we, for our parts, are accordingly impressed; but if Mr. Darwin had said, "Our ancestor was not an animal which breathed water, had no imperfect skull, and no great swimming tail, and was undoubtedly not a hermaphrodite," I question whether we should not have been equally accipient, and quite equally impressed. But now that Mr. Darwin has come after all to have as much confidence in genealogy as the author of the *Vestiges* himself, we have to see that it is the lepidosiren or mud-fish that is his greatest favourite in the propagation race. When Sir Charles Lyell ventures to say a word about "the necessity of the continued intervention of creative power," Mr. Darwin is immediately reminded of the mud-fish, and of the ease with which (to use his own expression) it will *floor* Lyell. "I cannot see this necessity," he says, "and its admission, I think, would make the theory of natural selection valueless. Grant a simple archetypal creature like the mud-fish or lepidosiren with the five senses and some vestige of mind, and I believe natural selection will account for the production of every vertebrate

animal!" Why the mud-fish is such a favourite with
Mr. Darwin probably is because, as he tells us, it is
intermediate "between reptiles and fish, between mammals and birds on the one hand and reptiles on the other
hand." The mud-fish, should we look it up, as we easily
may in any zoological primer, will be found a creature
something like an eel, and of no great size. When Mr.
Darwin asked to be allowed to endow it with "the five
senses and some vestige of mind," we may have thought
that he was only asking to be granted what the problem
itself amounted to; but should we look at the fish itself,
and consider what materials Mr. Darwin only asked for
in order to make it a man, I doubt not we shall admire
his modesty. For the commencement of all the marvels
of animal life, Mr. Darwin, as he says, would seem to
require only "a proteine compound chemically formed in
some little pond, with all sorts of ammonia and phos-
phoric salts, light, heat, electricity, etc., present;" but,
alas! as he very pointedly laments, "at the present day
such matter would be instantly devoured and absorbed,"
now that there are so many "living creatures" all about
(iii. 18). The want of this primordial life-matter, which
Mr. Darwin quite cheerfully opines might be quite easily
"*chemically* formed," does not discourage him from evolving all animals whatever from a single specimen of them
once he has got one—the mud-fish say, which for him,
too, has only to "appear." "I have long regretted," he
says (iii. 18), "that I truckled to public opinion, and
used the pentateuchal term of creation, by which I really
meant 'appeared' by some wholly unknown process."
This is how he recants the wind-up of his great book,
the *Origin*, "into that grandeur of view" which sees "the
Creator breathe life into a few forms or into one." No,
no! there can be no "creation," but only "modification;"
all the materials of which are imaginatively prepared for

it in the first imagined "appearance" out of the first imagined proteine. Then how he got to all this! He tells Dr. Asa Gray (ii. 79), as we saw once already. "All my notions about *how* species change are derived from long-continued study of the works of (and converse with) agriculturists and horticulturists;" and accordingly he admits, "I have found it very important associating with fanciers and breeders."

Nay, he even confesses that he did not disdain to find himself seated in pursuit of knowledge under difficulties "amongst a set of pigeon fanciers in a gin palace in the borough!" (ii. 281). It is, then, in consequence of what he has learned in this way about pouters and fantails, the horns of cattle and the wool of sheep, together with bands, stripes, or bars upon the backs and legs of horses and donkeys (ii. 111), that he feels himself empowered at last to declare that "all vertebrata have descended from one parent" (ii. 211), and that analogy leads him to the conclusion of the descent also "from one parent of the great kingdoms (as vertebrata, articulata, and the rest)" (ii. 212). Nay, so high did he mount in his rapture of discovery (imagination), "that he applied the theory of evolution to the whole organic kingdom from plants to man!" (ii. 6). What a wonderful thing that first only chemically-formed proteine must have been, which already contained in its invisible "seed-bags," as Jean Paul Richter might say, plants, animals, and man, Adam and Eve, and all! Nay, what a much more wonderful thing, if possible, is that spoon of mere individual difference by chance, which alone enables Mr. Darwin to dig into the initial material identity, and deal it out into the infinity of the infinitely varied plant life and infinitely varied animal life which we see around us! Once Mr. Darwin has finished with the vertebrata—*only* the vertebrata!—what a wonderful leap that is, *a salto mortale*, a flying leap on the single trapeze of "analogy," that enables him without more ado to find the articulata, insecta, mollusca, molluscoida, and what not, all in the same Noah's ark of a pedigree with man! It is not an expensive matter to philosophize in that way. The grandfather, Erasmus the first, said *omnia ex conchis*, or *ex conchis omnia*, "all from oysters;" Mr. Darwin surpasses his grandfather and cries all, oysters too, from proteine. For if one will consider of it, there is, at bottom on Mr. Darwin's part, certainly with illustrations enow, pictures enow, little more than a *cry*. Let us look back on what we have seen—let us turn up any one page as alluded to in Mr. Darwin, and we shall find, with all his illustrations, that the method of Mr. Darwin is one of hypothesis, supposition, probable conjecture only. It is so easy to prove this that, without troubling to look back and turn up pages behind us, I just open a book of Mr. Darwin's at random—I just positively take it up from my table, open it at random, and read what I see. I find I have opened at page 594 of the second edition of the *Descent of Man*. "At a very early period, before man attained to his present rank in the scale, many of his conditions would be different from what now obtains amongst savages. Judging from the analogy of the lower animals he would then either live with a single female or be a polygamist." (He would not have been a bachelor, it seems?) "The most powerful and able males would succeed best in obtaining attractive females." (We know that the weakest succeed now in that respect quite as well as the strongest!) "They would also succeed best in the general struggle for life. . . . At this early period the ancestors of man would not be sufficiently advanced in intellect to look forward to distant contingencies; they would not foresee that the rearing of all their children, especially their female children, would make the struggle of life severer for the tribe. They would be governed more by their instincts. They would not at that period," and so on. That is a perfect specimen of how the mind of Mr. Darwin works. Difference would be—difference would go on incalculably into new identities, not possibly turn back, as all facts past or present seem on the whole to suggest, into the old ones again. With him it is always so and so " would be." One correspondent seems to have objected to him his constant " I believe, or I am convinced," and to have advised rather what he might depend upon as " I prove " (ii. 240). " I cannot doubt " is another such expression of his. " I cannot doubt," he says, " that during millions of generations individuals of a species will be born with some slight variation profitable to some part of its economy." That is his whole doctrine in its one creative bud : individuals vary to advantage ; and it rests on a mere subjective " I cannot doubt," and that, too, in regard to a mere mental picture of millions !—millions of generations !—that some one individual, from time to time among them all, we may be safe to assume, will experience " some slight variation profitable to some part of its economy." The whole tendency of the natural indefinite picture, which, as such, we cannot well gainsay, is to blind us to the pure assumption of the single proposition — individual differences will so accumulate to advantage in millions of generations as to constitute a new species. Of course it is useless to ask for the proof which the correspondent suggested ; proof there can be none given ; naturally, that record of millions of generations can have a place only in the imagination ; and by way of proof there can be nothing for it but illustratively to allude to all manner of conjectural likelihoods and specious possibilities, which in a great many cases will be found to admit of a *no*, not one whit less satisfactorily than of a *yes*. To read what Mr. Darwin, in the *Krause-*

*book*, quotes from Mr. Lewes in regard to Erasmus Darwin, one is led to believe that Mr. Lewes had a very high opinion of that respected grandsire. That is certainly the impression Mr. Darwin desires to convey. We come to the very opposite conclusion, however, when we turn up the passage and read in Mr. Lewes himself, who tells us how Erasmus, "as he proceeds, gets more and more absurd;" how, "as a poet, his *Botanic Garden* by its tawdry splendour gained him a tawdry reputation;" and how, " as a philosopher, his *Zoonomia* gained him a reputation equally noisy and fleeting." The grandson speaks of his grandfather's "overpowering tendency to theorize and generalize." And certainly no one will dispute as much if he reads the *Zoonomia*. All life for Erasmus proceeds from an organic filament; there is a different one for the different kingdoms; yet, probably, he says at last, "one and the same kind of living filament is and has been the cause of all organic life." And here I, for my part, prefer the grandfather's *filament* to the grandson's *proteine*. Mr. Darwin conjectures seals to begin to feed on shore (ii. 339), and so, consequently, to vary; and yet he admits (ii. 336), "I know of no fact showing any the least incipient variation of seals feeding on the shore." The grandfather will have it, again, that all animals were at first fish, and became amphibious by feeding on shore, and so gradually terrestrial. This is vastly more wholesale than what the grandson says about seals, and yet I know not that the grandfather's teeming imagination ever gave birth to a more Brobdingnagian monster than this on the part of the grandson. At page 141 of the latest issue of the *Origin of Species* we read: "In North America the black bear was seen by Hearne swimming for hours with widely open mouth, thus catching almost like a whale insects in the water." A bear swimming and catching insects, even as a whale might—this on the part of Mr. Darwin is to make easy to us the transition of one animal into another. Truly, as I said, Mr. Darwin does not *always* scout genealogy! He could not stomach it in the case of Dr. Robert Chambers and the passage of a fish into a reptile; but in fifteen years—the interval between his reading and his writing—he has learned something—he has acquired himself a swallow wide enough for both a whale and a bear. The passage, it seems, according to a note in the *Life and Letters* (ii. 234), was omitted in the second edition. Nevertheless, it is to be read in the last issue now. Mr. Darwin, then, must have deliberately restored it. I say *deliberately*, for we find him, November 24, 1859, consulting Lyell about it. "Will you send me one line to say whether I must strike out about the whale? it goes to my heart!" Next day also we find him assuring this same Lyell, "I will certainly leave out the whale and bear." Nay, in September of the following year he cannot help writing once more on the subject to Lyell, but this time—so much has it gone to his heart—appealingly. "Observe," he cries,—"observe that in my wretched polar bear case I *do* show the first step by which conversion into a whale 'would be easy,' 'would offer no difficulty!'" He had already said in the first of these three letters, "In transitions it is the *premier pas qui coute*," and we are to understand, therefore, that supplied with the first step of the transition of a bear into a whale we could be at no loss in picturing to ourselves the easy remainder of the entire process. An easy remainder, surely, seeing we had to refer for it only to our own imaginations! It is to the imagination, at all events, that the grandfather testifies great gratitude. He cheerfully allows it a chief place in "*metamorphoses*," and surely with reason! It shall be the imagination of the mother that colours the eggs of her progeny; he even brings in the imagination of the father in a wonderful (*Shandy-an*) manner! Then it is by imagination afterwards of the original irritation of the lachrymal glands at birth that we are able during life to weep when in grief, as it is by imagination of our first cold shivering, also at birth, that when in fear we always tremble, etc. I suppose it is still the effects of imagination he alludes to when he says: "The tadpole acquires legs and lungs—when he wants them! and loses his tail —when it is no longer of service to him!" And certainly it is only by a signal effort of the imagination that he himself has been enabled to discover this astonishing rationale and causality of squinting (*Zoonomia*, ii. 143). "Squinting is generally owing to one eye being less perfect than the other, on which account the patient endeavours to hide the worst eye in the shadow of the nose!" We may break off here, and resume next week.

# GIFFORD LECTURE THE NINETEENTH.

Dr. Erasmus Darwin—Student scribbles on *Zoonomia*—Family differences, attraction and repulsion—The Darwins in this respect—Dr. Erasmus of his sons, Mr. Charles and Dr. R. W. —Dr. R. W. as to his sons—Charles on his grandfather, father, brother—Mr. Erasmus on his brother's book—On the *à priori*—On facts—Darwin's one method—Darwin and Hooker on facts—Family politics—Family religion—Family habits—Family theories—Mr. Darwin's endowments—His *Journal*—The *Zoonomia*—Theories of Dr. Erasmus—Paley—Instinct—An *idea* to Dr. E.—Dugald Stewart—Picture-thinking—Dr. E.'s method—Darwin's doubts—His brave spirit —The theory to his friends—Now—Almost every propos of the grandson has its germ in the grandfather (Krause)—Yet the position of the latter—Byron on—Mr. Lewes also—The greater Newton, original Darwinism now to be revived—Dr. E. admirable on design—Charles on cats made by God to play with mice!—Dr. E. on atheism—The apology—But will conclude with a single point followed thoroughly out: the Galapagos —Darwin held to be impregnably fortified there—The Galapagos thrown up to opponents at every turn—But we are not naturalists!—Dr. E. rehabilitates us—Description of the Galapagos from the *Journal*—The islands, their size, number, position, geographical and relative—depth of water and distance between —Climate, currents, wind—Geology, botany, zoology—Volcanoes, dull sickly vegetation, hills, craters, lava, pits, heat, salt-pools, water—Tortoises, lizards, birds—Quite a region to suggest theory.

WHEN we left off on the last occasion we were engaged in drawing illustrations in regard to the source and nature of the doctrine of natural selection from the special theories and peculiar character of Erasmus Darwin, the elder. We saw how it was the imagination that predominated, whether in the theories or in the man. A curious testimony to this on the part of general readers may be found in the scrawls and scribbles on the University copy of the *Zoonomia*. Some one has been wicked enough to tear out a good number of pages from one of the volumes. Of scrawls, there occur: " Imaginary—Darwin, beware! That is the rock you have split upon, Hypothesis, where other barks as well as yours have been wrecked;" and again, "Darwin's dreams!" One writer laments that Erasmus strayed beyond the *Botanic Garden;* had he not done so," the writer says,

"Then disappointment had not marked thy name;
And Darwin's laurels rivalled Newton's fame."

There may have been remarked a peculiarity in some families according as it shall be the principle of attraction or the principle of repulsion that rules in them. Of some the members are, as the Germans say, *spröde*, mutually repellent; they have no confidences with each other. That they are sons, brothers, sisters is, in respect of one another, a reason for depreciation and disregard, almost for offensive familiarity and contempt. They never think of the opinion of one of themselves as an opinion at all; and with one another there is no end to the liberties they take. With others, all that is reversed. *Their* geese are all swans. They support each other. In season and out of season they cry each other up. They never think of the members of other families, they never can see anything in them. All on the outside of themselves are the βέβηλοι, indifferent people, people of no account. Charles Darwin was a loyal, modest man, who was quite incapable of being unjust to others. Such a trait, too, is probably to be found, more or less, in all the Darwins. Still, on the whole, perhaps, the Darwins, at least of three generations, may be not too unrighteously admitted to have exhibited something of the mutual-admiration principle. The grandfather prints with pride the literary productions of his sons, "*Mr.*" Charles and "*Dr. R. W.*" Darwin. What a father Dr. R. W. again was to his two sons, Erasmus and Charles, the latter of them has expressly chronicled in the warmest terms. Of his grandfather he is correspondently eulogistic: "He (the grandfather) had uncommon powers of observation," he says. But as for his father, Dr. R. W., Dr. R. W. was to Charles "incomparably the acutest observer he ever knew," "the best judge of character he ever knew," "the wisest man he ever knew;" and he was also, as we have seen, "the largest man he ever knew!" Of his brother Erasmus, the opinion of Charles is that he was the "clearest-headed man whom he had ever known." Then this Erasmus, for his part, must be granted to have been equally true to the family principle. When his brother's book, the *Origin*, reaches him, and he reads it, he cannot help exclaiming to the author of it (ii. 233), "I really think it is the most interesting book I ever read.... In fact, the *à priori* reasoning is so entirely satisfactory to me that if the facts won't fit in, why, so much the worse for the facts, is my feeling." And here Erasmus, as I may observe, only expresses the same opinion as I have expressed in regard to his brother's method. There is an *à priori* theory, and then there is a miscellany of remark in regard to facts to support it. Erasmus is very honest in *his* avowals. The *theory* is the all and all to him, the *facts* but poor wretches that have only to knock under and adapt themselves. Indeed, this opinion about facts does not seem confined to Erasmus the younger; there would appear even some fatality incident to facts so far as they occur in natural history at all. Charles himself avows to his friend Hooker (ii. 45), "It is really disgusting and humiliating to see directly opposite conclusions drawn from the same facts;" to which remark Sir Joseph Hooker's reply must have been peculiar, for Charles (ii. 70) rejoins to it, "It is a melancholy, and I hope not quite true view of yours, that facts will prove anything, and are therefore superfluous!" But as regards the family, there is more than mutual love in it: there are family politics—they are all Whigs; and there is a family religion—they are all, we may say, in regard to the Creed, heterodox. Other things, too, run in it as a family, such as early rising, hatred of alcoholic beverages, and a practical love of natural history. In fact, there can be no doubt that we are right in this, that a family agreement, down to the most individual particulars, was the very hinge, as it were, on which the whole three of them, grandfather, father, and son, turned. The constitution even of their very minds seems to have been pretty well identical. As we have seen, the grandfather had an "overpowering tendency to theorize" (i. 6); the father "formed a theory," the son says, "for almost everything that occurred" (i. 20); and the son himself, as regards hypotheses, confesses (i. 103), "I cannot resist forming one on every subject." Mr. Darwin also admits that the "passion for collecting" was in him "clearly innate;" and again, that his "scientific tastes" were certainly innate. In fact, there cannot be a doubt that, than Charles Darwin, there never was a man born with a purer and stronger innate or inherited faculty to observe. Why, the love for everything that crawls was so absorbing in him that he put a black beetle into his mouth as another man might put a bon-bon! At Down there was not a bird's nest in his garden, or all about, that he did not know. Almost, it might be said, that there was not to be found on his grounds even a single worm that was not his familiar acquaintance. We have many journals of naturalists on scientific voyages, but never such a journal as that of Mr. Darwin in the *Beagle*. It is a practical lesson in geology, such as can be got nowhere else, even to read it. Then as regards animals and plants, during the whole expedition, not one sample of the one kind or the other seems to have escaped his recognition. There never was such a brain as that of Charles Darwin, stuffed full, teeming, and running over with a thousand facts that no one before him ever had a mind to think of, to notice, or to record. Then his ingenuity in adjusting fact to fact or in eliminating contrarieties and contradictions was marvellous — utterly unexampled — such success in these ways was never exhibited in a book before. Fancy the grandfather with similar powers, but free from the practice of medicine and the production of poetry, what a book the *Zoonomia* might have been! And see what it is instead! A crude melange of crass theories, and undigested, inconsistent, miscellaneous particulars! The author of it starts with his *à priori* theory of "all from oysters;" he submits it to the test of his *miscellany*, and that is the result! Fish which are generally suspended in water, and swallows which are generally suspended in air, have their backs, we are told, the colour of the distant ground and their bellies that of the sky. Why this? That the swallows may escape hawks which, being above them, will mistake their backs for the ground, while below them they will mistake their bellies for the sky! I suppose it is the pike that, as above or below, is similarly to be duped of his fish! Dr. Erasmus actually fancies insects to be undoubtedly formed from the sexual appendages of plants, the honey-loving stamens and pistils of the flowers, as he calls them, some acquiring wings, others fins, and others claws from their ceaseless efforts to procure their food, or to secure themselves from injury: "changes," he avers, "not more incomprehensible than the transformation of tadpoles into frogs and caterpillars into butterflies!" On another physico-metaphysical conceit of Erasmus Darwin's we have a commentary by Paley. "I am not ignorant," he says (*Natural Theology*, cap. 18), " of the theory which resolves instinct into sensation. Thus the incubation of eggs is accounted for by the pleasure which the bird is supposed to receive from the pressure of the smooth convex surfaces. . . . The affection of viviparous animals for their young is, in like manner, solved by the relief which they receive in suckling. . . . The salmon's urging her way up the stream of fresh-water rivers is attributed to some gratification or refreshment which, in this particular state of the fish's body, she receives from the change of element." It is not worth while quoting what Paley says in answer to all this. The groundless arbitrariness, perhaps even the *semi*-seriousness of such propos cannot escape us. As regards incubation, we know it to be a fact that such noxious and poisonous animals as snakes, serpents, boa-constrictors, and cobras will, as with a mother's solicitude, so obstinately sit on their eggs that they will rather die than leave them. Is such devoted affection in appearance only relief of a colic in fact? If you rescue a young sparrow fallen from the nest and expose it in a cage at your window, I wonder if it is only for relief to a pain in the stomach that the she-sparrow and the he-sparrow will, for many days, cling incessantly to the cage with food in their bills for their little one within it! Dr. Erasmus Darwin ventures, even in respect of what is purely metaphysical, to tell us what an *idea* is. To him it is, as it were, only the stamp on the body of the things without. He defines it "a contraction, or motion, or configuration of the fibres which constitute the immediate organ of sense." Of this definition Dugald Stewart remarks that it is " calculated to impose on a very wide circle of readers by the mixture it exhibits of crude and visionary metaphysics," and I think we may, without intolerable injustice, extend the criticism to all those semi-physical and semi-metaphysical reels in bottles, which men like the author of *Zoonomia* are so innocently busy, bee-like, to construct. Most unformed men do not reason, to call it reason. Proof with them is the instinctive recourse to a picture. They are, as Kant has it, only on such stage as the Egyptians or the Chinese, whose minds as yet are not fine enough for pure notions, and can only understand by the help of physical representations — not possibly by the mere letters of an alphabet. They think in tropes, they see in metaphors. The circulation of their brains is a circulation in images. Their metaphysics in general are so thickened with physics that they can only settle into what is bizarre and biassed, counterfeit and mock. For gold they can only offer us pinckbeck. Dr. Erasmus was a medical man, and medical men, at least, *had* not always then the advantage of courses in logic, metaphysics, and morals, they had not always then transformed their hieroglyphics into the letters of the alphabet. It is just possible that there is a little of that physical thinking even now-a-days, and not on the part of the Bob Sawyers alone.

The procedure of Dr. Erasmus Darwin, then, is altogether the method and manner of a man who starts with an *à priori* theory, and looks miscellaneously to heaven, and earth, and the sea, and all that in them is, for illustrations, mere pictures in proof. As Dr. Asa Gray objects to the natural selection of his grandson, in all that quasi-ratiocination, there is no point of departure undeniably and manifestly made good as a *vera causa*. Or as Professor Sedgwick similarly objected, there is no movement on the Baconian principle, no regular induction, from point to point, and step to step, accurately,

2 A

precisely, and convincingly carried out. "Many of his wide conclusions are built upon assumptions which can neither be proved nor disproved." There are times when, in respect of his own work, such objections start up in all their force even to Mr. Charles Darwin himself, almost as definite barriers to his own advance. To Asa Gray he fully admits (ii. 217) "that there are very many difficulties not satisfactorily explained by my theory." These difficulties, he confesses to Jenyns (ii. 219), "stagger him to this very day." Even to Mr. Huxley, as we saw, he writes, "I entirely agree with you that the difficulties on my notions are terrific" (ii. 354). In regard to these same difficulties, we have this further admission to Dr. Asa Gray (ii. 315), "I could myself," says Charles, "write a more damning review"—of his own book, that is—"than has as yet appeared." Whoever can read between the lines, however, in these writings of Mr. Charles Darwin's, will have no difficulty in discovering that he (Darwin) was, despite his doubts, as brave a man as ever lived. He cowers beneath his checks at times; but ever he whispers to himself, like a true Englishman as he is, "It's dogged as does it!" It is in few things more interesting than to watch him, during the incubation of his theory, in his various letters to his chosen friends. His despondent moods are interesting, and ever again his renewed courage. But what, perhaps, is still more interesting, is the persistent resolution he manifests to win these friends over, together with the shrewd, almost insidious, but never ignoble, adaptations and accommodations he sets into operation according to the peculiar character of each. Lyell, Hooker, Huxley, Carpenter, Gray are all most delicately handled. He says once to one of these, "Often and often a cold shudder has run through me, and I have asked myself whether I may not have devoted my life to a phantasy . . . but investigators of truth, like Lyell and Hooker, cannot be wholly wrong, and therefore I rest in peace." Still I know not that that peace was a well-assured one. There is ample evidence in these letters that Lyell, Carpenter, Gray, and, we may say, all his less-noted friends, were never believers in his theory, pure and simple. We have seen difficulties called ominous even with Mr. Huxley; and as regards Sir Joseph Hooker, it may be that he will march with his friend to the very end still—not that these letters show him to have been ever much more assured than Lyell, or Gray, or the rest were. And how is it, now, that the *Origin of Species* has been thirty years before the public? As regards the great outside world, while still caviare to the orthodox, it is understood among those who are above the Bible that natural selection is a demonstrated and established doctrine. It is not so certain, however, that as much is understood among experts. I don't know but what we begin to hear murmurs in camp. I cannot follow this farther now, however. I will only call to mind the last Presidential Address of the British Association, and its warnings against incautious assertions as to organic life.

And not quite to be misunderstood, I will add this, whatever I have said, I have no intention to deny that there may be at this moment many and good and worthy men, believers both in Mr. Darwin and their Bible. To me, however, the consideration of his grandfather's theories, as well in themselves as in their fortune and fate, give, if not warrant and assurance, at least suspicion, of a foundation of sand. With the single exception of what is meant by the one word "modification," I know of no genetic doctrine in the works of the grandson that will not be found, at greater or less length, suggested, mooted, propounded, discussed in the works of the grandfather. Dr. Ernst Krause wrote in the specially Darwinian number of the evolutionary journal, *Kosmos*, an essay, "The Scientific Works of Erasmus Darwin," which Mr. Charles Darwin so much relished that he wrote Dr. Krause "thanking him cordially . . . and asking his permission to publish an English translation of the essay." In this he was joined by his brother Erasmus the younger. Dr. Krause is a foremost evolutionist, and, with much else, writes a special work, *Charles Darwin and his Relation to Germany*. The translation in question was entrusted to Mr. W. S. Dallas, also a distinguished Darwinian, who executes the admirable index to the *Variation of Animals and Plants*, the translation of Fritz Müller's *Für Darwin*, and the glossary to the sixth edition of the *Origin*. To the resultant book by Mr. Dallas, Mr. Darwin contributes, in the shape of a " preliminary notice," more than one half of the whole. " Many persons," says Mr. Darwin in his autobiography, " have been much interested by this little life, and I am surprised that only 800 or 900 copies were sold." Other book-makers may be surprised, but hardly for Mr. Darwin's reason ! From all this, I think we may conclude that Dr. Krause can claim an absolute Darwinian approbation and endorsement, when, in said little book, he writes of Mr. Charles Darwin, that he " has succeeded to an intellectual inheritance, and carried out a programme sketched forth, and left behind by his grandfather. Almost every single work of the younger Darwin may be paralleled by at least a chapter in the works of his ancestor, . . . heredity, adaptation, the protective arrangements of animals and plants, sexual selection, insectivorous plants, and the analysis of the emotions and sociological impulses; nay, even the studies on infants are to be found already discussed in the writings of the elder Darwin, . . . who, a

Lamarckian before Lamarck first established a complete system of the theory of evolution." Of the parallel between the younger and the elder Darwin, that is to say more than even I mooted, and in such circumstances as to give an authority to the general position utterly beyond dispute. Are we to suppose, then, that the course of literary and philosophical history in Great Britain has gone all wrong? Before the culmination and success of Mr. Charles Darwin, whether in literature or philosophy the name of Erasmus Darwin had pretty well ceased to be heard of. As we knew that there had been a John Philips and a *Splendid Shilling*, or a Scotchman Wilkie and a thing called *Epigoniad*, or a Bishop Wilkins and his *Discovery of a New World*, so we knew of a *Botanic Garden* and a *Zoonomia*; but as we only knew *of* the former, so we only knew *of* the latter: we had never read either. As regards *Zoonomia*, we had taken Dugald Stewart and Dr. Thomas Brown's word for it: it was something merely crude and visionary, the mushroom product of uninitiated crassitude; and as for the *Botanic Garden*, we had, perhaps, heard the recitation from it of "Eliza on the wood-crowned height," or of the grand passage, "Roll on, ye stars! exult in youthful prime," or of the melancholy passage, "So the sad mother at the noon of night;" and had thought to ourselves always how happy was that line of Byron's that dubbed Erasmus but "a mighty master of unmeaning rhyme!"[1] In fact

---

[1] In *English Bards and Scotch Reviewers*, Byron exclaims in prose, "The neglect of the *Botanic Garden* is some proof of returning taste," while in verse he has these pretty plain lines:—

"Let these, or such as these, with just applause,
Restore the Muse's violated laws;
But not in flimsy Darwin's pompous chime,
That mighty master of unmeaning rhyme;
Whose gilded cymbals, more adorned than clear,
The eye delighted, but fatigued the ear;

on the whole matter we just took it for granted that when Mr. Lewes said, "tawdry splendour gained him a tawdry reputation," which, in another respect, proved " equally noisy and fleeting,"—we just took it for granted that when this was said all was said, and that, as regards Dr. Erasmus Darwin, we might, with perfect tranquillity, leave him henceforth quite undisturbed in the limbo of other poetasters and philosophasters. If, however, we are to believe the Herr Dr. Krause, all this is wrong,— all this is a sin, and a shame, and a disgrace,—all this is a flagrant injustice to one of the greatest scientific discoverers that ever lived—a discoverer that anticipated the discoveries of even the illustrious Charles Darwin, whom it has not been esteemed excessive praise of late to style "The Greater Newton." Nay, there are others, it seems, who surpass even the Herr Dr. Krause in his admiration of Dr. Erasmus. Dr. Krause tells us himself of a wish seriously expressed on the part of some to revive original Darwinism now. It is not so with him, however, let him admire the elder Darwin and Darwinism as he may. On the contrary, any such wish to him " shows a weakness of thought and a mental anachronism which no one can envy." And yet, I, for my part, after all that even Krause himself has told me, know not that, in reference to the origin and transformations of plants and animals, the thought and thoughts of the grandson differ from those of the grandfather, unless in so far as the former (Charles), unlike the latter, rejects the interposition of a designing cause: Charles Darwin

> In *show*, the simple lyre could once surpass,
> But now worn down, appear in native brass;
> While all his train of hovering sylphs around
> Evaporate in similes and sound:
> Him let them shun, with him let tinsel die:
> False glare attracts, but more offends, the eye."

has only one device for the creation of that whole marvellous panorama of life on earth; and, in two words, it is, *individual difference!* I, for my part, then, who stand up here for the certainty of Natural Theology and the cogency of all its arguments, ontological, cosmological, teleological, must believe Erasmus Darwin, the grandfather, to have been, in his reverence for design, much nearer the truth than Charles Darwin the grandson: I cannot forget the many passages I have seen in the former expressive of his deep sense of the reality in this world of an organization on ideas. All that contrasts to me wonderfully with the strangely young, the innocently simple admissions, which, as fruit of adequate reflection, the grandson so unmisgivingly imparts to the inexperienced youths who write to him for guidance. He seems to have been greatly exercised in mind that, given a beneficent and omnipotent Deity, flies should feed within the living bodies of caterpillars, or that a cat should play with mice (ii. 312). The grandfather, for his part, though, like the grandson, he " disbelieved in any revelation," could never see his way to give up his faith in the existence of God. He even published an ode on the folly of Atheism, of which this is the first verse:—

> " Dull Atheist, could a dizzy dance
> Of atoms lawless hurled
> Construct so wonderful, so wise,
> So harmonized a world?"

And now I have to say a word of apology. I cannot do that justice in these lectures to the whole theme of Darwinism for which I had prepared myself. I have by me, one way and another, not much less than a hundred and a half of closely-written quarto pages of extracts and memoranda, which were to serve me as mere core and nucleus to a complete statement on the whole subject.

The attempt to carry out this programme gave me great pain, and cost me much anxiety for long, inasmuch as, with the space at my command, I was simply endeavouring to reconcile impossibilities. I do not believe that even the whole course of lectures would have enabled me to exhaust the materials I had gathered. What I had to content myself with in the end was simply to sit down and write according as the information in my head prompted me. Even to turn up my authorities proved for the most part as distressing and as futile as to operate on a needle in a bundle of hay. It is for that, then, I apologise—that I have been able to present to you the subject only in a certain miscellaneousness.

In conclusion, however, I will now take up one point and follow it out. Every one who has at all approached this subject has heard of the Galapagos, the Galapagos Islands, or the Galapagos Archipelago. In the index to the *Life and Letters*, the fauna of them are named "the starting-point of investigations into the origin of species;" and Mr. Darwin himself more than once avows that it was what he had observed there led him to study the origin of species (i. 82, ii. 23, iii. 159); while it is well known that the adherents of Mr. Darwin generally throw up the bastion of the Galapagos as a barrier so strong that no enemy can carry it. But that being so, it is evident that there may be that there which, if seen and understood, would convince us too. We, too, have no interest but the truth. I, for my part, am quite willing to be convinced, if there be any evidence to convince, whether in the Galapagos or anywhere else.

For the information which is necessary to us here, we have to turn to that admirable volume which Mr. Darwin names his *Journal of Researches*. I have already mentioned how it is a work singular and single in its excellence. Mr. Darwin devotes one whole chapter in it, the seventeenth, to the Galapagos Archipelago; and it is to that chapter I have to direct your special attention. We have not the advantage of either the knowledge or ability of Mr. Darwin; but if these islands were of such a nature as to impress Mr. Darwin only in one direction, surely we must expect them, in the same direction, more or less to impress us too. No doubt there is an objection not unfrequently taken which would summarily sist the appeal to the possibility of any such influence for us: we are not naturalists, and only naturalists can judge of what is concerned in the Galapagos! Mr. Darwin himself, however, writes to Asa Gray: "I think it of importance that my notions should be read by intelligent men, accustomed to scientific argument, though *not* naturalists." There is, to be sure, a certain presumption, after all, in the assumption, and in the proceeding to judgment on the assumption of just as much as that—but perhaps a reference to the grandfather will put us right again, and pretty well confirm to us some *locus standi* in as great a matter as the present. We have seen that, in view of its excellence even in the direction of the grandson, whose peculiar lines it precisely anticipated, it has been seriously proposed to restore the elder Darwinism. Now, of the Bible of that Darwinism, the *Zoonomia*, this is the Dedication: "To all those who study the operations of the mind as a science, or who practise medicine as a profession." If only the word "practise" had been in the past tense, one might have been excused for the thought that, in no very distant regard, Dr. Darwin had been, to say so, almost prophetically personal! *Ne sutor supra crepidam* is, of course, the rule; but it need not prove exceptionless. I have the idea that Mr. Huxley would look a little *torvous*, did any man dispute his right to a judgment on Descartes!

The Galapagos are a group of small islands, of various sizes, and some thirteen in number, of which only two seem unnamed. Six of them may be regarded as outlying, and seven central. Of the former on the north, three, as scarcely referred to by Mr. Darwin, may be left out of count. On the east, Chatham Island is distant (say) 22 miles, and on the south, Charles Island 32 from the nearest central island. Twelve miles may be the greatest, and two or three the least, distance from one to the other among the central islands themselves. These measures, however, are dependent on Mr. Darwin's own map and scale in his *Journal*, and cannot be considered rigorously exact. The situations, and especially the distances, in each other's regard, are the important points in the consideration so far. We advance to a second important point when we recognise the position of these islands to be right under the equator in the Pacific Ocean, and (the third important point) at a distance of between five or six hundred miles west of South America. The climate of these islands, despite their position on the equator, is represented as far from being excessively hot, the great Polar current from the south, namely, surrounding them with a sea of a singularly low temperature. For winds these islands are exposed, of course, to the southern Trades, which blow over them as far as four degrees farther north; but above a certain height they are apt to be overhung with vapours. It is only under these vapours, and especially to windward, that vegetation can be said to thrive, for everywhere else these islands are of a monotonously repulsive sterile aspect. They are all volcanic, and supposed to be geologically recent. Some of the craters surmounting the larger islands are of immense size, and they rise to a height of between three and four thousand feet. The flanks of these as they rise are studded by innumerable orifices, and there must be in the whole archipelago at least two thousand craters. These craters have their southern sides either much lower than the other sides, or quite broken down and removed in consequence of the combined action of the Pacific swell and the southern Trades. Landing on these islands, nothing can be less inviting than the first appearance, says Mr. Darwin. A broken field of black basaltic lava, thrown into the most rugged waves, and crossed by great fissures, is everywhere covered by stunted, sunburnt brushwood, which shows little signs of life. The dry and parched surface, heated by the noonday sun, gives to the air a close and sultry feeling, like that from a stove: one fancies even that the bushes smell unpleasantly. The brushwood appears, from a short distance, as leafless as our trees during winter, even when it is in full leaf, nay, for the most part, even when it is in flower. The entire surface, he says once, seems to have been permeated like a sieve by the subterranean vapours: here and there the lava, while soft, has been blown into great bubbles; and in other parts the tops of caverns similarly formed have fallen in, leaving circular pits with steep sides. Of two of the islands Mr. Darwin reports: "Both are covered with immense deluges of black naked lava, which have flowed either over the rims of the great caldrons, like pitch over the rim of a pot in which it has been boiled, or have burst forth from the smaller orifices on the flanks; in their descent they have spread over miles of the sea-coast." "Scrambling over the rough surface" of this extraordinary region is most fatiguing, and Mr. Darwin describes how horribly disappointing it is when, "choked with dust" and thirst, one "hurries down the cindery slope eagerly to drink" from some solitary pool over a crater, one finds he has in his mouth only what is "salt as brine." As one walks, one finds the rocks abound with great black lizards, between three and four feet long, and on the hills an ugly yellowish-brown species equally common." On one occasion, "as I was walking along," he says, " I met two large tortoises, each of which must have weighed at least two hundred pounds (more than 14 stone): one was eating a piece of cactus, and as I approached, it stared at me and slowly stalked away; the other gave a deep hiss, and drew in its head. These huge reptiles, surrounded by the black lava, the leafless shrubs and large cacti, seemed to my fancy like some antediluvian animals. The few dull-coloured birds cared no more for me than they did for the great tortoises." We have a great deal more from Mr. Darwin about these huge hideous reptiles, whether tortoises or lizards, that is very interesting and strange. Both seem to swarm. The tórtoises for food are open to capture at any time. "It is said that formerly single vessels have taken away as many as seven hundred, and that the ship's company of a frigate some years since brought down in one day two hundred tortoises to the beach." Vapour-crowned volcanic heights studded with orifices; miles and miles of black lava, red scoriae, and dusty cinders; great black or yellow-hideous lizards sleeping in the sun; huge monsters of tortoises lazily crawling along paths they have worn through centuries to where water lies: how startling it must be in the midst of such lonely weird sights as these to come suddenly on the ghastly gleaming skull of a buccaneer captain who had been murdered by his crew!

One cannot wonder that such a region as this went to the heart of Mr. Darwin, and remained ever afterwards with him a constant problem of the most intent and absorbing interest,—one cannot wonder that it was here he found the motive for his peculiar theory. The spot was solitary and remote; and what life there was upon it, seemed to have for him only a strange, unnatural, and old-world look. The possible influence of isolation, simply as isolation, would probably first occur to him; and then, perhaps, the question, if the isolation had been the source of so many changed forms, how was it that there were others which had remained seemingly unchanged? Such conjectures appear at least not alien to the genius of a Darwin; but we must postpone our further consideration of these matters till the next week.

# GIFFORD LECTURE THE TWENTIETH.

The action—South American types, left here to themselves, change into new species from accumulation of their own individual spontaneous differences—The birds—Differences in the times and modes of arrival between land and sea birds—Carte and tierce—Contradiction—Parried by a word—An advocate's proof—The printer and Mr. Darwin's *woulds*—The sea-gull—The finches—Sir William Jardine—The process to Darwin—What was to him "a new birth"—Where the determinative advantage for these *different* beaks—The individual central islands *not* incommunicably separate—French birds at Dover—Isolation—*Ex-contrario*—Individual difference the single secret, that is the "law" which has been "discovered" of "natural selection"—Apply influence of external conditions to the Galapagos—Kant—The Galapagos rat and mouse—New beings but yet the old names—If difference goes always on only to difference without return to identity, why are there not infinitely more species?—Bowen—Darwin only empedoclean—Parsons—Lyell—Monsters (giants and dwarfs) sterile—Frederick's grenadiers, the pygmies—Divergent species at home—The Galapagos but the Mr. Jorkins of the Darwinians—The tortoise, where did it come from?—The amblyrhyncus similarly inexplicable—Lizards of the secondary epoch—The Galapagos Islands absolutely without a vestige of the struggle for life in any direction—The breeder, and nature, can act only on what is already there—The breeder deals in identity, not difference, and his breeds would all turn back to the original—No breeder a new species—Nature acts not on Darwin's method, but design—Toothed birds, the hipparion, the otter-sheep—Accidental individual difference to be the sole creator in the end of all that enormous and infinitely complicated concert to unity!—Farewell.

BEING now possessed of some idea of the scene of the action, we may proceed forthwith to this latter itself.

And that is, to this sole effect: That South American types of life became, in process of time, specifically changed in these islands of the Galapagos, in consequence of their isolation, as well partial as total. The types particularly selected to be dwelt on are the birds. "In the Galapagos Islands," says Mr. Darwin in the *Origin* (348), "there are 26 land-birds; of these 21 (or perhaps 23) are peculiar, whereas of the 11 marine birds only 2 are peculiar;" and this difference Mr. Darwin explained by difference in the *numbers* of the immigration and in the *times* of it. "Species," he said, "occasionally arriving after long intervals of time in a new and isolated district, and having to compete with new associates, would be eminently liable to modification, and would often produce groups of modified descendants." We are to understand, that is, this to have been the case with the land-birds: they only "occasionally" arrived "after long intervals of time," and they had to "compete with new associates." As for the sea-birds, the excess of *non*-modification in them was due, it is said, "partly" to their "having immigrated in a body, so that their mutual relations were not much disturbed," and "partly to the frequent arrival of unmodified immigrants from the mother-country, with which the insular forms have intercrossed." We see here that invariable felicity of Mr. Darwin that, if there is a foin in *carte*, it is as swiftly followed up by a fence in *tierce*. Few immigrants, at long intervals, give us modification—*carte;* but many immigrants, at frequent intervals, quite as much withdraw modification—*tierce!* Mr. Darwin blows hot and cold with equal vigour. It is only fair to observe, however, that Mr. Darwin has a reason why sea-birds have immigrated differently from land-birds. "It is obvious," he says, "that marine birds could arrive at these islands much more easily and frequently than land-birds." But even here, in his own facts, is there not pretty well his own contradiction ? If marine birds can immigrate more easily and frequently than land-birds, it at least sounds strange that, while there are 26 of the land, there are only 11 of the sea. It is quite possible, of course, as regards *new* species that the many come from the few, and, contrariwise, the few from the many. No one can doubt, at any rate, that Mr. Darwin's ingenuity could make it appear so. He can find a word at any moment that is an *open sesamè* to any difficulty. He says himself that, from end to end of it, his *Origin of Species* is "one long argument." And so it is! From end to end of it, it is what the Germans call an *Advocatenbeweis:* from end to end of it, it is an *advocate's proof.* Even in what lies at this moment before us, just in the same way as we saw already, he that continues to read will find almost every proposition conditioned by a *would.* It is always this *would* take place, and that *would* take place. In point of actual fact, there are so many *woulds* in Mr. Darwin's books on natural selection, that one may be forgiven if one finds oneself speculating, with some curiosity, about the resources of a printer's fount. In this reference, and as concerns the many from the few or the few from the many, *would* it be unfair to say that one *would* not expect such an animal as a gull to be one of the only two remarkably modified sea-birds ? One *would* expect it to arrive always in very large numbers, and on occasions of very frequent occurrence. From the known habits of the gull, one would expect this almost more in its case than in that of any other sea-bird—one *would* really, least of all, expect the gull to be the exceptional sea-bird to display in the Galapagos even as much modification as the land-birds. Mr. Darwin himself cannot help exclaiming here, "Considering the wandering habits of the gulls, I was surprised to find that the species inhabiting these islands is peculiar." It is a situation and a circumstance naturally to give exit to a whole flight of *woulds* and *would nots!* (*Journal*, 380).

But if the birds at the Galapagos are peculiarly selected for remark, of these it is the finches that, as Mr. Darwin would have it, are specially to be considered. "Ornithology—curious finches," are his own words in the heading of the chapter in his *Journal*. Of the twenty-six land-birds, in fact, the finches are so remarkable that they constitute one half of them. In the Galapagos Islands there are no less than thirteen new species of finches; and Mr. Darwin is so much impressed with them that he illustrates his description of them in the *Journal* by actual drawings of them. I have the book here, and they may be seen. The figures given are very evidently heads of finches even as we know them in this country. No. 1 refers to the *Geospiza magnirostris*, and is distinguished by a very full large beak. The beak of No. 2, the *Geospiza fortis*, is less large, but still strong. That of No. 3, the *Geospiza parvula*, is very much such as we may see in our own finches, sparrows, or even canaries. The beak of No. 4 is small and sharp, almost as in our own wrens. Between Nos. 1 and 3, it appears, there is not only one, but actually six intermediate species. "The perfectly graduated series in the size of their beaks," Mr. Darwin calls "a probable consequence of their numbers;" and it is by reason of these numbers that "one might really fancy," he says, "that from an original paucity of birds in this archipelago, one species had been taken and modified for different ends." Now, in these four finch heads we have what, in the mind of Mr. Darwin, was the motive and the generative speck of the whole ultimate theory. Because he found in these islands so many finches, and in the different islands different ones, Mr. Darwin was led to speculate on their possible origin. There was a common analogy in all of them; and that analogy was an analogy that bore only on a certain South American type. The obvious inference, accordingly, was that all these finches, however much they were modified, had been actually modified, one and all of them, out of a single characteristic type; and that type was to be found only in South America. As one sees, it is at once assumed here that the thirteen different finches constitute or represent thirteen different species; and, consequently, the first thing it occurs to us to ask is, What *is* a species? We remember how Mr. Darwin was himself put to it to determine a species in his Cirrepedes, and how he needs must laugh at his brother naturalists in the same endeavour generally. We are told that, be the differences what they may, these birds always bear to each other the closest resemblance. The thirteen males are all black, the thirteen females are all brown, and they are to be found, all, or the most of them, *feeding together*. We really should like to know if they cannot *pair together*. Mr. Darwin is chagrined; but it does not, at least at first sight, seem unnatural that Sir William Jardine, I suppose the greatest ornithological authority, thought that "some of the Galapagos so-called species ought to be called varieties," and that "some of the sub-genera, supposed to be wholly endemic, have been found on the continent" (ii. 246). On the whole, we really should like to know on what it was that the specific difference turned for Mr. Darwin himself. This is plain that, if they were *not* species, and species endemic to the Galapagos, Mr. Darwin must have made a bad start. But suppose them species, and that they were not specially or directly created, as seems to Mr. Darwin (though not to us), the only other alternative, how does he conceive his own process of modification, the pullulation of differences, to have *naturally* evolved them? As we see, and as is insisted on, they vary in their beaks. Is it there that Mr. Darwin finds his peculiar *pulse?* In the *Life and Letters*, he expressly exemplifies to us what he would call "a new birth." It is "a bird born with a beak $\frac{1}{100}$th of an inch longer than usual." That, evidently, to him is a good instance of the first step in a pullulation of differences. May we suppose, then, that he sees the beaks of these finches pullulate and pullulate into the new species which he describes and draws in his book? If Mr. Darwin asserts it, *we* cannot deny it. But when we look at his own pictures, great beaks, strong beaks, small beaks, tiny beaks, may we be allowed to ask on which side we shall assume the determinative "advantage" to lie—the determinative "advantage" that is always postulated in the theory? Shall it be the great beaks that have pullulated into strength, or shall it be the small beaks that have pullulated into fineness? We know that Mr. Darwin regards the isolation of these islands precisely as the one determining condition of this growth of species. But that being so, we cannot but recognise that his very condition must blow quite as vigorously cold as hot—fence quite as securely in tierce as in carte. If the strong and great are due to it, so also are the small and fine. Mr. Darwin sees so much potency in the *isolation*, and lays so much stress on it, that he attributes to it, not only the general difference of life in the archipelago from life on the continent, but even the individual difference of life on one island as compared with life on another. "By far the most remarkable feature in the natural history of this archipelago is, that the different islands to a considerable extent are inhabited by a different set of beings" (394); "Several of the islands possess their own species" (397); "Different islands have their representatives of *Geospiza*"

—the finch (395). To such expressions as these Mr. Darwin adds others to the effect that, in his belief, these islands are incommunicably cut off the one from the other. This latter circumstance, as in the interest of the view which it is his dearest wish to impress, he is even at some pains, in his usual colouring way, at least to accentuate. In the *Origin*, these islands, he says, " are separated by deep arms of the sea, in most cases wider than the British Channel: the currents of the sea are rapid, and sweep between the islands, and gales of wind are extraordinarily rare ; so that the islands are far more effectually separated from each other than they appear on a map." Now, as regards distances, the statement here must be confined to what I have called the outlying islands: it is wholly out of place when referred to those in the centre. At most, five or six miles will bring all the latter into connection, the one with the other; and these five or six miles concern only the separation of two from the other five islands, while, otherwise, all are very much nearer each other than even five or six miles. The Galapagos Islands, therefore, specially at least those that constitute Mr. Darwin's references, are not separated by arms of the sea " in most cases wider than the British Channel," which is a gap of twenty-five miles. Then the currents between may be "rapid;" but, in that respect, they must vary much with different states of the tides. Lastly, as regards gales of wind, they may be "rare;" but the very phrase allows them from time to time to exist. Nay, the very lizards would seem, numerous as they are, to be somewhat dependent on storms for their support. " They consume," says Mr. Darwin, " much of the succulent cactus, *the branches of which are occasionally broken off by the wind !*" We may remember, too, that the craters on these islands have their windward sides "either much lower than the other sides, or quite broken down and removed in consequence of the combined action of the Pacific swell and the southern Trades." Gales of wind, then, may be "extraordinarily rare;" but they *do* happen, and we can hardly conclude with Mr. Darwin, from the mere rarity of them, that "neither the birds, insects, nor lighter seeds would be blown from island to island." On the contrary, it does seem precisely certain that seeds, insects, and birds *would*, from time to time, not possibly escape being blown from island to island. But what of the prevailing serenity and calm ? Mr. Darwin describes, in the *Origin* (356), many of the birds as specially well adapted for flying from island to island : are we to suppose that two, or three, or five, or six miles would not, in such circumstances, prove to all such birds rather a temptation and an attraction than an intimidation and restraint ? Even the British Channel was but a step to the French birds that covered the cliffs of Dover when *liberté, égalité, fraternité* took, during the Revolution, to slaughtering them. On the whole, whether we look to Mr. Darwin's own measures or to Mr. Darwin's own facts, we are without any warrant to conclude that, in the Galapagos, island, isolated from island, stands a region of its own.

For the most part, Mr. Darwin is very resolute in his faith in isolation as a main element or agency in the birth of species; but there are times, especially latterly, when he actually seems to vacillate. He writes to Hooker in 1844 : " Isolation is the chief concomitant or cause of the appearance of new forms." As late as 1876, " it would have been a strange fact," he exclaims (iii. 159), " if I had overlooked the importance of isolation, seeing it was such cases as that of the Galapagos which chiefly led me to study the origin of species." Still, four years earlier, we can get such an avowal as this from him (iii. 156): "I rejoice to think that I formerly said as emphatically as I could, that neither isolation nor time by themselves do anything for the modification of species." What, however, is really emphatical here ought to fall on the words "by themselves." The declaration alluded to occurs in the fourth chapter of the *Origin*. There we find isolation described as "an important element in the modification of species," but not as an absolutely necessary and indispensable element. It is only important as giving the chance for variation. That, too, is the *rôle* of time in the process; and, says Mr. Darwin, "it has been erroneously asserted that the element of time has been assumed by me to play an all-important part in modifying species, *as if all the forms of life were necessarily undergoing change through some innate law.*" No; it is neither isolation, nor time, nor "*innate law*" that shall be allowed to interfere with what to Mr. Darwin, as to Mr. Huxley, is the central idea and quintessence of the system, *individual difference*. That—individual difference—is the law of natural selection which has been discovered; and years only corroborate and confirm Mr. Darwin's allegiance to the purity of it. So it is that he says in 1876 (iii. 159)—no doubt with isolation in his mind—" I cannot doubt that many new species have been *simultaneously* developed within the same large continental area;" while, two years later, as regards individual difference he writes (iii. 161) in this strong way: "As our knowledge advances very slight differences, considered by sytematists as of no importance in structure, are continually found to be functionally important." Evidently, it is more and more what depends on difference that occupies his thought and absorbs his attention. Nevertheless it was certainly isolation in the first place, the isolation of the Galapagos, that availed to suggest to him the possibility of new species forming themselves, or being formed, on the ordinary terms that are usual in nature. Then, undoubtedly, it had appeared to him that a changing organism, if left to itself, uncrossed and uninterfered with, would be in the precise position favourable for the transmutation of itself into a new species. Isolation might not create species, or could not create species, but it would be at all events the peculiar feeding-ground in which species, through the manifestation and accumulation of difference, would create itself.

If it is in the interest of modification, difference, as the centre of the theory, that Mr. Darwin may seem somewhat to vacillate as regards isolation, we may recollect that we saw some similar vacillation in respect to external conditions. In the first instance he appeared to have an implacable aversion to all such conditions as climate, etc., having had anything to do with the modification of organisms. By and by, as to Moritz Wagner in 1876, he admits that, in regard to "the direct action of the environment, there is now a large body of evidence." Well, now, is there any reason why we may not apply that here ? Everything was strange and new in these islands—how strange, how new! Craters and caverns, and black lava, and red scoriæ, and salt pools—suffocating heat—brown brushwood even when in flower, that smelt sickly—huge tortoises crawling, more than fourteen stone in weight—big black and yellow lizards on the rocks or in the cinders by thousands —how could we expect to find anything whatever the same here ? "In birds of the same species which have to live in different climates," says Kant (*WW.* vi. 321), "there are provisions for the growth of a new coating of feathers, should certain of them inhabit a cold climate, which provisions, however, in a temperate climate, are kept in reserve. Since wheat, in a cold country, must have more protection from wet and cold than in a dry and warm one, it possesses a natural capability of clothing itself in a gradually thicker integument. This forethought of nature, by calculated precautions, to prepare its creature for all future contingencies, in order that it may preserve itself and adapt itself to the diversity of climate and soil, is a just subject of wonder, and, with the migrations and transplantations of animals and plants, gives rise to new species in appearance, which are nothing else than races and varieties of the same kind, the natural, inborn capacities of which have variously developed themselves in long periods of time according to occasion." Thus, then, for the production of apparent new species, Kant points to innate original nature as respondent to the influence of the varying external conditions; whereas Mr. Darwin, for an equal result, depends on "accumulation of individual differences," and that, too, only "spontaneously," only by "accident," only by "chance," as, for example, in "a bird born with a beak $\frac{1}{100}$th of an inch longer than usual." But, after all, was not Mr. Darwin coming round to Kant's way of it, when, as late as 1876, he confesses (iii. 159): "In my opinion the greatest error which I have committed, has been not allowing sufficient weight to the direct action of environment, *i.e.* food, climate," etc.? In his earlier days, indeed, Mr. Darwin did admit as much as this even for the Galapagos. He found in them, he says, only two mammals, a rat and a mouse. The rat has evidently been imported, Mr. Darwin says, and "is merely a variety, produced by the new and peculiar climate, food, and soil to which it has been subjected" (378); nor, as regards the mouse, are we left in any doubt that his opinion was identical. Now, Mr. Darwin tells us in the *Origin* (113), that the rat and the mouse "have been transported by man to many parts of the world; they live under the cold climate of Faroe in the north and of the Falklands in the south, and on many an island in the torrid zones." If, then, the strange environment of the Galapagos could so change forms so persistent as these, that the one may almost be allowed to rank, and the other does rank, as a new species, why should we resort to a different genesis for the birds and the rest? Mr. Darwin says of these islands (*Journal*, 377 and 393) that in them "a vast majority of all the land animals, and more than half of the flowering plants, are aboriginal productions: it was most striking to be surrounded by new birds, new reptiles, new shells, new insects, new plants!" Mr. Darwin says this; he calls all these animals and plants new; and yet he gives to the whole of them all the old names! Of the twenty-six birds, thirteen are finches, three are mocking thrushes, and three tyrant fly-catchers, two are owls, and two are swallows; there are a hawk, and a wren, and a dove. If the animals themselves are new, and if, as Mr. Darwin says also, "most of the organic productions are aboriginal creations, found nowhere else," so that "we seem to be brought somewhat near to that great fact—that mystery of mysteries—the first appearance of new beings on this earth" (378),— how is it that we have in our ears all the old familiar sounds, and see before our eyes only all the old familiar names? New creations should be new creations, and quite unlike the old—new creations, consequently, should have names of their own, and not only misleadingly carry the appellatives of creations past. If, indeed, the peculiarities here have led Mr. Darwin to the discovery of the true rationale of creation, how is it that we have more to surprise us than even this strange matter of names?—how is it that new creations are not much more common experiences? In each of the million upon million of individuals that exist always and everywhere upon our globe an accumulation of differences ought to be going on constantly—ought to be the one event; and species, consequently, ought, by this time of day, to be absolutely innumerable. Something like this objection has been already made to Mr. Darwin; and, though he says little, I think he shows himself sensitive to it. Professor Bowen of Harvard writes once, " If the doctrine were true, geological strata would be full of monsters which have failed." Whereat Mr. Darwin contemptuously scoffs: "A very clear view this writer" (whom he afterwards styles "a singularly unobservant man ") " had of the struggle for existence " (ii. 304, 372)! We have only here again, however, the *earliest*—the Greek—suggestion of the struggle for existence and the survival of the fittest unwittingly come upon by Mr. Darwin. Empedocles fabled, as we have seen, that all sorts of organisms spontaneously take birth, but only those survive which are fit; and that is precisely the import of Mr. Darwin's scoff to Bowen: In the struggle for existence, namely, monsters would disappear. Professor Parsons, also of Harvard, seems to have repeated Bowen's objection. Mr. Darwin calls his whole paper "worth nothing" (ii. 331); but at the same time he writes, on the same day, to another correspondent, " If you see Professor Parsons, will you thank him for the extremely liberal and fair spirit in which his essay is written ? Please tell him I reflected much on the chance of favourable monstrosities," etc. Now these two professors are outsiders; but it is a strange thing that Sir Charles Lyell, who is no outsider, makes also to Mr. Darwin precisely the same objection (ii. 290). ' You ask (I see)," writes Darwin to Lyell, "why we do not have monstrosities in higher animals? but when they live they are almost always sterile (even giants and dwarfs are *generally* sterile)." There is a little addition here—sterility—to the Empedoclean idea; but may we not attempt to take the point off it, in Mr. Darwin's own manner, by counter-instances? To say "*generally*" is to say too much; for we know that the inhabitants of Potsdam are a tall race, inasmuch as they are the descendants of the Prussian king's seven-foot, eight-foot, and nine-foot grenadiers; and as for dwarfs, we are just on the point of hearing from Mr. Stanley about a whole nation of such, who, under the name of pygmies, have been fighting the cranes since the beginning of history!

But as regards the Galapagos organisms bearing the same names as those elsewhere—as regards the Galapagos birds, for example, being for the most part finches, one wonders that Mr. Darwin should have had any call to find his idea only in them or their neighbours. We have plenty of divergent species—finches, wrens, linnets, etc.—at home. Why go so far afield for an idea that we may find within our own doors? Nay, what, after all, does the whole thing come to? How is it that we are brought face to face with that mystery of mysteries, creation, any more here than, absolutely, anywhere else? No doubt Mr. Darwin's words have a peculiar excitation for us—" somewhat near to that mystery of mysteries, the first appearance of new beings on this earth!" We breathlessly read further, we feel an awe as though on the point of seeing the very veil at last upraised from the countenance of the universe, the secret of the birth of all the beings that have lived, the secret of the birth of man—is it any wonder that we are coerced, and constrained, and surprised into a mere "pshaw!" in the end, when all that we come to are these four finches? It has been well for the friends of Mr. Darwin that the Galapagos archipelago has been kept, as the ultimate referee, *only in its own cloud*. It was uncommonly convenient for Mr. Spenlow, in *David Copperfield*, to be able on occasion to point conclusively upstairs to the unseen Mr. Jorkins. Once seen, however, the terrible Mr. Jorkins proved to be the most harmless of mortals. Even so the Galapagos, when *seen*, are not seen to take us one step nearer the mystery of life. We have seen what has been said of the birds; but is it any better with the reptiles? The huge tortoise is called "aboriginal;" "it is found nowhere else in this quarter of the world;" "it may be questioned," Mr. Darwin avows, "whether it is in any other place an aboriginal." One asks with astonishment, then, where did it come from? No South American type will account for it here. And, pullulation of individual differences! are we to suppose that it pullulated out of the bare rock? Of what avail is the whole theory in such a case? Then are we one whit better off with the lizard, the amblyrhyncus? Mr. Darwin speaks of its progenitor "arriving" at the Galapagos; but he adds, "from what country it is impossible to say, as its affinity, I believe, is not very clear to any known species" (ii. 336). That is, he has no warrant but his own supposition for speaking of it as even "arriving." He warns the geologist who may "refer back in his mind" to the monstrous lizards of the Secondary epochs, "that this archipelago, instead of possessing a humid climate and rank vegetation, as was the case then, cannot be considered otherwise than extremely arid, and, for an equatorial region, remarkably temperate." From Secondary lizard to Galapagos lizard, were connection even possible, that is a vast difference, an incalculable difference, is it possible to suppose that the pullulation of difference could ever bridge it?

We have seen that Mr. Darwin speaks of the struggle for existence as an essential element of the theory, and we know it otherwise to be such; what countenance, then, does the very feeding ground, and breeding ground, and originating ground of natural selection show it? Why, none—absolutely none! Throughout the whole of the Galapagos archipelago there is not a vestige of the struggle for existence—not a trace! We have attempted to make good that there *are* storms of wind; but these, as Mr. Darwin says, are "extraordinarily rare." Then there is heat, but it is temperate, and, for the most part, there is no rain. The birds live there, if anywhere on earth, in perfectly halcyon weather, and they have all food; they have never the slightest occasion in that respect to affect the slightest quarrel with one another. Nor is it otherwise with the only other inhabitants, the lizards and tortoises. "The numbers of individuals of each species are extraordinarily great." Of the lizards, Mr. Darwin remarks, their numbers are such that "we could not for some time find a spot free from their burrows on which to pitch our tent." "This reptile," he says, "has no enemy whatever on shore." "They are not at all timorous." As they crawl, "they often stop and doze for a minute or two." "I have seen," says Mr Darwin, "these lizards and the huge tortoises feeding together." "I have seen," he says again, "one of the thick-billed finches picking at one end of a piece of cactus, while a lizard was eating at the other end; and afterwards the little bird, with the utmost indifference, hopped on the back of the reptile." Only "if two are placed on the ground and held together, they will fight and bite each other; but I," adds Mr. Darwin, "caught many by the tail, and they never tried to bite me." The tortoises have "broad and well-beaten paths in every direction from the wells down to the sea-coast: it was a curious spectacle to behold many of these huge creatures, one set eagerly travelling onwards with outstretched necks, and another set returning after having drunk their fill." "I frequently got on their backs," says Mr. Darwin, "and then giving a few raps on the hinder part of their shells, they would rise up and walk away." The female "drops her eggs indiscriminately in any hole"—she has no fear for them! To this entire scene of peace, and calm, and indolent enjoyment it cannot be said that even the hawk, "the carrion-feeding buzzard" as it is otherwise called, is a single exception; for only the young, newly-hatched tortoises are its prey. As for the old ones, they "seem generally to die from accidents, as from falling down precipices." It is maintained that nobody had ever found any one of them dead "without some evident cause." All living things on these islands, birds and all, even the carrion-buzzard, are of a tameness in the extreme: "all of them often approached sufficiently near to be killed with a switch, a cap, or a hat—a gun is here almost superfluous; for with the muzzle I (Mr. Darwin) pushed a hawk (the carrion-buzzard) off the branch of a tree!"

I need go no farther, *probatum est*; the case is now complete. This archipelago, whatever it was in the way of suggestion to Mr. Darwin himself, can hardly be allowed, so far as I see, to be anything better than a Mr. Spenlow's Jorkins to anybody else. As for "the central idea, the quintessence of Darwinism," the pullulation of differences, it is quite possible, as Mr. Darwin suggests, that there might be "a bird born with a beak $\frac{1}{100}$th of an inch longer than usual;" but is the conception of such initial step enough to enable us to picture even in imagination the eventual production of all those beaks, to say nothing of the various birds themselves? Individual does differ from individual; no two individuals are perfectly alike. Manifestly, then, there is development of difference, of difference after difference, of differences infinite. But is it so certain, as Mr. Darwin will have it, that difference goes on—that difference adds to itself—that difference never stops—*till* there emerges—what?—its own opposite, an identity, a fixed new identity that actually propagates its own identity, as a species, before our eyes, illimitably? But *does* the difference go on *only so?*—*does* the difference add to itself *only so? If* there is *advance* of difference into a *new*, is there not *return* of difference into the *old*, identity? We can see the latter at every minute of the day, and on all sides of us; but we never see the former —never have seen the former. No man, not even a breeder, has ever seen the former. A breeder, if he is to breed, must have his material to work on; he knows that to effect the modifications he wants, he can only take advantage *of what is already there*. Nay, it is not by the accumulation of differences that the breeder effects his purposes, but by the accumulation of identities. If he wants wool, he adds wool to wool; if he wants flesh, he adds flesh to flesh; if he wants bone, he adds bone to bone; if he wants weight, he adds weight to weight; if he wants speed, he adds speed to speed. But do as he may, the breeder knows well that, but for his artifices, his breeds would all turn back again to what they were at first. You must keep the coal up, if you would keep the fire up. But with all his skills, and all his contrivances, and all his perseverances, no breeder has ever yet produced *a new species*. We do not deny, any more than Kant, that nature *can* produce new species: we only deny that nature has no secret for the process *but* the accumulation of the differences of accident. We know no proof of this—toothed birds, the hipparion itself, and even the wonderful "otter" sheep notwithstanding. We claim design for nature, whatever we admit!

Mr. Darwin follows up his suggestion of the *accident*, the *chance*, of his 100th of an inch more than usual, in this emphatic way (iii. 33): "The more I work, the more I feel convinced that it is by the accumulation of such extremely slight variations that new species arise." That is as much as to assert that, out of an accidental speck of proteine, the accidental pullulation of difference (mere difference) produced,—without design,—mechanically, as it were,—you and me, the circulation of the blood, the respiration of the lungs, the action of a brain!

But I must break off here: these lectures are now at an end. It was to expound Natural Theology that this place was given me. The proofs for the being of a God *are* Natural Theology. These proofs I followed historically, on the affirmative side, with some fulness, almost from first to last. On the negative side, I had to make a selection of what history offered me there; but I endeavoured to meet the want by the production of what, on the whole, are generally and publicly esteemed the three authoritative degrees of the relative argumentation.

I beg to thank you for the great attention with which you have always honoured me, and to bid you respectfully, Farewell!

# INDEX.

Abdalrahman III., 275.
Abstraction, 136.
Action and reaction, 49, 50.
Actuality, 126.
Addison, 224, 231.
Advanced views, 14, 15, 222.
Affirmative, 35.
*Agis*, 226, 230.
Agnosticism, 15.
Agrippa, 68.
Alexandria, 166.
Alphonso of Castile, 57, 272.
Amalrich, 117.
Analogy, 268.
Anaxagoras, 39, 46–49, 55, 60, 65–67, 72, 73, 77, 80, 220, 346.
Anselm, 33, 34, 45, 173, 177–193.
Antisthenes, 345, 347.
Antithesis, 49, 160.
Ariosto, 236.
Aristophanes, 221.
Aristotle, 33, 41, 45, 49, 54, 60, 66, 77, 80, 82, 83, 96, 97, 124–156, 220, 236, 238, 346–349.
Aristoxenus, 220.
Arnobius, 180.
Ascent, The, 137.
Astronomy, 32, 33, 76–80.
Athanasius, 181, 347.
Atheists, 219, 221, 283, 374.
Athenagoras, 182.
Attraction, 50.
Aufklärung, 14–16, 115–124, 145, 163, 215, 232.
Augustine, 23, 28, 32–34, 189, 193, 320, 347.
Augustus, 108.
Aulus Gellus, 29, 160, 178.

Bacon, Lord, 49, 51–56, 67, 95, 96, 117, 220.
Baghavad Gita, 63.
Bakewell, Robert, 331, 332.
Basil, 347.
Baumgarten, 118.
Baur, F. C., 182.
Beaks, 387 sq., 392, 398, 399.
Bear, 360.
Begriff, 11, 12, 13.
Bekker, 154.
Belief, 17.
Bell, Sir C., 26.
Bequest, The, 5.
Berkeley, 67, 249, 354.
Bernard, St., 202.
Bible, The, 24, 28, 36, 149, 179, 181, 308, 345.
Biese, 153.
Blackie, Professor, 156, 175.
Blair, Dr. Hugh, 183, 224, 225, 232, 235, 244.
Blindness, 86.
Boethius, 190.
Bonitz, 151.
Books, Sacred, 18.
Boston, 238.
Boswell, 108, 109.
*Botanic Garden*, The, 373.
Bowen, Professor, 394.
Brahmanism, 207.
Brandis, 154.
Breeder, 339.
Bridgewater Treatises, 25, 169.
Brougham, Lord, 26, 223, 246.
Brown, Dr. Thomas, 178, 183, 281, 373.
Browning, 17.

Bruno, G., 69.
Buckle, 19, 49, 108, 223, 239.
Buffon, 150.
Burke, 241.
Burns, 284.
Burton, 280, 281.
Byron, 144, 373.
Bythos, 37.

Cæsar, Julius, 174, 272.
Cæsar, The, 164.
Cain, 16, 19.
Caligula, 272.
Calvin, 117.
Carlyle, 16, 17, 74, 80, 81, 120-122, 204, 213, 273, 276, 284.
Carpenter, Dr., 370.
Catechism, The Shorter, 12, 13.
Categories, 68, 294 sqq.
Catullus, 234.
Causality, 278-283, 292 sqq.
Causes, The Four, 41-44, 49-52, 54, 103, 137.
Cervantes, 17.
Chambers, Dr. R., 353, 361.
Charlemont, Lord, 233.
Charles II., 49.
Charles V., 274.
Chaucer, 231.
Chemistry, 32, 33.
China, 36.
Chinese, The, 369.
Christianity, 27, 34, 166, 204, 208.
Chrysippus, 160, 171, 257.
Chrysostom, 180.
Church, The, 214.
Churches, The Three, 10, 11.
Cicero, 23, 28, 108, 148, 168-177, 220, 225, 236, 245.
Clarke, 25, 124, 260.
Cleanthes, 171.
Clement of Alexandria, 180, 347.
Colebrooke, 36, 37, 39, 40, 102, 280, 345.
Coleridge, 14, 82.
Comparison, 277.
Condillac, 82.
Conditions, 335 sqq., 391 sqq.
Confucius, 18.
Consensus gentium, 179.
Constantine, 161.
Contingency, 69, 111, 112, 125, 126, 260, 305 sq., 351 sq.

Corneille, 231.
Corporeity, 49.
Cosmological Argument. 45, 124, 260 sqq.
Cowley, 234.
Creation, 344 sqq., 356, 393 sq.
Cudworth, 25, 44, 68, 220, 345, 346, 347.
Cuvier, 133, 154, 155.
Cyril of Alexandria, 180.

Dallas, W. S., 372.
Dante, 236.
Darwin, Charles, 127-134, 155, 219, 278, 323-400.
Darwin, Dr. Erasmus, 273, 323-400 passim.
Darwin, Mr. Erasmus, 365.
Darwins, The, 365.
David of Dinant, 117.
Davidson, Thomas, 337.
Day, The—its roar, 201.
Degrees, The Three, 323, 324.
Democritus, 159, 219.
Demosthenes, 225.
De Quincey, 28.
Derham, 25, 36.
Descartes, 22, 50, 51, 71, 117, 188, 193, 377.
Design, 57, 93-96, 100, 114, 127-137, 150, 168-175.
Diagoras, 220.
Dicæarchus, 220.
Dickens, 396.
Difference, 103, 353 sqq., 398-400.
Diogenes, Apol., 87.
Diogenes Laertius, 60, 158, 221.
Douglas, 226-230.
Dryden, 228, 231, 232.

Ear. See Eye.
East, The, 166.
Eckhart, Meister, 320.
Ecstasy, 161.
Egyptians, 29, 369.
Eleatics, 219.
Elliot, Sir Gilbert, 244.
Elliott, Ebenezer, 215.
Emerson, 4, 82, 199, 200, 206, 210, 212, 213.
Empedocles, 134, 219, 270, 384.
Encyclopedists, 120.

## INDEX.

Energy, 50.
Engadine, The, 236.
Ennius, 168.
Epictetus, 161.
Epicurus, 23, 158, 271.
Epigoniad, 239.
Erdmann, 72, 142, 186, 192, 281.
Erigena, Scotus, 267, 268, 282.
Essay, The Little Moral Philosophy, 183.
Esse, vivere, intelligere, 25, 319.
Essenes, 167.
Ethicality, 88-91.
Eusebius of Cæsarea, 181.
Evil, 160, 270 sqq.
Existence, 62.
Externalization, 69.
Eye and Ear, 77, 78, 84-87, 95, 101.


FAITH, 16, 215, 217.
Falklands, The, 393.
Families, 364.
Fanciers, 357.
Faroes, The, 393.
Fathers, The, 24, 27, 106, 177, 179, 182, 346.
Fénélon, 25.
Ferguson, 240, 242.
Fichte, 80, 151.
Fielding, 10, 224.
Filament, 360.
Finches, 385 sqq.
Finite, 191.
Fleming, Dr., 183.
Fontenelle, 236.
Forces, 48, 49.
Form, 43, 44, 54, 68, 136, 282, 283, 303 sq.
Franzius, 154.
Freewill, 13.
Froude, 273.


GALAPAGOS, THE, 332 sqq.
Gassendi, 51.
Gaunilo, 185.
Genealogies, 355, 376-400.
Genesis, 37.
Genlis, Mme. de, 145.
George IV., 223.
Germany, 240.
Gibbon, 118, 120, 202, 224, 240, 241, 275.

Gifford, Lord, 3-11, 32, 38, 62, 63, 197-216.
Gifford, W., 223.
Gnostics, 37, 38, 167.
God, 5, 6, 19, 22, 23, 24, 31, 34, 37, 38, 58, 62, 63, 70, 126, 138, 147, 192, 193, 252.
Gods, Pagan, 28, 29, 98.
Goethe, 93, 119, 121.
Goldsmith, 183, 224, 232.
Good, The, 106, 107, 160.
Gray, Asa, 327, 341, 342, 357, 369, 371, 377.
Grece, Clair, 128, 133, 346.
Gregory of Nyssa, 181.
Grew, 25, 36.
Grote, 67, 267.


HAMANN, 118.
Happiness, 145, 213, 274, 277.
Hearne, 360.
Heavens, The, 77.
Hebrew Scriptures, 18, 19.
Hegel, 45, 187, 280, 319.
Henry, 241.
Heraclitus, 23, 49, 219, 268.
Herder, 118.
Herschel, Sir John, 280.
Hesiod, 37, 40.
Hexaemeron, 25.
Heyder, 154.
Hilary, 347.
History, Course of, 162.
Hobbes, 14, 71, 117.
Hodgson, 74.
Hoffmann, 337.
Holbach, d', 258.
Home, John, 226, 238.
Homer, 153, 172, 225.
Hooker, Sir Joseph, 328, 330, 336, 337, 341, 365, 370.
Horace, 236.
Humboldt, 149.
Hume, 14, 19, 57, 82, 108, 117, 150, 183, 220, 222-285 *passim* to end.
Hutcheson, 22, 249.
Huxley, 224, 338-343, 370, 371, 377.
Hymn, Aristotle's, 139.


IDEAS, 250 sqq., 299 sqq., 368.
Identity, 103, 279.

Imagination, 361 sqq.
Immanent, 60, 64, 152.
Immortality, 72.
India, 36, 37, 38, 39, 280, 345, 347.
Infinite, 34, 35, 38, 191.
Irenæus, 179.
Isocrates, 174.
Isolation, 387 sqq.

JACOBI, 118.
Jardine, Sir William, 386.
Jeffrey, Francis, 223.
Jehovah, 179, 308 sq.
Jenyns, 370.
Jericho, 19.
Jerome, 181.
Jews, 18, 36.
John of Damascus, 181.
Johnson, Dr., 108–112, 183, 224, 275.
Jonson, Ben, 230, 231.
Jorkins, Mr., 396.
Julian, Apost., 180.
Juvenal, 29.

KANT, 45, 74–77, 80, 93, 101, 144, 219, 233, 238, 286–324, 369, 391.
Kepler, 32.
Klopstock, 118.
Krause, 326, 372, 374.

LACTANTIUS, 180.
Lagrange, 57.
Lamarck, 373.
Lamballe, Princesse de, 273.
Lao-tse, 36.
Lärm, Des Tages, 201.
Latinity, 174.
Lavater, 118.
Law, No innate, of evolution, 390.
Lecturer's purview, 7.
Lectures, The, how laid out, 400.
Leibnitz, 22, 74, 75, 125, 127, 188.
Leonidas, 222.
Lessing, 118.
Leucippus, 159.
Lewes, 185, 360, 374.
Light, 78, 85.
Linnæus, 133.
Lizards, 396.
Locke, 117, 249, 287.

λόγος ξυνός, 267.
Louis XI., 113.
Lucretius, 236.
Luther, 202.
Lyell, Sir Charles, 328, 336, 337, 341, 355, 370, 371, 384.

MACAULAY, LORD, 223.
Mackintosh, Sir James, 223.
Macrobius, 175.
Mahometanism, 12.
Maimonides, Moses, 71.
Malebranche, 259.
Malthus, 332.
Mankind, 141.
Matter, 43, 44, 54, 68, 136, 261, 267, 303 sq.
Maxwell, Clerk, 49.
Mendelssohn, 118.
Mesmerism, 215.
Metaphysic, 33, 51–56.
Meteyard, Miss, 326.
Method, 358.
Michelet, 154.
Middle Ages, 24, 25, 27, 106, 200, 320.
Mill, John Stuart, 222, 223.
Milton, 28, 57, 150, 184, 185, 231, 232.
Mind, 69.
Minucius Felix, 173.
Miracles, 17, 18, 214.
Modification, 344 sqq.
Molière, 236.
Monks, their life, 202.
Monotheism, 31, 34, 35, 36, 98.
Monsters, 394 sqq.
Montaigne, 24, 25.
Morality, 88, 91.
Mormonism, 12.
Mover, A First, 138.
Mud-fish, 355, 356.
Muir, Dr. John, 39.
Mukharjî, Râs bihârî, 37.
Müller, Fritz, 372.
Müller, J. v., 154.
Müller, Max, 39.
Murchison, Sir R. I., 353.

NAPOLEON, 150.
Natural Science, 32, 33.
Nature, 67, 68, 69, 143.

# INDEX. 405

Necessity, 111, 266.
Negation, 161.
Negative, 35.
Neo-Platonists, 161, 167.
Newton, 49, 57, 58, 59, 374.
Nice, Council of, 161.
Nicolai, 118.
No-God Men, 16.
*Nous*, 46 and *passim*, 61-67, 79, 84.
Numenius, 106.

OBJECT, 102, 349 sqq.
Ogle, Dr., 133, 135.
One and many, 69.
Ontological Argument, 39, 40, 45, 182-193, 259 sqq.
Origen, 347.
Origin, The, of species, 384.
*Othello*, 227-231.
Ovid, 236.
Oysters, 358.

PAINE, THOMAS, 15, 16.
Paley, Dr., 25, 26, 30, 36, 168, 368.
Paley, Mr., 40.
Pantheism, 62, 63, 64, 207, 211.
Parnell, 234.
Parsons, Professor, 353, 384.
Particular, 70.
Pentateuch, 356.
Percy, 73.
Pericles, 221.
*Phædo*, The, 46, 48.
Philip of Opuntium, 100.
Philips, John, 373.
Philister, 226.
Philo Judæus, 106, 172.
Philosophy, 31, 35, 53, 81, 209, 222.
Philosophy of religion, 26, 27.
Physical science, 32, 33, 34, 239.
Physical theories, 73.
Physics, 53.
Picture-thinking, 369.
Plato, 47, 54, 65, 68, 82, 92, 96-114, 159, 300.
Pliny, 29, 177.
Plotinus, 32.
Plutarch, 161, 220, 257, 258.
Polytheism, 31, 34.
Pompey, 108.
Pope, 183, 226, 231, 232, 234, 236.

Porphyry, 32.
Positive, 11, 12, 13.
Potentiality, 126.
Practice, 141.
Prantl, 154, 174, 185.
Prayer, 107.
Press, The, 16.
Proofs, The, 30, 31, 35, 45, 93, 182-193, 218, 256-324.
Proteine, 356, 360.
*Protoplasm, As regards*, 280.
Pygmies, 395.
Pythagoreans, 23, 61, 167, 219.

QUANTITY, 85.
Quintilian, 234, 243, 246.

RABELAIS, 282.
Racine, 226, 227, 231, 234, 236.
*Rasselas*, 275.
Rationalism, 13-16.
Ray, 25, 36.
Raymund of Sebonde, 24, 25, 27, 36, 218.
Reason, 13, 14.
Reflection, 162.
Reid, 42, 56, 74, 80, 181, 183, 281, 282, 289.
Reimarus, 118.
Religion, 4, 8, 11, 26, 34, 35, 107, 203.
Religion, Pagan, 35.
Religion, Philosophies of, 26-30.
Repulsion, 50.
Revolution, 163.
Revolution, French, 16.
Ricardo, 222.
Richter, J. P., 119, 357.
Roar, The, of the day, 201.
Robertson, 183, 224, 235, 240.
Rome, 164.
Rosenkranz, 249.

SACRED BOOKS, 18.
Salto Mortale,
Sandford, Sir D. K., 223.
Scepticism, 163.
Schelling, 54, 80.
Schiller, 93, 119.
Scholastics, 22.

Scotch, The, 239.
Scott, 284.
Scriptures, 18, 19.
Schwegler, 67, 151, 165.
Seals, 360.
Sects, The, 157-168.
Secularism, 15.
Sedgewick, Professor, 369.
Seghed, The Emperor, 275.
Selection, Natural, 325, 330 sqq. and *passim*.
Semler, 118.
Semper, 337.
Seneca, 177.
Septimius Severus, 275.
Sextus Empiricus, 171.
Seward, Miss, 326.
Shakespeare, 59, 210, 226-232.
Simon of Tournay, 117.
Singular effect, 255 sqq.
Skeptics, 157.
Smith, Adam, 44, 203, 222, 224, 240, 244, 245, 262, 271, 321.
Smith, Sydney, 337.
Smollett, 48, 224, 240, 241.
Socinians, 117.
Socrates, 46-50, 65, 87-96, 99.
Sophists, 115-124.
Sophists, The, Note on, 165.
Sophocles, 227.
Soul, 153.
Sound, 78, 80, 85.
Sound views, 7.
Space, 74-76, 83, 294 sqq.
Sparta, 222.
Species, 330 sqq., 386.
Speculation, 140.
Spenser, 231.
Spinoza, 14, 63, 71, 72, 117, 206, 207, 211, 281.
Squinting, 362.
Stahr, 154.
Stanley, 395.
State, The, 166.
Stewart, Dugald, 108, 109, 183, 281, 282, 268, 373.
Stilliugfleet, 25.
Stobo, 241.
Stoics, 159.
Strahan, 244, 245.
Strato, 220.
Struggle, 332, and *passim*, 396-400.
Style, 223 sqq., 243 sqq., 248.

Subject, 102, 349 sqq.
Subjective, 211.
Substance, 63, 206, 207.
Suetonius, 173.
Superstition, 107-115.
Swift, Dr., 235.
Syzygies, 37.

TACITUS, 177, 236.
Tages, Des, der laute Lärm, 201.
Tailor, The, 278.
Tasso, 236.
Taste, 225.
Tauler, 320.
Taylor, Thomas, 37.
Teeth, 96, 129-133.
Teleological argument, 38, 39, 40, 45, 46, 56, 93, 262-285, 299-305.
Terence, 234.
Tertullian, 180.
Thales, 219.
Theologies, 23.
Theology, 21, 33.
Theology, Natural, 6, 19, 21-26, 30-35, 41, 42, 53, 55, 56, 67, 79, 80, 84, 170, 198, 256-258, 287.
Theophilus, 182.
Theory, 141.
Therapeutæ, 167.
Thomson, Dr. A., 173.
Thomson, James, 87, 184.
Time, 74, 75, 76, 80, 83, 104, 105, 149, 294 sqq.
Tortoises, 396.
Trades, The, 277.
Trajan, 272.
Transcendent, 60, 152.
Trendelenburg, 154.
Trinity, The, 27, 28, 105, 106, 137.

UEBERWEG, 185.
Understanding, 14.
Unity, 153.
Universal, 69, 70.
Universe, 70.

VALENTINUS, 37.
Varro, 23, 24.
Vedas, 18.
*Vestiges, The*, 353.
Vinnius, 284.

Vrgil, 225, 234, 236, 284.
Voet, 284.
Voltaire, 14, 19, 117.
Vorstellung, 11, 12, 13.

WAGNER, 336, 391.
Waitz, 154.
Waller, 231.
Weathering, 73.
*Westminster Review*, 223.
Whale and Bear, 360.
Wilkie, 239, 373.
Wilkins, 373.

Wolff, 46, 188, 192.
Wordsworth, 275.
World, The, a life, 67, 68, 69, 77, 84-87.

XENOPHON, 47, 92, 93.

YOUNG, DR., 242.

ZELLER, 67, 154.
Zorzi, 68.

MORRISON AND GIBB, PRINTERS, EDINBURGH

*T. and T. Clark's Publications.*

**LOTZE'S MICROCOSMUS.**

Just published, Third Edition, in Two Vols., 8vo, price 36s.,

# MICROCOSMUS:
## CONCERNING MAN AND HIS RELATION TO THE WORLD.
### By HERMANN LOTZE.

CONTENTS:—Book I. The Body. II. The Soul. III. Life. IV. Man. V. Mind. VI. The Microcosmic Order; or, The Course of Human Life. VII. History. VIII. Progress. IX. The Unity of Things.

'These are indeed two masterly volumes, vigorous in intellectual power, and translated with rare ability. . . . This work will doubtless find a place on the shelves of all the foremost thinkers and students of modern times.'—*Evangelical Magazine.*

'The English public have now before them the greatest philosophic work produced in Germany by the generation just past. The translation comes at an opportune time, for the circumstances of English thought, just at the present moment, are peculiarly those with which Lotze attempted to deal when he wrote his "Microcosmus," a quarter of a century ago. . . . Few philosophic books of the century are so attractive both in style and matter.'—*Athenæum.*

'Lotze is the ablest, the most brilliant, and most renowned of the German philosophers of to-day. . . . He has rendered invaluable and splendid service to Christian thinkers, and has given them a work which cannot fail to equip them for the sturdiest intellectual conflicts and to ensure their victory.'—*Baptist Magazine.*

In Two Vols., 8vo, price 21s.,

# NATURE AND THE BIBLE:
## LECTURES ON THE MOSAIC HISTORY OF CREATION IN ITS RELATION TO NATURAL SCIENCE.
### By DR. FR. H. REUSCH.

REVISED AND CORRECTED BY THE AUTHOR.

Translated from the Fourth Edition

By KATHLEEN LYTTELTON.

'Other champions much more competent and learned than myself might have been placed in the field; I will only name one of the most recent, Dr. Reusch, author of "Nature and the Bible."'—*The Right Hon. W. E. GLADSTONE.*

'The work, we need hardly say, is of profound and perennial interest, and it can scarcely be too highly commended as, in many respects, a very successful attempt to settle one of the most perplexing questions of the day. It is impossible to read it without obtaining larger views of theology, and more accurate opinions respecting its relations to science, and no one will rise from its perusal without feeling a deep sense of gratitude to its author.'—*Scottish Review.*

*T. and T. Clark's Publications.*

Just published, in demy 8vo, price 16s.,

# HISTORY

OF

## THE CHRISTIAN PHILOSOPHY OF RELIGION

### FROM THE REFORMATION TO KANT.

By BERNHARD PÜNJER.

Translated from the German

By W. HASTIE, B.D.

With a Preface

By ROBERT FLINT, D.D., LL.D.,
PROFESSOR OF DIVINITY, UNIVERSITY OF EDINBURGH.

---

'The style is simple, natural, and direct; the only sort of style appropriate to the subject. The amount of information imparted is most extensive, and strictly relevant. Nowhere else will a student get nearly so much knowledge as to what has been thought and written within the area of Christendom, on the philosophy of religion. He must be an excessively learned man in that department who has nothing to learn from this book.'—*Extract from Preface.*

'Pünjer's "History of the Philosophy of Religion" is fuller of information on its subject than any other book of the kind I have either seen or heard of. The writing in it is, on the whole, clear, simple, and uninvolved. The translation appears to me true to the German, and at the same time a piece of very satisfactory English. I should think the work would prove useful, or even indispensable, as well for clergymen as for professor and students.'—*Dr. Hutchison Stirling.*

*T. and T. Clark's Publications.*

## KANT'S PHILOSOPHY OF LAW.

Recently published, in crown 8vo, price 5s.,

# THE PHILOSOPHY OF LAW.

AN EXPOSITION OF THE FUNDAMENTAL PRINCIPLES OF JURISPRUDENCE AS THE SCIENCE OF RIGHT.

### By IMMANUEL KANT.

*TRANSLATED FROM THE GERMAN BY W. HASTIE, B.D.*

'I have read the Preface with great interest and entire concurrence. I anticipate the best results from turning the thoughts of our young men back to the fountainhead of all sound speculation since the French Revolution.'— Professor LORIMER, LL.D., University of Edinburgh.

'I have examined one or two important passages, and think it an excellent translation. I shall have much pleasure in recommending it to my Students.' —Professor CAIRD, LL.D., Glasgow.

'The book will be helpful to us in Philosophy Classes, specially Ethical, as well as to Law Students.'—Professor CALDERWOOD, LL.D., University of Edinburgh.

'I do not see how the translation could well be better.'—J. HUTCHISON STIRLING, LL.D.

'Bellissima ed opportuna traduzione che farà conoscere all'Inghilterra maggiormente il piu potente pensatore della Germania.'—Professor CARLE, Professor of the Philosophy of Law in the University of Turin.

'Treffliche Uebersetzung.'—Dr. J. VON HOLTZENDORFF, University of Munich.

'A valuable translation of Kant's Philosophy of Law.'—Professor DIODATO LIOY, University of Naples.

'An excellent translation of this great work in its complete form . . . with an appreciative preface.'—*Journal of Jurisprudence.*

'Mr. Hastie has done a valuable service to the study of jurisprudence by the production of this work. His translation is admirably done, and his introductory chapter gives all the information necessary to enable a student to approach the main body of the work with sympathy and intelligence. The work supplies a defect hitherto regretted in the literature of jurisprudence in this country.'—*Scotsman.*

*T. and T. Clark's Publications.*

In demy 8vo, price 12s.,

## THE SCRIPTURE DOCTRINE OF THE CHURCH
### Historically and Exegetically Considered.

*(Eleventh Series of 'Cunningham Lectures.')*

By Rev. D. DOUGLAS BANNERMAN, D.D.

'Mr. Bannerman has executed his task with commendable impartiality and thoroughness. His learning is ample, his materials have been carefully sifted and clearly arranged, his reasoning is apt, lucid, and forcible, while he has none of the bitterness which so frequently mars controversial works of this class.'—*Baptist Magazine.*

'The matter is beyond all question of the very holiest and best. . . . We do not hesitate to give the book a hearty recommendation.'—*Clergyman's Magazine.*

'The Cunningham Lecturer has made out an admirable case. His book, indeed, while not written in a controversial spirit, but with calm temper, argumentative power, and abundant learning, is a very forcible vindication of the Presbyterian system, and one which, we suspect, it will be no easy task to refute, whether from the Romanist or the Anglican sides.'—*Scotsman.*

In Two Vols., 8vo, price 21s.,

## A SYSTEM OF BIBLICAL THEOLOGY,

BY THE LATE

W. LINDSAY ALEXANDER, D.D., LL.D.,

PRINCIPAL OF THE THEOLOGICAL HALL OF THE CONGREGATIONAL CHURCHES IN SCOTLAND.

'A work like this is of priceless advantage. It is the testimony of a powerful and accomplished mind to the supreme authority of the Scriptures, a lucid and orderly exhibition of their contents, and a vindication, at once logical, scholarly, and conclusive, of their absolute sufficiency and abiding truthfulness. It is a pleasure to read lectures so vigorous and comprehensive in their grasp, so subtle in their dialectic, so reverent in spirit, and so severely chaste in their style. There are scores of men who would suffer no loss if for the next couple of years they read no other book than this. To master it thoroughly would be an incalculable gain.'—*Baptist Magazine.*

'This is probably the most interesting and scholarly system of theology on the lines of orthodoxy which has seen the light.'—*Literary World.*

'This has been characterized as probably the most valuable contribution which our country has made to theology during the present century, and we do not think this an exaggerated estimate.'—*Scottish Congregationalist.*

*T. and T. Clark's Publications.*

---

In Two Volumes, 8vo (1600 pages), price 24s.,

## THE DOCTRINE OF SACRED SCRIPTURE:

A CRITICAL, HISTORICAL, AND DOGMATIC INQUIRY INTO THE ORIGIN AND NATURE OF THE OLD AND NEW TESTAMENTS.

By GEORGE T. LADD, D.D.,

PROFESSOR OF MENTAL AND MORAL PHILOSOPHY, YALE COLLEGE.

'This important work is pre-eminently adapted for students, and treats in an exhaustive manner nearly every important subject of Biblical criticism which is agitating the religious mind at the present day.'—*Contemporary Review.*

---

In post 8vo, Second Edition, price 7s. 6d.,

## BIBLICAL STUDY:

### ITS PRINCIPLES, METHODS, AND HISTORY.

By PROFESSOR C. A. BRIGGS, D.D.

WITH INTRODUCTION BY PROFESSOR A. B. BRUCE, D.D.

'We have great pleasure in recommending Dr. Briggs' work to the notice of all Biblical students; it contains much new matter, and presents even the old with the freshness which is inseparable from lively interest and earnest personal investigation.'—*Nonconformist.*

'Written by one who has made himself a master of the subject, and who is able to write upon it both with the learning of the scholar and with the earnestness of sincere conviction.'—*Scotsman.*

'Dr. Briggs' book is one of much value, not the less to be esteemed because of the moderate compass into which its mass of information has been compressed.'—*Spectator.*

'Dr. Briggs' long experience in teaching enables him to supply the student's precise needs. He expresses himself clearly and tersely, and stimulates thought as well as furnishes information.'—*Wesleyan Methodist Magazine.*

'We are sure that no student will regret sending for this book.'—*Academy.*

'A valuable introduction to the critical study of the Scriptures.'—*Aberdeen Free Press.*

---

BY THE SAME AUTHOR.

In post 8vo, with Maps, price 7s. 6d.,

## AMERICAN PRESBYTERIANISM:

### ITS ORIGIN AND EARLY HISTORY.

Together with an Appendix of Letters and Documents, many of which have recently been discovered.

'We have no doubt this volume will be read with intense interest and gratitude by thousands.'—*Presbyterian Churchman.*

'This book travels over a great extent of ground. It is packed with information, and appears to be the fruit of protracted and enthusiastic study.'—*Aberdeen Free Press.*

'An honest and valuable contribution to ecclesiastical history.'—*Glasgow Herald.*

'Dr. Briggs has succeeded by his researches in unearthing and rendering available to a large quantity of fresh and valuable information, which will make his book indispensable to all future students of the subject with which he deals.'—*Belfast Witness.*

*T. and T. Clark's Publications.*

# HERZOG'S BIBLICAL ENCYCLOPÆDIA.

Now complete, in Three Vols. imp. 8vo, price 24s. each,

## ENCYCLOPÆDIA OR DICTIONARY
### OF
### Biblical, Historical, Doctrinal, and Practical Theology.

*Based on the Real-Encyclopädie of Herzog, Plitt, and Hauck.*

EDITED BY PHILIP SCHAFF, D.D., LL.D.

'A well-designed, meritorious work, on which neither industry nor expense has been spared.'—*Guardian.*

'This certainly is a remarkable work. . . . It will be one without which no general or theological or biographical library will be complete.'—*Freeman.*

'The need of such a work as this must be very often felt, and it ought to find its way into all college libraries, and into many private studies.'—*Christian World.*

'As a comprehensive work of reference, within a moderate compass, we know nothing at all equal to it in the large department which it deals with.'—*Church Bells.*

---

SUPPLEMENT TO HERZOG'S ENCYCLOPÆDIA.

In Imperial 8vo, price 8s.,

## ENCYCLOPÆDIA OF LIVING DIVINES.

'A very useful Encyclopædia. I am very glad to have it for frequent reference.'—*Right Rev. Bishop Lightfoot.*

---

Now complete, in Four Vols. imp. 8vo, price 12s. 6d. each,

## COMMENTARY ON THE NEW TESTAMENT.
### With Illustrations and Maps.

EDITED BY PHILIP SCHAFF, D.D., LL.D.

| *Volume I.* | *Volume II.* |
|---|---|
| **THE SYNOPTICAL GOSPELS.** | **ST. JOHN'S GOSPEL** AND THE **ACTS OF THE APOSTLES.** |
| *Volume III.* | *Volume IV.* |
| **ROMANS to PHILEMON.** | **HEBREWS to REVELATION.** |

'A useful, valuable, and instructive commentary. The interpretation is set forth with clearness and cogency, and in a manner calculated to commend the volumes to the thoughtful reader. The book is beautifully got up, and reflects great credit on the publishers as well as the writers.'—*The Bishop of Gloucester.*

'There are few better commentaries having a similar scope and object; indeed, within the same limits, we do not know of one so good upon the whole of the New Testament.'—*Literary World.*

'External beauty and intrinsic worth combine in the work here completed. Good paper, good type, good illustrations, good binding please the eye, as accuracy and thoroughness in matter of treatment satisfy the judgment. Everywhere the workmanship is careful, solid, harmonious.'—*Methodist Recorder.*

*T. and T. Clark's Publications.*

# PROFESSOR GODET'S WORKS.
(Copyright, by arrangement with the Author.)

In Two Volumes, demy 8vo, price 21s.,

## COMMENTARY ON ST. PAUL'S FIRST EPISTLE TO THE CORINTHIANS.
BY F. GODET, D.D.,
PROFESSOR OF THEOLOGY, NEUCHATEL.

'A perfect masterpiece of theological toil and thought. . . . Scholarly, evangelical, exhaustive, and able.'—*Evangelical Review.*
'To say a word in praise of any of Professor Godet's productions is almost like "gilding refined gold." All who are familiar with his commentaries know how full they are of rich suggestion. . . . This volume fully sustains the high reputation Godet has made for himself as a Biblical scholar, and devout expositor of the will of God. Every page is radiant with light, and gives forth heat as well.'—*Methodist New Connexion Magazine.*

In Three Volumes, 8vo, price 31s. 6d.,

## A COMMENTARY ON THE GOSPEL OF ST. JOHN.
### A New Edition, Revised throughout by the Author.

'This work forms one of the battle-fields of modern inquiry, and is itself so rich in spiritual truth, that it is impossible to examine it too closely; and we welcome this treatise from the pen of Dr. Godet. We have no more competent exegete; and this new volume shows all the learning and vivacity for which the author is distinguished.'—*Freeman.*

In Two Volumes, 8vo, price 21s.,

## A COMMENTARY ON THE GOSPEL OF ST. LUKE.

'Marked by clearness and good sense, it will be found to possess value and interest as one of the most recent and copious works specially designed to illustrate this Gospel.'—*Guardian.*

In Two Volumes, 8vo, price 21s.,

## A COMMENTARY ON ST. PAUL'S EPISTLE TO THE ROMANS.

'We prefer this commentary to any other we have seen on the subject. . . . We have great pleasure in recommending it as not only rendering invaluable aid in the critical study of the text, but affording practical and deeply suggestive assistance in the exposition of the doctrine.'—*British and Foreign Evangelical Review.*

In crown 8vo, Second Edition, price 6s.,

## DEFENCE OF THE CHRISTIAN FAITH.
TRANSLATED BY THE HON. AND REV. CANON LYTTELTON, M.A.,
RECTOR OF HAGLEY.

'There is trenchant argument and resistless logic in these lectures; but withal, there is cultured imagination and felicitous eloquence, which carry home the appeals to the heart as well as the head.'—*Sword and Trowel.*

*T. and T. Clark's Publications.*

Just published, in post 8vo, price 7s. 6d.,

## THE LIFE AND WRITINGS OF ALEXANDER VINET.

By LAURA M. LANE.

WITH AN INTRODUCTION BY THE VEN. ARCHDEACON FARRAR.

'I may say, without hesitation, that readers will here find a deeply interesting account of a sincere and brilliant thinker. . . . The publication of this book will be a pure gain if it calls the attention of fresh students to the writings of a theologian so independent as Vinet was, yet so supreme in his allegiance to the majesty of truth.'—Ven. Archdeacon FARRAR.

'Miss Lane deserves the grateful thanks of all students of theology for her praiseworthy attempt to revive interest in a man whose views have a special message for these times, and whose lofty and beautiful spirit cannot fail likewise to attract all students of human nature.'—*Glasgow Herald.*

Just published, in demy 8vo, price 7s. 6d.,

## ELEMENTS OF LOGIC AS A SCIENCE OF PROPOSITIONS.

By E. E. CONSTANCE JONES,

LECTURER IN MORAL SCIENCES, GIRTON COLLEGE, CAMBRIDGE;
JOINT-TRANSLATOR AND EDITOR OF LOTZE'S '*Microcosmus.*'

'What strikes us at once about the work is the refreshing boldness and independence of the writer, which, however, is not mere waywardness or idiosyncrasy. In spite of the long-drawn previous history of the science and of its voluminous records, Miss Jones finds plenty to say that is freshly worked out by independent thought. There is a spring of vitality and vigour pervading and vitalizing the aridity of even these abstract discussions.'—*Cambridge Review.*

Just published, in demy 8vo, price 9s.,

## KANT, LOTZE, AND RITSCHL:

### A Critical Examination.

By LEONHARD STÄHLIN, BAYREUTH.

TRANSLATED BY PRINCIPAL SIMON, EDINBURGH.

'In a few lines it is impossible to give an adequate idea of this learned work, which goes to the very root of the philosophical and metaphysical speculations of recent years.'—*Ecclesiastical Gazette.*

'We are grateful to the publishers for this volume, which deserves to be carefully read and studied.'—*London Quarterly Review.*

'The book is worthy of careful study.'—*Church Bells.*

www.ingramcontent.com/pod-product-compliance
Lightning Source LLC
Chambersburg PA
CBHW020543300426
44111CB00008B/776